# How to use this book

Written for the new AQA specification, the features in this book include:

## Objectives

At the beginning of the double-pages, you will find a list of learning objectives. These are based on the requirements of the course – so you can ensure you are covering what you need to know.

## ▼ SOURCE  ▼ INTERPRETATION

**Sources** introduce you to material that is primary or contemporary to the period, and **Interpretations** provide you with different people's perspectives on the past.

## Practice Question

These are focused questions to help you practise your history skills, including evaluating sources or interpretations, and essay writing. They give you an idea of the types of questions you might get in an examination.

## Study Tip

These are hints to highlight key parts of **Practice Questions** and will help you answer the questions.

## Fact

Fascinating references, facts or anecdotes that will make you think and add to your knowledge and understanding.

## Work

The activities and questions aim to develop your knowledge, understanding and key history skills. They are designed to be progressive in terms of difficulty, and to get you to think about the topic, become familiar with the history, and apply what you have learned.

## Extension

This is an opportunity to challenge you to investigate the history more deeply through independent research and reflection.

## Key Words

The important phrases and terms are highlighted and are also defined in the glossary. Learn what they mean – and how to spell and use them correctly.

## Timeline

A short list of dates identifying key events to help you understand chronological developments.

## Key Biography

Details of a key person to help you understand the individuals who have helped shape history.

## Norman England

This was an extraordinary period that saw the end of the Anglo-Saxon dynasties and includes arguably the most famous battles in English history. Most of the changes imposed by William the Conqueror remained for centuries and many are still evident today. The Normans changed many areas of life in England from religion to the way local areas were governed and taxes were collected. Whilst the Normans have had a reputation for violence, it cannot be denied that this was one of the most exciting periods of English history.

**1066**
January - King Edward dies; Harold Godwinson crowned King of England

September - Battle of Fulford Gate; Battle of Stamford Bridge

October - Battle of Hastings

December - William crowned King of England

**1087**
Death of King William I; his eldest son, Robert Curthose, becomes Duke of Normandy and his second eldest son, William Rufus, becomes King William II

**1100**
King William II killed and his brother Henry crowned King Henry I

**1090**

**1080**

**1100**

**1075**
The revolt of the Norman earls

**1070**

**1096**
William Rufus recognised as the ruler of Normandy

**1066**

**1086**
The results of the Domesday Survey collated and the Domesday Book created

**1091**
Scottish rebellion; King Malcolm of Scotland killed in 1093

**1071**
The East Anglia rebellion of Hereward the Wake and his allies

**1069**
The Harrying of the North

**1088**
Norman barons and Robert Curthose rebel against William Rufus; Rufus responds quickly, cutting off their support

# Oxford AQA GCSE History

# British Depth Studies c1066-1685

Lorraine Waterson

Tim Williams

SERIES EDITOR
**Aaron Wilkes**

CONSULTANT
**J. A. Cloake**

**OXFORD**

# OXFORD
UNIVERSITY PRESS

Great Clarendon Street, Oxford, OX2 6DP, United Kingdom

Oxford University Press is a department of the University of Oxford. It furthers the University's objective of excellence in research, scholarship, and education by publishing worldwide. Oxford is a registered trade mark of Oxford University Press in the UK and in certain other countries



© Oxford University Press 2016

The moral rights of the authors have been asserted



First published in 2016



All rights reserved. No part of this publication may be reproduced, stored in a retrieval system, or transmitted, in any form or by any means, without the prior permission in writing of Oxford University Press, or as expressly permitted by law, by licence or under terms agreed with the appropriate reprographics rights organization. Enquiries concerning reproduction outside the scope of the above should be sent to the Rights Department, Oxford University Press, at the address above.

You must not circulate this work in any other form and you must impose this same condition on any acquirer



British Library Cataloguing in Publication Data Data available

978-0-19-8370123

Kerboodle Book: 978-0-19-8370161

10 9 8 7 6 5 4 3

Paper used in the production of this book is a natural, recyclable product made from wood grown in sustainable forests. The manufacturing process conforms to the environmental regulations of the country of origin.

Printed in China by Golden Cup Printing Co Ltd.

**Acknowledgements**

The publisher would like to thank the following for permission to use their photographs:

**Cover:** Dea Picture Library/Getty Images.

**p6tl:** Private Collection/Ken Welsh/Bridgeman Images; **p6b & p6tr:** Mary Evans Picture Library/Alamy Stock Photo; **p7tl:** Angelo Hornak/Alamy Stock Photo; **p7tr:** akg-images/Album/Prisma; **p7b:** World History Archive/Alamy Stock Photo; **p8bl:** kerenby/Shutterstock; **p8tl:** Mary Evans Picture Library; **p8tr:** Ian Dagnall/Alamy Stock Photo; **p8br:** Look and Learn; **p9t:** Peter Jackson/Look and Learn; **p9bl:** liszt collection/Alamy Stock Photo; **p9br:** 19th era/Alamy Stock Photo; **p12:** World History Archive/Alamy Stock Photo; **p15l:** The British Library Board; **p15r:** LatitudeStock/Alamy Stock Photo; **p16l:** The Art Archive/Alamy Stock Photo; **p16r:** World History Archive/Alamy Stock Photo; **p17:** INTERFOTO/Alamy Stock Photo; **p19:** North Wind Picture Archives/Alamy Stock Photo; **p20:** Cambridge University Library; **p21:** Popperfoto/GettyImages; **p22:** Private Collection/Ken Welsh/Bridgeman Images; **p27:** INTERFOTO/Alamy Stock Photo; **p29:** The Art Archive/Alamy Stock Photo; **p33:** Chetham's Library, Manchester, UK/Bridgeman Images; **p34:** Nasjonalgalleriet, Oslo/Public Domain Wikipedia; **p37b:** National Galleries Scotland; **p37t:** Look and Learn; **p38:** Mary Evans Picture Library/Alamy Stock Photo; **p42:** Look and Learn; **p43:** Dea/M. Seemuller/Getty Images; **p46l:** Mary Evans Picture Library/Alamy Stock Photo; **p46r:** Heritage Image Partnership Ltd/Alamy Stock Photo; **p47:** Jersey Post Ltd/www.jerseystamps.com; **p51:** Mary Evans Picture Library/Alamy Stock Photo; **p55:** akg-images/British Library; **p56tl:** World History Archive/Alamy Stock Photo; **p56tr-p56br:** The British Library Board; **p57:** Bibliothèque Nationale de France (BnF); **p62 & p64:** Alamy**p65:** pjr travel/Alamy; **p66:** Saint Anselm College; **p67:** akg-images /Album/Oronoz; **p70:** Holy Cross Monastry, County Down, Northern Ireland; **p71:** Mary Evans Picture Library/Alamy Stock Photo; **p72l & p72r:** The British Library Board; **p76:** Angelo Hornak/Alamy Stock Photo; **p77:** Look and Learn; **p78:** Bibliothèque Nationale de France; **p80:** Hulton Archive/Handout/Getty Images; **p81:** Acceptphoto/Alamy Stock Photo; **p83t:** Topham Picturepoint; **p83b:** World History Archive/Alamy Stock Photo; **p84:** Stapleton Collection/Corbis; **p86:** Look and Learn; **p89:** The Granger Collection/TopFoto; **p91l:** World History Archive/Alamy Stock Photo; **p91r:** The British Library Board; **p92:** Deborah Hayter/Oxfordshire History Centre./(MS. Archd. papers Oxon. b.41 f.99); **p94:** Phil Hynds/Alamy Stock Photo; **p95:** British Library Board/Bridgeman Images; **p96:** John D Clare; **p98:** The Granger Collection/Topfoto; **p99:** Royal Library of Belgium; **p101:** Neil Mcallister/Getty Images; **p102:** Andrew Palmer/Alamy Stock Photo; **p103:** Universal History Archive/Getty Images; **p104:** akg-images/Album/Prisma; **p105:** The British Library Board; **p106:** Museo di San Marco dell'Angelico, Florence, Italy/Bridgeman Images; **p107l:** Vale Royal Abbey; **p107r:** travelib/Alamy Stock Photo; **p108:** Aidan McRae; **p109:** Hulton Archive/Getty Images; **p110:** The Art Archive/Alamy Stock Photo; **p111:** Jeremy Pembrey/Alamy Stock Photo; **p112:** Alinari Archives/Corbis; **p113:** Look and Learn; **p115:** The British Library Board; **p116:** Look and Learn; **p119:** Alamy; **p120b:** Look and Learn; **p120t:** Private Collection/Bridgeman Images; **p122:** Parker Library/Corpus Christi College Cambridge; **p124:** Dirk Renckhoff/Alamy Stock Photo; **p125l:** British library; **p125r:** John Cleare/Fotolibre; **p127:** Whitworth Art Gallery, The University of Manchester, UK/Bridgeman Images; **p129:** Alamy; **p130:** The British Library Board; **p131:** British Library Royal MS, C vii, f. 133 (date: late 14th century); **p135:** RCAHMS Aerial Photography Digital; **p137t-p139t:** Look and Learn; **p139b:** AF archive/Alamy Stock Photo; **p140:** Universal History Archive/REX Shutterstock; **p141 & p145t:** Look and Learn;**p145b:** Corbis; **p147b:** Bettman/Corbis; **p147t:** The Print Collector/Corbis; **p148:** Hulton-Deutsch Collection/Corbis; **p150:** BBC 2423883; **p151tl:** The Print Collector/Corbis; **p151b:** Gianni Dagli Orti/Corbis; **p151r:** Leemage/Corbis; **p152:** The Parliamentary Art Collection; **p154t:** Bettman/Corbis; **p154b:** World History Archive/Alamy; **p155:** Reproduced with the kind permission of Lord Barnard, TD., Raby Castle; **p156:** Bridgeman Art Library; **p158:** Queen Elizabeth I (1538-1603) in Old Age, c.1610 (oil on panel), English School, (17th century)/Corsham Court, Wiltshire/Bridgeman Images; **p160:** Pictorial Press Ltd/Alamy; **p161:** Longleat; **p164t:** GraphicaArtis/Corbis; **p164b:** Bettman/Corbis; **p165:** MS Roy 18 AXLVMI The poet George Gascoigne (c.1525-77) presenting a manuscript to Queen Elizabeth I (1533-1603) (engraving) (b&w photo), English School, (16th century) / British Library, London, UK / Bridgeman Images; **p169t:** Dr William Gilbert (1544-1603) showing his Experiment on Electricity to Queen Elizabeth I and her Court, 19th century (oil on canvas) (see detail 99460), Hunt, Arthur Ackland (fl.1863-1913)/Private Collection/Bridgeman Images; **p169b:** The Alchemist, Teniers, David the Younger (1610-90) / Johnny van Haeften Gallery, London, UK / Bridgeman Images; **p162 & p163:** With kind permission from Brian Delf; **p166:** Ian Dagnall/Alamy Stock Photo; **p170:** A Rich Man Spurns a Ragged Beggar, from 'A Christall Glass of Christian Reformation' by Stephen Bateman, 1569 (woodcut) (b/w photo), English School, (16th century)/Private Collection/Bridgeman Images; **p172:** Lordprice Collection/Alamy; **p173:** Bridgeman Art Library; **p174:** Fotosearch/Getty Images; **p176:** Getty Images; **p178t:** kerenby/Shutterstock; **p178b:** Leemage/Corbis; **p179:** Baldwin H. Ward & Kathryn C. Ward/Corbis; **p180:** The Trustees of The British Museum; **p181r:** Derek Bayes/Lebrecht Music & Arts/Lebrecht Music & Arts/Corbis; **p181l:** College of Arms MS Miscellaneous Grants 1, f.148r (arms of John Hawkins). Reproduced by permission of the Kings, Heralds and Pursuivants of Arms; **p182r:** The Gallery Collection/Corbis; **p182l:** The Granger Collection/TopFoto; **p184l:** King Edward VI (1537-53) and the Pope, c.1570 (oil on panel), English School, (16th century)/National Portrait Gallery, London, UK/Bridgeman Images; **p184r:** B.Seed/Lebrecht Music & Arts/Lebrecht Music & Arts/Corbis; **p188:** Mary Evans Picture Library; **p189:** The British Library; **p192:** World History Archive/Alamy;**p193:** Bridgeman; **p190:** Hulton Deutsch Corbis; **p194b:** Victoria and Albert; **p194t:** Gustavo Tomsich/Corbis; **p195:** Mary Evans/The National Archives, London. England; **p196:** Lebrecht Music & Arts/Lebrecht Music & Arts/Corbis; **p197t:** Mary Evans Picture Library; **p197b:** Bridgeman Art Library; **p199:** Portrait of Philip II (mounted on a cow), the Duke of Alencon, the Duke of Alba, William of Orange and Queen Elizabeth I, Moro, Philip (d.1578) / Private Collection / Bridgeman Images; **p200:** The Print Collector/Corbis; **p201:** The Gallery Collection/Corbis; **p202:** Tarker/Corbis; **p203:** Hulton Archive/Getty; **p205l:** Mansell/The LIFE Picture Collection/Getty Images; **p205r:** North Wind Picture Archives/Alamy Stock Photo; **p208:** The British Library Board; **p209t:** Leemage/Corbis; **p209b:** Peter Jackson/Look and Learn; **p210:** The Print Collector/Corbis; **p212:** E M Ward / Look and Learn; **p214l:** Private Collection/De Agostini Picture Library/Bridgeman Images; **p214r:** Castle Ward, County Down, Northern Ireland/National Trust Photographic Library/Bridgeman; **p216:** The Print Collector/Corbis; **p217:** Ken Welsh/Design Pics/Corbis; **p220 & p218:** Bridgeman Art Library;
**p222:** 19th era/Alamy Stock Photo; **p223:** Look and Learn/Peter Jackson Collection; **p225:** Steven Vidler/Corbis; **p226:** EB65A100680s4 Houghton Library Harvard University; **p228:** james schutte/Alamy Stock Photo; **p229l:** Special Collections/Otago University Library, New Zealand; **p229t:** The Tate Art Gallery; **p231t:** Lebrecht Music & Arts/Lebrecht Music & Arts/Corbis; **p230:** Royal Collection Trust / © Her Majesty Queen Elizabeth II 2016; **p231b:** Government Art Collection (GAC); **p232:** AS400 DB/Corbis; **p233:** Stefano Bianchetti/Corbis; **p235:** Rita Greer; **p236:** AS400 DB/Corbis; **p237t:** Lebrecht Music & Arts/Lebrecht Music & Arts/Corbis; **p237b:** Bridgeman Art Library; **p239:** C L Doughty/Look and Learn; **p240t:** Brit Museum; **p240b:** Adam Woolfitt/Corbis; **p241r:** Chris Andrews; Chris Andrews Publications/Corbis; **p241l:** Melvyn Longhurst/Alamy Stock Photo; **p242l:** Lebrecht Music and Arts Photo Library/Alamy Stock Photo; **p242r:** Mary Evans Picture Library/Alamy Stock Photo; **p243l-p243b:** Lebrecht Authors/Lebrecht Music & Arts/Corbis; **p244:** Corbis; **p245:** Peter Jackson/Look and Learn; **p247l:** Wellcome Image Library; **p247r:** Hulton-Deutsch/Hulton-Deutsch Collection/Corbis; **p248:** Royal Astronomical Society/Science Photo Library; **p251:** Hulton Archive/Getty Images; **p253:** AS400 DB/Corbis; **p254:** Oliver Frey/Look and Learn; **p255:** Corbis; **p256:** Argostini Picture Library/Getty Images; **p257l:** Art Directors & TRIP/Alamy Stock Photo; **p258:** National Archives; **p259:** The National Library of Congress; **p260:** Liverpool Museums, Liverpool; **p261:** Corbis; **p257r:** Dr David Schlosberg; **p262:** Print Collector/Contributor/Getty Images; **p263t:** Collection Het Scheepvaartmuseum, Amsterdam; **p263b:** Look and Learn; **p264:** Derek Bayes/Lebrecht Music & Arts/Lebrecht Music & Arts/Corbis; **p267:** liszt collection/Alamy Stock Photo; **p269t:** R Smirke/Look and Learn; **p269b:** Corbis; **p270:** Leemage/Corbis; **p271l:** adoc-photos/Corbis.

We are grateful to the authors and publishers for use of copyright material and in particular to the following:

**AQA** for practice questions from the AQA GCSE History Draft Specimen for 2016 Paper 2 'Shaping the nation", copyright © 2016 AQA and its licensors. **Amberley Publishing** for extract from Peter Rex: *1066: A New History of the Norman Conquest* (Amberley, 2009). **Cambridge University Press** for extract from 'British Mercantilistic Policies and the American Colonies' by John J McCusker, in Stanley L Engerman and Robert E Gallman (eds.): *The Cambridge Economic History of the United States*, Vol 1 (Cambridge University Press, 1996). **Helen Mary Carrel** and the International Medieval Congress, for extract from her presentation, International Medieval Congress, July 2006, Institute for Medieval Studies, University of Leeds. **Express Newspapers**/N & S Syndication for extract from 'All the Queen's Men: Was Elizabeth I really the Virgin Queen?' by Jane Warren, Daily Express, 4 July 2014, copyright © Express Newspapers 2014. **Franciscan Media** for extract from John Duns Scotus, Saint of the Day, copyright © Franciscan Media, 28 Liberty St. Cincinati, Ohio 45202, USA. All rights reserved. **Haaretz** for extract from 'This Day in Jewish History, Jews Expelled from England' by David B Green, *Haaretz*, 1 Nov 2012. **Heritage History** for extract on the Anglo-Dutch War from www.heritage-history.com. **History Today Ltd** for extract from 'Roger Bacon: Doctor Mirabilis' by J J N McGurk, *History Today*, No 24:7, July 1974. **Ewan J Innes** for extract from 'The Strategies and the Tactics of the Scottish Armies1296-1314', *Scottish History*, 1989, www.scottishhistory.com. **Little Brown Book Group** for extract from the Prologue to *Rebel* by Jack Whyte (Sphere, 2012). **Military History** for extract from 'King Edward I, England's Warrior King' by Eric Niderost, *Military History*, No 6, Dec 2006, copyright © HistoryNet. **Nottingham Medieval Studies**, University of Nottingham for extract from 'Should I Stay or Should I Go? Robert Burnell the Lord Edward's Crusade and the Canterbury Vacancy of 1270-3' by Richard Huscroft, *Nottingham Medieval Studies* 45 (2001). **The Orion Publishing Group**, London for extract from *Charles II: His life and times* by Antonia Fraser (Weidenfeld & Nicolson 1993), copyright © Antonia Fraser 1979,1993. **Pearson UK**/ Pearson Education Ltd for extract from *The Long 18th Century: Literature from 1660 - 1790 - Companion*, by Penny Pritchard, York Notes Plus (Longman, 2010). **Peters Fraser & Dunlop** (www.petersfraserdunlop.com) on behalf of the Estate of Robert Latham for extract from *The Diary of Samuel Pepys: A New and Complete Translation* by Robert Lathem, published by HarperCollins. **Q-files.com**, the free online children's encyclopedia, for extract from www.Q-files.com. **The Random House Group Ltd** for extract from *London: A Novel* by Edward Rutherford (Century, 1997). **The Simon de Montfort Society** for extract from the website www.simondemontfort.org. **Stirling District Tourism** for text on Sir William Wallace from The National Wallace Monument, www.nationalwallacemonument.com. **Telegraph Media Group Ltd** for extract from Michael Gaskill's review of Jenny Uglow's book *A Gambling Man, Daily Telegraph*, 4 Oct 2009, copyright © Telegraph Media Group Ltd 2009. **Tribune Content Agency** for extract from 'The Real Medieval History behind Game of Thrones trial by combat' by Spencer Kornhaber, *theatlantic.com*, 2 June 2014, copyright © The Atlantic Media Co 2014. All rights reserved. **University of Wales Press**/Gwasg Prifysgol Cymru for extract from *Llywelyn ap Gruffudd: Prince of Wales* by J Beverley Smith (U Wales Press, 2014).

We have made every effort to trace and contact all copyright holders before publication, but if notified of any errors or omissions, the publisher will be happy to rectify these at the earliest opportunity.


**Approval message from AQA**

This textbook has been approved by AQA for use with our qualification. This means that we have checked that it broadly covers the specification and we are satisfied with the overall quality. Full details of our approval process can be found on our website.

We approve textbooks because we know how important it is for teachers and students to have the right resources to support their teaching and learning. However, the publisher is ultimately responsible for the editorial control and quality of this book.

Please note that when teaching the AQA GCSE History course, you must refer to AQA's specification as your definitive source of information. While this book has been written to match the specification, it cannot provide complete coverage of every aspect of the course.

A wide range of other useful resources can be found on the relevant subject pages of our website: www.aqa.org.uk.


Links to third party websites are provided by Oxford in good faith and for information only. Oxford disclaims any responsibility for the materials contained in any third party website referenced in this work.



From the author, Tim Williams:
I would like to thank all those who have worked hard in turning what I have written into this book, and for their support throughout the process. I would like to thank Becky DeLozier, Janice Chan, Tamsin Shelton and Sarah Flynn for their patience and guidance, Aaron Wilkes for his creativity and expertise and Jon Cloake for his honest feedback, and the ongoing support and advice that he is always ready to provide. Finally, thank you to my family and friends who have listened patiently every time I have been excited by some new piece of information or historical source.

The publisher would like to thank the following people for offering their contribution in the development of this book: Aaron Wilkes, J.A. Cloake, Fran Robertson, Helen Reilly and Indexing Specialists (UK) Ltd.

# Contents

# Introduction to the Oxford AQA GCSE History series

The Oxford AQA GCSE History series have been specially written by an expert team of teachers and historians with examining experience to match each part of your AQA course. The chapters which follow are laid out according to the content of the AQA specification. Written in an interesting and engaging style, each of the eye-catching double-pages is clearly organised to provide you with a logical route through the historical content.

There is a lively mix of visual **Sources** and **Interpretations** to enhance and challenge your learning and understanding of the history. Extensive use of photographs, diagrams, cartoons, charts and maps allows you to practise using a variety of sources as evidence.

The **Work** activities and **Practice Questions** have been written to help you check your understanding of the content, develop your skills as a historian, and help you prepare not just for GCSE examinations, but for any future studies. You can develop your knowledge and practise examination skills further through the interactive activities, history skills animations, practice questions, revision checklists and more on *Kerboodle*.

## British Depth Studies

British Depth Studies focus on key developments and events in the history of Britain. You will study in detail one of the following periods: Norman England and the establishment of the Norman rule; Medieval England and the reign of Edward I; the last 35 years of Elizabethan England; and the Restoration of the monarchy in England. You will look at economic, religious, political, social and cultural aspects of the period in question. You will also investigate a historic site (such as a castle, battle site, house or religious building) and its context, to help you understand the relationship between a place and historical events.

Understanding history requires not just knowledge, but also a good grasp of concepts such as causation, consequence and change. This book is designed to help you think historically, and features historical **interpretations**. These interpretations will encourage you to reflect on the different ways in which the past may be seen by historians.

We hope you'll enjoy exploring the British Depth Study –

*Jon Cloake*
Series Consultant

*Aaron Wilkes*
Series Editor

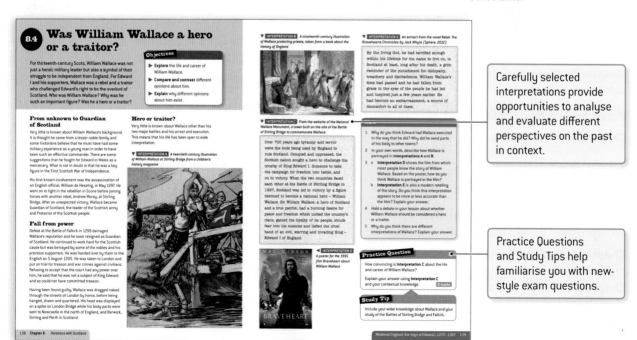

Carefully selected interpretations provide opportunities to analyse and evaluate different perspectives on the past in context.

Practice Questions and Study Tips help familiarise you with new-style exam questions.

*British Depth Studies*

# Medieval England

Edward I was a powerful and intimidating king, succeeding a man who had shown himself to be a weak leader – his father Henry III. He oversaw huge changes to the legal system, made Parliament more representative and made England a powerful player in world trade. His conquests of Scotland and Wales were brutal affairs bringing him into conflict with Llewelyn ap Gruffydd and William Wallace, national heroes in their countries to this day. It was a time of great political, social, cultural and economic change and Edward was at the heart of it.

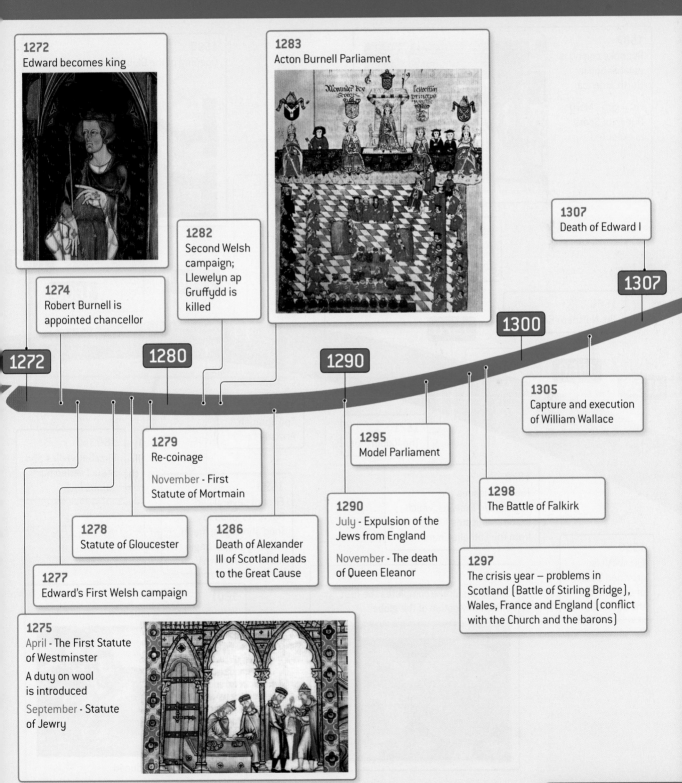

**1272**
Edward becomes king

**1283**
Acton Burnell Parliament

**1307**
Death of Edward I

**1282**
Second Welsh campaign; Llewelyn ap Gruffydd is killed

**1274**
Robert Burnell is appointed chancellor

**1272**

**1280**

**1290**

**1300**

**1307**

**1279**
Re-coinage

November - First Statute of Mortmain

**1295**
Model Parliament

**1305**
Capture and execution of William Wallace

**1278**
Statute of Gloucester

**1286**
Death of Alexander III of Scotland leads to the Great Cause

**1290**
July - Expulsion of the Jews from England

November - The death of Queen Eleanor

**1298**
The Battle of Falkirk

**1277**
Edward's First Welsh campaign

**1297**
The crisis year – problems in Scotland (Battle of Stirling Bridge), Wales, France and England (conflict with the Church and the barons)

**1275**
April - The First Statute of Westminster

A duty on wool is introduced

September - Statute of Jewry

# Elizabethan England

Elizabeth I grew up surrounded by people who said that no woman was capable of ruling England. Yet the Elizabethan age saw great change in all areas of society. From the exploration of Walter Raleigh and Francis Drake to the plays of Shakespeare, and from the defeat of the Spanish Armada to the first Poor Laws, the queen was at the heart of it all. In this British Depth Study, you will gain an understanding of the complexities of Elizabethan society and how its different aspects fit together.

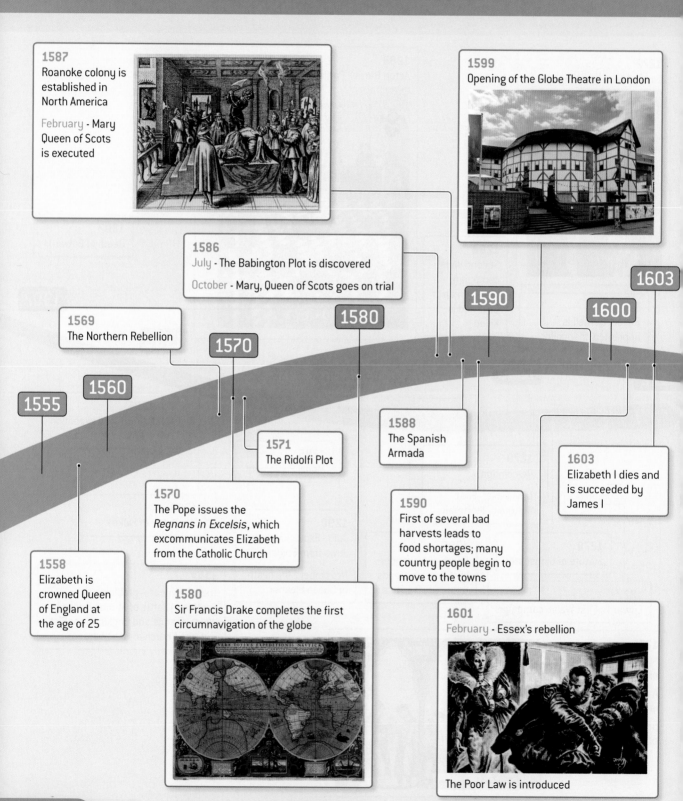

**1587**
Roanoke colony is established in North America

February - Mary Queen of Scots is executed

**1599**
Opening of the Globe Theatre in London

**1586**
July - The Babington Plot is discovered

October - Mary, Queen of Scots goes on trial

**1569**
The Northern Rebellion

**1603**

**1590**

**1600**

**1580**

**1570**

**1560**

**1555**

**1571**
The Ridolfi Plot

**1588**
The Spanish Armada

**1603**
Elizabeth I dies and is succeeded by James I

**1570**
The Pope issues the *Regnans in Excelsis*, which excommunicates Elizabeth from the Catholic Church

**1590**
First of several bad harvests leads to food shortages; many country people begin to move to the towns

**1558**
Elizabeth is crowned Queen of England at the age of 25

**1580**
Sir Francis Drake completes the first circumnavigation of the globe

**1601**
February - Essex's rebellion

The Poor Law is introduced

# Restoration England

When Charles II rode into the streets of London in 1660 the crowds cheered and celebrated, believing a better time was coming after civil war. England had beheaded one king and was now welcoming his son onto the throne. From political conspiracies to the comedies of Restoration theatre, and from the hysteria of the Popish Plot to the rampaging of fire through the streets of London, Restoration England was a time of great political, social, cultural and economic change.

**1660**

May - Charles rides into London having been officially returned to the throne

London theatres reopen

August - The Indemnity and Oblivion Act fulfils Charles's promise to pardon all those who fought against his father apart from the regicides

**1679**

Lord Danby is forced to resign and narrowly avoids trial in the House of Lords for secret negotiations with the French

**1670**

The Secret Treaty of Dover

**1680**

The Exclusion Bill Parliament

**1683**

The Rye House Plot

**1674**

The end of the Cabal and the rise of Lord Danby

**1660**

**1668**

The Cabal Ministry rises to power after the downfall of Clarendon

**1670**

**1680**

**1685**

**1685**

Death of Charles II; the Duke of York becomes James II

**1673**

The Test Act bans Catholics from holding public office

**1666**

The Great Fire of London

**1661**

The Cavalier Parliament is formed; the Clarendon Ministry takes power

**1665**

The Great Plague

1665–67 The Second Anglo-Dutch War

**1672**

The Royal African Company is given the right to trade slaves

1672–75 The Third Anglo-Dutch War

**1678**

The Popish Plot

**1662**

The Licensing of the Press Act limits the freedom to publish anything that challenges the Church of England

April - Charles marries Catherine of Braganza and receives the Indian port of Bombay as part of her dowry

July - The First Navigation Act

**1667**

The Dutch raid on the Medway

# England before 1066

This topic focuses on the arrival of the Normans in England and the establishment of their rule between 1066 to around 1100. To understand this period, you will need to begin by exploring what England was like prior to this time.

Before 1066, England was a sophisticated and civilised society with around two million inhabitants. Religion was an important feature of society: everyone followed Catholic Christianity and accepted what the Church said as absolute fact. King Edward the Confessor had ruled since 1042 and his reign had been stable and largely peaceful. Prior to this, England had been ruled by Edward's half-brother, Harthacnut, whose father was Danish. Danish Vikings had been invading England for many years, and the 'English' kings were often Danish themselves. An '**earl**' was a man of great influence who ran his own area of the country, or 'earldom'. Arguably the most important earl was Godwin, Earl of Wessex.

## Who were the Godwins and why were they important?

The Godwins were a powerful ruling family in Norman England. As you can see in Map A, they controlled a large area of England by 1066.

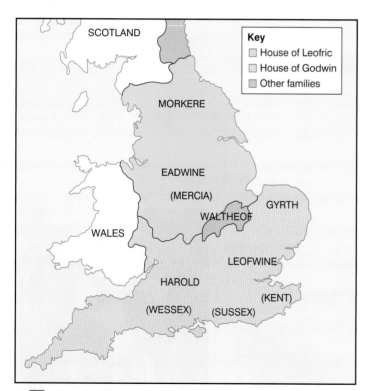

**Key**
- House of Leofric
- House of Godwin
- Other families

SCOTLAND

MORKERE

EADWINE
(MERCIA)

GYRTH

WALTHEOF

WALES

LEOFWINE

HAROLD

(WESSEX)  (SUSSEX)  (KENT)

▲ **A** *The map shows the English earldoms in 1066; borders often changed according to who was earl and how much power they had; the king could take land away or reward land depending upon the relationship he had with the earl*

## The rise of the Godwins

Godwin had a major dispute with King Edward in 1052 which resulted in him being **exiled** from England. Godwin was unhappy with the king's favouritism to his Norman friends to whom he gave many positions in his court. This was unpopular with all of the Anglo-Saxon earls, not just Godwin. Upon his return, Godwin's military forces met King Edward's. Godwin's forces were greater; however, Godwin agreed to publically apologise to Edward. Following Godwin's apology, the king reinstated the earls, their lands and their power, and the power of the Godwins increased. Godwin made his peace with his king and died in King Edward's bedchamber in 1053. His son, Harold, was given Wessex as his earldom; Tostig Godwinson was given Northumbria, but was replaced due to his inability to run his earldom.

## Key Biography

### Earl Godwin (1001–53)

- Born in Sussex and died in Winchester. Wessex was his earldom.
- Wife: Gytha Thorkelsdóttir, a Danish Princess
- Related to kings: father in law of King Edward the Confessor, related to King Cnut through Gytha
- Relationship with King Edward: Godwin's relationship with King Edward was complex and the men often disagreed on important issues

## Government

England was ruled by King Edward the Confessor. The country was divided into areas ruled by earls.

## Lay of the land

Most of the southern half of England was covered in forest. There were small villages where the forest had been cleared and land was farmed.

## Society

The population was organised into a hierarchy. People were ordered by their level of importance, with the king at the top, followed by the Church and the earls, and the peasants at the bottom.

## Religion

Anglo-Saxons were very religious people and were all Christians who followed the Roman Catholic religion. The head of the Roman Catholic Church was the Pope and he lived in the Vatican in Rome. Catholics believed that the Pope was God's personal representative on earth. The Church played an important role in society at this time for a number of different reasons: it provided rules for living; was a major landowner; heard legal cases on its land; and set rules on marriage and **inheritance**.

## England before 1066

## Population

There were around 2 million people living in Britain, but few lived in the northern and western parts of the country. There were hardly any castles so England was not very well defended.

## Defence

The king and earls had around 2500–3000 **housecarls** who were professional, well-trained soldiers. The earls could call upon their peasants to fight for them when necessary.

## Wealth

England was very wealthy and was often a target for foreign raiders such as the Vikings. It had many natural resources which meant that it could establish good trade links with other countries. Previous kings had encouraged more trade with Scandinavian countries, such as King Cnut (1016–1035) who encouraged trade with Norway and Denmark as he was also king of those countries. King Edward had been brought up in Normandy, so England had strong trade links with France as well. England had a sophisticated **minting** system – it made its own coins and had a treasury which made it one of the most advanced economic systems in the known world.

▼ **B** *Simplified Godwin family tree; dates given are dates of death*

Earl Godwin = Gytha

Sweyn 1052 | Harold II 1066 | Edith 1075 | Tostig 1066 | Gyrth 1066 | Leofwine 1066 | Wulfnoth 1094

With Edith Ravenhair

With Eadgyth Swan-neck

Harold Godwin MacHarold — Edmund MacHarold — Magnus MacHarold — Gytha M.Malcolm of Scotland

Harold Haroldson — Ulf Haroldson — Gyrth Haroldson — Edgar Haroldson

## Work

1   What was England like before 1066? Think about both the positive and the negative aspects.

2   Who were the Godwins?

3   Which members of the Godwin family were most important in England? Why were they so important?

4   How important were they and what were the key reasons for their importance?

# Who were the Normans?

In 911, a Viking leader named Rollo attacked northern France. Although he was unsuccessful, the French king, called 'Charles the Simple', realised he was unable to drive Rollo out of France so he proposed a truce. The king offered Rollo an area in the north western part of France in exchange for his **allegiance**. The area was under constant attack from the Vikings, so by putting a Viking in charge it spared the French from having to deal with the problem. Rollo named his new land 'Normandy'. The name was taken from the Scandinavian word *Normandie*, which means 'Northman' and refers to Rollo's place of birth.

**Objectives**

▶ **Identify** the area of Normandy.

▶ **Explain** how William and Edward were related.

▶ **Evaluate** the importance of Normandy at this time.

## What was England's relationship with Normandy?

King Edward the Confessor's mother was Emma, who was the sister of Duke Richard II of Normandy, a distant relative of Rollo. When her Anglo-Saxon husband King Ethelred died in 1016, she sent her sons, Alfred and Edward to live in Normandy with her relatives. They were Ethelred's sons and, for their safety, she sent them to their uncle. When Emma married King Cnut an agreement was made that when he died the throne of England should be passed to their son, rather than Cnut's son, Harold, from a previous marriage. But when King Cnut died in 1035, it was Harold I who inherited the throne, while Emma's son Harthacnut inherited the Danish throne. Emma was determined to have her son Harthacnut crowned king of England, so she summoned her elder sons, Alfred and Edward, back to England in 1040 in order to support their half-brother Harthacnut's claim to the throne. Alfred was captured by Earl Godwin and died of his injuries, whereas Edward was eventually accepted into King Harthacnut's court and was named as his heir. Upon the death of King Harthacnut in 1042, Edward inherited the throne and became king.

During his time as king, Edward brought many of his Norman friends over to England as advisors. The Norman influence was one of the reasons Godwin and Edward argued in 1051 and resulted in Edward reducing the importance of his Norman advisors to avoid conflict with the Anglo-Saxon earls. Many of the Norman advisors went back to Normandy and were replaced by powerful Anglo-Saxons, including several members of the Godwin family.

## The significance of Normandy

William inherited Normandy at the age of seven from his father, Duke Robert I, in 1035. Normandy was a rich area in north western France, and it had been the site of many violent events as the result of Viking invaders. Norman dukes

▼ **INTERPRETATION A** *The picture shows the baptism of Rollo, from a fourteenth-century French manuscript in the Toulouse Library*

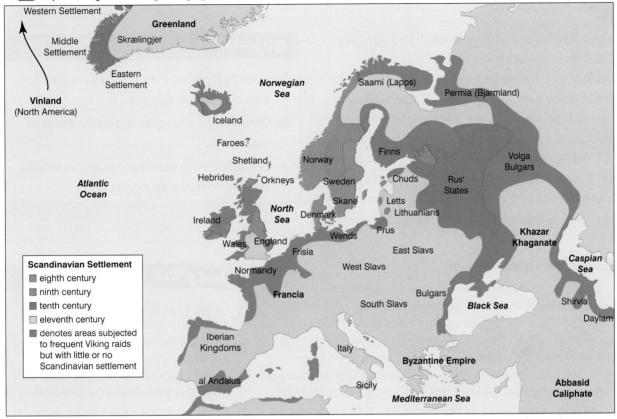

had to acknowledge that French kings were superior, however they could raise their own armies, carry out their own justice and demand their own taxes, so they were independent rulers in their own right. From the moment of Robert's death, there were many attempts to assassinate William by older earls who wanted to replace him as the Duke of Normandy. Duke Robert had not been married to William's mother, Herleva, which meant that William was an illegitimate child. His enemies used this as an opportunity to humiliate him, calling him 'William the Bastard'. William had to learn to fight for himself from an early age, and proved himself to be a shrewd politician and a successful general. William earned himself the title 'Conqueror' because of his successful campaigns in Maine and Sicily in the early 1060s, thus proving that the Normans were a force to be reckoned with.

William was related to King Edward through Emma, who was the sister of William's great grandfather Richard II, Duke of Normandy. This made William a distant cousin of Edward's. In addition, as Edward had been raised in Normandy with Emma's family, William was friends with the English king and visited him in England.

## Extension

Research the history of the Vikings in England up until 1066. Go back to the time of Alfred the Great and make a note of the dates of battles between Vikings and Anglo-Saxons. Plot the dates on a timeline. Do you notice a pattern? Are there any periods of intense warfare or relative peace?

## Key Words

allegiance

## Study Tip

Maps are really useful when studying history as they can show how countries relate to each other. This is vital when considering the importance of the Vikings. The Vikings had a large sphere of influence in the eleventh century, which caused conflict in the countries they invaded.

## Work

1 Where is Normandy?
2 Who was Rollo and how did he manage to gain control of Normandy?
3 How was William related to Edward?
4 Why do you think Normandy was so important at this time?

# The rivals for the throne

When Edward the Confessor died on 5 January 1066 he had no children. As a result, it was unclear who was to become king. After Edward's death there were many powerful men who put forward their claim to the throne, four of whom presented the strongest claims. However, the claimants came from different countries and had differing levels of support. This, in turn, meant that whoever became the new king had the potential to change England forever.

**Objectives**

▶ **Identify** the claimants and their reasons for their claims to the throne.

▶ **Compare** the strengths and weaknesses of each claim.

▶ **Evaluate** the arguments and draw conclusions about who had the strongest claim.

## Rules of inheritance

At this time in history there were several different ways in which the throne could be passed on. Firstly, a son of the king could inherit the title, though it did not necessarily have to be the eldest son. If the king had no sons, then a male relative of a previous king could be chosen instead. The second way was **post obitum** which meant 'after death' and was a nomination or bequest, in this case of the throne of England. Alternatively, the king could name an heir of his choice; if this decision was made on his deathbed it was known as **novissima verba**. The **Witan** (a group of nobles and leading churchmen) could either suggest an heir or support the king's own choice. Finally, there was the use of force: claimants could challenge each other for the throne, and the successful man was then crowned.

**Study Tip**

Family trees are useful ways of making sure you understand how everyone relates to the events you are studying. It is useful to plot the people and key events (such as start and end dates of reigns) on a timeline of the period. Keep plotting events on your timeline as you learn them. Then use one colour per person to highlight events they were involved in to see the impact that person had.

▼ **A** *This family tree shows the ties between some of the claimants and their families*

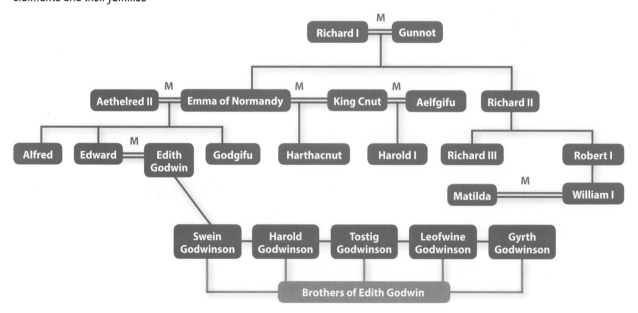

## The four claimants: Who do you think had the strongest claim to the throne of England?

### Key Biography

#### Edgar the Outlaw (c1051–c1126)

- Edgar (also known as the **Aethling**) was the great nephew of Edward the Confessor. He was related through the male line, so had the closest blood tie to Edward.

- Edgar was born in Hungary as his father, Edward the Exile, had been sent there by King Cnut to prevent him from causing trouble after Cnut took the English throne. King Edward called for Edgar to return to England in 1057 as he had not managed to produce an heir himself. However, Edward did not name Edgar as his heir.

- Edgar and his sister had lived with Edward and his wife, Edith, since they were small children. Edgar was treated as Edward's adopted son, and many people thought of him as such.

- Edgar was an Anglo-Saxon and had the support of many earls.

- Edgar was known as an outlaw due to his actions after 1066; he took part in a number of rebellions against the Normans.

### Work

1. Make a list of the ways in which the throne of England could be inherited.
2. Why did Hardrada think he had a claim to the throne?
3. Why did Edgar think he had a claim to the throne?
4. Who do you think had a stronger claim: Hardrada or Edgar? Give reasons for your choice.

### Fact

Historians sometimes add a 'c' before dates. This stands for 'circa', which means 'around' or 'approximately'.

### Key Biography

#### Harald Hardrada ('hard ruler') (1015–1066)

- Harald was the King of Norway, and was a powerful Viking with a large and successful army.

- Harald was related to King Cnut (reigned 1016 to 1035). His claim was that, as Edward had no sons a relative of the previous king should be chosen, therefore he himself should be king.

- It was said that Hardrada's father, Magnus, had been promised the throne by Cnut's son, Harthacnut. Therefore, Hardrada believed he had a claim to the throne through his father. However, when Harthacnut died, Edward claimed the throne instead of stepping aside for Hardrada.

## Key Biography

### Harold Godwinson (1022–1066)

- Harold was the most important earl in England as Earl of Wessex.
- Harold was '**sub-regulus**', a deputy king who ran England for Edward and represented him in battle from 1060 onwards.
- Harold said that Edward had promised him the throne on his deathbed; he was supported by all of the English nobles (except Tostig, Harold's brother – the pair had fallen out) and had the support of the Witan.

## Key Biography

### William, Duke of Normandy (c1028–87)

- William took over as Duke of Normandy aged seven, and faced many attempts on his life due to his position.
- William was a successful and brutal warrior. In 1047, William and his army won the battle of Val-es-Dunes and cut off the hands and feet of enemies after they made comments about his mother.
- William was a distant cousin of Edward through Edward's mother, Emma.
- William claimed that Edward had promised him the throne earlier in his reign. In 1051, the Godwins had rebelled against Edward; William travelled to England to give his support to Edward and, as a result (according to William), Edward promised him the throne.
- William said that Harold had sworn to support his claim to the throne in 1064.

### Who did Edward support?

There were a number of reasons why King Edward the Confessor might have supported Harold Godwinson. Harold was the most powerful earl in England because he was the Earl of Wessex, the richest earldom in the land, and was the eldest member of the Godwin family after his brother and his father died in 1052. Harold was also Edward's brother in law as Edith Godwin had married King Edward in 1045. However, King Edward and the Godwin family had a complicated history and there had been occasions in the past where they had rebelled against the king. King Edward also had family ties to Normandy. It is unclear as to who was promised what in the years before King Edward died, and this is what caused the crisis over who would be king in 1066.

▲ **INTERPRETATION B**  *A section of the **Bayeux Tapestry**, apparently showing Harold Godwinson swearing on holy relics; it is thought he is promising to support William's claim to the throne in front of William himself*

▼ **INTERPRETATION C**  *Adapted from 'The Norman Conquest' by N. J. Higham, Sutton Pocket Histories 1998:*

On his deathbed in the presence of his wife, his steward and the archbishop, Edward nominated Harold as his successor. With William's candidacy unsupported in England, Tostig in exile and Edgar inexperienced, Edward had little option but to reinforce the candidacy of his brother in law and sub regulus.

## Extension

One of the most important pieces of evidence for this period is the Bayeux Tapestry. The Tapestry was made in Normandy in the 1070s and was commissioned by Bishop Odo, William's brother in law. We have to be careful when studying the Tapestry as it was made after the event at a time when William wanted to show the English that he was the rightful heir to the throne.

Research more sections of the Bayeux Tapestry that relate to who the rightful heir to the throne was. Does the information change who you think had the best claim to the throne? If so, why?

## Work

1  a  Copy and complete the following table to assess the different claims to the throne. For each claimant, tick the box if the condition for a claim to the throne applies to that person. Then, underneath your table, write a brief explanation of how it applies.

1  b  Prioritise the claims to the throne from strongest to weakest. Which person do you think had the most convincing reasons for their claim? Explain why you have chosen them and not the other three.

|  | Edgar the Outlaw | Harald Hardrada | Harold Godwinson | William of Normandy |
|---|---|---|---|---|
| Family ties |  |  |  |  |
| *Post obitum* |  |  |  |  |
| *Novissima verba* |  |  |  |  |
| Election or selection |  |  |  |  |
| Force or power |  |  |  |  |

2  Imagine you are the campaign manager for one of the claimants to the throne. Design a campaign poster for your chosen potential successor. Include a slogan, a picture that will capture the imagination of the English people, and one reason why the person you have chosen should be the new king.

3  Read **Interpretation C**. Why did King Edward the Confessor nominate Harold Godwinson to be king? Who does the interpretation suggest King Edward really wanted to be his successor? Why could King Edward's wishes not be fulfilled?

### Practice Question

Explain what was important about William, Duke of Normandy's claim to the English throne.        **8 marks**

### Study Tip

You could think about where William was from and why this was important. You could also consider who else had a claim to the throne and the problems William's claim created for them.

# William prepares to invade

When King Edward the Confessor died on 5 January 1066, Harold Godwinson was crowned King of England the very next day. However, William, Duke of Normandy, expected the throne to pass to him. William claimed he was promised the throne by Edward in 1051 during the dispute with the Godwin family. William started to **mobilise** his forces in preparation for an invasion of England as soon as he found out about Harold's **coronation**. William did not invade straight away; instead, he chose to take a long-term strategy and amass his military forces whilst also preparing political and religious support for his campaign.

## Objectives

▶ **Summarise** William's preparations for invasion.

▶ **Identify** the strengths of the preparation plans.

▶ **Assess** William's preparations.

## William's invasion preparations

### French support

William had conquered the French province of Maine in 1063 and had a good relationship with the previous French king, Henry. Henry's son was 14 in 1066 so was too young to present a threat to Normandy. There was civil war in Anjou, and William was the most powerful man in north-west Europe as he had the most support. William had a secure base around Normandy as he had extended his area of authority over neighbouring provinces, and even as far away as Sicily, before invading England.

▲ **A** Map showing William's power and the areas that he controlled

### Getting across the channel

The ships and men were gathered together for a long period, but William ensured that they were well fed so they did not suffer. He also moved his fleet from the mouth of the River Dives to the mouth of the River Somme at Valery, halving the journey to England to around 33km (20 miles).

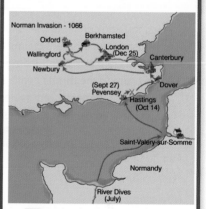

▲ **B** Map showing the relocation of William's fleet

### Support from God

William sent Lanfranc, a leading member of the Norman church, to Rome, where he persuaded the Pope that the English Church needed reforming and William was the man to do it. This led to the Pope giving a **Papal Banner** to William, which meant William had the Pope's support in what was now a **Holy War**.

## How did William prepare to invade England?

### Military preparations: the army

Once William had the Papal Banner, he recruited men from all over France – from Aquitaine, Flanders, Central France, Maine and Brittany – and also Sicily. Many men joined because they wanted to be part of a Holy War, but recruits were also promised land and riches. Eventually, around 8000 men were ready to cross the English Channel.

### Military preparations: the fleet

William did not have a navy so he built a large number of flat-bottomed boats that could transport horses. Weapons were produced and 'flat pack' castles were made, so that when the Normans landed, they could put up the temporary castles very quickly.

## Timeline: Events of 1066

| 5 Jan | 6 Jan | 8 Sept | 20 Sept | 25 Sept | 28 Sept | 6 Oct | 11 Oct | 14 Oct |
|---|---|---|---|---|---|---|---|---|
| King Edward the Confessor dies | King Edward buried and Harold Godwinson crowned king | King Harold has to disband his fleet and southern army | Battle of Fulford Gate | King Harold beats Harald Hardrada's invading forces at the Battle of Stamford Bridge | William, Duke of Normandy, lands at Pevensey | King Harold arrives back in London | King Harold leaves London | Battle of Hastings |

▼ **INTERPRETATION C** *Norman invaders landing on the English coast in 1066*

## Landing in England

The wind had been blowing in the wrong direction at the River Dives and this led to the relocation of the fleet. William eventually landed at Pevensey on 28 September 1066. During the summer months Harold had waited in the south with an army but when William didn't come, many of the English soldiers had been allowed to return home. Harold himself had travelled north with his elite soldiers to fight off an invasion from another contender – Harald Hardrada at the battles of Fulford Gate and Stamford Bridge. Upon arrival, William's troops immediately built a castle using the 'flat pack' structures they had brought with them. They could now defend their landing spot.

## Key Words

mobilise    coronation
Papal Banner    Holy War

## Work

1. Create bullet points to summarise William's preparations for invasion. Use the spider diagram on page 18 to help you.

2. Look again at the spider diagram of William's invasion preparations. Create a table showing the measures William took to prepare for the invasion and then identify strengths and weaknesses. Why did William not invade as soon as Edward died?

3. Why was Harold not there to fight William as soon as he landed at Pevensey?

4. Assess William's preparations overall. How effective do you think they were? What problems did he create for Harold?

### Practice Question

Explain what was important about William's preparations for the invasion.    **8 marks**

### Study Tip

You should consider the military, political and spiritual preparations.

# Harald Hardrada invades

From the moment that Harold Godwinson was crowned, he was aware that he faced a number of challenges to his throne. He marched south with part of his army to prepare for an invasion by William, Duke of Normandy, and he left the rest of the army under the command of his brothers in law, earls Edwin and Morcar. What happened to the earls and the northern army? And how did Harold react?

**Objectives**

▶ **Describe** the Battle of Fulford Gate and the Battle of Stamford Bridge.

▶ **Explain** why Hardrada won the Battle of Fulford Gate but not Stamford Bridge.

▶ **Relate** the defeat of Hardrada to the threat King Harold faced from William, Duke of Normandy.

## Hardrada prepares to strike

Harold waited for William during the spring and summer months, but he had to allow the ordinary peasant soldiers (known as the **fyrd**) to go home on 8 September because they needed to harvest their crops. It was at this point that Harald Hardrada of Norway launched his invasion. Hardrada sailed up the river Humber with 300 ships and landed 16 km (10 miles) from the city of York. Earls Edwin and Morcar were waiting for him with the northern army and attempted to prevent the Norwegian forces from advancing to York. The battle between the two sides was known as the Battle of Fulford Gate (see Fact, right).

▲ **INTERPRETATION A** *A thirteenth-century portrayal of the Battle of Fulford Gate from* The Life of King Edward the Confessor *by English chronicler Matthew Paris*

**Extension**

Research the Battle of Fulford Gate. Documentaries and re-enactments (acting out past events) are useful as they can show the lie of the land. Once you have more details, write a newspaper account of the battle from either the Viking or the Anglo-Saxon point of view.

**Fact**

### The Battle of Fulford Gate

**Date:** 20 September 1066

**Place:** Fulford, just outside York

**Invaders:** Hardrada, King of Norway; Tostig, younger brother of King Harold; and around 7000 Viking soldiers.

**Defenders:** The Anglo-Saxon earls, Edwin and Morcar, and around 3500 members of the English northern army.

**Outline of the battle:** Only a few Norwegians arrived at the battleground at first, and the English won an advantage through superior numbers and the element of surprise. However, as the battle continued, more Viking troops arrived and their numbers eventually overwhelmed the Anglo-Saxons.

**Outcome:** Hardrada and the Vikings won, but both sides suffered losses. The northern army was disorganised and scattered, and Edwin and Morcar were forced to flee.

## Battle of Stamford Bridge

The loss at Fulford meant that King Harold had to move quickly to deal with the Viking invasion. Harold had already disbanded the southern army earlier in the month, so he moved north with his private army and gathered forces as he went. The journey of 306km (190 miles) was covered in four days, and King Harold reached Tadcaster, a town on the outskirts of York, on 24 September. He waited overnight with his troops and on 25 September he entered York and came upon the Viking troops at Stamford Bridge. The Anglo-Saxons had the advantage of surprise as the Vikings were not expecting King Harold to reach York so quickly. The Vikings were camped on the opposite side of the river Derwent from the English and had not defended the bridge across the river properly. The resulting battle was long and bloody, and Hardrada and Tostig were both killed. However, King Harold's victory was short lived. Three days later on 28 September, William, Duke of Normandy, landed on the south coast of England.

> Hardrada was not expecting King Harold so soon. His army was split on both sides of the river Derwent and most were not wearing their armour.

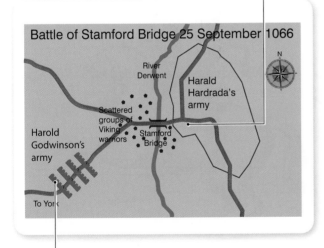

Battle of Stamford Bridge 25 September 1066

River Derwent

Harald Hardrada's army

Scattered groups of Viking warriors

Stamford Bridge

Harold Godwinson's army

To York

> Harold marched his men north to Tadcaster, and then on to Stamford Bridge.

> The battle raged on but King Harold won and Hardrada was killed. According to sources, only 24 out of the 300 ships that landed in England were needed to return the survivors to Norway.

▲ **INTERPRETATION B** The Lone Norseman, *painted in the 1970s*

### Key Words

fyrd

### Fact

Some historians believe that there was a giant Norwegian who stood on the bridge with an axe and killed 40 Anglo-Saxons. He was killed later by some cunning Anglo-Saxons who floated under the bridge in a barrel and stabbed him between his legs.

### Work

1. Describe the Battle of Fulford Gate using as many adjectives as you can.

2. Why did Hardrada win the Battle of Fulford Gate but not Stamford Bridge? Make a list of advantages and disadvantages he had at both battles to help you explain your answer.

3. How did the defeat of Hardrada relate to the threat King Harold faced from William, Duke of Normandy? Think about the geography of the battles, the outcomes of the battles and the preparations of William and the Normans.

### Practice Question

How convincing is **Interpretation B** about the Battle of Stamford Bridge? Explain your answer using **Interpretation B** and your contextual knowledge.

**8 marks**

### Study Tip

Consider the organisation of troops, the main events, and the outcome. How is the interpretation convincing when you judge it against what you know?

# 2.3 Harold versus William: who will win?

King Harold was in York, recovering from the Battle of Stamford Bridge, when he heard about William's invasion fleet landing in Pevensey. Harold's armies were exhausted from long marches and the battles with the Vikings. King Harold was faced with a dilemma. Should he march straight to the south coast with his weary troops to surprise William? Or should he take time to rest and gather more troops before marching south?

## Objectives

▶ **State** the strengths and weaknesses of the armies of King Harold and William.

▶ **Evaluate** who might win: Harold or William?

▶ **Justify** your choice of the potential winner of the battle.

## Harold's decision

Harold's difficult decision as to whether to launch a surprise attack on William or allow his soldiers to rest was soon decided for him. Harold heard news that William and his Norman forces were attacking villages on the south coast and were making their way to London. So Harold left immediately and marched his tired army south to confront the invading Normans.

**INTERPRETATION A** *Adapted from the* Anglo-Saxon Chronicle, *the only English account of the Battle of Hastings:*

> William came upon King Harold by surprise and before his army was drawn up in battle array.

▲ **B** *A Norman knight in chain mail armour*

### Study Tip

**Interpretation A** shows that Harold had managed to surprise William. However, other sources say that William had sent out scouts so he was in fact aware that Harold and his army were there. The Anglo-Saxons were camped on Senlac Hill, so William had to attack them there if he was to be successful.

## Timeline: Build-up to the battle, 1066

| 11 Aug | 28 Sept | 6 Oct | 11 Oct | 13 Oct |
|---|---|---|---|---|
| William ready to launch an invasion from Normandy | William lands at Pevensey; King Harold marches south | King Harold and the remnants of his army reach London | King Harold leaves London, choosing not to wait for 30,000 reinforcements, and marches to meet William | King Harold reaches the South Downs |

# Who was more prepared to win?

|  | King Harold and the Anglo-Saxons | Duke William and the Normans |
|---|---|---|
| **Type and size of army** | Fyrd; around 7000 | Mixture of trained **mercenary** forces from Normandy and Western Europe; around 7000 |
| **Specialist soldiers** | Housecarls and **thegns** | Knights, trained from the age of three, riding horses that were trained to kick and bite in battle. |
| **Weaponry and armour** | Double-handed axes, pikes, large circular shields; Housecarls had armour; peasants used pitchforks, farming equipment, and weapons and armour taken from fallen soldiers. | Bows, large tear-shaped shields that covered from chin to knee, pikes, armour |
| **Battle style** | **Shield wall** formation: interlocking round shields to prevent enemy soldiers from penetrating the line; use of double-handed axe. Most soldiers were foot soldiers or **infantry**. King Harold was positioned in the centre of his troops on foot as Anglo-Saxons did not use horses in battle. | Various: infantry attacked on foot, archers were used to wear down the enemy. Troops were organised into divisions: each division commander used a system of flags to communicate so they could change tactics in battle. William rode a horse. Knights on horseback carried **lances** and made up the **cavalry**. |
| **Position in battlefield** | Positioned at the top of Senlac Hill | Arrived at the battleground first. Chose a site at the base of Senlac Hill, on an old Roman road which ran over the top of the hill. There was marshy land on either side so the road itself became the battlefield. It was an important road – Harold had to use it to get to William, and William had to use it to get to London. It was a site that would change the course of English history. |
| **Previous experience in battle** | King Harold was an experienced general and had successfully fought against the Welsh and Vikings. | Duke William had conquered many areas around Normandy and as far afield as Sicily. |
| **State of the army** | King Harold had marched his army north in four days to face Harald Hardrada on 25 September. He then marched his army south, arrived in London on 6 October, and left London on 11 October to face William. His army was exhausted. | William had landed at Pevensey on 28 September. The Normans erected a castle and then made their way along the south coast, burning villages as they went. They arrived in Hastings and had several days to rest and prepare for the battle with King Harold and the Anglo-Saxons. William brought plenty of horses and supplies so the army could refuel before the battle. |
| **Extra support** | King Harold was a popular king amongst most Anglo-Saxons and had the support of the Witan and some of his brothers. | Duke William had the support of the young King Philip I of France. He also had the Papal Banner from the Pope in Rome (and therefore the support of God). |

## Extension

On a map of England, plot King Harold's journey from London to Stamford Bridge, and then back south to Hastings. Look back through what you have learned so far to recall how far his troops had to march and how long it took. Can you work out an estimated marching speed per hour?

## Key Words

mercenary   thegn   shield wall   infantry   lance   cavalry

## Work

1. Look at the table above. Make a list of the strengths and weaknesses of each army.

2. a. Who do you think would win the battle?
   b. Justify your choice of winner by explaining why they are more prepared and what advantages they have over the other. Think about how they would overcome the strengths of their opponents.

# Historic Environment: The Battle of Hastings

## 2.4A

Norman battles were very advanced in terms of their tactics and weaponry for the medieval period, although the outcome of battles was always difficult to predict. Both long-term and short-term planning played a vital role alongside advanced tactics, weaponry and organisation of troops. There were other factors that could also be decisive; for example, mistakes made by the opposition, geographical factors, and even luck. What were Norman battles like? What happened at the Battle of Hastings, and how do we know about it?

### Objectives

▶ **State** the events and outcome of the Battle of Hastings.

▶ **Compare** the strategy and luck of both sides.

▶ **Analyse** whether the outcome of the battle was affected by its location.

## Norman warfare

The Normans used a variety of tactics in order to win battles. Knights on horseback, called cavalry, were trained from the age of three, and the horses were trained to kick and bite. Archers were also used frequently. The army was divided into divisions, and flags called **gonfanon** were used to signal manoeuvres on the battlefield. The Norman army was made up of professional soldiers who spent many hours practising.

## What happened at Hastings?

William and his troops landed in Pevensey. King Harold was still in the north dealing with Harald Hardrada's Viking invasion. William was keen to deal with King Harold and provoked him by making his way up the coast towards London, attacking and burning villages as he went. He arrived in Hastings and decided to make his stand 11 km (7 miles) outside the town at the crossroads of the old Roman road to London. William arrived at the battle site and chose to site his troops at the bottom of Senlac Hill.

**1** The battle started at 9am as Norman archers walked up to Senlac Hill and fired a volley of arrows. However, the archers were too close to the hill and the arrows flew over the heads of the Anglo-Saxons. Some of the Norman infantry charged up the hill but were blocked by the housecarls. The Anglo-Saxons' main form of defence was the shield wall. Housecarls overlapped their circular shields and this was a very effective way of defending their position.

**2** After the first Norman attack failed, a section of the Norman army ran away from the Norman line. Members of the fyrd ran after them but became stuck in the marshy land at the bottom of the hill. The Normans turned and slaughtered the Anglo-Saxons who had chased them. This tactic became known as the **feigned retreat** and it slowly drained the shield wall of Anglo-Saxon soldiers.

**3** At around midday, there was a break in the fighting to allow both sides to remove their dead and wounded. William changed his tactics and moved his archers from the front of the battlefield to behind the infantry. The change in position of the archers meant that, rather than flying over the heads of the housecarls, their arrows hit the Anglo-Saxon army squarely and caught them by surprise.

**4**

William ordered the cavalry to charge, which led to heavy casualties on both sides. Harold's troops managed to stay in formation but the Normans deployed their feigned retreat again. Both sides suffered heavy losses and William ordered his knights to dismount and attack on foot. At the same time his archers fired their arrows and the knights and infantry charged at the Anglo-Saxons.

**5**

By 4pm, the Anglo-Saxon shield wall was beginning to disintegrate and the Normans began to attack and break through the sides of the wall. The remaining housecarls fell into a defensive position around Harold. It was at this time that King Harold was killed. Seeing his death, the fyrd broke ranks and fled.

## Factors that influenced the outcome of the Battle of Hastings

- King Harold hurried to face William: he could have waited for between 20–30,000 extra troops from the south-west, but he chose to go straight to Hastings.
- Harold had fought alongside the Normans in 1064 and was aware of their tactics, but still used the old Anglo-Saxon shield wall technique.
- Harold chose to fight on foot rather than horseback, so it was difficult for him to communicate with his troops or to give orders once the battle began.
- Harold had split his army in the spring of 1066; when the northern army was defeated by Hardrada, it had to march south and fight the Normans.
- Both Hardrada and William decided to launch their invasions at the same time.
- The weather delayed William's invasion; this gave Harold time to defeat the Vikings before William arrived.

- Some say that some of William's soldiers ran away, which led to the feigned retreat.
- William chose to delay his invasion; the long wait **demoralised** Harold's soldiers.
- The double invasion occurred during the harvest season, which led to **desertions** in Harold's fyrd.
- William gained the Papal Banner so his soldiers believed they had God's blessing to fight and, if they died, they went to heaven.
- William had time to rest his army and train them on the actual battle ground. He brought all of the equipment he needed to build castles and feed his army and horses.
- William chose the site of the battleground.
- William took his time invading; he ensured that he had made all the preparations necessary.
- William's troops were highly organised into divisions with a system of communication.
- William was on horseback so had more control of his troops and could be more responsive.

## Work

1  Why did William win? Make a list of reasons. Then, group them into pre-battle preparations and events that occured during the battle.

2  a  Look at the table of factors above. Divide the factors into 'Harold's mistakes', 'William's superior tactics' and 'luck'.

   b  Did William win because he was superior or was it down to bad luck for Harold? In pairs, argue each side of the case.

3  How might the features of the location of the battle have influenced its outcome?

# Historic Environment: The Battle of Hastings

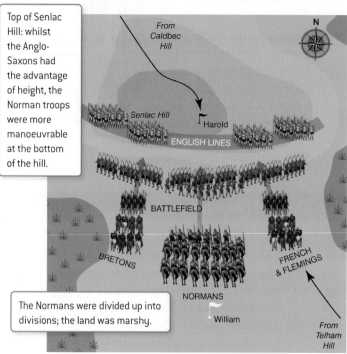

Top of Senlac Hill: whilst the Anglo-Saxons had the advantage of height, the Norman troops were more manoeuvrable at the bottom of the hill.

The Normans were divided up into divisions; the land was marshy.

▲ **A** *The battleground at Hastings at 9am*

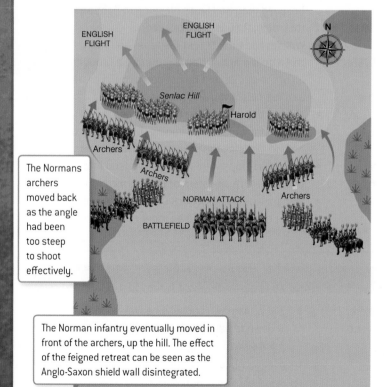

The Normans archers moved back as the angle had been too steep to shoot effectively.

The Norman infantry eventually moved in front of the archers, up the hill. The effect of the feigned retreat can be seen as the Anglo-Saxon shield wall disintegrated.

▲ **B** *The battleground at Hastings at 5pm*

## What is the historical debate surrounding Norman tactics?

Some historians think that William's victory was down to his brilliant military leadership; others think it was down to luck, and the fact that King Harold made a number of mistakes. In order to be able to assess which view is the most accurate, it is essential to study the environment of the battle ground. There has been much debate over the most radical of William's strategies: the feigned retreat. This was when a section of the Norman army ran away and the enemy followed them; when the Normans were out of sight they turned and massacred all of the attacking enemy troops. This tactic was repeated to wear down the opponent and was made more effective as the Anglo-Saxons were slowed by the marshland at the bottom of the hill. Anglo-Saxon writers describe it as being an unplanned move that William turned to his advantage. However, Norman writers state that this tactic had been successfully used before by William in campaigns in Sicily. Whilst the debate rages on, the question remains: why did William choose to assemble his troops at the bottom of Senlac Hill and give the advantage of height to his enemy?

## What can we learn from the Bayeux Tapestry?

The Bayeux Tapestry features images of weaponry and tactics and as such is considered by many to be a piece of Norman **propaganda**.

The Tapestry was a record of events from the Norman perspective and it helps to explain why William invaded in the first place. One of the reasons Duke William gave for the invasion was that he had been promised the throne by King Edward the Confessor. In 1064, Harold Godwinson had visited Normandy and Duke William had reported that Harold had sworn an oath on holy relics to support his claim to the throne.

## Key Biography

### Bishop Odo of Bayeux (1036–1097)

- Bishop Odo was the half-brother of William, Duke of Normandy, as they had the same mother but different fathers.
- He was an experienced soldier but also an administrator.
- He fought with Duke William at Hastings and this is shown in the Bayeux Tapestry by him wielding a club.
- He was very loyal to Duke William up until the mid-1070s, and was rewarded with lands and titles after the battle. However, he later led a revolt against William's son.

## Key Words

propaganda    fealty    apologist

▼ **INTERPRETATION D** The History of William the Conqueror (c1073) by William of Poitiers; Poitiers was first trained as a soldier and then became a priest in William's household:

> As before, several thousand [English] were bold enough to rush forward, as if on wings, to pursue those who they took to be fleeing, when the Normans suddenly turned their horse's heads, stopped them in their tracks, crushed them completely and massacred them down to the last man.

▼ **INTERPRETATION C** *Norman cavalry attacking Senlac Hill, from the Bayeux Tapestry*

However, when we look at other evidence from the time, the issue of the oath becomes unclear. The Anglo-Saxon Chronicle, an English interpretation, does not mention the oath at all. Orderic Vitalis, an Englishman writing 40 years after Hastings, does mention the oath, but not when it was made or why it was made. If Harold made an oath of **fealty** to Duke William, this did not necessarily mean he had to hand the crown over to him.

Why are these accounts so different? The Bayeux Tapestry and other Norman sources, such as William of Poitiers and William of Jumieges, were writing in the time after the Battle of Hastings, when William was trying to gain control of England. As such they are known as Norman **apologists**, which is to say that they were recording the events of Hastings but in a way that would make William more acceptable to the English (and to make Harold Godwinson less popular). We can explore this by comparing the Tapestry to English accounts of the events.

## Work

1. When and why was the Bayeux Tapestry made?
2. Recall the Battle of Hastings and make a chronological list of the main events.
3. Explain which interpretation is the most reliable for telling us about what happened at Hastings?
4. How useful is the Bayeux Tapestry?

### Study Tip

Firstly, consider what decided the outcome of battles at this time. What were the reasons for William's success at the Battle of Hastings? Did a combination of factors lead to Harold's defeat? You should consider the terrain over which the battle was fought. Who had the advantage? Who was the better leader? What were their plans? Think about the decisions they made at different points in the battle. Was there a turning point? How did the troops and equipment on each side compare? Were they equally matched? Lastly think about the element of luck. Was the battle decided by something neither side could have predicted or prevented?

# Historic Environment: Norman castles

Between 1066 and 1086, the Normans built around 500 **motte and bailey** castles: about one every two weeks. These castles were part of William's long-term strategy to secure his position on the throne of England. As soon as he landed in Pevensey, he rebuilt a Roman castle as a base from which to move along the English coast towards London. Although he had won the Battle of Hastings it did not mean that he had conquered England. Defeated Anglo-Saxons did not want him as their ruler, and building castles was a key way to control their anger and possible retaliation. What can we learn about the historical period from these first Norman motte and bailey castles?

**Objectives**

▶ **Identify** why the Normans built a castle at Pevensey.

▶ **Explain** the features and functions of a Norman castle.

▶ **Assess** the impact of Pevensey Castle on the surrounding area.

## The purpose of castles

Anglo-Saxons had built royal castles, or 'burghs', as defensive features. In contrast, the Normans built castles as bases for offensive patrols into the surrounding area: from castles, the Normans could attack angry Anglo-Saxons who aimed to overthrow their Norman rulers. While Anglo-Saxon castles were built for the king, Norman castles were primarily built by the nobility to protect themselves from hostile locals. Castles symbolised Norman suppression of the Anglo-Saxons as they were physically higher than the English. Norman castles were large, imposing buildings that were built to intimidate, bully and to administrate the local area; they showed who the foreign conquerors were and that the Normans were never far away. They commanded the landscape in every direction and were a visible distinction between the rulers and the ruled. Castles could terrorise the local population, so perhaps William's building of Pevensey Castle was the reason why Harold came down so quickly after Stamford Bridge to defend his territory.

## Motte and bailey castles

Motte and bailey castles were quick and easy to erect and made use of existing geographical features, such as hills. The motte was the mound or hill that the **keep** was built upon, and the bailey was the outer area that surrounded the motte. The first motte and bailey castles were made out of wood which the Normans brought with them from Normandy. Pevensey Castle is a good example of this.

Wooden motte and bailey castles were built until 1070. After this date, stone keeps were added and by 1100 all new castles were made from stone. A contemporary source records that there were 48 large castles by 1086, although there were many smaller castles around the land.

## Where were castles built?

Castles were built at sites that were strategically important. For example, there was a high density of castles along the Welsh border **marchlands** to protect the Normans from English and Welsh rebels living in the troublesome border regions. William personally ordered the building of a number of castles, including the ones at Colchester, the Tower of London, Hastings, Windsor and Warwick. Castles were often built near existing towns, on high ground and close to a water source. Often, land had to be cleared to build the houses within the castle grounds, so any buildings in the area were knocked down; this was a very unpopular policy with the Anglo-Saxons. The location of castles was extremely important as they had to be high enough to see attackers coming, defend important routes such as the old Roman roads or river crossings, have easy access to resources such as wood, food and water, and also have natural advantages for defence. Castles were often located near a bend in a river or on the coast as the water would provide a natural moat.

## Work

1   Describe the different uses of Norman castles.

2   How were the sites of castles chosen?

3   Study Map A. Which areas of the country had more castles than others? Can you think of the reasons for this?

▼ **INTERPRETATION B**   *A section from the Bayeux Tapestry showing the construction of the motte and bailey castle at Pevensey; this image shows that the mound is composed of alternate layers of soil and shingle mixed with stone, giving it a solid foundation which stopped it from being quickly eroded; the Tapestry makers have shown this as different coloured layers*

## Practice Question

How convincing is **Interpretation B** about Norman motte and bailey castles?

Explain using **Interpretation B** and your contextual knowledge.   8 marks

## Study Tip

You should aim to explain why the Normans used motte and bailey castles, in particular the one they built at Pevensey. You could also think about the interpretation itself, and how your knowledge confirms and supports what it shows or tells you. Look back at the previous pages on the Bayeux Tapestry to help you.

# Historic Environment: Norman castles

## The first castle: Pevensey

In addition to being the first Norman castle, Pevensey was typical of castles built at this time: a lot of Norman castles have similar histories and features. Pevensey castle was created as a temporary shelter for William and his nobles and as a base from which to launch their invasion of England. Pevensey was seen as the gateway to Britain as it was a coastal location at the time. There were already the stone remains of a Roman **fort**, which William built on and incorporated into the castle. Pevensey Castle continued to develop as an important site from the times of the Romans through to the end of the Norman period and beyond.

**Outer bailey:** the area within the outer wall that surrounded the motte and any other buildings, including houses, which needed to be kept safe. Defenders could push attackers off if they did manage to scale the wall. The Normans extended the existing Roman ruins by building a wooden, and then stone, motte and bailey. The old Roman road runs through the bailey.

**Outer bailey wall:** very high walls with plenty of lookout posts. The slightly raised ground leading up to the outer bailey wall made the castle difficult to attack.

**Moat:** Not to be confused with the motte, the moat was a river, stream, sea, or manmade ditch that ran around the base of the bailey. Most moats, including Pevensey's, were dry ditches and were created when the earth was dug up to make the motte. At Pevensey, the Normans cleaned out and repaired the old Roman ditch. Defenders could throw missiles at attackers attempting to cross the ditch.

**Keep:** made from stone (originally wood) and built on a motte, raised high above the surrounding area. Soldiers were positioned on the walls of the keep at all times to keep a lookout for any threats. The keep had high straight stone walls which were difficult to scale. There were also three guard towers. In addition, the keep contained a steep narrow staircase, which made it more difficult for attackers to advance and easier to defend. Norman nobles and their families stayed in the keep if they were attacked.

**Gateways and gatehouses:** the ways by which people could enter the different areas inside the castle. There was an old Roman gateway into the outer bailey and another gateway into the inner bailey. Soldiers were positioned on top of the gateways so that they could keep a lookout for trouble and also so that they could attack enemies by shooting arrows or missiles at them, while staying safely out of range of enemy attack. Some castles had a drawbridge as part of the gatehouse, which could be raised to stop attackers entering.

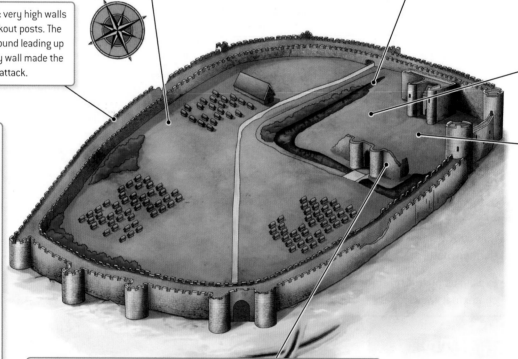

▲ **C** *There is debate among historians about what Pevensey Castle would have looked like in Norman times; this is an artist's impression*

▲ **D** *A typical Norman keep had a narrow staircase and crenellations; Pevensey's keep would have looked a bit different from this*

### Fact

## Crenellations

These formed a **rampart** (wall around the top of the castle) that had regular gaps through which to fire arrows. A wooden hatch was located in between the stone gaps, so that defenders could raise it to fire arrows and lower it for defence.

### Work

1  Why did the Normans build a castle at Pevensey?

2  What advantages did the site at Pevensey have for castle building?

3  How did the castle change over time?

4  What were the functions of Norman castles? Explain you answer.

5  Assess the impact of castles on the local area: think about what they allowed the Normans to do and the impact they would have had on the local population.

**Inner bailey:** The area within the inner wall. It protected the keep itself and was designed to be the last line of defence if attackers had managed to get through the outer bailey wall.

**Motte:** A mound, often steep-sided, around which the castle was focused. At Pevensey, the motte is less pronounced, as the whole area within the outer bailey wall is slightly raised.

### Study Tip

The Normans built many castles in England. Why were they so important? The location of a Norman castle will have been chosen carefully. What was special about the siting of a Norman castle? What was the purpose of the castle? It might guard a natural feature, such as a river crossing, or give a good view over the surrounding countryside. You should consider what it was about the design and features of a castle, such as Pevensey, that made it strong. Lastly think about how castles helped the Normans to keep control of England.

### Timeline: History of Pevensey Castle

| 286 | 450 | 1066 | 1088 | After 1100 |
|---|---|---|---|---|
| Roman fort built between 280–300AD | The Saxon invasion begins and the fort is sacked. It remains in Anglo-Saxon hands until the Norman invasion | William and his Norman army land at Pevensey and construct a temporary wooden motte and bailey castle. After the Battle of Hastings, William gives Pevensey to his half-brother Robert of Mortain and builds a more permanent stronghold inside the fort | King William's son, William Rufus, invades and besieges the castle; Robert of Mortain holds out for six months but ultimately loses, though William Rufus allows him to keep the castle | A large stone keep is built |

# William, King of England

William, Duke of Normandy, won the Battle of Hastings on 14 October 1066. However, he was not in control of the rest of England: the country was full of defeated, angry Anglo-Saxons, many of whom were still loyal to the king William had just killed. Two powerful Anglo-Saxon earls, Edwin and Morcar, had not been at Hastings, and there were still significant English forces ready to oppose William. If an Anglo-Saxon leader could be found, English troops could rally and attack William and his Normans. So how did William defeat this resistance and become King of England by Christmas Day, 1066?

## Objectives

▶ **State** William's opponents.

▶ **Summarise** the ways in which he dealt with his opponents.

▶ **Assess** how William dealt with his opponents.

## William's next steps

After Hastings, William moved east to Kent to secure the ports, stopping Anglo-Saxon trade and allowing entry of supplies from Normandy. William strengthened his **fortifications** and moved on to Canterbury, the heart of the English Catholic Church, in order to assert control over it. William then attempted to attack London but was fought off by the Anglo-Saxons. In retaliation, William burnt the area of Southwark. The Normans then moved west and gained control of Winchester, which was the centre for the **treasury** and also a very important city for the Church. In November 1066, Archbishop Stigand tried to put Edgar the Aetheling (Edward the Confessor's nephew) forward as king. Although Edgar's claim to the throne was backed by the Witan he did not receive enough support. Whilst Edgar posed a threat to William, he did not succeed in preventing him from becoming king.

### Key Biography

### Archbishop Stigand (died 1072)

- Stigand had been a bishop since 1043 and had acted as a mediator between King Edward and Godwin in 1052 during their disagreement.
- He was made Archbishop of Canterbury (the highest position in the Catholic Church in England) and he was also the Archbishop of Winchester.
- William refused to be crowned by Archbishop Stigand due to his corruption, and was crowned by the Archbishop of York instead. William removed Stigand from his position in 1070.

A meeting was held at Berkhampstead where William received an oath of fealty from Edgar, earls Edwin and Morcar, bishops, and leading men of London. William then ordered the burning of land between Berkhampstead and London, which gave him complete control of the area. By the time he was crowned on Christmas Day 1066, he had enough power to claim to be the King of England. This did not mean that William had total control of England: he still faced threats from within England and also from abroad. Whilst Hardrada had been defeated at Stamford Bridge, there were a number of other Vikings who were looking for an opportunity to attack England and take some of its riches.

In 1067, William distributed lands to his loyal barons and gave men land in areas of potential rebellion.

## Timeline

| 1066 | 1067 | 1068 |
|---|---|---|
| **25 Dec** William crowned King of England | **March** William returns to Normandy; unrest in Herefordshire and Wales | Rebellions in the south west |
| | **Dec** William returns to England | Siege of Exeter by William |
| | William distributes land in areas of potential rebellion to his loyal barons | Earls Edwin, Morcar and Edgar the Aetheling flee north |

▼ **A** *A map to show William's progress to London and the crown of England*

**Stamford Bridge**
Harold defeats Danes
25 September

**Berkhamsted**
Saxon earls submit
end October

**Wallingford**
Archbishop of
Canterbury submits
late October

**London**
William repulsed
at Southwark
mid October.
William crowned
25 December

Canterbury

Winchester

**Pevensey**
William lands
28 September

**Battle of Hastings**
William defeats Harold
14 October

## Key Words

fortifications     treasury     negotiation
siege     ravaging

▼ **INTERPRETATION C** *Adapted from a history textbook by Toby Purser, 2004; Purser is a specialist in Norman history and his book focuses on how Anglo-Saxon England was transformed into Anglo-Norman England:*

> William put the rebellions down with great brutality; any pretence he had to being the legitimate heir of Edward the Confessor ended during this period. To underpin his occupation he built hundreds of castles across the kingdom, garrisoned by armed mounted troops.

◀ **B** *The coronation of King William I; this scene was missing from the Tapestry when it was discovered and was completed by embroiderers in 2014*

## Work

1 Make a list of the people who opposed William.
2 a William dealt with his opponents and gained control in different ways. Which of the following methods did he use to deal with each opponent? **Negotiation**, strengthening areas, force, **siege**, **ravaging**, coronation. Name the opponents and the evidence for the methods he used with them.
   b Which method do you think was most effective, and why?

## Practice Question

How convincing is **Interpretation C** about the way in which William dealt with rebellions? Explain your answer using **Interpretation C** and your contextual knowledge.

**8 marks**

## Study Tip

You should aim to think about the methods that are shown in **Interpretation C** and examples of when William used these methods. You also need to think about the other ways in which rebellions were dealt with, and give examples.

| 1069 | 1070 | 1072 | 1075 | 1076 |
|---|---|---|---|---|
| **Jan** Rebels burn Norman Earl Robert of Commines to death in Durham<br><br>Rebellion spreads to York<br><br>Vikings invade<br><br>Revolts in Dorset, Somerset, Staffordshire and Cheshire<br><br>King Malcolm of Scotland marries Edgar's sister, Margaret | 'Harrying of the North'<br><br>Unrest in East Anglia | Scotland invades northern England | Revolt of the Norman earls | Last English earl, Waltheof killed by beheading<br><br>Scottish raids in Northumbria |

# Rebellions against the Normans

King William returned to Normandy between March and November 1067, as he now had two realms, England and Normandy, to run. Whilst he was away, tensions began to increase and revolts broke out in different areas of England. So who made up the opposition to King William?

## Objectives

▶ **Identify** areas of rebellion.
▶ **Outline** who gave support to the English rebels.

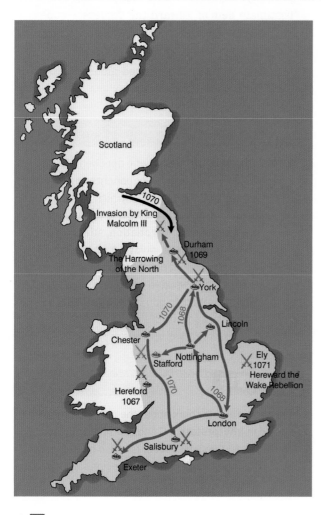

▲ **A** *The location of the English uprisings and the movements of King William's forces sent to deal with them*

## The suppression of Edwin and Morcar

The first rebellion against the new king came from Edwin and Morcar, the two most powerful remaining Anglo-Saxon earls:

▼ **INTERPRETATION B** *Adapted from* A New History of the Norman Conquest *by historian, Peter Rex, 2011; Rex argues that William's claim to the throne was deceptive:*

> Edwin and Morcar had led a rebellion in London immediately after the Battle of Hastings. William of Poitiers claimed that the movement was capable of raising a 'numerous and formidable force'. However, William sent his knights to deal with the rebels and the knights at once inflicted 'great sorrow upon London by the death of many of her sons and daughters.' It was perhaps this that finally moved the leading citizens of London to give hostages and to submit themselves. Edwin and Morcar submitted to William at Berkhampstead, whereupon William returned all of their possessions and titles to them.

## Rebellion of the Welsh border

The Welsh borders had always been a problem as they were an area of wild, untamed land that was a refuge for English outlaws and difficult to rule. Trouble broke out in 1067 when a Herefordshire thegn, Edric the Wild, started a revolt with a large number of English followers.

▼ **INTERPRETATION C** *Edric is sometimes featured as the leader of the mythical 'Wild Hunt'*

He gained the support of the Welsh Princes and managed to steal property along the border. Edric failed to take control of the area but launched another attack in 1069, reaching Cheshire and Staffordshire. When he and his followers approached the Norman castle at Shrewsbury, the commanders at the castle held them at the gates and William led his forces personally to meet them in battle. The rebels were soon defeated.

## The revolt of Eustace

Soon after the Welsh rebellion, King Edward's brother in law, Eustace Count of Boulogne, attacked Dover Castle in Kent. William of Poitiers suggested that the thegns in Kent invited Eustace and offered him their support, although this was not true. Eustace was defeated by the knights in the castle. He later made peace with William along with Edric the Wild.

## The south west and Exeter

When the city of Exeter rebelled against William's rule in 1068, the king dealt with it by besieging the city with an army of Normans and Englishmen. The city held out for 18 days, however Exeter was forced to surrender and the king built a castle on the highest ground, leaving his half-brother Robert of Mortain in charge.

On his way back to London, William supressed Bristol and Gloucester. This was not the end of the matter as three of Harold Godwinson's sons landed on the Somerset coast in an attempt to defeat William, though they were unsuccessful.

## The rebellion of the Norman earls

In 1075 William faced a rebellion from his own Norman earls. Ralph de Gael was the leader and was joined by Roger de Breteuil. Roger was the Earl of Hereford and the son of William FitzOsbern. William had forbidden Ralph's marriage, and his sheriffs had been hearing legal cases in Roger's lands instead of Roger himself. Roger may also have been unhappy that, under William, he did not have the same power that his father had.

The Norman earls had support from a variety of people, including the English Earl of Northamptonshire and Huntingdonshire, Waltheof. In addition, King Philip I of France encouraged Roger to rebel. Philip did not want Normandy to be more powerful than the rest of France, so he was eager to distract William's attention away from the area. Ralph and Roger were also promised other aid from overseas, so their rebellion posed a serious threat to William.

However, William did not deal with the rebellion himself but left this to his trusted **regents**, Lanfranc and Odo. Lanfranc sent troops to Herefordshire and Odo forced Ralph to retreat to Norwich, and eventually to Brittany. The English earl Waltheof tried to make peace with William but was beheaded in 1075. During the Christmas of 1075 William had the rebels blinded and murdered. Earl Roger was imprisoned, probably spared from death because of the friendship between his father and William. Whilst William would have to deal with some unrest up until his death in 1087, the organised rebellion of his own earls in 1075 was the last if the serious threats to his reign.

## Work

1. Which areas were affected by English rebellions? Use the map to help you.
2. For each rebellion, make a note of who was rebelling and the reason for it.
3. Add who supported each rebellion, using different colours to show individuals, English earls, English people and foreigners.
4. Draw a table and label the columns 'serious threat' and 'not serious threat'. In the different columns, make a note of the nature of the threat Hereward posed.

## Practice Question

How convincing is **Interpretation B** about how William dealt with Edwin and Morcar?  `8 marks`

## Study Tip

Consider what you know about the brothers and their relationship with William. How else had he dealt with them? What does the interpretation lead you to believe? Does it leave anything out?

# The Harrying of the North

The north of England was the most rebellious area, as it saw itself as semi-independent from the rest of the country. There was also a large number of people who were of Danish Viking descent who sympathised with their country of origin. To help secure himself against rebellion, King William tried to make alliances with the remaining English earls, Edwin, Morcar and Waltheof, however the English earls refused to be ruled by William.

**Objectives**

▶ **Describe** the **Harrying** of the North using interpretations.

▶ **Compare** and contrast interpretations of the Harrying of the North.

## What was the 'Harrying'?

In 1068, Edwin and Morcar, with Edgar the Aetheling, fled William's court, and went north. As a losing contender to the throne, Edgar needed allies in order to continue his pursuit of the crown. King Malcolm of Scotland gave Edgar his support against King William. Malcom had just married Edgar's sister so was now related to him. Events in the north spiralled out of control in January 1069 when the Norman Earl Robert of Commines and his men were murdered by English rebels. In addition, the bishop of Durham's house was set on fire and Edgar attacked the city of York. To make matters worse, Danish Vikings in 240 ships invaded in the summer of 1069 and joined up with an English army led by the English earls, Edgar and Waltheof. The joint English and Danish army defeated the Norman forces outside the castle in York and captured the castle itself. However, as William approached, the Vikings returned to their ships and William paid them money to leave, which they accepted. In response, William laid waste to vast areas of land around York, burning and **salting** the fields and killing any living creature. The event became known as the Harrying of the North. The Domesday Book, written in 1086, records that 80 per cent of Yorkshire was known as 'waste', which means it was uncultivated and unpopulated. This may have been a direct result of the Harrying.

## How devastating was the Harrying of the North?

There are differing interpretations on the extent of the devastation of the Harrying of the North. How and why do these accounts differ?

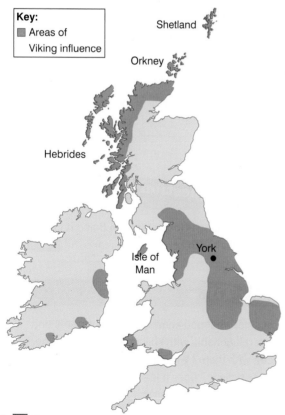

Key:
■ Areas of Viking influence

Shetland

Orkney

Hebrides

Isle of Man

York

▲ **A** *The areas of Viking influence were known as the* **Danelaw** *region; people in this region tended to be more rebellious and caused problems for William*

▼ **SOURCE B** *Adapted from the* Anglo-Saxon Chronicle, *1069:*

And there came to meet them Prince Edgar and Earl Waltheof and Gospatric with the Northumbrians and all the people marching with an immense army rejoicing exceedingly, and so they all went resolutely to York and stormed and razed the castle and captured an incalculable treasure and killed many hundreds of Frenchmen and took many with them to the ships. When the king found out about this he went northwards with all his army that he could collect, and utterly ravaged and laid waste to that shire.

▼ **INTERPRETATION C** *Adapted from William the Conqueror's deathbed confession, recorded in a church history book called The Ecclesiastical History (1123–1141) by Orderic Vitalis:*

> William fell on the English of the northern shires like a ravening lion. He commanded their houses and corn, with all their possessions, to be burnt without distinction, and large herds of cattle and beasts of burden to be butchered wherever they were found. And by doing so alas he became the barbarous murderer of many thousands, both young and old, of that fine race of people.

▲ **INTERPRETATION D** *An artist's impression of the 'Harrying of the North' from a children's educational magazine in 1978*

## Key Words

Harrying        Danelaw        salting

## Practice Question

Explain what was important about the Harrying of the North for Norman England.        **8 marks**

## Study Tip

Consider the effects or consequences of the Harrying. You could look at the consequences for: the farming population; the English earls; the other rebels.

## Key Biography

### King Malcolm III of Scotland (1031–93)

- King Malcolm III or Malcolm Canmore (this means 'big head' in Gaelic) was king of Scotland between 1058 and 1093.

- After the Battle of Hastings, Malcolm gave rebellious Anglo-Saxons a home in Scotland and protected them.

- Malcolm was married twice; after his first wife died he married Margaret Aetheling, Edgar's sister.

- After Edgar's failed rebellion in 1069, Malcolm invaded the north of England in 1070. William assembled his troops and marched on Scotland, meeting Malcolm's army in Perth. Malcolm was forced to sign the Treaty of Abernethy in 1072, in which he acknowledged William as his overlord, and exiled Edgar the Aetheling from his court as a sign of good faith to William. In return, he was given lands in Cumbria.

- Peace between Scotland and England lasted until 1093 when, after a disagreement with King William Rufus (William I's son), Malcolm was killed at the Battle of Alnwick.

## Work

1  Read the interpretations on these pages. Make a note of any words you are unsure of and look them up in a dictionary.
2  How does each interpretation describe the Harrying of the North? Make a note of as many adjectives as you can find in the interpretations.
3  What is significant about the provenance of each interpretation ('provenance' means where and when it came from and who created it)?
4  How has the interpretation of the Harrying of the North changed over time? Compare the interpretations to consider this. Make sure you consider the interpretations' provenance.

## Extension

Why was the 'Harrying of the North' so important? Conduct some research on the event and find out what happened to the people there. How long did it affect the region for? What effect did this have on William's ability to control the English?

# Why did Hereward the Wake rebel?

After the Harrying of the North in 1069, the English earls Edwin and Morcar continued to cause problems for William. They went to East Anglia where they met up with King Swegn of Denmark and an English thegn called Hereward the Wake (Wake means wary). The rebellion of Hereward the Wake was one of the most famous English rebellions from the Norman period. Why was the rebellion so famous and did it achieve its aims?

## Objectives

▶ **State** the reasons for the rebellion.

▶ **Consider** how serious the rebellion of Hereward the Wake was.

## Key Biography

### Hereward the Wake (1035–1072)

- He is believed to be the son of Leofric, the English Earl of Mercia.

- In his youth he was wild, and his father persuaded King Edward to make Hereward an **outlaw** as he could not control his son.

- He held land in Warwickshire and Lincolnshire during the time of King Edward the Confessor.

- He became an English hero after he rebelled against the Normans in East Anglia.

▼ **A** *A map of East Anglia, showing the location of Ely*

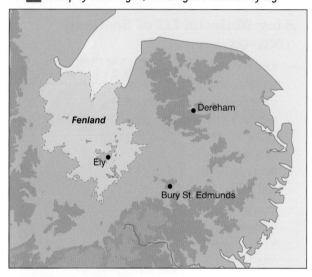

## What happened?

Hereward had a grudge against William and his Norman earls as they had confiscated lands from his father and killed his brother. He joined a rebellion with the English earls and their foreign supporters. Hereward, King Swegn and Morcar launched a series of **guerrilla**-style attacks in the marshes and **fenlands** of East Anglia. The most famous attack was on Peterborough in 1070, where they looted and burned the Abbey. The local geography was a great advantage for the rebels. They set up a base in an Abbey on the Isle of Ely, where they built up large amounts of supplies to survive a siege. They also used local guides to move easily around the marshy terrain. William was not able to use his usual tactics to defeat Hereward and the rebels due to the position of Ely, and the fact that it was so well defended by the marshes and Hereward's network of informants. Therefore, William had to develop a different tactic to defeat him.

▼ **INTERPRETATION B** *An 1870 engraving featuring Hereward the Wake*

# Events at Ely

**1.** William besieged the Island of Ely.

**2.** William built a rampart to cross the marshland. At 3 km (2 miles) long and with a castellum (a defensible platform) on the track, the rampart was an impressive achievement in Norman warfare.

**3.** Too many Norman soldiers crossed the rampart at once so it sank into the marshland.

**4.** William built a siege tower and, according to some accounts, brought in a local witch to torment the rebels. The witch stood at the top of one of the towers and shouted abuse and chanted spells.

**5.** Hereward set fire to the area, and the siege tower and part of the bridge caught fire.

**6.** Hereward was betrayed by Monks who told William about a secret route to Hereward.

**7.** The rebels surrender and Hereward disappears

## Key Words

outlaw   guerrilla   fenlands

## Extension

Look at **Interpretation B**. How is Hereward shown in this image? What do you think Hereward's place in English History is? Research Hereward the Wake to find further evidence to help back up your opinion.

## Work

1   Why did Hereward rebel against King William?
2   How serious was the rebellion? What did it take for William to defeat Hereward?
3   Design a front cover for a children's book on Hereward's rebellion that is biased towards either William or Hereward.

▼ **INTERPRETATION C**   *Adapted from* The Feudal Kingdom of England 1042–1216 *by Frank Barlow; Barlow specialises in biographies of medieval figures which use many primary sources:*

> Order was fast returning to the English kingdom. Only in the fens, where Hereward and his companions in possession of Ely Abbey, was the country unsubdued. The king decided to suppress this last centre of disaffection. A short campaign based on Cambridge cleaned up the Fens. Hereward escaped and his future actions belong to folklore rather than history.

## Practice Question

How convincing is **Interpretation C** about the rebellion of Hereward the Wake? Explain your answer using **Interpretation C** and your own knowledge.   **8 marks**

## Study Tip

You could make a list of threats Hereward posed to William and consider how William dealt with the rebellion and how difficult it was. You could then compare this with **Interpretation C** and consider whether or not it supports your findings.

# How did William use land to help him control the country?

Before the Normans arrived in 1066, the English were ruled by the King and the Anglo-Saxon **aristocracy** – the earls. England was divided up into earldoms (areas of land). The king could make anyone an earl, and give them an earldom, but he could also take land away. He could request the support of troops from earls during a time of war and the earls had to give the service of their housecarls and fyrd if they were to keep the king happy. So did things stay the same under the new king? How did William control his new kingdom?

### Objectives

▶ **Define** the key term '**feudal system**'.

▶ **Explain** why William tried to retain leading Anglo-Saxons but failed to do so.

▶ **Analyse** the different forms of feudalism in England under Edward and William.

## What happened to English landowners?

When William was recruiting mercenaries and Norman men to fight in 1066, he wanted to reward their loyal service with land as well as money. However, that did not mean that he wanted to replace every Anglo-Saxon landowner with a Norman. That being said, by 1076 the last English earl, Waltheof, had been beheaded, and there were only two Englishmen who held land directly from the king: Thurkill of Arden and Colswein of Lincoln. By 1096, all of the senior positions in the Church were held by Normans. So whilst William wanted to retain some of the Anglo-Saxon earls, their lack of loyalty meant that they were replaced by Normans. The Anglo-Saxon form of feudalism had involved lordship and **patronage**; however, the Norman feudal system that was introduced into England was based on William favouring and giving land to those who had helped him to conquer his new kingdom.

## To what extent was the Norman feudal system a change for English society?

Before William became king, people would have seen themselves as a member of one of three groups: churchmen, noble warriors or workers. The small number of nobles (or earls) fought in battles and ran the **administration** of the country as very large landowners. Most of the population were peasant workers, who were divided further; thegns could own land in villages and bailiffs enforced

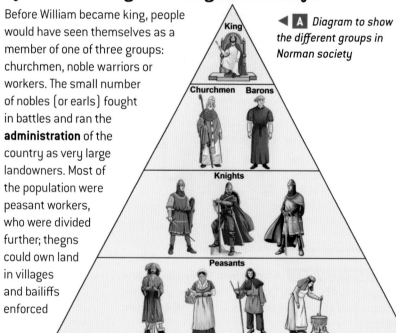

◀ **A** Diagram to show the different groups in Norman society

Timeline

| 1068 | 1075 | 1075 | 1076 | 1085 | 1086 |
|---|---|---|---|---|---|
| Fyrd used to deal with rebellion at Exeter | Fyrd used to deal with Rebellion of Norman Earls and the rebellion in East Anglia | Waltheof, last remaining English earl, removed from position | Waltheof beheaded | Survey of England agreed | Domesday Survey |

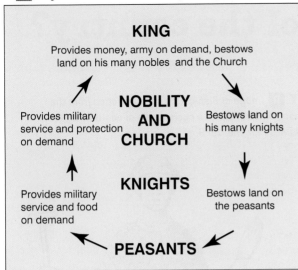

**▼ B** *Diagram to show how the Norman feudal system works*

**KING**
Provides money, army on demand, bestows land on his many nobles and the Church

**NOBILITY AND CHURCH**

Provides military service and protection on demand

Bestows land on his many knights

**KNIGHTS**

Provides military service and food on demand

Bestows land on the peasants

**PEASANTS**

law and order. At the lower end of society, **villeins** worked in fields.

The diagrams above show how the Norman feudal system was organised. Feudalism was based on a system of give and take, and was very similar to what had already existed in England before the Norman Conquest. However, unlike the previous form of feudalism, land ownership remained with William himself, and there were many more nobles such as **barons** who helped William run the country. The king gave land and titles to his barons and in return they gave him their loyalty and military service. The barons gave protection, shelter, food, and sometimes land to their knights, and in return the knights gave their loyalty and military service. The knights gave peasants food, protection, and shelter, and in return peasants worked in fields and gave their military service as part of

## Practice Question

Write an account of the ways in which the feudal system changed under the Normans.

**8 marks**

[Taken from AQA 2016 Paper 2 specimen material]

## Study Tip

This question asks you to analyse change. You should aim to consider the extent of change as well as the type of change. Try to use historical evidence to support your answer. Have a look at the Extension task before you attempt this question as it will help you to consider your answer.

## Key Words

aristocracy   feudal system   patronage
administration   villein   baron   social hierarchy

the fyrd. In this way, everyone knew their position in the **social hierarchy**, what was expected of them, and what they needed to do for the people above and below them in the system.

## Extension

Look at diagrams A and B. How does the feudal system compare with the way in which your school, or another organisation you know, is organised? Are there any similarities or differences? Research the feudal system and consider the question: 'How different was life in England after the Norman version of the feudal system was introduced?' You need to think about what changed and what stayed the same, and also consider who life changed for – was it everyone or only certain people?

**▼ INTERPRETATION C** *Adapted from an educational History website:*

It seemed to historians that the feudal system was a way in which a king could rule a violent society, with access to a large army of knights, whilst the majority of the population provided them with the resources to do so. The feudal system gave Norman kings an army. The feudal system was the basis of the class system – it defined who the 'haves' were and who were the 'have-nots'. But, it did not stop barons rebelling against the king, or from torturing and slaughtering their peasants.

## Work

1   Write a definition for the feudal system in the time of King William.

2   What were the similarities and differences in the forms of feudalism under Edward and William?

3   Why did William try to keep some of Edward's earls and leading churchmen after he had conquered England? Give some examples.

4   Why was William largely unsuccessful in retaining leading Anglo-Saxon earls and churchmen in their positions?

# How did William use land to help him control the country?

## Who were the new Norman barons?

Those people who were given land or a 'fief' directly by the King or had their possession of it confirmed by him were his **tenants-in-chief** or 'barons'. The Domesday Book shows that by 1086 the Church owned about a quarter of the land in England. Half of the rest of the country was owned by about 180 tenants-in-chief. But of this half was then owned by only ten men, an inner circle of the most powerful tenants-in-chief. By a process known as **subinfeudation**, tenants-in-chief could reward their own followers, usually knights, with smaller grants of land. The tenants-in-chief and knights made up the aristocracy.

England had a small number of earls who ranked just below the king (the aristocracy). In 1050, these was Mercia, Northumbria, Wessex and East Anglia. William created smaller earldoms after the Conquest linked to Chester, Hereford, Huntingdon, Kent, Norfolk and Shrewsbury. Others were added later on. Baron was a term used in north-west France that was not a title but was used generally for a powerful Norman nobleman who did not quite have the status of an earl.

Under the feudal system, knights had to provide service to the king; however, they could avoid this service by paying **scutage** which was a form of taxation that was paid, even during times of peace. This system in which land was given by the king (patronage) in return for oaths of fealty, paid with military service and/or money, was called **fiscal feudalism**.

## The promise of land

Land was used as a reward. William's aristocracy and barons had to give him military service in return for their land. Whilst all of the members of the aristocracy played an important role in maintaining control of England, there were a few men who played crucial roles in controlling the country for William. Bishop Odo, for example (the man who most likely ordered the Bayeux Tapestry to be made), was one of William's regents. When William took control of England after Hastings he had claimed all of the land. However, he gave back around 25 per cent to the Church, which therefore remained a very important land owner in its own right.

▼ **D** *Image of Bishop Odo, an illustration from the book* Illustration for a cyclopaedia of costume *by James Planche, 1879*

### Key Biography

#### Robert of Mortain (c1031–90)

- Robert was Bishop Odo's brother and William's half-brother.
- He gave William the use of his ships for his invasion of England. In return Robert was given land in 20 counties, the most important area of which was the land around Pevensey.
- He fought for King William in 1069 against Danish invaders.
- He went to Normandy to help run the area for William.

## How did William control the lawless Welsh border?

The Welsh borders were a particular problem for William after he was crowned king. The area was lawless and many English rebels fled into Wales to seek protection and to regroup after they had been defeated by William. This area of land was known as the Welsh Marches, and King William needed someone efficient and loyal to sort out the problems in the area for him. This person was William FitzOsbern. He became a powerful 'Marcher Lord' and had wide-ranging powers over the south Wales border region. He made Hereford his base and recruited a formidable force of soldiers, relatives and other Norman nobles to support him. He built castles and **garrisons** at Monmouth, Clifford and Wigmore and an impressive castle at Chepstow. Chepstow Castle became FitzOsbern's base from which he launched attacks into Wales, and it is the oldest standing stone castle in Britain today.

### Key Biography

#### William FitzOsbern (1020–71)

- FitzOsbern, a distant cousin of Duke William, was brought up in William's household and he was to become one of the most important men in William's kingdoms.

- His father had been William's steward (a man who acted as a teacher and advisor), but had died trying to protect William during an assassination attempt when the Duke was a young child.

- FitzOsbern was a loyal soldier and fought in battles for William in the 1040s and 1050s.

- In 1066, he was Duke William's steward, and they were very close. FitzOsbern helped William to recruit mercenaries to fight at Hastings and fought alongside the Duke himself.

- He was also one of King William's regents and served him loyally during the Harrying of the North and in battle in south Wales.

- He was given lands all over the south of England, including Oxfordshire, Dorset and Berkshire, as reward for his service.

- FitzOsbern was killed in battle in Normandy in 1071.

### Extension

Research William FitzOsbern further. Why was he so important to King William? Create a timeline showing the key events in FitzOsbern's life and highlight key times when he demonstrated his importance to King William.

### Work

1 Define the following key terms: feudal, aristocracy, fealty.

2 How did King William use land to control people?

3 Look over all of the information on pages 40 to 43 and consider the question: How did King William use land to help him control the country? Make notes on how successful you think this strategy was.

# What does the Domesday Book tell us about King William's England?

In 1085, King William faced the threat of invasion from Danish Vikings and the Count of Flanders, so he called a war council together in Gloucester. He needed to enforce a **geld** (a form of tax) to pay for his army; however, the invasion forces never came. Soon after, William ordered an inventory (a list) to be drawn up in order to help him raise this tax. This became known as the Domesday Survey. What sort of information did it give William?

## Objectives

▶ **State** why William ordered the Survey.

▶ **Compare** life in England in 1066 and 1086.

▶ **Evaluate** the impact of the Normans on landholding.

## What are the theories about the purpose of Domesday?

The exact purpose of the survey is not known but there are a number of theories. It could be a 'tax book' with the aim of finding out how much people owned, so that they could be correctly taxed in order to pay bribes to Vikings in order to prevent war. It could also have been commissioned so that King William could be better informed about the best way in which to raise tax, and so that a formal written record of England at the time of the introduction of the Norman feudal system could be created.

Domesday did allow William to ensure that he got as much money as possible from taxes. He could also make sure that his feudal lords were not withholding money, which could have made them a threat to his power. In addition, William could legalise and record arguments over the ownership of land. Therefore, whilst the true purpose of Domesday is unclear, it provides valuable evidence of not only what life was like in England after the Battle of Hastings, but also how much it changed as a result of the Norman Conquest.

## What did William own?

As all of the Anglo-Saxons had, according to William, supported King Harold, their land was taken from them. William, therefore, owned all of the land in England and it was up to him who he gave land and titles to. It was not King William's intention to have no English earls; however, he wanted to reward the loyal service of the men who fought for him at Hastings. He certainly would not tolerate disloyal or rebellious English earls.

The Survey showed that King William and his family owned about 20 per cent of the land in England; the Church around 25 per cent; about 10 members of the Norman aristocracy held a further 25 per cent of land; and the remaining 30 per cent of land was held by 170 people. Land was therefore controlled by around 250 people, which was very similar to the situation in the time of King Edward the Confessor. However, the main difference was that under King Edward the land belonged mostly to Anglo-Saxons; under William, it was owned mainly by foreigners.

▼ **INTERPRETATION A** *From* The Feudal Kingdom of England 1042–1216 *by Frank Barlow, 1999:*

> Although King William I in 1086–87 may have considered reforming in his own interest this valuable inheritance from his cousin, the Domesday Book proved to be more a record of ancient customs than a blueprint for an improved system.

## Extension

According to **Interpretation A**, why did William order the Domesday Survey? Note down ideas and then discuss in small groups.

# What questions were asked in the Domesday Survey in 1086?

A document known as the Ely Inquiry shows what questions were asked in the Domesday Survey. It also states that the sheriff, local baron, priest and villagers had to swear an oath to answer questions honestly.

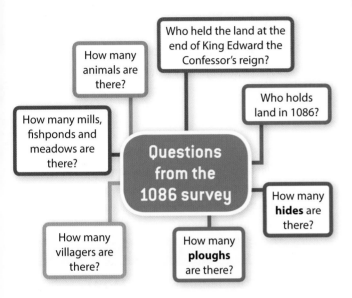

**Questions from the 1086 survey**

- Who held the land at the end of King Edward the Confessor's reign?
- How many animals are there?
- How many mills, fishponds and meadows are there?
- Who holds land in 1086?
- How many villagers are there?
- How many **ploughs** are there?
- How many **hides** are there?

# When did the Domesday Survey become the Domesday Book?

The Survey was suggested in 1085 and carried out in 1086; however, it was only written in book form in the time of William II. The Survey became known as 'Domesday' which means 'Day of Judgement'. The term 'Domesday Book' was only used in the twelfth century because by then the legal authority of the Survey was seen as being equal to that of God's authority on Judgement Day.

# What does Domesday tell us about life in England?

Apart from who owned the land, the Survey also sheds light on England's population and how much wealth that population did or did not have. It shows that in 1086, there were around 2000 knights in England with probably 10,000 Norman settlers. The total population of England was between 1.5 and 2 million people. The survey recorded the estimated value of land under Edward the Confessor and King William, and also how land holding had changed over the same period; however, some places were left out, for example London and Winchester, perhaps because the Survey was left unfinished.

## Key Words

geld    hides    ploughs    hundred

▼ **SOURCE B** *Section taken from the Domesday Survey showing details on the area of Buckinghamshire:*

- **Hundred:** Rowley
- **County:** Buckinghamshire
- **Total population:** 62.5 households (very large).
- **Total tax assessed:** 0.5 geld units (very small).
- **Taxable units:** Taxable value 1 geld units.
- **Value:** Value to lord in 1066 £10. Value to lord in 1086 £16.
- **Households:** 11 smallholders. 2 slaves. 26 burgesses.
- **Plough land:** 8 plough lands. 2 lord's plough teams. 3.5 men's plough teams.
- **Other resources:** Meadow 8 ploughs. 1 mill, value 0.7.
- **Lord in 1066:** King Edward.
- **Lord in 1086:** King William.
- **Tenant-in-chief in 1086:** King William.

## Work

1 Look at **Source B** and answer the following questions:

   a Who was the Lord in charge of Rowley in 1066 and in 1086?

   b What was the value of the land in 1066 and in 1086?

   c What had happened to the ownership and value of the land between 1066 and 1086?

2 Why do you think there was a difference in the value of land between 1066 and 1086? Use your own knowledge to help you.

3 Why did William order the Survey? What information did he get as a result, and how could he use this information?

# Who killed William II?

King William I had three sons: Robert, William and Henry. In 1087, as King William lay dying, he promised Normandy to Robert and England to William. The youngest prince, Henry, was to receive £5000. However, Robert was not satisfied and he fled to his uncle in Flanders, Belgium. But King William had refused to give in to Robert's previous demands to rule England as well as Normandy, which led to years of bitterness and resentment between them. Robert was also bitter towards his younger brother, and when William II became the new king of England, Robert rebelled against him.

## Accident or assassination?

William II's inheritance of the throne of England was the cause of disagreement between him and his brothers. This led to disasterous consequences for him. In 1100, William II travelled to the New Forest in Hampshire to go hunting, where he reported that he had a bad dream in which he had been killed. Whilst hunting that day the new king was shot through the heart by an arrow. To this day, historians are not sure exactly what happened. Was it an accident, or was King William II murdered?

### Key Biography

#### King William II, also known as William Rufus (1056–1100)

- 'Rufus' (meaning 'red' in Latin) was William II's nickname, as he had red hair.

- During a Scottish rebellion in 1091, William managed to force King Malcolm of Scotland to acknowledge him as the overlord of Scotland. When the Scottish rebelled again a couple of years later, William was victorious at the Battle of Alnwick and Malcolm was killed.

- In 1096, his brother Robert went on a crusade and **mortgaged** Normandy to William II, who had to pay £10,000 for it. The money was raised by taxes in England, which were deeply unpopular.

### Key Biography

#### Robert Curthose (1054–1134)

- Robert was given the nickname 'Curthose' by his father, King William I. Robert was short and stout, and 'Curthose' means 'short boot' in French.

- He was ambitious, and had demanded that he be allowed to rule Normandy as early as 1077.

- He participated in the First Crusade (1096–99) and was very successful in the campaigns.

- In 1105–06, Henry I invaded Normandy and Robert was captured and imprisoned in Wales, where he lived until his death.

## Timeline

| 1082 | 1087 | 1088 | 1089 | 1093 |
|------|------|------|------|------|
| Robert rebels against his father and is exiled to Italy | Robert becomes Duke of Normandy | Rebellion against William II led by Robert and his uncle, Bishop Odo of Bayeux | William II claims Normandy and wages war on Robert, whom he defeats | William II argues with the Archbishop Anselm of Canterbury, because William was too involved in Church affairs |

▼ **INTERPRETATION A** *Adapted from a church history book called* Historia Ecclesiastica *(1123–1141) by Orderic Vitalis; it discusses King William I's attitude towards his son Robert, just before his death in 1087:*

> Before I [William] fought against Harold on the heath of Senlac, I granted the dukedom of Normandy to my son, Robert, because he was the eldest. He has already received the homage of nearly all the barons of this land. The grant thus made and confirmed I cannot undo. But I know for certain that the country which is subject to his dominion will be truly wretched. He is proud, silly and reckless, and will long have to suffer severe misfortune.

▼ **INTERPRETATION B** *From Spartacus Educational, a history website aimed at school children:*

> During the hunt, Walter Tirel fired an arrow at a stag. The arrow missed the animal and hit William Rufus in the chest. Within a few minutes the king was dead. Tirel jumped on his horse and made off at great speed. He escaped to France and never returned again to England.

▼ **INTERPRETATION C** *Adapted from the* Anglo-Saxon Chronicle, *which is a record of events in English History. There are many versions of this book:*

> William II was very harsh and fierce in his rule over his realm and towards his followers and to all his neighbours and very terrifying. Influenced by the advice of evil councillors, which was always gratifying to him, and by his own greed, he was continually exasperating this nation with unjust taxes. In his days therefore, righteousness declined and every evil of every kind towards God and man put up its head...Therefore he was hated by almost all his people and abhorrent to God...

▼ **INTERPRETATION D** *From a school History textbook:*

> King Henry gave jobs and land to important families soon after Rufus' death, particularly to the Clare and Giffard families. Tirel's wife came from the Clare family and two other family members were in the hunting party on the day that Rufus died. Tirel was also related to the Giffards.

**Key Words**

mortgage

▼ **INTERPRETATION E** *A stamp from the Island of Jersey, 1987*

**Work**

1 Make a list of the key suspects of the crime.

2 Identify a motive or a reason for these suspects to want William II dead. Think about what they had to gain, or what he had done to them previously.

3 Suggest the person who you think is responsible for William II's death.

4 Choose the role of either the prosecution or the defence in the legal case examining the death of William II. Build a case either defending or prosecuting each of the suspects. Justify your case by referring to the interpretations on these pages.

| 1097 | 1100 |
| --- | --- |
| Archbishop Anselm leaves England for Rome and William II seizes his estates | Robert attempts an invasion of England, which fails<br>William II killed by an arrow to the heart in mysterious circumstances. He is immediately replaced by his brother, Henry I |

**Extension**

You could extend Activity 4 further by finding out more background information on your key suspects and seeing if you can identify any other suspects.

# Keeping law and order

The Anglo-Saxon law and order system was very effective and in many ways was superior to the Norman system, so William retained many English practices and merely introduced a few Norman changes. Many English laws were also introduced in Normandy. William used the best of both systems to ensure that he maintained control in both kingdoms. So how much of the Anglo-Saxon legal system did King William keep, and how much did he change after 1066?

**Objectives**

▶ **Outline** the changes to law and order.

▶ **Explain** systems of trial and punishment used by the Normans.

▶ **Compare** and contrast the methods of maintaining law and order.

## Keeping the peace

Look through the following information carefully. It outlines the extent to which William changed law and order.

### Shire courts

**Continuity:** Under the Anglo-Saxons, England was divided into shires, and the shire court met twice a year when cases involving land disputes, crime, taxes and rebellions were heard by the **sheriff**. There were changes in the shire courts, but they remained the main method of enforcing law and order in local areas under the Normans.

**Change:** Large Anglo-Saxon earldoms had been replaced with smaller Norman earldoms, often based around shire towns, such as Chester and Shrewsbury. In addition, castles were built in shire towns and the administration and law and order were based there, including the sheriff and court. The importance of shire courts declined due to the increasing role of the **honorial** courts, where tenants could appeal cases with their lord. Sometimes royal household officials were sent to shire courts to oversee proceedings, and **juries** were introduced in some cases.

▼ **A** *Map showing Anglo-Saxon earldoms in 1045*

◀ **B** *Map showing the new Norman earldoms in 1087; note the decrease in the size of earldoms*

## Hundred courts

**Continuity:** In Anglo-Saxon times shires were divided into 'hundreds', which were 100 hides in size with each hide being about 120 acres. However, hundreds could vary in size as shires themselves also varied in size. Hundred courts continued under the Normans: they looked at local issues in each hundred, normally land issues.

**Change:** The hundred courts met more frequently than shire courts and were run by the sheriff's deputy (second in command).

## Inheritance

**Continuity:** Under the Anglo-Saxons, it was common to divide up land holding amongst families.

**Change:** When the Normans introduced the feudal system it was vital that the new earldoms remained intact and were not split between an earl's sons after their father's death, or the whole system was in danger of collapsing. **Primogeniture** refers to the process by which the eldest son inherited land or titles from his father. This meant that younger sons or daughters would be left with nothing.

## The oath system

**Continuity:** Anglo-Saxons placed a high value on people's word or promises. People were persuaded to make an oath of allegiance known as 'the common oath', which meant that they promised not to be involved in any major crime. If they did then their entire family was punished. Cases such as theft were heard in the hundred courts and the punishments were decided there. Punishments could include exile for the criminal and their family.

**Changes:** The Normans introduced **murdrum fines**. If any Norman Earl was murdered then the entire area around where the criminal lived was heavily fined. The law was extended to include any Norman who was attacked or injured by Anglo-Saxons. The law was introduced because of the large number of new Norman earls who were vulnerable to attack by the local Anglo-Saxon population.

### Key Words

sheriff honorial court jury primogeniture ecclesiastical murdrum fine

### Fact

King's court: upheld the laws of the king and was presided over by the king or a designated official

Local courts: various types existed in Anglo-Saxon England

County courts: presided over by a sheriff

Hundred courts: presided over by the head of a family, so dealt with very local issues

Feudal courts: introduced by the Normans and dealt with disputes in manors

**Ecclesiastical** courts: presided over by Abbots and Bishops and dealt with issues within the Church, or on Church land

### Practice Question

Write an account of the ways in which law and order changed under the Normans.

**8 marks**

### Study Tip

You should aim to talk about what changed, who this affected and to what extent. You should also consider what changed and what remained the same. You could conclude by stating what you think the most significant changes were and which areas had the least change.

### Work

1 Make a list of Anglo-Saxon laws that the Normans kept.

2 Make a list of laws that the Normans changed.

3 Why did primogeniture and murdrum fines have to be introduced?

4 a Rank the methods of keeping law and order according to the amount of change introduced by the Normans.

   b Which change do you think was the most significant and why?

# Keeping law and order

## How much did the Normans change the legal system?

The changes to inheritance laws and the introduction of fines rather than brutal punishments show a more modern approach by the Normans in comparison to the old Anglo-Saxon ways. The Normans ended the practice of criminals paying compensation to the families of victims and introduced the concept of paying fines to the government. Another way in which the legal system became more modern was that laws were written rather than oral, which made them easier to enforce.

### Changes to language in law

As well as English and French, Latin was spoken and written by some people in England after the Norman Conquest. Latin was used by literate people such as monks and churchmen, who were responsible for copying books and texts. As time went on, people of Norman descent spoke more English and English people began to use French words. However, written English declined after 1066 as all writs and charters (the way in which laws were recorded) were written in Latin. Latin was by far the most common written language and was used for ecclesiastical writs (Church laws), other laws, letters, and literary texts such as histories and fiction. Even church sermons, works on science, law, and theology were all written in Latin. Latin became the language of government. It was therefore essential for the important people in society to learn it, and parish schools and universities all taught in Latin.

### Punishments to fit the crime

In addition to the changes to the laws of England, the Normans changed the ways in which people were punished in order to maintain control over the population. As with laws, punishments were often an extension to existing Anglo-Saxon customs rather than a complete change to the system. The Anglo-Saxon system was brutal, using capital punishment, **mutilation** and the grisly **'ordeal'** system. This system was used by the Normans, but they could often be more brutal than their Anglo-Saxon predecessors.

▶ **C** *A representation of ordeal by fire: an accused person holds a red hot iron bar*

## The ordeal system

Trial by ordeal had been used in England since the ninth century and was based on the belief of *'Judicium Dei'*, or 'the Judgement of God', to prove a person's guilt or innocence. Often a guilty person would confess rather than endure the ordeal. People believed that if a person

### Ordeal by fire

This involved a person putting their arm into a cauldron of boiling water or holding a red hot iron bar and walking three paces. The wound was bandaged and if it started to heal after three days the person was innocent; if it did not they were guilty.

### Ordeal by water

A suspected person was strapped to a chair and thrown into a lake. If they sank they were innocent; if they floated they were guilty, and then they were executed. The accused died in any case, either by drowning or by execution.

was innocent of a crime then they would be saved by God. However, this did not mean they were saved from the ordeal. The Anglo-Saxons used ordeal by fire or water, and the Normans extended this by introducing ordeal by combat.

### Ordeal by combat

This ordeal was introduced by the Normans. If a nobleman was accused of a crime he would fight his accuser, and whoever won the fight was thought to be right. The loser was wrong and was also usually dead by the end of a fight.

▼ **INTERPRETATION D** *A fifteenth-century representation of ordeal by combat*

### Extension

Complete the following table, which will help you to complete the Practice Question. You will need to refer back to the previous pages to complete your table.

| Method of control | Anglo-Saxon | Norman changes | People who it affected in society |
|---|---|---|---|
| Shire courts | | | |
| Hundred courts | | | |
| Primogeniture | | | |
| Oaths | | | |
| Murdrum fines | | | |
| Ordeals | | | |
| Harrying of the North | | | |
| Forest laws | | | |

### Forest laws

King William was an avid hunter and did not tolerate the general population hunting on his lands. Prior to the Conquest, most of England was covered in forest and local people hunted animals such as deer and smaller mammals in order to supplement their diets. The Normans introduced Forest Laws which meant that if anyone was caught hunting in forests they could be fined, mutilated (for example, blinded), or even executed.

### Practice Question

Explain what was important about the reforms to law and order under William I.        **8 marks**

### Study Tip

Think about what changes were made and who this affected. You should aim to consider how the changes in law affected the whole of English society. You could do this by looking at the different sectors of society – the peasants, land owners and Norman aristocracy – and conclude with how important the reforms were for each sector, and then for society as a whole.

### Work

1 How did the Normans punish people? Explain your answer fully by giving examples. Use the representations of ordeals to help you.
2 Which punishments did the Normans introduce?
3 Which laws did the Normans introduce?

# What did a Norman village look like?

90 per cent of people lived in the countryside during this period. There were small clusters of houses with between a hundred and several hundred people living together. The villages were controlled by the lord of the manor who lived in the **manor house**. The Domesday Book records that there were around 13,400 villages in 1086. What was life like in a Norman village?

## Objectives

▶ **Describe** the features of a Norman village.

▶ **Evaluate** who had the most important role in a village.

## An overview of villages

For the majority of peasants, the Norman Conquest had little impact. Indeed, apart from the fact that they had a new Norman landlord, their lives more or less remained the same. Peasants lived in cottages, grew crops on strips of land and grazed their animals on common land. The ploughs used to farm were made of metal and pulled by oxen. The land was farmed in strips because it was easier for the oxen to pull the plough in a straight line. The main crops were wheat, oats, barley and rye. Villages were organised around common areas of land. Houses were built along roads and were clustered together. There was a clear division between land for houses, farm land, pasture for animals, and the woodland that was often located near the village.

## Important buildings in the village

At the centre of the village was a church made of stone: this was the most important building in the village. The church tower had a bell that was rung to tell villagers when to start and finish work. Peasants spent most of their free time in the church as there were services not only on Sundays but also on feast days and holy days (these days became known as 'holidays' because people did not work on them). In addition, the church had to be sturdy as it was used to store goods, to serve as a prison and, in times of danger, to act as a fortress.

## The open field system

The farmland within and around a village was divided into fields surrounded by hedges. Some fields were used to graze cattle and others were used for growing crops. The fields for crops were divided into individual strips of land, but the strips were not separated from each other by fences, walls or hedges; this is known as the open field system. About 25 to 35 per cent of the land was kept for the use of the lord and the rest was divided among the peasants. Each peasant was responsible for farming a number of strips and paid the lord rent for the land in the form of money or a share of the crops.

▼ **A** *A plan of a typical village during Norman times*

Examples of crops that were grown are grain, vegetables and herbs. Peasants had to make enough food to feed themselves and also to give to their lord as rent. They also made beer for the lord of the manor. Some fields were left **fallow**, which meant that they were left empty for a year or two: this gave the soil time to recover so that it would produce better crops when it was planted again.

## A case study: **Wharram Percy**

The village of Wharram Percy does not exist any longer but archaeologists have discovered the remains of the village, and we can learn a great deal about life in Norman villages as a result of their studies. The village lay about 29 km (18 miles) north-east of the city of York in the north of England. The village developed in the Iron Age and grew during the Roman occupation of Britain between 55BC and AD410.

▼ **INTERPRETATION B** *An artist's impression of Wharram Percy, created in the 1970s; you can see how the different parts of the village were linked together via roads, and the thatched roof of St Martin's Church*

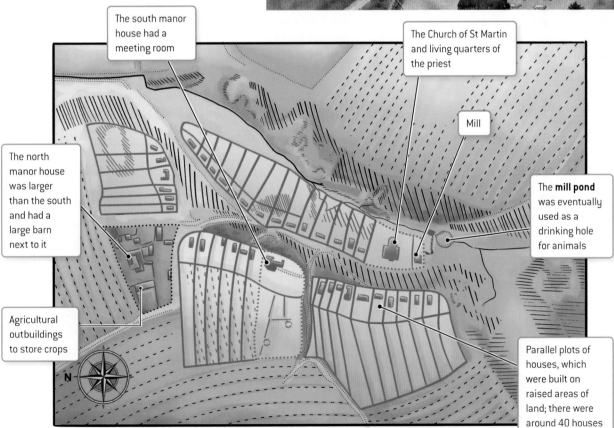

The south manor house had a meeting room

The Church of St Martin and living quarters of the priest

Mill

The north manor house was larger than the south and had a large barn next to it

The **mill pond** was eventually used as a drinking hole for animals

Agricultural outbuildings to store crops

Parallel plots of houses, which were built on raised areas of land; there were around 40 houses

▲ **C** *A plan of Wharram Percy*

## Work

1  What proportion of people lived in villages in the Norman period?

2  Who controlled the villages?

3  Describe the open field system.

4  What does the case study of Wharram Percy tell us about life in a Norman village?

# What did a Norman village look like?

## A peasant's home

The poorest peasants, called **serfs** or villeins, lived in houses around the lord's manor. They were not allowed to leave the area without the permission of the lord. Most serfs were farmers but others worked as servants or craftspeople. The quality and layout of homes in Norman times depended upon where you fitted into society. Peasants' homes were cold, damp and dark with floors made of packed mud. Often it was warmer and lighter outside than within. A peasant's home had very small windows to help keep it warm and to prevent people from breaking in. Peasant families ate, slept and relaxed in a single room; only a few had two rooms. Houses had thatched roofs and could be easily destroyed by fire.

## Manors

**Manors** were specific areas within villages that included the manor house, barns, churches, villager's houses, grazing land, and mills, and had many roads running through them. The group of peasants who lived in the manor were known as **freemen**. They still had to pay rent and work for the lord of the manor during sowing and harvest time. Peasants did not own land but thegns, knights and barons often owned land of around 485–730 hectares (1200–1800 acres) in size. They would also have owned houses, barns, woods, forests and lakes. The collective term for all land owned by a lord was a '**demesne**'. The lord's manor house and the houses of the peasants who worked for the lord could be found there. Manor houses were made from stone rather than wattle and daub and were warmer and more secure. Peasants could not leave the manor unless they had the permission of their lord and their lives revolved around obeying his rules.

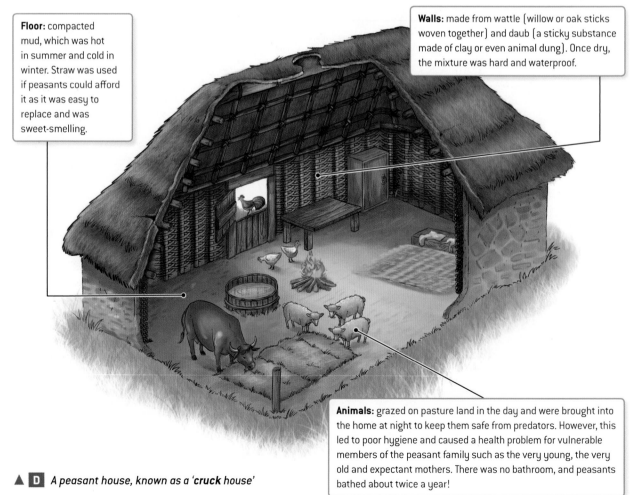

**Floor:** compacted mud, which was hot in summer and cold in winter. Straw was used if peasants could afford it as it was easy to replace and was sweet-smelling.

**Walls:** made from wattle (willow or oak sticks woven together) and daub (a sticky substance made of clay or even animal dung). Once dry, the mixture was hard and waterproof.

**Animals:** grazed on pasture land in the day and were brought into the home at night to keep them safe from predators. However, this led to poor hygiene and caused a health problem for vulnerable members of the peasant family such as the very young, the very old and expectant mothers. There was no bathroom, and peasants bathed about twice a year!

▲ **D** *A peasant house, known as a 'cruck house'*

## Roles and responsibilities

In addition to peasants and lords of the manor, there were a number of other key people who ensured the smooth running of each village.

**Reeve:** senior official who worked on behalf of the Crown in local areas, for example, as a chief magistrate. After the Conquest, the reeve's job was reduced to the day-to-day management of a manor and its peasants, an essential role to ensure that everyone did their jobs. The reeve was a peasant, chosen by the lord or through a vote by the peasants.

**Bailiff:** in charge of collecting taxes for the crown and ensuring that crops were gathered and debts repaid.

**Priest:** ran the local church; he was responsible for ensuring marriages and wills were legal.

**Miller:** produced grain to make bread for the area. Bread had to be baked in the ovens of the lord of the manor and the lord decided how much money the miller paid for this.

### Key Words

serf   manor   freemen   demesne   cruck   reeve   bailiff

▲ **INTERPRETATION E**   *A painting of a reeve managing peasants*

### Work

1   Describe the house of a peasant.
2   Describe the house of the lord of the manor.
3   Who was responsible for making sure the village ran properly? Who had the most important role? Justify your choice.
4   Write a short essay comparing the main features of a Norman village and houses with those of today. You could think about heating, lighting and building materials, for example.

### Practice Question

What was important about the organisation of a Norman village?   **8 marks**

### Study Tip

You could think about what was important in terms of how the land was used, who owned the land and how it helped the Lord of the manor control the local population. Remember to include specific examples like Wharrem Percy.

# 5.2 A peasant's year

The life of a peasant child was not a pleasant one. Many died before they were six months old and those who survived worked with their parents on the land. Children cleared stones to stop the tools from breaking and chased birds away at harvest time. They were not educated in schools and were expected to work from the moment they were able to stand and hold something in their hand. Life did not get any easier for adult peasants as they worked during daylight hours and rarely had any time off. But was life all bad for peasants?

## Objectives

▶ **Describe** the life of a peasant.

▶ **Evaluate** the effect of the lord on a peasant's life.

## Seasonal life in a typical year

Most peasants were farmers and they worked in fields owned by their lords. Their lives were dictated by the farming year. In fact, from lord to peasant, all village people's lives were dependent upon the seasons and farming. Late spring was the hardest time of year as supplies were running out. Poor harvests during the previous year meant peasants might starve to death.

## A day in the life of a peasant

### Work and food

Peasants usually got up half an hour before sunrise and ate a form of porridge called pottage. When it got light they started working. At various times of the year, peasant farmers ploughed the land and then sowed (planted) crops, carried out reaping (cutting crops for harvest with a **scythe**, **sickle** or reaper) and haymaking

### Spring: sowing seeds

▲ INTERPRETATION A  *Spring: Painting of peasants sowing seeds in the fields*

### Summer: harvesting crops

▶ INTERPRETATION B  *Summer: Peasants bringing in the harvest on an August day*

### Autumn: ploughing fields

▲ INTERPRETATION C  *Autumn: Peasants ploughing with oxen*

### Winter: surviving

▲ INTERPRETATION D  *Winter: The land could not be farmed so peasants lived off food stored from the harvest*

(cutting the grass to make hay). Following this they carried out binding and thatching (processing the hay to move or store it) or threshing (beating the plant to separate grains and seeds).

Not all peasants were farmers – some were millers or brewers, and their day started equally early as they had to process everything by hand. Brewers made beer from crops but could not sell it until their lord decided upon a price. Millers ground corn into flour, and if they used hand mills they were fined by the lord. They were not allowed to bake bread in their own home and had to use the lord's ovens, which was expensive.

### Food and drink

During the day peasants would have a light meal of rye bread (a dry hard bread), and work only finished when the sun went down. They would have an evening meal late at night which would have been mostly vegetables that they grew themselves. Drink would have been homemade beer or cider. Meat was rarely eaten by peasants as it was expensive. Sugar and fruit were also rare and expensive; the only sugar peasants would have had would have been honey that they found locally. The lord of the manor and richer theqns would have eaten meat and fish on a daily basis. They would also have enjoyed sugar in the form of honey, cakes and pastries. Meats were bacon, salted beef or mutton. River fish were eaten by everyone if they could get hold of them. A woman would only finish work after her husband and children had finished eating and she had cleared away dishes.

▼ **INTERPRETATION E** *Painting showing the typical work of the peasants*

### Time off

Peasants worked six days a week, so there was little time for fun, and the only time they had off was during a Holy Day or Sundays. Holy Days would start with a church service and would be followed by entertainment. Men wrestled, or took part in shin-kicking, cock fighting or wrestling. Sometimes the village would be visited by a travelling musician or someone with a bear to entertain the crowds.

## What made life difficult for peasants?

Peasants known as freemen were technically free to farm for themselves but they had to do 'born work' for the lord when required; this could include ploughing or bringing in the lord's harvest instead of their own. Villeins were peasants who only had a small plot of land but had to work for the lord for at least one day per week, every week of the year, weeding, mending fences, and removing stones from fields. During harvest time, they had to work for their lord for up to five days a week. Peasants were supervised by a bailiff to ensure that they were working properly.

Peasants paid money in taxes or rent to their landlord and a tax to the Church called a **tithe**. This was a ten per cent tax on all of the farm produce over a year. If a peasant could not pay in money he could pay in seed or equipment. When the Church collected these taxes they stored them in huge barns called tithe barns. Peasants also had to work for free on Church land. After all of the taxes were paid, peasants could keep what was left. From this money they had to pay for the seeds for the next season and sometimes they did not have enough money left to do this.

### Work

1   Look at **Interpretation E**. What does the source show about the work of a peasant? Describe the work you can see being carried out.

2   When was the busiest time of the year for a peasant? Explain your answer using examples.

3   Evaluate the impact that a lord had on the life of a peasant. How far did the lord make a peasant's life better or worse?

# 5.3 How much did towns grow under the Normans?

There were a number of established towns in England before the Normans arrived, for example Winchester, Chester and York. After the Norman Conquest some existing towns grew as important military, religious or administrative centres. King William encouraged the growth of towns in order to increase trade and taxes to the Crown. What economic impact did the Conquest have on England, and how was this seen in towns?

## Objectives

▶ **Give** facts about Norman towns.

▶ **Explain** how towns changed under the Normans.

▶ **Compare** Norman towns and villages.

## Growing settlements

London became increasingly important, as did Norwich. The city of Winchester, which was one of England's largest and most important towns in Anglo-Saxon times, did start to decline in importance; however, King William built a new cathedral there so its religious importance increased. Smaller towns grew due to their markets, for example Bury St Edmunds. The Norman nobles encouraged local towns to develop as this would increase trade; this was especially the case for towns in the south as they had more links with Normandy and the continent. Between 1066 and 1100, 21 new towns were created around the country.

## What evidence is there of the growth of towns?

Evidence of the growth of towns can be found in the Domesday Survey of 1086. It recorded the two largest towns as London, with 10,000 inhabitants, and Winchester, with 6000. Norwich, York and Lincoln had between 4000 and 5000 people. Many towns developed around new cathedrals and became important religious centres; for example, Durham, Ely, Salisbury, Winchester and Lincoln.

The Normans built many castles, initially to defend the new Norman nobility, but they soon became centres for trade. Houses in many towns such as York and Lincoln were destroyed to make way for castles, as an important part of their military control over local people. However, by 1086 the Domesday Book also recorded that new houses had been built, for example 300 in Bury St Edmunds.

A good indicator of the size and development of a town was the number of **burgesses** who lived there. A burgess was a town dweller from the upper ranks of townspeople. They owed services and taxes to a lord and could buy and sell property. Lincoln, for example, had 970 burgesses. Burgesses had legal and administrative responsibilities but the amount of power they had did vary from town to town. In some towns, they handled legal issues for the shire or the hundred.

## Features of a Norman town

Houses in towns were built closely together and conditions were cramped.

▼ **A** *An artist's impression of a Norman town*

# How did trade affect the growth of towns?

Trade played an important role in the growth of towns during the Norman period. Trade links with France were strengthened at the expense of Scandinavian links; however, the Normans brought stability in trade and this led to the development of many towns.

### Key Words

burgess  guild  franchise  grant

### The salt trade

Salt was a very important product as it was used for cooking and to preserve food. The town of Droitwich, for example, grew rapidly due to the production and sale of salt. The Domesday Book shows that there were 13 salt houses in Droitwich and that three salt workers paid their tax to the king in the form of salt.

### Metalwork

The production of iron and lead was very important in Norman England for building houses and making weapons. Towns that specialised in metalworking were often situated near woodland, because wood was used in the furnaces needed to melt and shape the metal. One of these towns was Gloucester, which sourced wood from the Forest of Dean.

### The wool trade

Wool was in great demand in England and neighbouring countries for making clothes. It was produced in the countryside, but was brought along major rivers to markets in towns such as York and Lincoln. Wool was often exported abroad to towns such as Flanders in Belgium, so some English coastal towns grew as centres of international trade, including Boston, London, Sandwich and Southampton. This trade in wool created links for trading fine cloth and wine too, so towns such as Bristol grew as a result of the trade in wine from Gascony, France.

### Guilds

Burgesses might be craftspeople, such as weavers, goldsmiths or leatherworkers, or conduct trade as bakers, butchers, fishmongers and merchants. Each of these groups joined together to form specialist associations called **guilds**. The guilds began to grow and often had considerable power.

### Markets and fairs

Markets and fairs could only be held if a **franchise** (authorisation for a group of townspeople to carry out business activity) was given in the form of a **grant** from the king or his government. After the Norman Conquest 2800 grants were given. The first grant was given by King William to the Bishop of Winchester to hold a 'free fair' at St Giles Hill.

Whilst markets gave traders a place to buy and sell their products, fairs marked religious events and were an occasion for celebration. However, fairs were also important economically. They were sponsored by the Church, which made money from them. Traders bought and sold products there, and there were also entertainers such as stilt walkers, musicians and singers.

### Work

1 How many new towns appeared between 1066 and 1130?

2 Write a sentence or two about the following trades: salt trade, metalwork, wool trade.

3 Which trade led to the most change in towns? Explain why this was important.

### Practice Question

Write an account of the ways in which town life changed under the Normans.    **8 marks**

### Study Tip

When considering this type of question, think about what changed and what remained the same. Name Norman towns as specific examples, and write about how they developed under the Normans and the growth of trade and fairs.

## 5.4 Did the Norman Conquest change everyday life?

When the Normans began to rule England in the years after 1066, things certainly changed. A new foreign king was now the King of England, and lots of French-speaking nobles came over to England to help him and live in their new castles. But to what extent did everyday life change? Did life change for all English people? Were the changes greater for different groups?

**Objectives**

▶ **Outline** the ways in which the Normans changed life in England.

▶ **Assess** to what extent the Normans changed life in England.

### Land

#### Norman aristocracy

At first, William tried to retain as many Anglo-Saxon landowners as he could. However, many took part in rebellions and had to be replaced. Before the Conquest, a few earls owned vast areas of land. After the Conquest, King William took possession of all of the land. He gave some to the Church, kept some for himself, and divided the rest between mainly Norman earls. As a result, smaller earldoms and a greater number of earls made it harder for a significant group to set themselves up to oppose the king. Most of their time and energy was spent travelling between the areas they were in charge of, checking that things were running smoothly.

A new social class was introduced in the form of knights, who could also be landlords. For the first time, the Domesday Book recorded landholding and wealth.

#### Peasants

Although the nationality of many of their landlords changed, life for peasants did not change significantly in terms of their relationship with the land.

▼ **A** *Land owned by King William in 1087, shaded in pink*

### New laws

#### Norman aristocracy

King William was impressed by the Anglo-Saxon financial system, so he retained it and introduced the Exchequer (where the king's money was kept) and minting system (the creation of coins) to Normandy. The Normans introduced trial by jury and trial by combat, which only the Norman aristocracy had the right to demand.

#### Peasants

Some new laws did affect the peasant way of life. Previously, peasants had hunted to supplement their diets, particularly in the winter and early spring when food supplies were running low. New forest laws meant that peasants faced fines, imprisonment or even death if they hunted in the forest. Murdrum fines also had a big impact on peasant life; the whole area could be fined if a Norman was killed. As a result, peasants were less likely to support rebellions.

## Castles

### Norman aristocracy

In order to protect themselves from the local Anglo-Saxon population and maintain their status, the earls built castles on their land. The role of castles developed over time so that, as well as being important for defence, they also became centres for trade and commerce.

### Peasants

Castles were built very quickly, which must have impressed as well as intimidated the local population. The peasants' land may also have been cleared to make way for a castle. However, many locals, such as the blacksmith, carpenters and trades people, lived and worked within the walls of the bailey. So a motte and bailey castle also defended them from attack.

▼ **INTERPRETATION B** *A modern interpretation of a motte and bailey castle, showing peasants living within the bailey*

## Language

### Norman aristocracy

As the vast majority of earls were Norman, the language of the new English aristocracy became French rather than English. Norman French became the language used at court, in law and for government. However, the language of religion was still Latin.
As time went on, the Norman French and Anglo-Saxon languages started to merge to create the 'Anglo Norman' language.

### Peasants

Peasants continued to speak the English they were used to for some time after the Conquest. However, Norman words crept into everyday use; for example, veal, arrow, bow, armour, battle, castle, baron, knight and earl.

## By how much did life really change?

The Normans did change life in England. However, the extent of change differed according to social status. For those at the very top of the hierarchy when the Normans arrived, the Norman impact was significant. There was an almost complete change from the Anglo-Saxon system. However, for the peasants at the bottom of the social scale, there was little change. King William's intention was never to change every aspect of English life and make it completely Norman. Instead, he took positive aspects from both systems to make sure that the governments of England and Normandy were successful, efficient, profitable and, most importantly, secure.

## Practice Question

Write an account of the ways in which life in England changed under the Normans.

**8 marks**

## Study Tip

Think about what the Normans changed, who felt the change more, and how much changed. Use the information throughout this chapter to help you.

## Work

1   a   List the ways in which the Normans changed life in England.

    b   List the ways in which life in England stayed the same after the Normans arrived.

2   Create a graph to record the impact of change on everyday life. List the changes you noted in Activity 1 along the x-axis and label the y-axis 'Significance of change'. Plot points in one colour for the Norman aristocracy and in a different colour for the English peasants. You need to decide how significant each change was, plot it on the graph, and then connect the points.

# How religious were people in Norman times?

Religion was very important in Norman England. Like the Anglo-Saxons before them, the Normans believed in God and practised a type of Christianity called Roman Catholicism. What happened to them after death was important; for them, heaven and hell were real places. If you led a good life on earth and went to church regularly, the Church promised that you would go to heaven. However, if you were a bad person and did not go to church, you would suffer the horrors of hell. Although the Church was led by the Pope in Rome, it was still subject to England's laws.

## Objectives

▶ **Summarise** the roles of the Church.

▶ **Explain** how religious people were in Norman times.

▶ **Assess** how important the Church was in England.

## How did people know about heaven and hell?

Many people could not read, and they could not understand church services or read religious texts because they were mainly in Latin. The Normans thought this was the proper language for religion, so they introduced more Latin than there had been in Anglo-Saxon times. People learned about heaven, hell and Bible stories through paintings on the church walls and stained glass windows.

## What were the roles of the Church in Norman England?

**Religion:** The main role of the Church was to ensure that people demonstrated their belief in God by going to church, that they lived a good life and went to heaven.

▼ **SOURCE A** *Doom paintings such as this one were intended to warn people about heaven and hell and remind them to follow the Church's advice*

**Economics:** The Church was a major landowner. Peasants had to work on Church lands for free, which took them away from working on their own lands. They believed God would know if they did not work on Church land and would punish them.

The Church also collected tithes (a 10 per cent tax people had to pay to the Church). The tithe was a tax on all that a farm produced in a year and could be paid in money, seeds or equipment. It was stored in huge tithe barns.

**Law:** The Church heard court cases for crimes carried out on Church lands; for example, theft, or marrying a relative, which was considered a serious offence as the Church had forbidden it. The Church then handed down justice in the king's name.

**Politics:** Leading members of the Church advised the king on important national matters as members of the Witan. Archbishops, bishops, abbots, and occasionally abbesses (female leaders of convents) and priests were members of the Witan. The archbishops of Canterbury, York and Winchester (important religious centres) were senior members.

**Education:** The Church was the only institution that produced books. The printing press was not invented until the sixteenth century, so texts were copied and illustrations were painted by hand by monks in order to make new books. In addition to religious texts, monks copied other important works including medical texts for doctors. In this way the Church could control which books were published.

▼ **INTERPRETATION B** *From* The Feudal Kingdom of England 1042–1216 *by Frank Barlow, 1999:*

> Church laws were still under royal supervision, and although the church was allowed its own law and its own courts, the king was the judge of the limits of Church power.

**Health:** People in the twelfth century did not understand the causes of diseases and thought they were a punishment from God. As a result, priests tried to cure the sick by praying for them or recommending they pay a penance in the form of money, pain or prayer.

## What was the role of the priest?

Priests played a central role in the community. In addition to helping the sick, they led church services, heard confessions, married people and baptised children. All members of the community went to the village church, from the lord of the manor to the youngest peasant, so the local priest could advise all members of the community, rich or poor.

## Why did people go on pilgrimages?

**Pilgrims** are people who went on a journey, or pilgrimage, to a religious place in order to feel closer to God and heaven. Those who could afford to went to the **Holy Land** of Jerusalem, or to the Church of Saint Etienne in Normandy to visit the tombs of William I and his wife Matilda. Many others made pilgrimages to **abbeys** and **monasteries** in England.

### Work

1   What were the different roles of the Church in Norman England?

2   Look at **Source A**. What does this doom painting show and what is it encouraging people to do or not do?

3   Explain how religious people were in Norman England.

4   How important was the Church in England? Think about other factors as well as religious ones.

### Practice Question

How convincing is **Interpretation B** about the role of the Norman Church?

Explain your answer using **Interpretation B** and your contextual knowledge.     **8 marks**

### Study Tip

Think about the different roles of the Church in Norman England. Which role does the interpretation show and which ones does it not reflect?

# How did the Normans influence religion in England?

King William I was a deeply religious man. He was aware that the people who ran the English Church were not following the rules set by the Pope in Rome. William was keen to **reform** the Church in England as he had done in Normandy, and this was one of the reasons why the Pope granted him the Papal Banner to fight at Hastings. Once William was crowned king, he set about changing and improving the English Church to get rid of the old practices.

## How religious was William I?

William showed how religious he was, and also how grateful he was for God's support at Hastings, by building many new churches and cathedrals in England. He built an abbey on the site of the Battle of Hastings and enormous cathedrals such as the one at Winchester. In Durham and Rochester, cathedrals were built next to castles, which would have made both buildings look even more impressive.

▼ **A** *A photograph of Battle Abbey near Hastings*

## Was the need to reform the English Church as urgent as King William thought?

During the reign of King Edward, a number of bishops attended European councils and were aware of reforms going on in Europe. The reform movement was centred around a monastery in Cluny, France.

### Fact

**Holding positions of power in the Church**

The following practices were banned by the Catholic Church, but William believed these rules were being broken in England and elsewhere.

Pluralism: holding more than one position or job in the Church

Simony: selling positions or jobs in the Church

Nepotism: giving a job or office to someone only because they were a friend or relatives of someone in the Church

Marriage: members of the **clergy** were not allowed to marry or have children (they should have remained **celibate**)

Pope Leo IX started the reform and this was continued by Pope Gregory VII. King William had been reforming the Norman Church before his invasion. He was so concerned about the **corruption** of the Church that he refused to allow Stigand, the Archbishop of Canterbury, to crown him. Stigand held multiple positions of leadership in the Church; this was known as pluralism and was not allowed.

# King William's changes to the Church in England after 1066

William made a number of changes to the way in which the Church was run. Some changes were to bring the English Church more in line with the rules from Rome; others were to enable the Church to help run the country; and some changes benefitted William himself.

## Key Words

reform    clergy    celibate    corrupt    Romanesque    diocese    Benedictine

| Area | Reform |
|------|--------|
| Bishops | Whilst William wanted to reform the English Church he was not prepared to do this at the expense of his own power. Anglo-Saxon bishops and archbishops were removed and replaced with Normans. Archbishop Stigand was replaced by Lanfranc. By 1080, there was only one Anglo-Saxon bishop left. |
| Architecture | At first Normans stole the treasures of many of the 49 English monasteries and took the Church's land. However, the Normans soon began rebuilding churches and cathedrals in the **Romanesque** style (which was already familiar to them), including Rochester, Durham, Norwich, Bath, Winchester and Gloucester. This style favours clean lines, with simple yet impressive design. |
| Organisation | After 1066, the Church became better organised. **Dioceses** (areas of land served by a church or cathedral) were divided into archdeaconries, which were further divided into deaneries. New cathedrals were built in more important towns and cities, such as Coventry, Salisbury and Lincoln. |
| Legal issues | In 1076, the Council of Winchester ordered that only Church courts could try the clergy, meaning that people who worked for the Church would be tried for their crimes in Church courts rather than in local courts. Also, William adhered to Papal law by reintroducing a tax of one pence, which every household had to pay to the Pope. However, William did interfere when Bishop Odo was arrested in 1082 for attempting to take a group of knights to the continent; William insisted on him being tried as the Earl of Kent rather than the Bishop of Bayeux so that he would go to the King's court. |
| Parish priest | Peasants did not experience changes to their religious experience under the Normans, since most Anglo-Saxon priests remained in their jobs. Local priests were poorly educated. Some were married and remained so even after the reforms. |

## Key Biography

### Archbishop Lanfranc (1010–1089)

- Early in his career, he was an Italian **Benedictine** monk and abbot of Bec Abbey who was exiled by William after he opposed William's marriage to Mathilda.

- In 1066 he went to Rome to obtain the Papal Banner for William before the invasion.

- He advised King William on religious affairs, and played an important role in King William's reform of the Church in Normandy and England.

- He became the Archbishop of Canterbury in 1070.

## Work

1 Define the following terms: simony; nepotism; pluralism.

2 Why did William reform the Church in England?

3 Consider the ways in which William reformed the Church. Draw a table and organise the reforms into:

a changes that benefited William

b changes that brought the English Church in line with Rome

c changes that enabled the Church to help run the country.

Do any fit into more than one category?

# How did the Normans influence religion in England?

## The relationship between the Norman kings and the Pope

In 1066 William, Duke of Normandy, enjoyed the support of Pope Alexander II as he was granted the Papal Banner to fight in Hastings. However, King William's relationship did not remain so positive throughout his reign. Immediately after the battle, Pope Alexander ordered King William and his men to do **penance** for all of the killing and destruction they had caused during the campaign. As a result, King William built Battle Abbey which was finished in 1095. King William used a geld (a form of tax) to extract money from religious houses and this was continued by his son William II. Both William I and William II used religious positions to promote or reward people, but it was only the Pope or the Church who had the power to do this, not kings. This led to disagreements between William II and Archbishop Anselm.

## The Normans and the wealth of the Church

Both William I and William II used the Church for their own personal gain. There are accounts of Normans taking hold of Church offices and stealing from English churches. In the monastery at Abingdon, for example, a Norman monk melted down a chandelier for £40 worth of gold and silver (roughly £35,000 in today's money) and carried off precious dishes to Normandy. At Ely statues of the Virgin and Child were stripped of the gold, silver and gems that decorated them. Normans often stole from English Churches to enrich Norman ones. However, these accounts were written by chroniclers who likely wanted to portray the Normans unfavourably.

## How important was Anselm?

When Archbishop Lanfranc died in 1089 King William II did not replace him, but instead took money from Church property while he managed the area himself. William II had to deal with a number of rebellions during his reign and an invasion by King Malcolm and the Scots in 1091; the money he had acquired after Lanfranc's death helped to pay for this. King William II refused to appoint anyone to the role of Archbishop of Canterbury. However, when he became ill in 1093, he thought his illness might be due to his lack of **piety** and his greed and, believing he was going to die, asked Anselm to

> ### Key Biography
>
> ### Archbishop Anselm (1033–1109)
> - In 1060 Anselm joined the Benedictine monastery in Bec, where Lanfranc had been.
> - In 1063 Anselm was made **Prior** of Bec monastery (and later abbot), where he was highly respected, and wrote books about the existence of God and faith.
> - Anselm was summoned to England to succeed Lanfranc as Archbishop of Canterbury in 1093.
> - Anselm had many arguments with King William II and King Henry I about their abuses of the Church. He was banished on two occasions and went to Rome to support the Church. He remained Archbishop of Canterbury until he died and always put the Church before his king.

hear his confession and administer his **last rites**. Soon after, he appointed Anselm Archbishop of Canterbury in gratitude for his service and acknowledged Urban II, whom Anselm supported, as Pope.

▼ **INTERPRETATION B** *This statue of Archbishop Anselm was created for Saint Anselm College, Manchester, in 1987*

Anselm proposed reforms for the Church in Europe that were based on those instigated by Pope Gregory between 1050 and 1080, which were designed to deal with the morality and independence of the clergy. In 1097, William II and Anselm argued over a campaign in Wales. So when Anselm asked if he could leave England and go to Rome to see Pope Urban II, William agreed. This was not the first time Anselm had fled to Rome and showed that he accepted the authority of the Pope over the king in Church affairs.

## The Church reforms of Pope Gregory, 1073–1085

Pope Gregory believed that the Church should:

- be independent of the monarchs of Europe and take care of its own affairs

- remove corruption within the Church

- develop the moral principles of the clergy

- ensure that monks and priests were celibate.

However, in 1075 Henry IV of France (who was also the Holy Roman Emperor and ruled a large area on central Europe) refused to accept Pope Gregory's reforms. As a result, the Pope **excommunicated** Henry the following year. This meant that he was no longer part of the Church: the worst punishment the Church

▼ **INTERPRETATION C** *This image shows Henry IV in front of Pope Gregory; Henry was forced to plead for his excommunication to be reversed*

**Key Words**

penance     piety     prior
last rites     excommunicate

could enforce. In 1078 Pope Gregory banned kings from appointing bishops and abbots, in order to keep the Church's independence. This led to a struggle between the Pope and the monarchs of Europe over who could appoint senior members of the Church. This became known as the Investiture Controversy and it lasted from 1075 to 1122.

### Work

1  How did the Norman kings make money from their reforms of the Church?

2  Examine the reforms that King William I introduced. What changed?

3  Discuss with a partner the reasons for the change in the relationship between the Norman kings and the Pope.

### Extension

What was the biggest change in the relationship between the Norman kings and the Pope? What caused it? Are there any patterns that emerge?

### Practice Question

Explain what was important about the Norman reforms of the Church.

**8 marks**

### Study Tip

Think about the relationship between the Norman and English Churches. William made a number of different reforms for different reasons. You could think about reforms that improved the way the Church was run; reforms that improved the situation for William; and reforms that reflected changes he had already made in Normandy.

# 6.3 Historic Environment: Norman cathedrals

Religious buildings such as monasteries, abbeys and cathedrals, constructed during Norman times, were often very large and grand. Norman cathedrals were built as an expression of devotion to God in stone. They were designed to be magnificent and, seen from miles around, with high ceilings, clean lines and symmetrical columns. What were the main features of Norman cathedrals? What was the purpose of a cathedral, and how did they show Norman control?

## Objectives

▶ **Explain** the significance of Norman cathedrals.

▶ **Investigate** how a specific cathedral, Durham, reflects Norman control over England.

## What were Norman religious buildings like?

Norman religious buildings were Romanesque – a style of building that was found across Europe at this time. King Edward had started to use the style but the Normans used it extensively. It was very different to the smaller, more modest style of the Anglo-Saxon churches, which had been built to serve the community, and of which few remain today. Norman cathedrals were used as a form of intimidation in the same way that castles were. They were often built on top of a hill to give them prominence. Durham Cathedral, for example, occupies a strategic position on high ground above the River Wear. Its massive structure dominated the local landscape and reminded the locals that the Normans were in control of England. Durham also has a fortified castle, which provided additional protection to the area.

The scale of and beauty of cathedral and abbeys were designed to show the strength of the Norman religious faith; cathedrals were built in a cross to symbolise the crucifixion of Jesus and most housed monks. Cathedrals were also powerful political bases as bishops played an important role in running the country. They also attracted pilgrims, as they often contained **shrines** to important saints or holy relics (items that had religious significance).

## Durham Cathedral–a typical Norman cathedral

Durham was politically important. It was the main English town within the **buffer zone** along the border with Scotland. Earls found it difficult to control the area, so the Norman kings gave the Bishop of Durham additional secular powers (this meant he had legal powers outside of the Church) as people were likely to obey the authority of the Church. From 1075, the bishop became a prince bishop. This meant he could raise an army, impose taxes and mint coins in order to raise revenue (income), as long as he defended the border for the king. The prince bishop ruled over a large, rich area, so ambitious rather than religious men were often attracted to the role.

### Key Biography

#### Ranulf Flambard (1060–1128)

- In 1099, Flambard succeeded William de St Calais as the second Norman Bishop of Durham. He had been a royal clerk under King William II.

- Flambard meant 'fiery'. He was a successful Crown prosecutor (he fought legal cases on behalf of the king) and an excellent public speaker. He was generous to his friends and the poor, but he could be greedy and extravagant.

- Flambard was responsible for the start of construction on Durham Cathedral.

### Timeline: Durham Cathedral

| 1072 | 1075 | 1093–1133 | 1096 | 1128 |
|------|------|-----------|------|------|
| Norman Chapel built | Bishop of Durham becomes Prince Bishop of Durham | Cathedral is built over a 40 year period | The **quire** is completed | The **nave** is completed |

In 1093 building work started in Durham on a monastic cathedral for Benedictine monks. Construction was started under William of Calais and finished by Ranulf Flambard, both Bishops of Durham. It was also intended to house the shrine of St Cuthbert, perhaps the most famous Anglo-Saxon saint, and attract pilgrims.

## Key Words

shrine    buffer zone    quire    nave
benefactor    perpendicular style

Nave: The building of this started in 1092, also in the Romanesque style. The window at the back has a pointed top: this is known as the **perpendicular style** and shows that the window was added later; in this case it was made from stained glass and was a gift from benefactors. This was a common feature in Norman cathedrals and abbey churches.

The Norman chapel: Located in the cathedral itself and dating back to 1072, it was built in the Romanesque style with clean lines, rounded arches and vaulted ceilings. Chapels can be found in most cathedrals and abbey churches and are usually paid for by **benefactors**.

▲ **A** *Durham Cathedral's key features are typical of Norman cathedrals*

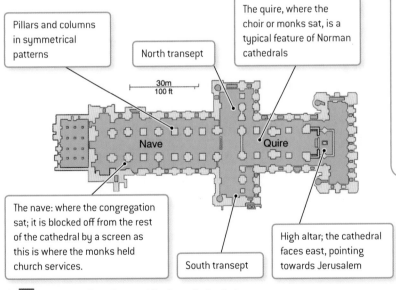

Pillars and columns in symmetrical patterns

North transept

The quire, where the choir or monks sat, is a typical feature of Norman cathedrals

30m
100 ft

Nave

Quire

The nave: where the congregation sat; it is blocked off from the rest of the cathedral by a screen as this is where the monks held church services.

South transept

High altar; the cathedral faces east, pointing towards Jerusalem

▲ **B** *The floor-plan shape of Durham Cathedral represents the cross on which Christ died*

## Study Tip

The Normans built many magnificent cathedrals throughout England. Why did they do this? Think about how the new cathedrals related to the way the Normans changed the Church in England. What would local people have thought about the new buildings and their builders? Consider the important design features of cathedrals such as Durham. What was different and impressive about the scale and style of cathedrals?

## Work

1   Why was Durham important in England?

2   Describe the key features of Norman cathedrals.

3   Why was Scotland a threat to the Norman kings? Refer to your prior learning on Scottish invasions.

4   Compare cathedrals to castles as a method of control, listing similarities and differences.

## Extension

On a blank map of the British Isles, label Durham Cathedral, London and the Scottish borders. Research Norman cathedrals and make a note of them on your map. What do you notice about the distribution of the cathedrals? Why do you think they were built in the locations you have noted?

# The life of a monk

Male monks and female nuns dedicate their lives to the worship of God and doing his work. Most monks live in places called monasteries or abbeys. The terms 'abbey' and 'monastery' mean the same thing: a church with domestic buildings attached. Most nuns live in nunneries, or convents. Their way of life is known as **monasticism**. When the Domesday Book was written there were 35 monasteries and nunneries in England. So what was daily life in a monastery like? And how did the Normans change monasticism in England?

## What were religious orders?

An 'order' is a group of religious people who follow the teachings of a particular holy person. In Norman times the most influential person was St Benedict, whose teachings had been followed since the sixth century. The first order to follow them were known as the Benedictine monks. However, as time went on, people's interpretations of the teachings of St Benedict changed and new orders were created.

## The Order of St Benedict

St Benedict was born in Nursia, Italy. He studied in Rome, but then decided to live away from everyday life in order to focus on worshipping God. He founded a monastery in Monte Cassino where he wrote a set of rules for the monks to live by. After he died, the Rule of St Benedict became the basic guide for life in all monastic institutions. The community Benedict founded became known as the Order of St Benedict. The order includes monks and nuns, who train for four years as **novices**. Then they have to agree to live by four vows – poverty, chastity, obedience and stability. Many also have to take a vow of silence.

▼ **INTERPRETATION A**

*St Benedict, c480–547*

## Benedictine vows

**Vow of poverty:** Monks and nuns have to give up all wealth and personal possessions when they join a monastery.

**Vow of chastity:** This vow means abstaining from sex, but also from other physical pleasure such as eating sweet food or drinking alcohol.

**Vow of obedience:** Monks and nuns have to obey the teachings of God through the Bible, their **abbot** or **abbess**, and the rules of their order.

**Vow of stability:** They promise never to leave the monastic community and for some this means not even leaving their monastery.

## A day in the life of a monk

| | |
|---|---|
| 00:00 | First prayers of the day (Matins) |
| 03:00 | Morning prayer (Lauds) |
| 06:00 | Get up; wash; church service (Prime) |
| 07:00 | Meet for day's instructions |
| 08:00 | Private reading and prayer |
| 09:00 | Church service (Terce and Mass) |
| 12:00 | Church service (Sext): meal |
| 14:00 | Rest |
| 15:00 | Church service (None) |
| 16:00 | Farming and housekeeping |
| 18:00 | Church service (Vespers) |
| 21:00 | Night prayer (Compline); bed |

# Work done by monks

The life of a monk was meant to be harsh, uncomfortable and sometimes painful. Monks lived in isolation away from the distractions and corruption of everyday life. As a result, monasteries and nunneries had to be **self-sufficient**, so they produced their own food and materials. Monks and nuns often carried out the work themselves, or the religious houses employed **lay brothers** to carry out this work.

It was thought that because Jesus Christ suffered on the cross, monks should suffer to try to be closer to God. However, some people joined holy orders to escape the harsh realities of life; this was particularly true for younger sons, who would inherit no land. The vast majority of a monk's life was devoted to prayer. They prayed in the belief that they were helping other people go to heaven. Ordinary people could pay monasteries to pray in the hope of getting to heaven more quickly. This made them benefactors to their chosen monastery.

All the work monks did was considered to be divine – on behalf of God. The printing press was not invented until 1440 so monks copied books by hand in monastery **scriptoriums**. Monks also completed divine work each day, which could include tending to the sick, working in almonries giving alms (clothes, food, etc.) to the poor, teaching in the community, and some monks even advised the king.

## How did the Normans reform monasteries?

► **INTERPRETATION B**

*A nineteenth-century illustration; the Benedictine monks were known as the Black Monks due to their clothing*

## Key Words

monasticism    novice    abbot
abbess    self-sufficient    lay brother
scriptorium    priory

In the tenth century the Cluniac order, developed within Cluny Abbey in France, reinforced the Rule of Benedict more strictly. King William I gave gifts of land and money to French monasteries and he asked Cluny Abbey to send monks over to England. Initially the abbot St Hugh refused but one of William's earls, William de Warenne, persuaded him to send a prior and three monks to help set up a **priory** near de Warenne's castle at Lewes between 1078 and 1082. By the end of the eleventh century there were 36 Cluniac monasteries in England.

This led to the revival of monasteries and abbeys in the north of England. Spectacular abbeys were built, such as Whitby Abbey on the north-east coast. Monks were brought from Normandy to run the new abbeys and monasteries. Abbots became tenants, governing large areas of land, and so had to provide knights as part of the feudal system. King William and his earls gave large amounts of money to the abbeys and monasteries as part of their penance for the Battle of Hastings. This penance could also include giving a child to become a monk or a nun, which might also be a convenient way to deal with a younger son who could not inherit land, or a younger daughter who could not be married off.

## Work

1  Outline the main teachings of St Benedict.
2  Why did people choose to become monks?
3  How did the Normans reform monasteries?
4  Look at 'A day in the life of a monk'. What conclusions can you draw from this information?

## Extension

Explore the world of a medieval monk. Research medieval monasticism, choose one order to investigate; for example, the Benedictine; Cluniac; the order of St Cuthbert; or an abbey such as Whitby Abbey, and find out what life was like in those orders or that particular building.

# Educating England

Education was first promoted in England by the Romans, who had specialist schools with full time teachers. However, when the Romans left Britain, these schools closed down and education was taken over by the Church. At that time, Church schools used the local language more than the Latin used by the Romans, and the teachers were monks or nuns. When the Normans arrived in 1066, schools once again moved out of monasteries and convents into the towns and cities. So how much education did children receive under the Normans?

## Objectives

▶ **Describe** how education changed over time.

▶ **Define** key terms.

▶ **Evaluate** how the Normans changed education.

## How did the Normans change education?

As the size and number of towns increased under the Normans, so did the need for a better education system. People who lived and worked in the towns needed better literacy and numeracy skills in order to conduct trade. Also, the Norman barons and knights who lived in England wanted their children educated to the highest possible standards.

▼ **INTERPRETATION A** *Aelfric, the first person to translate a Latin textbook into English*

In addition, reforms within monasticism meant that children were no longer allowed within monasteries or convents. Therefore, schools moved out of religious grounds and became separate buildings. There was also an explosion in the number of schools. By the twelfth century there were 40 schools and by the thirteenth there were 75. French was spoken, although the French language began

▶ **SOURCE B**

*A painting of the Tower of Babel from the introduction to Aelfric's book*

## Timeline: Education in England before the Normans

| 43 AD | 400 AD | 400–500 AD |
|---|---|---|
| The Romans introduce schools in major towns. Only the children (usually boys) of the richest people are educated. The schoolmasters teach grammar and **rhetoric**, so that the children can speak and write Latin correctly. Latin was the main language used by the Romans. | Britain is becoming Christian so reading and writing in Latin continues to be important. Towns are declining, so schools are closed down. As a result, monks take over the teaching role and Church schools open in monasteries. The number of Latin speakers declines and the **vernacular** (local language) – English – is used more. | Welsh, Irish and English become more widely spoken and used for poetry, local laws and customs. Latin is still used for religious and educational texts. Teachers develop ways of teaching foreign grammar and this becomes the basis for learning French, German and other languages. |

to influence the English language (and vice versa). However, Latin was still used for writing and was also seen as the language of Christianity

## How did education develop

Archbishops Lanfranc and Anselm were key people in reforms to the education system after the Norman Conquest. Lanfranc had created a school in Normandy in 1042 and taught there for three years. He later taught theology at a monastery, also in Normandy, for 18 years. The monastery became the most famous in Europe and the future Pope Alexander II and Anselm were students of his. In 1077, Anselm wrote a book, *Monologium*, in which he considers the attributes of God.

Archbishops Lanfranc and Anselm promoted education and built libraries. One function of the Church schools was to produce clergy (priests and members of the holy orders) and lay people who were literate. A number of grammar schools were built for this purpose; for example, in Northampton, Exeter, Lincoln and Oxford.

## What happened in grammar schools?

At the age of ten some children moved on to grammar schools, which were distinct from Church schools. Schoolmasters in small towns often taught children of all ages, while in larger areas they specialised in teaching either older or younger students. Students stayed at grammar school for at least four years, depending on the career path they intended to follow. They learned about Latin grammar in detail, as well as how to write and speak the language. Notes were written on boards made of stone which could be wiped clean; paper was only introduced after 1400.

The school year started in September and there were three terms, with the final term ending in June. This enabled students from peasant families to concentrate on bringing in the harvest in July and August. The school day started as soon as the sun was up and ended late afternoon, with breaks in the middle of the morning and for lunch. During lessons, the teacher sat in the middle of the room and children sat on benches around the outside, answering questions directed at them by their teacher.

If students were successful at school, they moved on to university where all books and lectures were in Latin. Students who did not go to university could become merchants, parish clergy or secretarial clerks. Subjects such as maths, accountancy and law were not taught in grammar schools and were taught when students started work.

### Practice Question

Write an account of the ways in which education changed under the Normans.    **8 marks**

### Study Tip

You could think about: what education was like before the Normans; who received it and where; and in what language. You could also consider how important individuals changed education.

**600–1000 AD**

Monks and nuns continue to teach pupils, a few of whom are girls. They are taught subjects such as theology, medicine and history, which at first requires reading and writing in Latin, but from the ninth century lessons are taught in English.

**990 AD**

A monk named Aelfric is the first person to translate a Latin textbook into English, which is used in England until after the Norman Conquest.

### Work

1   Write a sentence to explain each of the following terms: vernacular; church schools; rhetoric.

2   Look at the timeline. Can you identify key turning points in education?

3   Compare education under the Normans with education today. What are the similarities, and what are the differences?

# How to... analyse interpretations

> William was certainly effective, as the English earls found to their cost, having had their lands taken from them or at least lowered in status as landholders, and even killed or driven into exile as a consequence of resistance.

## Study Tip

Remember that an interpretation is a person's view of an event or an experience that has happened in the past. Every person's view depends on their background and circumstances, so different people may have completely different opinions about how William changed England. You could consider all of his changes — those that were seen as beneficial (and who felt the benefit of those changes) and those that weren't interpretations of the same event.

## Practice Question

How convincing is **Interpretation A** about the way in which William I changed England? Explain your answer using **Interpretation A** and your contextual knowledge.  **8 marks**

## Study Tip

Remember that this type of 'convincing' interpretation question in your Paper 2 British Depth Study exam is different from the 'how far' interpretation question in your Paper 1 Period Study exam. This one is based on the writings of a historian or someone who has studied the event or period. Consider: What do you know about the event? How far do you agree with this interpretation?

## Over to you

This type of question wants you to decide how **convincing** an interpretation is. In other words, how far does the interpretation fit with what you know about the history of the event, person or issue?

1. You could usefully begin by showing that you understand the main points of the interpretation by summarising the interpretation *in your own words*. For example, you could consider what you know about the history of the ways in which William changed England that matches or confirms the main point of the interpretation.

2. You may not be totally convinced by the interpretation: this means you may not believe that the interpretation is completely correct or you may not agree that the interpretation is the best way to understand the events. Can you suggest different interpretations of the changes William made, or different ways the issue can be seen? For example, do you think that all of his changes had a negative impact on the English people?

3. Finally, do you agree with the interpretation? In other words, did you find the interpretation convincing? (Even if you agree with the interpretation that the English earls were treated badly, you could still try to describe other groups of English people who did benefit or even English earls who were treated well.) Try to write a few concluding sentences in which you make a judgement about how persuasive or accurate the interpretation is compared to any alternative interpretation. It is important to explain why you have come to this conclusion based on the history of the event.

4. What are the strengths and weaknesses of the following essay introduction to the question?

Interpretation A says that William was 'certainly effective' however the earls found this to their cost, 'having had their lands taken away from them or lowered in status as landholders'. This is referring to the changes that were felt by the earls and thegns who lost land. For example, Edwin and Morcar both had their earldoms greatly reduced. It also says that some of the earls were 'even killed... or driven into exile' because they rebelled against William due to the changes to landholding. For example, Earl Waltheof was beheaded. However, the interpretation does not mention the changes to the Church or the ways in which the life of peasants changed. Therefore I agree that the source is a convincing interpretation about the ways in which life changed for the earls and the landowning classes but not for the vast majority of the population — the peasants.

# How to... tackle the Historic Environment question

**Practice Question**

'Luck was the main reason for the outcome of battles in this period.'

How far does a study of the battle of Stamford Bridge support this statement? Explain your answer.

You should refer to Stamford Bridge and your contextual knowledge.    **16 marks**

**Study Tip**

Resist the temptation to write down everything that you know about the Battle of Stamford Bridge because you won't have enough time in the exam. The question asks 'how far' a study of the battle supports the statement, so you should try to consider whether factors *other than* luck had an impact on its outcome.

## Over to you

Before your exam, you will have learned a lot about a specific historic site or building. This type of question asks you how your knowledge of a particular site helps you understand a key feature of the Norman period. In other words, what can a study of the **historic environment** tell you about people or events at the time? The environment may have influenced the outcome of the battle or conflict, so you could consider:

1  *Motivation*: Why was the battle fought?

2  *Location*: Why was it fought in that particular place? What are the main landscape features?

3  What happened at the battle? Why was the battle fought in the way that it was? What were the battle plans and how were forces deployed? How did the battle develop, and what were the key moments?

4  Who fought in the battle?

5  Questions 1 to 4 will be helpful for battle sites, but if you are studying a building, such as Durham Cathedral, you could consider different questions such as:

   a  *Motivation*: Why did someone want to build this specific building?

   b  *Location*: Why did they build it in that particular location?

   c  *Function*: Why was it built in that particular way? Consider the shape and design of the building or its layout. People design buildings to work and look in particular ways. Firstly, buildings have to function in a particular way, for example for safety, defence, comfort, or pleasure. Can you identify and explain specific building features, and the job they do?

   d  *Purpose*: What would the building be used for? Who lived or worked there?

6  Note that you don't need to use all the knowledge from your answers to questions 1 to 5 in order to answer the Practice Question. Select *relevant* information from the answers to write a response to the specific aspect of the historic environment you are asked about. The question asks '*how far*' the battle shows that Norman battles were often decided by luck, so you will need to say whether the outcome of the Battle of Stamford Bridge was decided more by luck or other factors, such as tactics.

7  Now try to answer the Practice Question yourself!

# 1.1

# What sort of a man was Edward Longshanks?

This topic focuses on the reign of Edward I of England between 1272 and 1307. To understand this period properly, you need to examine Edward's life before he became king. When he became King of England it was a role Edward had spent his whole life preparing for. His stormy relationship with his father, Henry III, the troublesome rebellions of men like Simon de Montfort and adventures in the **Crusades** all helped prepare the young prince for the throne. How did Edward's early experiences shape his character?

## The warrior prince

Edward was very tall for his time, and his height earned him the nickname 'Longshanks'. His stature enabled him to become an excellent horseman and his long arms gave him an advantage in any swordfight. He also had a thirst for adventure. From an early age, Edward was involved in English politics. He was not afraid of publicly disagreeing with his father over important issues. He supported the **barons** in their calls for more rights in 1258, putting himself on the opposite side of the argument to the king. As the barons' power increased, he switched sides to support his father in 1261 and was even for a time held captive by the barons' leader, Simon de Montfort. Edward proved his skills as a warrior and leader when he led the final defeat of Montfort in 1265. Some saw his changing position as a sign of untrustworthiness.

▼ **SOURCE B** *Adapted from the 'Song of Lewes' written in around 1264:*

Where unto shall the noble Edward be compared? Perhaps he will be rightly called a leopard. If we divide the name it becomes lion and pard; lion, because we saw that he was not slow to attack the strongest places, fearing the onslaught of none. A lion by pride and fierceness, he is by inconstancy and changeableness a pard, changing his word and promise, cloaking himself by pleasant speech. When he is in a strait he promises whatever you wish, but as soon as he has escaped he renounces his promise.

▼ **SOURCE A** *A contemporary portrait in Westminster Abbey that is believed to show Edward I*

## The crusader

In August 1270, Edward left England with around 250 knights and 1000 men to join one of the last Crusades. These were a series of wars in the Middle East encouraged by the **Pope**. Their aim was to capture the **Holy Land** for Christianity. Crusaders believed they were doing God's work and many European knights, princes and kings joined the campaigns. Edward's successes were limited and although he and his soldiers fought hard, the much larger Muslim forces proved too much. After recovering from being wounded by an assassin's poisoned dagger Edward left for Sicily and never went on crusade again.

## Destined for great things?

A famous story about Edward involved a giant stone falling and smashing a chair where he had just been sitting and playing chess. His survival was explained as a miracle. Along with his survival of the poisoned dagger wound during the Crusades, this was seen as a sign that God had an important purpose for Edward. From an early age, he had been fascinated by the story of King Arthur and spent his life trying to live up to the legend. The **chivalry** of the Knights of the Round Table did much to inform Edward's views on how war and society should work. He believed that, like Arthur, he was destined to be a great king.

### Key Words

Crusade    baron    Pope
Holy Land    chivalry    bishop
clergy    civil war    Magna Carta

## Edward's father: King Henry III (reigned 1216–72)

▼ **INTERPRETATION C** *A nineteenth-century illustration of Henry III*

HENRY III.    1216–1272.

Most historians agree that Henry III's reign was troubled and that he was a weak king. Edward certainly held that view. By surrounding himself with French friends Henry angered many English nobles who felt shut out of power. His appointments of foreign **bishops** in the Church also upset the English **clergy**. As a devoted Christian, he built new churches with money raised through increased taxes on ordinary people, which made him unpopular.

One of Henry's biggest problems were his disastrous wars. Defeats in the French regions of Aquitaine in 1229 and Gascony in 1242 were not only embarrassing but also expensive. When taxes were raised once again, Henry's barons had had enough. Led by Simon de Montfort, the barons met in Oxford in 1258 and demanded more influence in government. Henry agreed to these 'Provisions of Oxford'. Although Henry had accepted the Provisions, by 1261 he was ignoring them, and this caused a **civil war** between Henry and the barons led by Montfort. Henry was on the verge of giving up when his son came to the rescue and led the defeat of Montfort in 1265.

### The Provisions of Oxford, 1258

- A council of 15 barons would advise Henry. He could make no decisions without their agreement.
- Taxes would be decided locally, not by the king.
- No foreigners could hold senior positions.
- The king and the barons had to take an oath of loyalty to uphold this agreement.
- In 1259, the Provisions of Oxford were replaced by the Provisions of Westminster, which introduced even more restrictions on the king, particularly on tax collection.

### Work

1  Describe Edward's experiences of the Crusades.

2  Look at **Source A**. What impression does this source give of Edward? Explain your answer.

3  In pairs, draw an outline of Edward on a piece of A3 paper (remember he was very tall!). Inside the outline write down as many words as you can that describe what sort of man he was.

4  a  Why do you think Henry III is seen as such a weak king?

   b  What impact do you think the reign of Henry III would have had on his son, Edward?

### Fact

The First Barons' War (1215–17) was fought between a group of barons and King John, Edward's grandfather, and was the result of John's refusal to follow **Magna Carta**, which he had agreed to do in 1215. The Second Barons' War refers to the struggle between Henry III and Simon de Montfort from 1264 to 1267.

# 1.2 What problems did Edward face when he became king?

When Henry III died in 1272, his son and **heir**, Edward, was away from England. He was told the news when he reached Europe but did not rush to return to his new kingdom. He knew that the situation was stable and he was still recovering from the assassin's poisoned dagger. He was well aware that when he did arrive he would have a lot to deal with. Many of the problems that his father had struggled with remained and he was determined not to make the same mistakes.

## Objectives

▶ **Describe** the problems Edward I faced when he first became king.

▶ **Explain** how Henry III's mistakes might influence how Edward dealt with these problems.

▶ **Assess** why Edward was keen to be a different kind of king from his father.

## A strong king?

Edward had witnessed the problems that a king's weakness could create. His father's disastrous wars and poor decisions had plunged the country into civil war. The barons were still a powerful force. Edward felt he was a better military leader than his father and believed he was destined to be a great king.

## A father's failures: the Second Barons' War

Simon de Montfort emerged as a key figure in the negotiations between Henry III and the barons. Montfort openly criticised the king on several occasions, yet Henry seemed unable to do much about it. In 1260, he called Montfort to appear before a court but the trial never took place (Henry was distracted by a Welsh uprising) and the baron remained a powerful figure. When civil war broke out in 1264, Montfort not only had great success against the king in battle but also took both Henry and Edward prisoner. Now able to do as he liked, he placed his supporters in powerful positions and let his sons take control of land across the country. It was not until Edward escaped that Montfort was defeated in 1265 at the Battle of Evesham. Montfort had made Henry look weak. Edward was determined that he would never find himself in this position.

▼ **INTERPRETATION A** *Adapted from the website of the Simon de Montfort Society:*

> The story of Simon's life shows that he was a man of considerable talents: soldier, administrator, diplomat, scholar, ardent Christian, loyal husband and father. Whilst he always pursued his own financial and other self-interests, there is no doubt that Simon also promoted justice and the idea that parliament should be powerful.

## Key Biography

### Simon de Montfort (c1208–65)

- He was a French nobleman who became the Earl of Leicester in 1239.
- He led a rebellion against Henry III in what became known as the Second Barons' War.
- After capturing and imprisoning the king in 1264 at the Battle of Lewes he ruled England for a year.
- His rule ended when he was killed at the Battle of Evesham in 1265 and his forces were defeated.

# Edward's problems

After his father's death, Edward returned from the Crusade as King of England, but immediately faced several difficulties. Despite England being at peace and politically stable, Edward knew from his father's experiences that this could change very quickly.

## Key Words

heir    noble    customs    homage

## The barons

Edward knew how big a threat to his power a few unhappy **nobles** could be. He could not rule without them but he needed to arrange a settlement with the barons that would secure his own position but allow them to feel that they were not being ignored. He certainly was not willing to accept anything close to the Provisions of Oxford but he also knew he could not simply do as he liked.

## Finances

Henry III's expensive wars and mismanagement of the country's finances left Edward with little money. Henry's attempt to raise taxes had contributed to his conflict with the barons and so Edward would have to tread carefully. His own desire to wage war would be costly and he soon recognised that trade could be the solution, in particular **customs** payments. Beginning with the wool trade in 1275, the new king quickly established an effective system to bring in large sums to the Crown.

### Practice Question

Explain what was important about how Edward's experiences in the Second Barons' War might influence his rule. **8 marks**

### Study Tip

Remember, the focus of this type of question is the consequences of the event rather than a retelling of the event itself.

## The new king's problems

### Fact

Historians sometimes add a 'c' before dates. This stands for 'circa', which means 'around' or 'approximately'.

## Wales

Edward saw it as an annoyance that Wales was such a troublesome place. Regular rebellion in a land that bordered England was a real threat to the security of Edward's kingdom. Llywelyn ap Gruffudd, the Prince of Wales, had become increasingly powerful during Henry's reign and, in 1275, he refused to pay **homage** to Edward (a ceremony in which he would publicly show that Edward was superior to him and that he owed him support and loyalty). Edward, remembering his father's experiences with Montfort, could not let this disrespect pass.

## War and foreign policy

One way to prove he was a stronger king than his father would be to win back the lands in France lost by Henry. Edward remained the Duke of Aquitaine (in south-west France), a title he inherited from his father. This was a difficult position to hold as it made him answerable to the King of France. Edward could never accept that the King of France was superior, and someone to whom he owed homage. He also hoped to lead another Crusade that would unite the European countries in the fight to bring Christianity to the Holy Land. Uniting Europe would prove a great challenge.

## Work

1   Why was Edward's defeat of Simon de Montfort such an important victory?

2   Look at **Interpretation A**. How fair an assessment do you think this is of de Montfort's life?

3   Imagine you are an advisor to Edward I. For each of his problems in the spider diagram, write down the advice you would give him.

4   How might the experiences of Henry III influence how Edward dealt with Llywelyn ap Gruffudd?

### Extension

Although it happened before Edward's reign, the Second Barons' War' had a huge impact on the king that Edward became. Spend some time researching the war. What happened? Who was involved?

# How did Edward deal with the nobility?

Henry III's relationship with his barons could not have been worse. His agreement in 1258 to the Provisions of Oxford was a huge concession that meant that he could no longer make any decision without the support of the barons. This was a humiliating position for a king to be in. The Second Barons' War (1264–67) saw Henry imprisoned by one of his barons, Simon de Montfort. Edward needed to have a much better working relationship with the barons if he was to be a successful king. Who were the barons and why were they so powerful? How did they respond to their new king? Did Edward learn from his father's mistakes?

▶ **Examine** who the barons were and what their role was.
▶ **Describe** how Edward dealt with the barons.
▶ **Explain** why his methods proved effective.

## Who were the barons?

The original English barons were the Norman supporters of William the Conqueror who had played a role in his invasion of England in 1066. In order to establish his authority and reward their loyalty, William awarded areas of land to them. They paid rent on the land to the king and agreed to provide soldiers if they were needed. The king relied on the loyalty of the barons to be secure in his position. Edward I's grandfather, King John (reigned 1199–1216), lost their loyalty and was forced into signing Magna Carta. He even fought against the barons in the First Barons' War (1215–17) before being effectively forced from power by the time of his death. His young son,

Henry III, aged just nine when he became king, was never able to gain the upper hand over the barons. By Edward's reign, the king could no longer be sure of their loyalty. Many barons paid little in tax and their private armies could be a threat to the king.

**Fact**

'Nobility' is the term used to describe the ruling class of a country, just below royalty. Nobles have titles such as 'earl' and 'lord'. These individuals are known as 'nobles'.

## A new approach

Edward had a reputation for a short temper and terrified some members of the nobility who had had little respect for his father. When dealing with the barons he needed to establish two things. Firstly, that he was willing to work with them and include them in his government and, secondly, that he would not tolerate any disrespect and challenges to his authority. One of his first actions was to remove many of his father's ministers and officials. He appointed his close associate, Robert Burnell,

▼ **INTERPRETATION A** *An eighteenth-century image of Edward I and some of the barons*

80 **Chapter 1** Henry III's legacy

as **Chancellor**, a key position that made Burnell effectively Edward's Chief Minister. Edward made use of **Parliament** to listen to advice and to enact his ideas into law but they were *his* laws. He cleverly used Parliament as a way to involve the barons in the process without giving them too much power.

## Returning powers to the king

During Henry III's reign, power had moved away from the king and towards various nobles around the country who had control of much of his land. Edward set about getting this back. Many nobles had established significant power

▲ INTERPRETATION B *The Round Table, displayed in the Great Hall in Winchester; although it was painted at least 200 years later, the table itself is believed to have been Edward's; the king had a keen interest in the legend of King Arthur*

including the right to raise taxes and hold courts. In 1278, Parliament passed the Statute of Gloucester, which aimed to reclaim the lands and the powers for the king. To carry out the law, men known as **General Eyres** travelled the country on behalf of the king visiting and investigating landowning nobles. This process was known as ***Quo Warranto***, which means 'by what warrant?' Any baron who could not produce proof that the land he claimed was his or the power he held was legal, in the form of a royal licence or that he had owned it since 'time immemorial' (set as 1189, when King Richard I came to the throne), would have to return it to the king. A large number of barons lost their power and influence as a result of this action and it caused great anger but it established that all rights and power ultimately belonged to the king. He could give power but he could also take it away. The General Eyres followed the law closely so that the king could not be accused of seizing lands or being unfair to the barons.

### Key Words

| | |
|---|---|
| Chancellor | Parliament |
| General Eyre | *Quo Warranto* |

### Practice Question

Write an account of the ways in which Edward gained the upper hand over the barons.

**8 marks**

### Study Tip

Focus on how Edward's actions moved the balance of power away from the barons towards the king.

### Work

1 Who were the original English barons?

2 Why do you think Edward appointed such a close associate of his as Chancellor?

3 Create a poster to tell the barons about Edward's new rules about owning land. Make sure you include what they will need to produce in order to prove their rights and use the key terms in your work.

4 How effective do you think Edward's approach to dealing with the barons was? Explain your answer.

5 Look at **Interpretations A** and **B**.

   a What does **Interpretation A** suggest about Edward's relationship with his barons?

   b How far does **Interpretation B** suggest a different approach?

   c Based on what you know so far, which interpretation is the most accurate?

# 1.4A 1297: a difficult year for Edward

Edward's careful management of the country had led to a relatively peaceful period in the first 20 years of his reign. The death of his beloved wife, Eleanor, in 1290 affected him deeply, but it was seven years later that Edward faced the biggest challenges of his reign. 1297 saw one crisis after another both at home and abroad. It took all of Edward's political skill to survive them. What went wrong in 1297? Why did Scotland, Wales and France become such a big problem? And how did the barons react when Edward needed them?

**Objectives**

▶ **Describe** the events of 1297.

▶ **Explain** why these events challenged Edward.

▶ **Identify** links between the events and crises in 1297.

## The crisis of 1297: trouble abroad

Edward's early reign had seen peace with Scotland, increasing control of Wales and calm in his French **duchy** of Gascony. Study the map below to see how these three areas caused serious problems for the king in 1297.

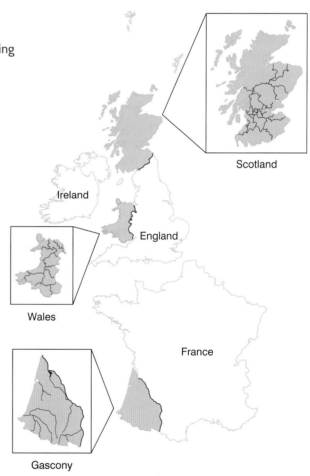

### Scotland

Until the 1280s there were few disagreements between England and Scotland. Although Edward saw himself as the **overlord** of the Scottish king, Alexander III, he was willing to accept that King Alexander should pay homage only for the lands he owned in England. The problem arose when the Scottish king died in 1286. His heir was his three-year-old granddaughter, Margaret, who sailed from Norway but died during the journey to Scotland. This left no obvious heir and caused a succession crisis known as the **Great Cause**. Edward agreed to help decide who had the best claim to the throne. He eventually backed John Balliol, who became king in 1292. Edward continued to involve himself in Scottish affairs, calling the new Scottish king to appear before the English Parliament and trying to establish himself as the overlord of Scotland.

King John Balliol grew increasingly unhappy with Edward's interference. The final straw was when Edward demanded that Scottish barons send men to help him fight the French. The Scottish barons attacked the English town of Carlisle in 1296. Edward's response was swift and brutal. He invaded Scotland, crushing his opponents at the Battle of Dunbar and stealing the Stone of Scone, used in Scottish coronation ceremonies. Balliol and the Scottish nobles were humiliated. It seemed Scotland had been crushed. However, in 1297, a new rebel leader, William Wallace, inflicted a humiliating defeat on the English at the Battle of Stirling Bridge. Full scale war in Scotland was now unavoidable.

## Wales

By the 1280s, Edward had nearly destroyed all opposition in Wales and had begun a huge castle building programme to create bases from which he could control the Welsh. Although many of the Welsh remained hostile, a level of order was established, but at a price. The castles had cost a fortune to build and it was now going to be difficult to pay for expensive wars in France and Scotland – and Edward still couldn't take his eyes off Wales because he was concerned that the Welsh would rebel against him at any time.

## Gascony

As Duke of Aquitaine, Edward had always taken a great interest in Gascony, a wealthy area in south-west France within the region of Aquitaine. As a child, it had been run for him, often brutally, by Simon de Montfort but once he was king, he took an active role in its governance. The problem, however, was how Gascony fitted into the rest of France. As a duchy it was technically under the rule of the French king, making Edward one of his **vassals** or underlords. Edward was even required to pay homage to the King of France, which he did in 1286. The situation remained uneasy, however, and when a group of French ships was captured by the English, who also attacked the French port of La Rochelle, the relationship between the two kings was in crisis. Seizing an opportunity to gain a victory over his rival, King Philip called Edward to do homage once again in 1294. Edward failed to appear and Philip declared that he had lost Gascony. By August 1297, Edward was ready for war and set sail for Flanders. Unfortunately for him, his allies in Flanders had already been defeated and he faced a challenge that was impossible to overcome.

▼ **SOURCE A**  *An illustration from a medieval manuscript showing Edward I paying homage to Philip IV of France in 1286*

▼ **SOURCE B**  *An image from a medieval manuscript showing Edward (centre), King Alexander III of Scotland and Llywelyn ap Gruffudd, Prince of Wales; the three men never actually came together all at once*

## Work

1  In what ways was Wales still a problem for Edward by 1297?

2  Explain how war with France came about.

3  Describe what you can see in **Source A** and **Source B**. What does **Source B** suggest about the relationship between the English, Welsh and Scottish rulers? Explain how and why these illustrations could not represent the situation in 1297.

# 1297: a difficult year for Edward

## How did trouble abroad lead to trouble in England?

The challenge of wars in Scotland and France, as well as keeping his hold on Wales, was going to be expensive for Edward. He needed money to pay for his wars and men to fight them. The **feudal system** that had existed in England since the Norman Conquest in 1066 required barons to pay taxes and supply soldiers when they were needed. For the first 20 years of Edward's reign he had done much to repair the damage done by his father and grandfather, and the barons had, for the most part, shown the loyalty that was required of them. In 1297, however, he asked for more than he ever had before.

## Taxes and the Church

In order to fund his wars in Scotland and France and keep the peace in Wales, Edward collected over £200,000 (equivalent to over £105 million today) in taxes in just three years. In addition, he ordered that farmers should give more of their crops to feed the army; he seized wool and animal hides for clothing and increased the tax on wool. In 1294, Edward had told the Church that it must pay half of what it earned in taxes. The Pope sent a message to the English Church saying that it should not pay but the Church eventually backed down in 1296 and Edward received some money. The majority of his funds still needed to come from elsewhere, however.

### Key Biography

**Roger Bigod (c1245– c1306)**

- He was the Earl of Norfolk from 1270.
- As a baron he held huge power on his own lands but was also a Member of Parliament.
- He served as Marshal of England, one of the king's senior military figures.
- He served the king in Wales in the 1280s.
- In 1302, Bigod, who had no children, agreed to make King Edward his heir in exchange for an annual sum of money.

▼ **INTERPRETATION C** *An illustration from* A Chronicle of England BC 55 to AD 1485 *by James E. Doyle (1864) showing Edward threatening Roger Bigod and the Earl of Hereford*

▲ **D** *Roger Bigod's coat of arms*

# A constitutional crisis

The standoff with the Church was difficult but nothing compared to what was to come in 1297. With wars in Scotland and France and a peace to maintain in Wales, Edward went to his barons to ask for the support they owed him. As he prepared to sail to Flanders to support his allies, the Flemish, in their fight against the French, he needed men to sail to Gascony. Edward went to Parliament in February to ask for soldiers and was told by a leading baron, Roger Bigod, that there would be no soldiers. Bigod, who was **Marshal of England**, told the king that the feudal system required barons to provide soldiers to fight *with* the king abroad. If Edward was going to Flanders, he could not ask Bigod to send men to Gascony. Some accounts suggest that the king threatened Bigod, saying, 'By God, Earl, you shall either go or hang,' and that Bigod replied, 'By the same oath, O king, I will neither go nor hang.' It was not clear who was in the right but it was Bigod and the barons, with control of their armies, who held the power.

Aware of their strong position, Bigod and another baron, the Earl of Hereford, drew up a list of demands for the king. These **Remonstrances** called for the end of high taxes. When the king left for France in August, with far fewer men than he wanted, Bigod went to the **Exchequer** in London and stopped the collection of any more taxes. The country was on the verge of another civil war.

# Crisis averted, by a new crisis

Just as things seemed to have slipped beyond Edward's control, the Battle of Stirling Bridge took place on 11 September 1297. With William Wallace's heavy defeat of the English, the barons and the king united to face the Scottish threat, although this only happened after Edward promised to follow the rules of Magna Carta. Despite problems elsewhere, the standoff between Edward and Roger Bigod was perhaps the biggest threat to the king's rule in the whole of his reign. The crisis in France was not ultimately ended until the marriage of Edward to the French king Philip IV's sister, Margaret, in 1299.

## Work

1. According to the feudal system what two things were barons required to give to the king?
2. Explain why Edward needed so much extra money.
3. Look at **Interpretation C**. How convincing do you find this image as an account of Edward and Roger Bigod's argument?
4. Create a mind-map on a piece of A3 paper that shows the problems Edward faced in 1297 and how they were connected to each other.
5. How successfully do you think Edward dealt with the crisis year of 1297?

## Key Words

feudal system
Marshal of England
remonstrance    Exchequer

## Practice Question

Write an account of the events of 1297.    **8 marks**

## Study Tip

You should try to show how the different events and problems of 1297 are linked together and have a direct impact on each other.

## Extension

Historians need to be able to compare the relative importance of different events. Challenge yourself by answering the following question: 'Which of the crises of 1297 was the biggest danger to Edward's rule?'

## Extension

1297 was a year of crisis for Edward. Challenge yourself by considering: 'How far were the problems of 1297 of Edward's own making?' Be sure to explain your answer fully.

# The feudal system

Medieval society was very structured. People knew their place and what their role was. Everything was based on a system known as feudalism. You have already come across this in the relationship between the king and his barons, but the system went right across society and it is impossible to understand the medieval world without understanding the feudal system. So how did the system work? Where did each group in medieval society fit in the system? And why was the system so important in medieval life?

## Objectives

▶ **State** the features of the feudal system.

▶ **Explain** how the system worked and the role everyone played.

▶ **Evaluate** the effectiveness of the system and whether it could lead to problems.

## How did medieval society work?

When William of Normandy conquered England in 1066 he brought many customs and traditions with him. One of these was a structure for society. England had had kings for many years and the idea of some people having more power and influence than others was nothing new, but what William brought was a rigid structure. The Norman feudal system was based on give and take and was very similar to what had already existed in England before the Norman Conquest. The king gave land and titles to his barons and in return they gave him their loyalty and military service. They were given the title of earl, which was passed from father to son. As vassals to the king, they had to pay homage to him. The barons gave protection, shelter, food and sometimes land to their knights and in return the knights gave their loyalty and military service. They were vassals to the barons. The knights gave peasants food, protection and shelter and in return peasants worked in the fields and gave their military service. There were two types of peasants. Most were **villeins**. Villeins could not leave the land or even marry without the permission of their lord. A few peasants were **freemen** who paid rent to the lord but owed him less in the way of loyalty. Everyone knew their position in the **social hierarchy**, what was expected of them and what they needed to do for the people above and below them in the system.

THE CEREMONY OF FEUDAL HOMAGE, 12TH CENTURY.

▲ **INTERPRETATION A** *An illustration from* The Historical Scrap Book *(1880) showing a knight paying homage to his baron*

### Fact

The Church owned immense areas of land in medieval England and bishops held the same position as barons with the same level of control over their lands. This made the Church very powerful.

## The feudal pyramid

The feudal system worked liked a pyramid with one man at the top and the largest group at the bottom. Each owed loyalty to those above them and offered protection and land to those below. The diagram on the next page will help to explain the structure.

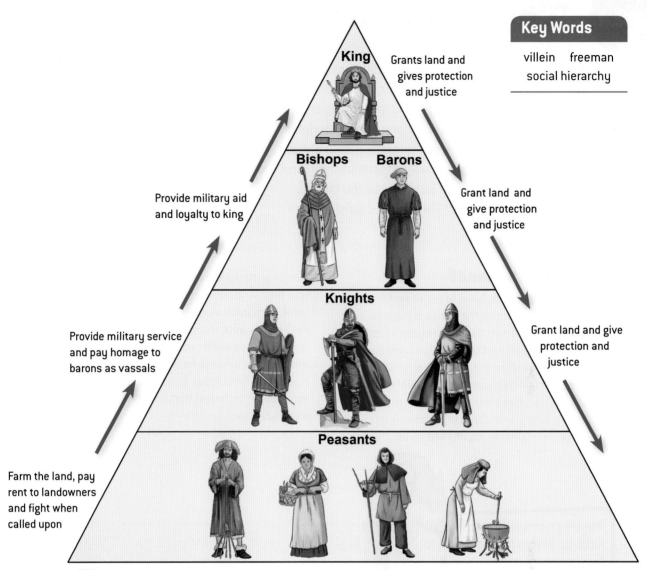

King — Grants land and gives protection and justice

Bishops    Barons

Provide military aid and loyalty to king

Grant land and give protection and justice

Knights

Provide military service and pay homage to barons as vassals

Grant land and give protection and justice

Peasants

Farm the land, pay rent to landowners and fight when called upon

▲ **B** *The structure of the feudal system*

## Work

1 Who was at the top of the feudal system and who was at the bottom?

2 Explain the relationship between the knights and the peasants.

3 Working in a group, come up with your own way of explaining the feudal system. This could take the form of a performance, a song, a rap or a model.

4 Look at **Interpretation A**. What evidence of the feudal system is present in this picture?

5 Are there any potential problems with the feudal system? Explain your answer.

## Extension

Although bishops were part of the feudal system and owed loyalty to the king, they also owed loyalty to the head of the Church: the Pope. How might this split loyalty cause problems? Look back at the previous chapter for a specific example to help you.

# The importance of land

Edward ruled a kingdom based on the feudal system. This affected people's social position and their relationship with each other. But an even more important effect was on the land. In medieval England, land was completely interlinked with the feudal structure and was therefore widely divided up. Edward was very keen to remind people that their land ultimately belonged to the king. So why was the land so important in the feudal system? How did Edward change the system?

## Who owned the land?

The feudal system was the basis of medieval society. Look back at the diagram on the previous page to remind yourself about how the feudal system worked. According to this system, other than that owned by the Church, all land was ultimately the king's. Land was then divided through a process called **subinfeudation**. This meant that land was transferred down the feudal hierarchy. The king granted land to his barons in exchange for their support, loyalty and taxes. The barons were the **tenants-in-chief**. The barons then split their land between knights and demanded the same from them as they themselves gave to the king. The knights were the **mesne lords**. They divided their land among peasants who would farm it. The peasants would be responsible for their land. These agreements would pass from father to son through inheritance. Subinfeudation meant that, ultimately, all of the land was traced back to the king.

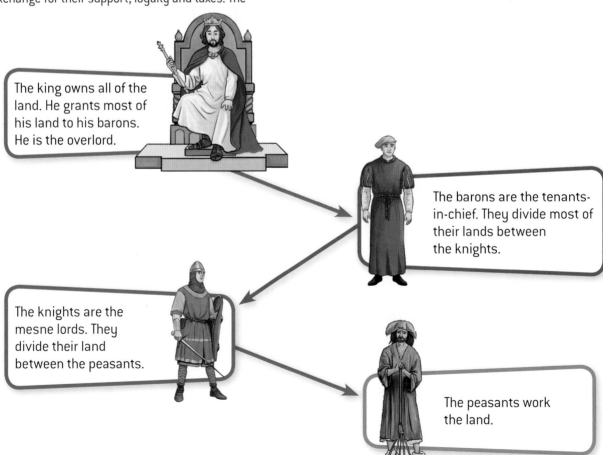

The king owns all of the land. He grants most of his land to his barons. He is the overlord.

The barons are the tenants-in-chief. They divide most of their lands between the knights.

The knights are the mesne lords. They divide their land between the peasants.

The peasants work the land.

## Lost in translation?

In medieval times, a lot of official business and documents were conducted in Latin or Norman French. Here are some of the key words and phrases (refer back to this table whenever you come across a new phrase).

| Key word or phrase | Translation and meaning |
| --- | --- |
| *De donis conditionalibus* | 'The donor's will shall be observed' – a person's wishes must be observed when they die |
| Frankalmoign | 'Free mercy/pity'– the act of giving land to the Church |
| General Eyres | The men who carried out *Quo Warranto* |
| *Quo Warranto* | 'By what warrant' (do you have this power/ own this land?) |
| Mesne | Middle/intermediate |
| Mortmain | Ownership that never ends because the owner is an organisation rather than a person, e.g. the Church |
| *Quia Emptores* | 'Because the buyers'– a law that changed the way land could be bought and sold |
| Subinfeudation | Splitting **estates** into smaller estates within the feudal system. The previous holder becomes the mesne lord of the new tenant |
| Substitution | Transferring land from one person to another without becoming their feudal lord |

▼ **INTERPRETATION A** *An illustration from an early fifteenth-century French manuscript showing peasants working the land with their lord's castle in the background*

### Key Words

subinfeudation   tenant-in-chief
mesne lord   estate   Hundred Rolls
First Statute of Westminster

## Edward shows who's in charge

When Edward became king, he quickly wanted to re-establish the idea that all land ultimately belonged to him. The tenants-in-chief and mesne lords had become very powerful during his father's and grandfather's reigns and the king wanted to remind them who the land really belonged to. He sent investigators, known as General Eyres, to discover how the barons had gained their land – *Quo Warranto* ('By what warrant...?'): was it through royal licence or unofficial means? If they could not produce a licence, the land automatically returned to the king. This investigation, along with others, produced a document known as the **Hundred Rolls** and gave Edward a detailed insight into who occupied what land.

The investigation had shown that there were big problems within the feudal system. For example, some land was being bought and sold or split further into even smaller estates. Each time this happened, subinfeudation meant that new mesne lords were created. Edward had made the point that all authority and land came from the king and this was established in law in the **First Statute of Westminster** (1275). It was the first in a series of laws by which Edward firmly established that all land ultimately fell under the king's control. The only way for a lord to keep land was to provide proof of ownership in the form of a royal licence or demonstrate that he had owned it since 'time immemorial' (1189 – the coronation of Richard I).

### Work

1 Who was the overlord?

2 Explain the term 'mesne lord'.

3 Working with a partner, create your own version of the diagram to explain how subinfeudation worked.

4 What did **Quo Warranto** show Edward?

5 What was the purpose of the First Statute of Westminster?

6 Look at **Interpretation A**. How far does this accurately show the feudal system?

## The Years of the Statutes (1274–90)

In the years that followed the Hundred Rolls and the First Statute of Westminster, Edward and his Parliament (made up of his barons and close advisors) passed a number of important laws that completely changed the law relating to land ownership. He broke with many of the traditions of the feudal system. The First Statute of Westminster re-established that all power and land came from the king, but Edward's investigation showed that the law was a mess. So he decided to pass more statutes to tighten up the laws about land ownership and inheritance. He also looked at the control the Church had over large areas of land.

## The issue of inheritance

The Hundred Rolls showed that land was passing between mesne lords and even between peasants through sale or as a wedding gift. Some people also gave land to the Church. These decisions often went against the heir's wishes, who had no say in the matter whatsoever. Disputes about the true ownership of land often ended up in court. The Second Statute of Westminster (1285) sought to deal with this problem. The statute included a section called *De donis*

*conditionalibus*. This clause made it clear that the wishes of a landowner must be followed. This could include restricting the heir's right to sell the land by saying that they must pass it on to their heir in full. Estates would therefore not be broken up and the feudal system would remain intact.

## The end of subinfeudation

The system of subinfeudation meant that when land was transferred between one person and another, the original holder of the land became the feudal lord of the new holder. As more land was transferred this created more mesne lords. In 1290, Parliament passed the Third Statute of Westminster, known as *Quia Emptores*, which banned subinfeudation. Instead, when land was sold, the previous tenant would have no further claim to it. They would not be a mesne lord to the new tenant. When land was bought under this system of **substitution** (they were 'substituting' themselves for the previous tenant), buying and selling land became entirely a business and financial transaction. New tenants did, however, have to accept and remain loyal to the feudal lord who had originally granted the land.

Although the statute undermined the feudal system at the bottom, it actually strengthened the king's power at the top. He reserved the right to stop a transfer of land and the barons still needed a licence from the king to grant lands to their vassals.

**Before**

▲ *Subinfeudation – land is divided by lords as part of the feudal system; as more land was divided more and more mesne lords were created, making the feudal system ever more complex*

**After**

▲ *Substitution – land is transferred from one person to another without the previous owner becoming a mesne lord*

| Date | Statute |
|------|---------|
| 1275 | First Statute of Westminster |
| 1279 | First Statute of Mortmain |
| 1285 | Second Statute of Westminster (*De donis conditionalibus*) |
| 1290 | Third Statute of Westminster (*Quia Emptores*) |
| 1290 | Second Statute of Mortmain |

## The great landowner: the Church

The Church owned a huge amount of land across England in the thirteenth century that was the Church's alone. The Church was not answerable to any feudal lord and even the king had limited power in its lands. Many people chose to give lands to the Church when they died but some mesne lords noticed that there was a loophole in the feudal system. They realised that if they transferred their lands to the Church as a gift (known as **frankalmoign**) and then leased it back from them, they could save money by avoiding paying rent to their lord or having to provide military service. Edward was determined to put a stop to this and had the full support of his barons. The Statutes of Mortmain in 1279 and 1290 closed this loophole and the *Quia Emptores* strengthened the law further.

### Key Words

substitution    frankalmoign

### Work

1. What did *De donis conditionalibus* ensure?
2. What is the difference between subinfeudation and substitution?
3. Why was frankalmoign seen as a problem?
4. Create an illustrated timeline to show the laws passed during this period.
5. **Source B** shows Parliament. Why do you think Parliament was willing to pass these laws? Look back at Chapter 1 to remind yourself of the role of Parliament in the thirteenth century.

### Practice Question

Write an account of the ways in which Edward's changes to land law affected the feudal system.

**8 marks**

### Study Tip

Remember to address the question from both sides: Edward's changes to how land could be transferred undermined the system but his changes also strengthened the power of the king at the top.

# What were the Hundred Rolls?

The new laws that Edward and his Parliament introduced between 1274 and 1290 changed the way land ownership and feudalism worked. As you have learned, they were all based on the *Quo Warranto* investigations and the Hundred Rolls. For historians, the Hundred Rolls are a very important document. What exactly were the Hundred Rolls? What did Edward hope to discover and what did he actually find out? And what can historians learn from the Hundred Rolls about Edward and medieval England?

## Objectives

▶ **State** the reason for the Hundred Rolls investigations.

▶ **Analyse** the results to learn about medieval England.

▶ **Investigate** the findings of the Hundred Rolls.

## Edward's investigations

King Edward set out to discover exactly who lived in England and, more importantly, what land they owned and what rights they held over it. The investigation was a **census** and is sometimes seen by historians as a second **Domesday Book**, the famous census carried out by William the Conqueror after his invasion of England. It took place between 1274 and 1275 and again between 1279 and 1280. Investigators went all over the country to find out exactly what obligations each person owed to their lord and how each lord was operating their estate. The aim was to find out whether barons and mesne lords had a royal licence to run their estate and collect rent from their tenants or whether they had gained it through some other means. The investigation was partly aimed at re-establishing the king as the ultimate owner of all land but it also gave the government a much clearer record of the situation. The results were collected in what became known as the Hundred Rolls (a 'hundred' being the small area of a county by which the results were organised).

▼ **SOURCE A** *Edward's official commissioning writ. He explains his reasons for the investigation:*

> Because of various encroachments made on us and others, rich and poor, within our kingdom, in **demesne**, fees, feudal rights, liberties and other things of various kinds, we and other men are suffering, and will suffer, loss. In order that, in future, that which is and ought to be ours and that which is and ought to be theirs may be clear, we commission [the following inquiry].

▼ **SOURCE B** *A copy of the Hundred Rolls entry for Somerton, a village in Oxfordshire; it outlines how the land was split by the mesne lord, Robert de Grey, among a number of peasants and how much rent they paid*

## What did the Hundred Rolls show?

The Hundred Rolls gave Edward a very detailed picture of England, going far beyond anything collected before. Unlike the Domesday Book, the Hundred Rolls go into specific detail about individual people and their property. The survey showed Edward that the feudal system was beginning to break down as lands were transferred from one person to another or to the Church. As land had been unofficially changing hands for many years, land disputes were constant. This also caused confusion about who owed what to feudal lords in terms of rent and military service. The information provided by the Hundred Rolls prompted Edward to bring in the statutes that changed land law in England.

The Hundred Rolls did not just show who owned land at the point of the survey but also how they had come to hold it. The Rolls also gave a message to the nobility: Edward was in charge, and all major decisions relating to land were to be decided by him! Not all of the Rolls survived but those that did are useful to historians both in understanding Edward's decisions and also what life was like in the 1200s.

▼ **SOURCE C**  *An extract from the Hundred Rolls:*

> The jury say that the king holds the **manor** of Middleton with Marden in his own hand. Then they say that Minster and Salmoneston used to be in the king's hands in ancient time and now the abbot and convent of St Augustine Canterbury holds these, they do not know from what time nor by what warrant. Then they say that Monkton at some time used to be in the hand of the ancient kings and the prior and convent of Christchurch Canterbury now hold it, they do not know from what time nor by what warrant.

▼ **SOURCE D**  *Adapted from the Hundred Rolls:*

> Then they say that John Monsel held a part of Bilsington and after his death the lord king received it and gave it to the lord Peter de Pynibus by his charter and the same Peter sold it to John Andrew of Winchelsea and the same John exchanged it with Sir John of Sandwich who now holds it and it is worth 100s. each year.

## Extension

Very few of the Hundred Rolls have survived but most of those that have are now available online. The sources above are taken from Kent. Investigate further by visiting *kentarchaeology. ac:* click on 'Hundred Rolls' and select the PDF file of the Kent Hundred Rolls Project. Look for examples of land changing hands but also investigate how mesne lords held courts and gave out punishments. The Rolls looked into whether they actually had any official right to do this.

## Key Words

census    Domesday Book
demesne    manor

## Fact

Although The Domesday Book is more famous, the Hundred Rolls was a much larger investigation – the biggest there had ever been into who owned what in England.

## Work

1   Where does the name 'the Hundred Rolls' come from?

2   a   What was the Domesday Book?
    b   Why do historians see the Hundred Rolls as more useful?

3   According to **Source A**, why did Edward commission the survey? Refer to the source in your answer.

4   Look at **Source C**.
    a   Who holds Minster and Salmoneston?
    b   Who had previously held these places?
    c   Who holds most of the land described in this source?
    d   Do they have any legal claim to it?

5   Look at **Source D**.
    a   How did Peter de Pynibus acquire the land?
    b   How did it pass to John Andrew of Winchelsea?
    c   What does this source suggest about land in the thirteenth century?

# Why was Robert Burnell an important figure in Edward's government?

**2.4**

One of the key figures in Edward I's government was Robert Burnell. He was at Edward's side through the majority of his reign and was responsible for many key policies. As Chancellor he not only held one of the most important positions in England, but he arguably increased its importance during his time in post. Who was Robert Burnell and how did he become so powerful? What role did Burnell and Edward play in the development of Parliament?

## Who was Robert Burnell (c 1239–92)?

Burnell was a low-ranking official in the court of Henry III but quickly developed a close relationship with Prince Edward. When Edward went on a Crusade he left Burnell in charge of his affairs in England. After King Henry died, Burnell served as **regent** until Edward returned. This meant he ran the country on Edward's behalf, which gave him both experience of governing and also of managing the barons. When Edward became king, he soon appointed Burnell as his Chancellor, in 1274. This effectively made him Edward's Chief Minister. With important plans to put into practice, Edward needed someone he could trust in such a senior position to carry out his policies. Burnell was given responsibility for *Quo Warranto* and played a key role in the statutes that followed.

Burnell was also the Bishop of Bath and Wells from 1275. It was not unusual for the king's close advisors to be bishops as well as holding government positions as it gave the king influence within the Church. With this in mind, Edward tried twice to appoint Burnell to the most senior position of Archbishop of Canterbury but was blocked by the Pope who did not want a close friend of the king's in such a powerful role.

## The king's right-hand man?

Until Burnell's death in 1292 he was Edward's key advisor. He worked to ensure the co-operation of Parliament and other senior figures and was known to have a calmer and more even-tempered approach to government than the king. He firmly established the power of the Chancellor (a position that still exists in today's government as the Lord Chancellor). For the first time the **Chancery** was permanently based in London and no longer travelled with the king. From this position of power, Burnell could exert great influence and often dealt with problems before they even reached Edward.

▼ **INTERPRETATION A** *Adapted from* Britain, Ireland and the Crusades c1000–1300 *by the historian Kathryn Hurlock (Palgrave Macmillan, 2012):*

> By the time Edward returned to England [from the Crusade] in August 1274, Burnell had exerted his own personality and influence to become the dominant figure in royal government and he was ready to take on the chancellorship. In his master's absence he emerged from the shadows of the royal household to assume that role at the centre of national affairs which he was to play for the next two decades.

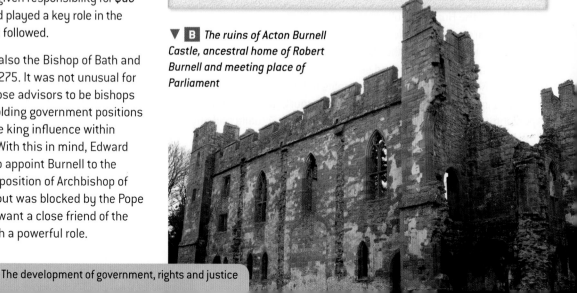

▼ **B** *The ruins of Acton Burnell Castle, ancestral home of Robert Burnell and meeting place of Parliament*

## Parliament at Burnell's house

Parliament before Edward's reign was a loose term for the collection of advisors, mainly barons, that surrounded the king and took part in discussions. It met wherever the king was and therefore moved around the country. On one occasion it met at Acton Burnell Castle in Shropshire, the home of Robert Burnell. The meeting, thought to have taken place in 1283, was significant because it marked the first time that commoners, non-nobles such as wealthy urban merchants, had attended a session of Parliament. It had always been restricted to the barons before this. However, the Parliament that met this time consisted of some of the richer citizens of the big towns as well as a number of knights.

As with many of Edward's decisions, his reason for holding the Parliament was financial: he needed money to fight in Wales. Shropshire was important strategically as it bordered Wales and he wanted ordinary people to support him. Edward further developed this idea of representation after Burnell's death. In 1295, he called what became known as the **Model Parliament**.

### Key Words

regent    Chancery    Model Parliament

### Work

1. Why do you think Edward wanted Burnell to be Archbishop of Canterbury?
2. Explain why the Parliament at Acton Burnell Castle was important.
3. What was the Model Parliament?
4. How important was Robert Burnell?

### The Model Parliament of 1295

Edward summoned Parliament on 13 November 1295, saying that 'what touches all, should be approved of all'. The Parliament included not just barons and bishops but also knights and wealthy commoners from every English county. Edward's aim was not democracy; he was once again short of money! It was now established that taxes could not be raised without Parliament's consent. It was the most representative Parliament that there had ever been and served as a model for future Parliaments.

▲ **SOURCE C** *A contemporary drawing showing the Model Parliament*

### Extension

Challenge yourself by answering this question: 'Edward's changes to the law and Parliament show that he believed in the rights of ordinary people.' How far do you agree with this statement? Use the whole of this chapter to help you answer.

### Practice Question

How convincing is **Interpretation A** as an account of Robert Burnell's rise to power?

Explain your answer using **Interpretation A** and your contextual knowledge.

**8 marks**

### Study Tip

Remember, you are free to agree or disagree with the interpretation. The important thing is that you explain why you are convinced by it or not.

# The development of towns under Edward I

The reign of Edward I saw increasing numbers of people leave the countryside for the growing towns of England. Towns offered a completely different way of life and Edward was keen for them to develop. What was life like in a medieval town? Why was Edward so keen for towns to develop?

## Objectives

▶ **Describe** life in a medieval town.

▶ **Compare** town and country life.

▶ **Explain** how and why towns developed.

## A country of villages

At the time of Edward's reign, around 90 per cent of the population lived in villages and farmed the land. Life was tough and everything depended on the success of the harvest. Unlike today, food was not readily available all year round and peasants had to work hard to make sure they grew enough food to survive winter. A bad harvest could mean starvation. Yet village life was well organised and structured. Officials, like the **bailiff** and the **reeve**, were responsible for organising the agricultural work. A manor court, run by the mesne lord, dealt with crime by imposing fines. The success of the village relied on everyone playing their part.

## The boom in urban living

Although towns were not new, under Edward I they grew in number. Towns could only be created if the king granted permission with a **royal charter**. Edward created many towns because it was in his interest to do so. Firstly, towns were centres of trade and business, and by adding a tax to the products bought and sold, the king could make money. Secondly, towns could be used as a base for securing an area or launching an attack on another area (such as Wales or Scotland).

As towns grew people were drawn to them to sell their **surplus** crops or do business. For freemen, they

▼ **INTERPRETATION A** *An illustration for a 1997 children's history textbook by John D. Clare*

also offered an opportunity to make a living away from the feudal lord. As feudalism broke down with Edward's reforms, more and more peasants moved to towns permanently.

## How did medieval towns work?

A successful town needed merchants to sell goods and a royal charter gave towns the right to hold a market. The charter also meant that taxes went directly to the king. The more a town grew, the more taxes could be collected. The charter gave towns other rights too. They could build walls with gates that protected the residents. This was particularly important in the towns that Edward built in Wales. These towns, known as **bastides**, were built as part of his castle building plan. In Welsh bastide towns, the Welsh were not allowed into the towns after dark: as a conquered people they were still not trusted by the English. Strangers entering town would be asked about their business and people considered untrustworthy could be banned.

Specialist craftsmen, like shoemakers or stonemasons, formed organisations called **guilds** to protect the quality of their products. Guilds also ensured that apprentices were well trained in order to preserve their trades' reputations. Mayors and officials were chosen from within their guilds. Town officials would ensure that market business was being conducted fairly and that traders were not cheating.

Charters gave towns a level of independence from the feudal system; they could have their own laws and enforce them using their own court and punishments. The feudal lords still had influence but power was in the hands of the merchants.

## Life in a thirteenth-century town

Medieval towns may not have been clean by modern standards, but it would be unfair to say that all towns at this time were absolutely filthy. It is true that towns *could* be dirty places to live but some had sewage systems, for example, and local officials prided themselves on the supply of water to the town. Some towns had public toilets too, and paid specialist cleaners, called 'gongfarmers', to clear them out. Sometimes rubbish was thrown in the streets, and rats, lice and fleas would have been common in the rushes strewn over the clay floors of houses.

### Key Words

bailiff    reeve    royal charter
surplus    bastide    guild

### Extension

A key part of medieval towns was the development of guilds. Challenge yourself by researching guilds in a nearby town or city. You could use the Internet or visit the local library. Does the town have a guildhall? This might be a good place to start!

### Practice Question

How convincing is **Interpretation B** about life in a medieval town?

Explain your answer using **Interpretation B** and your contextual knowledge. **8 marks**

### Study Tip

Remember that parts of the interpretation may be accurate and parts may be inaccurate. You should aim to include both in your answer.

▼ **INTERPRETATION B** *Adopted from Q-Files.com, an online children's encyclopaedia:*

The marketplace was alive with noises and smells on market day. Most townspeople kept pigs as they were cheap and a good source of food. But they were often let out into the streets to forage. The streets of a medieval town were dirty and smelly. Open drain channels ran along the sides or down the middle. People often threw dirty water out of their windows. The streets were also lively places – particularly on market days. Jugglers, jesters and even dancing bears entertained the crowds.

### Work

1   Describe three features of village life.

2   Explain the term 'guild'.

3   Create a spider diagram about medieval towns. Include what happened in them, who lived there and who was in charge.

4   Look at **Interpretation A**.
    a   Describe five accurate features of life in a medieval town that are shown in this picture.
    b   How far do you think this image is an accurate representation of medieval life?

5   Explain how and why towns developed during the reign of Edward I.

# Why was wool so important in medieval England?

One of the most important factors in the English medieval economy was wool. It played a vital role in England's growing wealth. Through the medieval period, wool had gone from simply being something that farmers wore, to England's biggest **export**. Edward worked hard to establish an important trade within England and across Europe. He also recognised that wool provided a great opportunity to raise money through taxation! How did the wool trade work and how did it develop under Edward?

## Objectives

▶ **Explore** the development of the wool trade.

▶ **Consider** why Edward encouraged its development.

▶ **Explain** how Edward encouraged the development of the wool trade in England.

## The wine of England?

Before the Norman Conquest of 1066, people produced wool for their own use and for small amounts of trade within or between villages. As the number of towns with markets grew, wool increasingly became a **commodity**, something to be bought and sold. The best wool was produced in Wales, South West England and Lincolnshire. This was sold across the country and increasingly by the twelfth and thirteenth centuries to Europe, particularly to the growing centres of clothmaking like Bruges and Ghent. Just as France was known for its wine, England became known for having the highest quality wool in Europe.

▼ **SOURCE A** *A man shearing a sheep from a twelfth-century manuscript*

Wool was very profitable and more and more English peasants and lords began to raise sheep. The number of sheep someone owned was a key indicator of their wealth. Wool merchants were common in English markets, buying wool and then taking it to the ports to send it to the Continent. Barons and mesne lords became increasingly involved in the trade themselves, but unlike the peasants, they could make deals directly with the clothmakers and consequently made more money by cutting out the merchants.

## Medieval agriculture

The success of the wool trade was built on the strictly organised system of medieval agriculture and wool was just one of the products that was produced. Although an increasing number of towns were established during Edward's reign, most people still lived in the countryside and worked on the land. Agriculture was based on the feudal system with peasants working a strip of land as tenants for their lord. The strip would usually include some good and some bad quality land. Country life was organised around the farming year. Crops were grown in spring and summer, and a bad summer meant a bad harvest. Autumn and winter were spent on preparation. If a harvest was bad, taxes still had to be paid and the family fed so it was vital that food was stored in years of surplus. It was a tough life with back-breaking manual labour but a vital part of the success of Edward's England.

## King Edward sees an opportunity

Edward constantly needed money to pay for his wars in Wales, Scotland and France. The easiest way to raise funds was through taxation but he knew he could only raise taxes so much before he faced serious opposition. The booming wool business gave him the opportunity to generate new income. In 1275, Edward introduced a wool **duty**, so when wool was sold, money had to be paid to the king. It was now in Edward's interest to ensure the wool industry grew and that transactions took place. He particularly wanted to encourage trade with foreign merchants, which brought in significant sums: in 1286–87, exports from Southampton raised duties of £696 (around £350,000 today).

▼ **SOURCE B** *A thirteenth-century image showing Belgian merchants visiting England to buy wool*

## Dealing with debtors

In order to make money out of duties, Edward needed to encourage trade to take place. One concern was the lack of payment of debts by merchants who bought the wool from the producer and sold it to the cloth makers. There was little protection for merchants who were owed money and Edward was concerned that foreign merchants were avoiding England because of this.

In 1283, the **Statute of Acton Burnell** (passed when Parliament met at Acton Burnell Castle) was introduced. It gave the mayors of London, Bristol and York the right to force debts to be repaid and to imprison debtors who were unable to pay what they owed. The statute was not successful in dealing with the problem. Only three city mayors were given the power and their right to collect the money was limited. They could force the sale of goods to collect debts but could not seize land or property that the debtor owned.

In 1285, the **Statute of Merchants** was introduced to try to tighten these loopholes. Mayors in other cities were given the powers and the right to imprison straight away. Importantly, they could also hand control of debtors' land to the person they owed money to.

### Work

1   Why do you think wool was such an important part of the English economy?

2   Explain what is happening in **Source B**. Use the source and your own knowledge.

3   How did King Edward make money from the wool trade?

4   a   What did the Statute of Acton Burnell hope to achieve?

   b   Why was it unsuccessful?

   c   What was different about the 1285 Statute of Merchants?

### Practice Question

Explain what was important about the wool trade during the reign of Edward I.

**8 marks**

[Taken from AQA 2016 Paper 2 specimen material]

### Study Tip

Consider how Edward made money from the wool trade in your answer.

# Historic Environment: Fortified manor houses

Most feudal lords had a manor house. This was not only his home but also where he oversaw his land and organised the peasants living on it. The size and grandeur of the manor house depended on the power of its lord. The rise of merchants under Edward I led to a huge change, however. Men who were not lords of the manor began to have the power and funds to build themselves large country houses that showed their new-found wealth and status. How did merchants become so wealthy? And what were the key features of a manor house?

## Objectives

▶ **Describe** the features of medieval fortified manor house.

▶ **Explain** how they demonstrate the prosperity (wealth) of the owner.

▶ **Explore** how a specific house, Stokesay Castle, shows the wealth brought to England by trade.

## The Medieval manor house

The central feature and focus of life in a medieval manor house was the Great Hall, based on the halls that had existed before the Norman Conquest. The lord and his family would eat and entertain guests in the Great Hall and hold meetings with people from their estates. It would have a large open fire. The servants would often sleep here while separate rooms were provided for the lord and his guests. In the thirteenth century **fortified** manor houses were built. The Great Hall remained the centre but more rooms were added, including the **solar**, a private living area for the lord and his family, and a separate kitchen.

Fortified manor houses, built of brick or stone, were designed with security in mind. They had as few windows as possible and may have had a **moat** and a **drawbridge**, which could be pulled up if the house was attacked. Although nowhere near as strong as a castle, a fortified manor house did offer some protection at a time when England was an unstable and unpredictable place. They were also homes and, unlike in castles, comfort was just as important as defence.

## The rise of the wealthy merchants

During the reign of Edward I, wool became England's most important product. Edward encouraged the industry's growth and English merchants made large amounts of money by selling wool in Europe, particularly in the Netherlands, and to visiting foreign merchants. Welsh wool in particular was sought after and English merchants living near the Welsh border were able to make their fortune. These rich men looked to establish their new-found status and a number of them bought land and built large houses. One such merchant was Laurence of Ludlow.

## Stokesay Castle: the home of a merchant

Laurence of Ludlow had made his fortune in wool from the Welsh Marches (the area of England that borders Wales). He had sold across Europe and had offices in London and Shrewsbury. By 1280, he was the richest wool merchant in England. In 1281, he bought land close to his main business interests near the Welsh border

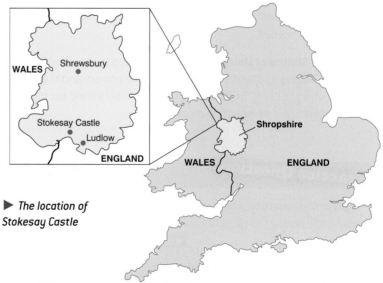

▶ *The location of Stokesay Castle*

and began building a home for himself. Work began in around 1285 and Laurence moved in a few years later. The building was designed to show his wealth and be a comfortable place to live. It also gave him the opportunity for more income as it included a large amount of agricultural land that could be rented out. In 1291, Laurence requested permission from the king to fortify the house and added the South Tower, a much more castle-like structure than the rest of the house. The house did not become known as Stokesay Castle until around the middle of the 1500s.

▼ **A** *Stokesay Castle as it looks today; although there have been changes since the thirteenth century, including the building of a gatehouse, the main structure remains the same*

▼ **B** *Features of Stokesay Castle*

## Key Words

fortified    solar    moat    drawbridge

## Work

1   What was the purpose of the Great Hall?
2   a   Explain the term 'fortified manor house'.
    b   What were its features?
3   Some historians suggest that Laurence of Ludlow was more concerned with comfort than security when he built Stokesay Castle. Is there any evidence to support this? Explain your answer.

**South Tower:** the castle design was made to resemble the castles that King Edward was building in Wales. Laurence was a merchant and wanted to show that he now considered himself among the nobility – an impressive castle could do this. It is self-contained and can only be accessed via a staircase on the outside. At the time it was used for business and accommodation.

**Great Hall:** the centre of public life in the house, a place for eating and for entertaining guests. The glass windows show Laurence's wealth (glass was very expensive). Most fortified houses avoided lots of glass.

**High windows:** for security, although attacks were unlikely.

**Thick, strong walls:** built more to match the style of King Edward's castles than for security. A gatehouse in the eastern wall would have been guarded to control who came in.

**North Tower:** the main living accommodation. Designed to look impressive to potential trading partners but also provide comfortable living.

**Solar block:** the family's private living area, which was connected to the Great Hall.

### Study Tip

A Medieval manor house can tell us a lot about the people who built it and life at the time. What was it like to live in for both its owners and their servants? What are the advantages of its location? A manor house, like Stokesay Castle, would be a place of safety and security. How was this achieved? Why was it needed? Which features of the building show the wealth of the owner?

# 3.4 How did Edward fund his government?

Edward's plan to establish himself as a strong king involved the dominance of England over its neighbours: Wales, Scotland and France. This meant that England would inevitably have to go to war. However, wars were very expensive and his father, Henry III, had left him with very little money. Edward needed to raise funds quickly, so how did he do it?

## Why did Edward need money?

During his reign, Edward fought a great many wars. He was determined to crush the Welsh once and for all, initially by launching a military crackdown against the rebels and then embarking on a massive castle building programme. In the 1280s and 1290s, relations with Scotland and France deteriorated leading to two more wars. The near constant waging of wars would take its toll on any economy but for Edward the situation was complicated by recent history. The reigns of his father and grandfather had shown that he could not simply tax the barons as much as he liked.

## Tax and trade

The easiest source of income was direct taxation: all his subjects had to give a portion of their own wealth to the king. Edward raised taxes but could not keep doing so; indeed he almost faced a rebellion in 1297 when one of his barons physically blocked the collection of taxes at the Exchequer. Another way to generate income was through duties, another form of taxation. A duty could be placed on any product and meant that a percentage of the sale would go to the king. A key duty of Edward's reign was on wool. It was first introduced in 1275 but was increased in 1294. For duties to be collected Edward needed to encourage trade and to do this he needed to deal with the coin problem.

## The coin problem

When Edward became king, England's coins were very old and worn and some had been deliberately damaged. Coins were made of silver and clipping was the removal of small amounts of the metal from a coin. If only a small amount was taken from each coin it would not be noticeable and the coin could still be used.

Clippings could be collected together and then sold as silver. This crime damaged England's economy because it led to people believing the coins were worth less, so traders and producers raised prices to compensate (**inflation**), which harmed trade. Foreign merchants would not accept damaged coins. Anyone involved in financial work was suspected of coin clipping, with Jewish people, a great many of whom worked as money lenders, being particularly under suspicion. It was difficult to prove who had clipped coins, but Edward needed to do something about the problem quickly. He introduced harsher punishments in 1275 and many people were arrested. In November 1278, 270 Jews were executed for involvement in the practice.

The problem, however, did not go away and in 1279 Edward ordered the replacement of all coins with newly minted ones. It would be harder to clip the new coins without it being noticed and so traders could be sure that what they were receiving was worth what was claimed. The re-coinage encouraged trade, which led to more duties being paid, which in turn gave the king a greater income.

▼ **SOURCE A** *A coin from Edward's 1279 mint*

## The Italian bankers

Although taxes and duties were helping to pay for Edward's wars, they were not enough. It took a long time to collect all the taxes and the king needed money immediately. He turned to the bankers of Italy. In the 1270s and 1280s, he struck a deal with the Riccardi bankers from the city of Lucca. In return for lending Edward money to fight his Welsh wars whenever (and as quickly as) he wanted, the Riccardi would manage the collection of taxes and duties. By doing the collecting themselves, the Riccardi might have been able to raise more money. The Riccardi also dealt with the collection of wool duties (around £211,000, or nearly £107 million in today's money, roughly half of what Edward borrowed from them). Edward got his money quickly and the Riccardi would get a longer term return on their loan.

For groups like the Riccardi, kings were lucrative but dangerous men to do business with. When war broke out between England and France in 1294, Edward demanded more money. Unfortunately for the Riccardi, their money was in France and the French king simply stopped them from accessing it. They couldn't give Edward what he wanted and he ended the deal between them. Instead, he immediately made a similar deal with another group of Italian bankers, the Frescobaldi.

▼ **SOURCE B** *An illustration from a fourteenth-century manuscript showing Riccardi bankers*

**Practice Question**

Write an account of the ways Edward funded his government.

**8 marks**

**Study Tip**

You should aim to include the following: taxes, duties (particularly wool) and loans from Italian bankers. You could consider how other policies, like re-coinage, helped increase these sources of funding.

**Work**

1  a  Why did Edward need money?
   b  How did he raise money?

2  How did the crime of coin clipping work and why did it cause concern for Edward?

3  How did Edward clamp down on coin clipping?

4  Why did Edward turn to the Italian bankers for money?

5  You are Edward in 1294 and you need new bankers. Write a letter to the Frescobaldi explaining what you need and why. Include: why you need money, why you were forced to get rid of your old bankers, what the new bankers' responsibilities would be.

# 3.5 Why did Edward force all of the Jews to leave England?

The first Jewish community in England was invited to come by William the Conqueror when he became king in 1066. In the next 200 years they played a key role in English society and were offered royal protection. Jews' lives changed dramatically in 1272 when Edward became king and in 1290 he announced that all Jewish people had to leave England. Why were Jewish people such an important part of medieval life? Why, and how, did Edward turn on them? And why were the Jews eventually expelled from England?

## Objectives

▶ **State** the importance of Jews in medieval England.

▶ **Describe** the changing policies toward Jews.

▶ **Explain** the reasons for the Statute of the Jewry and the Edict of Expulsion.

## The Jews in England

William the Conqueror invited Jews to live in England because he felt that they would be useful in building a strong country. Unlike Christians, Jews were allowed to lend money to people and make a profit by charging **interest**. William recognised that loans were necessary to develop the country and Jews could provide them. Because of their importance, Jews were given royal protection; anyone caught harming them would be guilty of damaging royal property! The success of England after the Norman Conquest would not have been possible without the Jews. They lent money not only to ordinary people but also to barons, bishops and kings, paying for armies, castles and cathedrals. The Jewish population increased greatly during the next two centuries.

## Outsiders

Many Jews became wealthy from their money-lending businesses but despite their royal protection they often faced hostility. Many Christians saw them as untrustworthy outsiders with their different religion and culture. **Anti-Semitism** was common and Jews were often **persecuted** and treated unfairly. Much of this may have been jealousy of the wealth that many Jews achieved but a key factor was that loans had to be repaid, something many people were reluctant to do! Violence against Jews was common, with mobs often seeking out loan records and attempting to destroy them.

## The end of royal protection

Royal protection had advantages for Jews but it also had a down side: the king could treat Jews as he wished. Increasingly, in the thirteenth century, Jews were taxed heavily and by the time Edward became king it had become impossible to raise their taxes any more. He felt they had outlived their usefulness and he needed the support of others to fund his wars in Wales. In 1275, Edward introduced the Statute of the Jewry. The law made life difficult for Jews in a number of ways, but most significantly, it banned them from practising **usury** (charging interest on loans), deprived them of their business and cancelled many of the debts they were owed. The law made many Jews bankrupt.

▼ **SOURCE A** *A contemporary French illustration of Jewish money lenders*

## The Expulsion of the Jews, 1290

Edward issued a new order 15 years after the Statute of the Jewry. The Edict of Expulsion (18 July 1290) called for all Jews to leave England or face execution. The official reason given was that the 1275 statute had not been obeyed but in reality it was about money. By expelling the Jews Edward was freeing many nobles from debt and making them much more willing to support taxes that would pay for war. Many Jews had already left England after the statute but those who remained left in a largely peaceful way. It would be almost 400 years before Jews were allowed to return to England.

▼ **SOURCE B** *A contemporary illustration showing the expulsion of the Jews*

▼ **INTERPRETATION C** *Adapted from an article on* Haaretz.com, *the online edition of the* Haaretz *newspaper published in Israel, 1 November 2012:*

Edward very quickly showed his readiness to adopt anti-Jewish measures. These included a prohibition on money-lending by Jews, a genuine blow, since this was a principal form of livelihood for members of the community. By July 18, 1290, when the king ordered their departure, the Jews were not making a significant contribution to the royal treasury and were the objects of popular hatred, as well as ecclesiastical [religious] discrimination, so that banishing them was not a difficult decision.

# Edward and the Church

The medieval Church was immensely powerful. It owned land and had great influence all over Western Europe. At its head was the Pope, whom Christians believed was God's representative on Earth. One of the biggest challenges for any medieval king was how he dealt with the Church. Edward's relationship with the Church was generally good but on a number of occasions things went very wrong. What made the Church so powerful? How did Edward deal with the Church? Can Edward's reign really be described as a quiet time for relations between the crown and the Church?

## Objectives

▶ **Describe** Edward's relationship with the Church.

▶ **Explain** how disagreements came about.

▶ **Assess** whether Edward's relationship with the Church was largely positive or negative.

## The medieval Church

Religion played a very important part in the lives of ordinary people in medieval England. People firmly believed in Heaven and Hell and that you should live your life in a good way and avoid sin. By far the majority of people were Christians, which in medieval times meant that they were **Catholic**. They looked to the

▼ **SOURCE A** *A medieval **doom painting** showing people suffering in Hell; these images would appear in church to remind people of the consequences of a sinful life; most people could not read or write so images were the best way to get across a message*

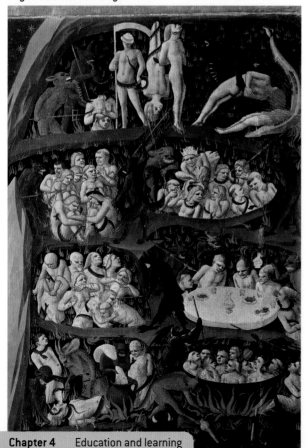

Church for guidance on how to live their lives, which made it very powerful. The Church was also immensely rich because it owned so much land. As you know, many people left their land to the Church when they died.

As head of the Church, the Pope's power was believed to come directly from God, meaning that he was not answerable to any king. This placed bishops in a potentially confusing situation: if there was a disagreement, did they owe their loyalty to their king or to the Pope?

## A difficult relationship

The relationship between the king and the Church was often a challenging one. It was in the best interests of both sides to work together and much of the time this was possible – medieval kings were Christians, after all. Yet at times the relationship was strained, particularly when it came to taxes and the law. The Church had rights over the lands it owned and could also hold its own courts outside of the country's legal system. For Edward I, careful management of his dealings with the Church would be essential.

### Fact

Unusually for a royal medieval marriage, contemporary accounts suggest that Edward and his first wife, Eleanor of Castile, were very much in love. When she died in 1290 in Lincoln, a heartbroken Edward had her body transported back to London. In an act that showed both his faith and his love for Eleanor, Edward had a stone cross built at each resting place on her body's journey back to London. Beginning in Lincoln, there are 12 Eleanor crosses, with the last at Charing Cross in London.

## Edward's plans

Edward was a devout Christian. He had fought in the Crusades for the Christian faith and the way he memorialised his dead wife, Eleanor, shows that he was a religious man. During his reign he spent a great deal of money on new religious buildings and monuments. One of his projects was to build a new abbey in Cheshire for Cistercian monks. Edward founded the abbey in 1270, two years before he became king. When he was caught in a storm at sea in 1263, Edward had prayed for his survival and promised to build the grandest abbey ever seen if he was spared. Vale Royal Abbey was the result. Although the abbey was built and monks lived there, it never reached the grandeur of the original plan, mainly because of a lack of funds. Money was often at the centre of Edward's dealings, and it was this that led to most of his difficulties with the Church.

### Key Words

Catholic    doom painting

### Extension

The Eleanor crosses are one of the most visible features that Edward left behind. They can tell us a lot about Edward, his love for his wife and what sort of place England was at the time. Spend some time researching the Eleanor crosses. You could choose one to research or look at the journey as a whole. Think about what they can teach us about medieval England.

▼ **B** *Vale Royal Abbey, Northwich, Cheshire as it looks today; it became a country house in the sixteenth century and is now a golf club*

▲ **C** *The Eleanor cross in Grantham*

### Work

1   Who was the head of the medieval Church?

2   Explain two things that made the medieval Church powerful.

3   What evidence is there that Edward was a devout Christian?

4   Look at **Source A**.
    a   What does this image show?
    b   What was the purpose of this image?
    c   How far do you think it was people's fear of Hell that made the Church powerful?

# Edward and the Church

## Edward and the archbishops

One of the most powerful positions in medieval England was that of Archbishop of Canterbury. As the most senior priest in the kingdom he had control and influence over the Church and its land. He was also answerable to the Pope as well as the king. Although Edward had influence over the decision, only the Pope could choose the Archbishop of Canterbury. However, Edward tried three times to get his friend and adviser, Robert Burnell, appointed to the post, but each time it was blocked by the Pope. Edward's relationship with the Church and his archbishops was generally good but on two occasions there were significant disagreements.

## Disagreement one: Archbishop Peckham

John Peckham became Archbishop of Canterbury in 1279. He was appointed by the Pope after King Edward had tried unsuccessfully to get Robert Burnell the job. So Peckham's relationship with Edward did not get off to the best start and the two clashed over several issues.

Peckham was keen to reorganise the way the Church was run and set about more effectively organising the collection of taxes on Church lands. He angered the king early on by insisting that a copy of Magna Carta was displayed in every cathedral, a document that Edward was not particularly keen that people should be reminded of as it was a reminder of the power the barons could wield over a weak king. Peckham's interpretation of religious law was very strict too; for example, he considered it a sin to borrow money from Jews, something that Edward and other nobles did regularly.

Edward was concerned with the Church's power on its own lands and its ability to collect taxes, which he felt undermined his own power. He was also concerned that Peckham made repeated use of **excommunication**. Being excommunicated meant that you were officially no longer a member of the Christian Church and so would go to Hell. This was viewed as an extremely serious punishment in the medieval world. Peckham's ability and willingness to use excommunication made him very powerful. Nothing a king could do was worse than eternal pain and suffering!

To try to limit Peckham's powers, the king issued a special document in 1286, entitled *Circumspecte Agatis*, which specified what types of cases Church courts could hear. While Church courts remained powerful, the king had made the point that the **secular** courts were the most important.

Peckham pushed hard to stop priests from holding more than one position within the Church, known as **plurality**. Some priests might be responsible for two or more parishes (sometimes miles apart), drawing a salary from each. Likewise, other priests would spend years living away from the parish and never visit while still being paid. Peckham saw this as corruption and wanted to stamp it out. His interference in the way other, lower-ranking, bishops organised their areas of responsibility caused many disagreements, which eventually forced him to back down.

While in principle Edward was not against improvements to the Church, he was concerned by Peckham's approach to his role. He did not want a powerful archbishop with his own taxes and laws rivalling his own, and was very keen to ensure that the Church contributed properly to his ambitious plans for the country and his reign. Peckham ultimately backed down on many of his reforms and Edward was able to show who held the higher authority in England. Church and king continued to have a relatively good relationship. When Peckham died, however, his successor would present Edward with even more challenges.

▼ **D** *Archbishop Peckham's tomb in Canterbury Cathedral*

## Disagreement 2: Archbishop Winchelsea

When Robert Winchelsea became Archbishop of Canterbury in 1293, he immediately caused friction between himself and the king. When he swore his oath of allegiance he added a section that said he only owed Edward loyalty in secular matters, not spiritual. At a time when Edward increasingly needed money for war in Wales, Winchelsea refused to allow Edward to tax the Church beyond a tenth of its earnings, which was much less than Edward wanted. In 1296, the Pope announced that the Church would not have to pay any money to a secular government. Winchelsea obeyed and refused to give any more money. He eventually relented and allowed other bishops to make up their own mind as to whether or not to pay. Winchelsea himself continued to refuse. Edward reacted by seizing some of his lands.

The disagreement was finally sorted out in July 1297 but the problem could not have arisen at a worse time. As you know, 1297 was a crisis year for Edward. With wars in Wales, France and Gascony and a very real threat of rebellion from some of his barons led by Roger Bigod, his disagreement with Winchelsea was one more crisis in a very challenging year. Edward never forgave the Archbishop and eventually forced him into exile in 1306 after accusing him of plotting a rebellion.

▼ **INTERPRETATION E** *An eighteenth-century illustration of Edward I meeting his bishops*

### Key Words

excommunicate
secular    plurality

### Work

1 Explain the term 'plurality'.

2 Explain why Edward and Peckham had disagreements.

3 Why could Edward's disagreement with Winchelsea be described as bad timing?

4 In a pair, each person takes the role of one of the archbishops for a debate. It is your job to argue that your archbishop caused Edward more problems than your partner's.

5 Who do *you* think caused Edward more trouble: Peckham or Winchelsea? Explain your answer.

### Practice Question

Explain what was important about Edward's relationship with the Church.    **8 marks**

### Study Tip

Remember that Edward's relationship with the Church was mostly good, despite his disagreements with Peckham and Winchelsea.

# 4.2 How did universities develop during Edward's reign?

The medieval period saw the development of the first universities. These new centres of learning, which had grown over several centuries to become important and influential places, played a key role in England during the reign of Edward I. What were these new universities? Who went to them and why? Why did they play such a key role in Edward's reign?

### Objectives

▶ **Describe** medieval universities.

▶ **Examine** the role played by universities in England.

▶ **Evaluate** the importance of Oxford and Cambridge to the reign of Edward I.

## Medieval universities

The first universities emerged in the eleventh century but these had grown out of much older institutions called monastic schools. Monastic schools were run by monks in monasteries, whereas universities became independent organisations. At first, classes were taught wherever there was space, such as in churches and in people's homes. A university was not a building to which people went, but a collection of individuals who studied together. Soon, however, universities began to construct or buy buildings so students had a particular place to go to study. Initially the focus was on the training of clergy but as time went on there was a movement towards the education of other men in the subjects of law and medicine. Young men studied for bachelors' and masters' degrees, while a small number went on to study for doctorate degrees.

▼ **SOURCE A** *A fourteenth-century illustration showing a lesson at the University of Paris*

All lessons were taught in Latin, so students would have to learn this language. Those who went to university tended to be from the **gentry** class and it was seen as a way to raise social standing and secure a profession. No women went to university and the male students would begin their studies around 14 years of age. Others, including many priests, spent their whole lives at the university itself as teachers and **scholars**.

Medieval universities could be paid for in three ways. Some were funded by the students (either by their family or another wealthy person sponsoring their studies). Many were paid for by the Church and were influenced directly by the Pope and other senior clergy. Finally, as was the case with England's first universities, some were funded by the Crown.

## Oxford and Cambridge

The first two universities in England were Oxford and Cambridge. Oxford was formed at some point at the end of the eleventh century or the beginning of the twelfth. Historians are unsure of the exact date. It grew dramatically in size after 1167 when English students were banned from studying at the University of Paris. Cambridge was founded in 1209 when, after a disagreement with the local authorities, a group of scholars left Oxford and gathered in Cambridge. By the time of Edward I's reign, both universities were well established. Both institutions were funded by the crown but individual parts of the universities (known as colleges) were often paid for by wealthy donors including senior members of the

Church and close associates of the king. This gave them influence with the universities, but Edward was determined to maintain their independence by protecting the scholars from interference in their work, even by those who were paying for it.

▼ **B** *Peterhouse College is the oldest college in Cambridge University and was granted its charter by Edward I in 1284*

## Why did Edward want Oxford and Cambridge to succeed?

King Edward wanted the universities of Oxford and Cambridge to be successful. This was because he recognised the benefit of having access to men who were respected across Europe for their learning and intelligence. They were useful to him as government officials. Coming from a lower class they would be loyal to the king in running his administration, unlike the nobility who might, with their own financial means, be more independent.

Edward's reign was dominated by his reforms to English law, including statutes that aimed to limit the power of the Church and the long established rights and powers of a number of barons. The legal experts of Oxford and Cambridge played a key role in this. They were able to demonstrate that what Edward was doing was based on the law and not just an attempt to gain more power.

This need for expert advice was even more pressing when it came to disagreements in Scotland over who should be on the Scottish throne and exactly what their relationship was with the English king. Lawyers who had studied at the universities were respected by all and so their opinions mattered. Edward also recognised the importance of written records and university graduates played a key role in ensuring that these were created. Well-organised documents would stop future disagreements like the ones that occurred at the beginning of Edward's reign.

## Work

1  When did the first universities appear in Europe?

2  Explain the three ways in which universities were funded.

3  Why do you think it is so hard to say exactly when Oxford University was founded but we know exactly when Cambridge was founded?

4  Look at **Source A**. What does it suggest about the role of the Church in medieval universities?

5  How important were the two universities to Edward and his aims? Think about how he wanted to respect their independence.

## Fact

Oxford and Cambridge were the only universities successfully established in England until the founding of the university of Durham in 1832.

## Extension

Choose either Oxford or Cambridge University and spend some time researching its early years. How was it founded? Who studied there? What did they study?

# The key thinkers of Edward's reign

Two great thinkers of Edward I's reign were Roger Bacon and John Duns Scotus. Both were influential at the time and their ideas have been seen as important in the centuries since. One was a religious thinker and one took a more scientific approach. Who were these two men and what were their ideas? Why have their ideas been seen as so important? And what did people think of them at the time?

## The religious thinker: John Duns Scotus

▼ **INTERPRETATION A** *A fifteenth-century painting of John Duns Scotus by Joos van Ghent, a Dutch artist*

John Duns Scotus was one of the most important religious thinkers of his age but very little is known about his life. He was a Scottish priest ('Scotus' means Scottish) who was born in the town of Duns. His writings, however, have survived. Respected for his intelligence, Duns Scotus was nicknamed Doctor Subtilis (the 'subtle doctor') because of his reputation for careful thought. He worked on many important issues, building on and challenging the ideas of philosophers like Aristotle and Aquinas. In 1303, he was forced to leave the University of Paris rather than support the King of France over the Pope in a dispute.

▼ **INTERPRETATION B** *From the Christian website AmericanCatholic.org:*

In an age when many people adopted whole systems of thought without qualification, John Duns Scotus appreciated the wisdom of Aquinas, Aristotle and the Muslim philosophers – and still managed to be an independent thinker. That quality was proven in 1303 when King Philip the Fair tried to enlist the University of Paris on his side in a dispute with Pope Boniface VIII. John Duns Scotus dissented and was given three days to leave France.

### Two key ideas of Duns Scotus

#### Immaculate conception

*A disagreement existed within Christianity over whether Jesus's mother, Mary, had been born without sin – an 'immaculate conception'. Christians believed that everyone carried the original sin of Adam and Eve, except for Mary. There was no recognised explanation for how this was possible and some respected religious thinkers questioned it. Scotus said that Jesus's crucifixion had removed any sin from his mother, and this explanation came to be widely accepted.*

#### Proof of God's existence

*Scotus made a detailed argument for the existence of God. The argument is complex, but to put it very simply: everything that exists comes from something: for example, parents produce a child. A higher power must have begun this process. This higher power must be greater than anything else and, as it was not created, it must have always existed (be infinite). This higher power must be the Christian God.*

# The scientific thinker: Roger Bacon

Bacon was concerned with scientific investigation and some see him as an early supporter of modern, evidence-based science. He worked at the Universities of Oxford and Paris where he focused on the ideas of the Ancient Greek philosopher Aristotle. He became a **friar** in 1256 and his superiors immediately limited his right to spend time on his academic work. His ideas took a much more logical path than many were happy with. Bacon's luck changed drastically in 1265 with the election of a new Pope, Clement IV. Clement told Bacon to continue his work in secret. The Pope's support allowed Bacon to investigate a wide range of ideas and issues. In 1268, he sent Clement his *Opus Majus* ('greater work'), which suggested how logical and scientific thinking could be introduced to Christianity. When Clement died and a new Pope was chosen, Bacon faced opposition and was put under house arrest. Many of his ideas were ridiculed.

▲ **INTERPRETATION C** *Roger Bacon sending his* Opus Majus *to the Pope; illustration for* La Ciencia Y Sus Hombres *by Luis Figuier (1876)*

## Bacon's ideas and theories

- Explored why people make errors or fail to learn things (e.g. following unreliable evidence or people)
- Argued that Bible was the starting point of all scientific understanding and should be studied in its original language
- Developed the Gregorian calendar (the one we use today)
- Studied optics and built a relatively accurate explanation of how the eye works
- Studied experimental science by looking at such things as the manufacture of gunpowder and the size and shape of the planets

## Key Word

friar

## Practice Question

How convincing is **Interpretation D** about Roger Bacon? Explain your answer using **Interpretation D** and your contextual knowledge. **8 marks**

## Study Tip

Remember to examine each point that is made in the interpretation but there is no need to copy out large parts of it.

▼ **INTERPRETATION D** *Adapted from an article in the monthly magazine* History Today, *published 7 July 1974:*

A stern and bitter critic of his contemporaries, a controversial figure in his Order, the Franciscans, an eccentric in thirteenth-century philosophic circles, a bold innovator in experimental science, brilliant teacher, theologian and scientist, Roger Bacon was all of these and more. Yet many of his writings were condemned and soon went into oblivion, so that within a century of his death the only reputation he gained was as a magician, and this endured until the seventeenth century.

## Work

1. Choose one of Duns Scotus's theories. In pairs come up with a way of explaining the theory. Be as creative as you can.

2. Which of Bacon's theories would have made him unpopular with some religious leaders? Why?

3. Look at **Interpretation B**.
   a. What impression does this give of Duns Scotus?
   b. How fair is this interpretation?

4. If we were going to build a statue to one of these men, which should it be? Think about what each achieved and their influence on people at the time and since. Make sure you talk about both men in your answer.

# 5.1 How did the medieval legal system work?

The medieval legal system was very different to today's. The legal system was interlinked with the feudal system with feudal lords acting as judges over those below them. The system had remained largely the same since 1066 until, shortly before Edward's reign, a man named Henry de Bracton began to try to improve the system. When he became king, Edward wanted to make further changes. How did the legal system work? What role did the king and his barons play? And what did Henry de Bracton change?

## Objectives

▶ **Describe** the system of justice in medieval England.

▶ **Examine** the work of Henry de Bracton.

▶ **Assess** why Edward might have wanted to change the system.

This diagram shows how the justice system worked in England when Edward came to the throne.

### Laws passed by the king

Laws were passed by the king and Parliament in the form of statutes, and courts had the responsibility of enforcing the law. The Church also had its own laws that dealt with religious matters. This was known as **canon law** and was set by the Pope in Rome. The idea of being innocent until proved guilty did not really exist. It was as much the job of the accused to prove that they had not committed the crime as the victim to prove that they had.

### Enforced by feudal lords

England's legal system was based on the feudal system. Other than for crimes like treason, any dispute or crime committed within a particular area was dealt with by the feudal lord. This was their **jurisdiction**. A case would only usually be heard if the victim requested it. A **jury** of local people may have been present but it was the lord who made the decision and handed out punishment, usually a fine, which had to be accepted. The only way to challenge it was a direct appeal to the king. This power was important to the lords as it provided a significant amount of their income.

### Enforced by guilds in the towns

In the towns the powerful guilds ran the court system. This meant that power was less likely to be in the hands of one person, but otherwise they tended to work in a similar way to the feudal courts.

### Church courts

Church courts included priests and bishops, and had absolute power over those who stood before them. There was not even a right to appeal to the king. Officially only issues of canon law could be dealt with by Church courts but often they dealt with other matters that arose on their lands.

### Justice in England at the start of Edward's reign

## The work of Henry de Bracton

During the reign of Edward's father, Henry III, there was an attempt to make the legal system more equal across the country. In around 1235, Henry de Bracton, a priest, legal expert and a key figure in Henry's government, published *De Legibus et Consuetudinibus Angliae* ('On the Laws and Customs of England'). He argued that when deciding if someone is guilty of a crime, not only their action should be taken into account but also their intention; for example, in the case of murder, did they intend to kill? This idea of *mens rea* or criminal intent still exists in English law. Bracton also gave guidance for other aspects of criminal trials including how the trial was conducted and the different jurisdictions of Church and state courts. Perhaps most controversially, Bracton stated that if a king did not act within the law, he could not call himself a king.

Bracton worked as part of a committee that heard the appeals of those barons who had sided with Simon de Montfort against Henry III. For Bracton, the law should be applied in the same way to all: no one was above it.

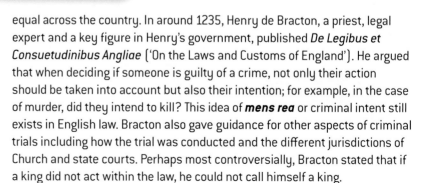

▼ **INTERPRETATION A** *Adapted from an article in the online newspaper* The Atlantic *published on 2 June 2014:*

> In societies around the world throughout history, guilt and innocence has more-than-occasionally been ascertained in 'trial by ordeal'. In some cases, the accused were made to pluck a stone from a cauldron of boiling water, oil, or lead; if their skin didn't burn off, they were judged innocent. In other cases, the guilty were believed to be those who suffered grave injuries from walking across hot iron, or ingesting poison.

## Edward's reign

Despite Bracton's work, the weakness of Henry III meant that the barons could largely do as they pleased. When Edward became king in 1272, four years after Bracton's death, the system of feudal justice remained largely intact. Lords dealt with crimes as they saw fit. Edward's desire to return power to himself, however, meant that this situation could not continue.

▼ **SOURCE B** *Henry de Bracton's 'On the Laws and Customs of England'*

## Key Words

canon law    jurisdiction

jury    *mens rea*

### Fact

Although most disputes and accusations were dealt with by the lord, more extreme methods could be used, including trial by combat (the two people involved or a chosen representative would duel in order to settle their differences) or trial by ordeal, when the accused would be subjected to great danger. Both of these worked on the belief that God would protect the innocent person.

### Work

1   Explain the term 'jurisdiction'.

2   How were feudalism and the justice system connected?

3   Look at **Interpretation A**:

 a   What does this interpretation suggest about medieval justice?

 b   How fair a representation is this of medieval justice?

4   Explain the term '*mens rea*'. Why do you think this is considered an important change?

5   Create a spider diagram to show Henry de Bracton's key ideas.

6   Why do you think Edward was keen to make changes to the system that existed when he became king? Explain in as much detail as you can.

# Crime and punishment

Today when people talk of 'medieval punishments', they usually mean that a punishment is particularly brutal. In fact, this view of punishments in medieval times is reasonably, but not totally, accurate! For example, punishments could be very harsh and violent, but simple fines were also very common. The aim of punishment was as much about discouraging other people from committing the crime as punishing the criminals themselves. Therefore the emphasis was usually on making sure others saw the punishment being carried out, rather than making the criminal suffer for the sake of it. What crimes were common in medieval England? What typical punishments were given out? Was effort made to make the punishment fit the crime?

## Objectives

▶ **Describe** the crimes and punishments of medieval England.

▶ **Consider** the reasons behind these punishments.

▶ **Evaluate** the medieval approach to punishment.

## The crimes of medieval England

The crimes committed in medieval England varied from begging and stealing bread to treason and murder, and all of these tended to receive harsh punishments. One of the most serious crimes was stealing because it affected people's livelihoods. Having a sheep or cow stolen was very serious indeed. While feudal lords could give out brutal punishments, it usually required the victim to make the accusation and other members of the community to apprehend the accused; there was little in the way of investigation. During Edward I's reign it was often more powerful, visiting judges who worked directly for the king who would deal with the more serious crimes and harsher punishments.

▼ **INTERPRETATION A**  *A twentieth-century illustration of a man being punished in the stocks*

▼ **INTERPRETATION B**  *Adapted from a lecture given by the historian Helen Mary Carrel in 2006 at the International Medieval Congress, at Leeds University:*

The common view of the medieval justice system as cruel and based around torture and execution is often unfair and inaccurate. In fact, medieval townspeople saw it as their Christian duty to show mercy to offenders who were sent to prison. Prisoners were obliged to pay fees to their gaolers for their upkeep, so they depended upon being given alms as a means of obtaining food, drink and other necessities. Consequently, prisons were much more public than nowadays – passersby could often see prisoners through the bars and gave them charity. Solitary confinement was usually a sanction only to be used against the very worst offenders because it removed the possibility of receiving alms from the charitable.

## Extension

'Medieval punishments fit the crime.' How far do you agree? Challenge yourself by trying to answer this question. You will need to do some extra research to add to what you have learned on these pages.

# Medieval punishments

### Minor crimes
Drunkenness, selling bad products, minor assault, causing a disturbance

### Punishment by public humiliation
The stocks
The pillory
A fine

### Capital offences
Murder, very violent assault, theft of valuable goods from the feudal lord (including animals), heresy (going against the official Church beliefs)

### Capital punishment
Hanging
Burning at the stake
Beheading (for nobles)

### More serious crimes
Repeated stealing, burglary, stealing from the feudal lord, violent assault, forgery

### Violent punishments
Fingers, hands or ears cut off
Flagellation (whipping)

### The most serious crime of all
Treason (attempting to kill or overthrow the king or betraying the country to an enemy)

### Capital punishment
Hanged, drawn and quartered: hanged until almost dead, followed by drawing (pulling out the criminal's insides and then burning them in front of their eyes), before cutting off their head and cutting their body into pieces (quartering). The aim would be to keep the criminal alive for as long as possible. A skilled executioner would keep them alive until the beheading!

## Practice Question

How convincing is **Interpretation B** about medieval justice?

Explain your answer using **Interpretation B** and your contextual knowledge.

**8 marks**

## Study Tip

When approaching an interpretation you should begin by deciding what opinion it is putting forward and then use your knowledge to judge whether this conclusion is accurate.

## Work

1. What sort of crime would be punished with the stocks?
2. What was the purpose of the public humiliation of criminals?
3. Why was stealing animals seen as such a terrible crime?
4. You are a local crime reporter. Write a short report of crimes and punishments in your village during a week. You can choose which crimes to write about, but remember minor crimes were much more common than more serious ones!
5. Why do you think treason was dealt with so harshly?

# What did the Statutes of Gloucester and Winchester change?

Edward's priority when he became king was to regain the power his father had lost. During Henry III's reign the barons had become increasingly powerful. The powers they had gained included a great deal of legal authority: the right to hold courts and give out punishments. In principle this was fine, but Edward wanted to make it clear that all authority ultimately came from him. He also recognised that the justice system needed to be improved and two statutes were passed to try to achieve these ambitions. What was the Statute of Gloucester and how did it help Edward establish his authority? What was the Statute of Winchester?

## The Statute of Gloucester, 1278: Edward takes power from the barons

When Edward became king, the years of open conflict between the king and the barons were over and England was stable. The problems of Henry III's reign had, however, left their mark. Over many years, the barons had become more and more powerful in the areas they controlled. They had gained more land but had also increased their judicial powers (the right to hold courts and punish criminals). Edward did not want to remove this right completely (it was an important part of feudalism) but he was concerned how much power the barons had.

In 1278, Parliament passed the Statute of Gloucester. As you already know, the *Quo Warranto* investigations had aimed to discover which lands and rights barons had been officially given and which they had just taken on themselves. They either had to produce a royal licence issued by the king or prove that their families had held the land since 'time immemorial' (since 1189, Richard I's coronation). The new statute increased the effectiveness of these investigations. It also sent General Eyres around the country to carry out the investigations and also to hear criminal cases. This challenged the rights of the barons to deal with crimes within their jurisdiction. The statute's impact was limited as most barons remained powerful but it had a clear symbolic impact: all legal power came from the king, and the courts (whether run by barons or General Eyres) received their powers from him.

## The Statute of Winchester, 1285: the beginning of policing?

Having established his authority, in 1285 Edward and Parliament began reforming the justice system. The Statute of Winchester aimed to give communities more responsibility for dealing with issues of law and order. The law reintroduced **watchmen**, a job that had disappeared in the previous century in many towns and cities. This group of local men would ensure order was kept after the town's gates were closed and could be summoned by the constable to establish order if there was a problem at other times.

▼ **INTERPRETATION A** *Adapted from* A History of Police in England *by Captain W. L. Melville Lee (1901):*

This Winchester statute is especially important to our inquiry, because it sums up and gives permanency to that which was introduced in former reigns, which were considered important for the protection of society; and because it presents to us a complete picture of that police system of the middle ages which continued with but little alteration for more than five hundred years, and which even now, though greatly changed in its outward appearance, is still the foundation upon which our present police structure is built.

**Extension**

**Interpretation A** argues that the Statute of Winchester was very significant. How far do you agree with the author's arguments? Think about what it changed at the time and how far it has continued to affect policing down the centuries. Use the information on these pages and your own research.

A key element of the Statute of Winchester introduced **hue and cry**. According to this rule, anyone who witnessed a crime must raise the alarm ('hue and cry'). If they heard the shouts, all able-bodied men had to help pursue the criminal. Ignoring a crime was punishable, as was raising a false hue and cry. The statute also stated that 'the whole hundred [ … ] shall be answerable': if a criminal was allowed to escape, the rest of the village would be held responsible!

Some historians argue that the Statute of Winchester was the beginning of what eventually became the modern police force. At the time, it established that everyone was responsible for ensuring that order was maintained, not just the barons, and that crimes must be punished.

## Why was Edward concerned with law and order?

Edward approached law and order from two directions. The Statute of Gloucester aimed to establish that all justice comes ultimately from the king, and the Statute of Winchester made it clear that everyone held responsibility for ensuring criminals were caught and crime was prevented. In fact, it could be argued that both of these had the same aim: to undermine the barons' power. Gloucester proved that the king held the power while Winchester established that ordinary people, not just nobles, held responsibility.

**Work**

1   Why did Edward want to change the justice system?

2   What was the purpose of the Statute of Gloucester?

3   Create a guide for medieval people about the new law of hue and cry. What should they do? What could happen to them if they do not follow the new rules?

4   What changes did Edward make to law and order in England? Explain your answer in as much detail as you can.

# What was a medieval battle really like?

The medieval period in England was often unstable and therefore extremely violent. Battles were a fact of life and took place not just between countries but also between people in the same country. Who fought in medieval battles? What weapons were used and what were the tactics? How did medieval battles work?

**Objectives**

▶ **State** the features of a medieval battle.

▶ **Examine** the weapons and tactics used.

▶ **Explain** why kings wanted to avoid battle.

## Setting the scene

Full scale medieval battles were not common, mainly because they were so unpredictable. When two armies met factors beyond their control (weather, terrain) could have as much impact on the battle as the number of men or the tactics used. Battles were sometimes necessary, however, and were brutal, bloody affairs that could last for hours and even days. Medieval battles would often take place in open fields with the two opposing armies facing each other. The army that arrived first would establish itself in the best position, most likely fighting downhill. A typical army would consist of:

- Rich, land-owning nobles as the commanders making the key decisions. They would often be inexperienced at hand-to-hand combat. The king might join them too.

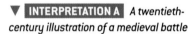 **INTERPRETATION A** *A twentieth-century illustration of a medieval battle*

- Nobles made up the heavy **cavalry** too: strong and well armed, ready to charge the enemy on horseback.
- Light cavalry came next, usually wealthy commoners. They could move quickly and were often used as scouts in battle to ride ahead and report back.
- **Infantry** came next, made up of archers and crossbowmen: inexperienced peasants who had been called to fight for their lord.
- **Mercenaries** fought too: men paid to fight for a particular side.

## The battle

Battles would begin with the order from a commander to charge. The heavy cavalry would usually then ride at full speed towards the enemy to try to break through the enemy's line, damage their defences and bring disorder to their ranks. The defending army would attempt to form a defensive wall if they had time. They may have formed a shield wall, although these were becoming less popular. **Pikes** were often used to create a defensive layer and were used most effectively by the Scottish in their **schiltron** formation. The ability of the heavy cavalry to break through the defences was the key to victory. One of the most important features of medieval battles were the archers. Used effectively, arrows could destroy an army by hitting the troops further back, behind the defences. Medieval warfare involved very close combat. Archers and crossbowmen might stand as little as 150m from each other when firing while others battled hand-to-hand. Battles ended when one side was no longer able to fight.

▼ **INTERPRETATION B** *An eighteenth-century Scottish engraving showing Edward I's first attack on the Scots*

Chivalry played an important part in warfare. Banners were commonly used to identify particular nobles, including the king, and it was widely accepted that nobles should seek out their equals to fight. The disadvantage of easily identifiable leaders was that they became targets. Capturing nobles to use as bargaining tools or to raise a ransom was common. The capture of Henry III at the Battle of Lewes in 1264 placed England under the control of Simon de Montfort.

## Key Words

cavalry    infantry    mercenary    pike    schiltron

### Pike

A 2m-long steel-tipped pole. Perfect for soldiers facing men on horseback. The cavalry could be brought down by large groups of pike-wielding men who stabbed the horses.

### Siege warfare

An important tactic was siege (from the French 'sieger', meaning 'to sit'). Attacking soldiers would camp outside and wait for the castle's food and water to run out whilst stopping anyone from getting in or out of the castle. The occupants would then be forced to surrender or starve. The most effective castles were ones that had ways of coping with a siege.

### The crossbow

Crossbows could fire from 100m and needed less skill to use than longbows. They were very accurate weapons, with more penetrating power but much heavier to use than a longbow.

### Medieval weapons and military tactics

### Mace

Used from around 1300, the hand-held mace was most effective when it could be brought crashing down on opponents.

### Battleaxe

Battleaxes could cut a man in two but required a huge amount of strength and energy and a lot of space to use.

### Schiltron

A defensive tactic that involved up to 2000 men with 3.5m pikes or spears forming huge circles or rectangles. The weapons pointed outwards like a giant lethal hedgehog. When used effectively, as by the Scots, these could be impossible to break through.

### The longbow

Could be fired from up to 200m away, much further than previous bows. Used to rain arrows down on the enemy and to hit individual targets. A skilled archer could fire up to 10 arrows per minute.

### Swords and daggers

For hand-to-hand combat. Used by knights and infantrymen.

## Work

1   a   Why did kings prefer to avoid battles?
    b   What were the advantages of a position at the top of a hill?

2   Explain the role of the heavy cavalry.

3   Choose one of the weapons above. Create an Internet selling page for this weapon. Include as much detail as you can about what makes it so effective. You can include images and customer reviews.

4   Look at **Interpretations A** and **B**.
    a   What features of a medieval battle can you see?
    b   Do you think either interpretation is convincing in how it shows a medieval battle? Explain your answer using both interpretations.

## Extension

GCSE

To understand the key battles of Edward I's reign, it is important to have a strong understanding of medieval warfare. These pages give you the important information but challenge yourself by discovering more. Why not research the tactics and technology or a famous siege, such as that of Stirling Castle?

# Why did Edward go to war in Wales?

Shortly after he became king, Edward launched a full scale attack on Wales. The rebellious Welsh were not only a challenge for Edward but also risked making him look weak, something he needed to avoid at all costs. Why was Edward so concerned with Wales? Why did he put so much effort and money into his conquest? Why did he and Llywelyn ap Gruffudd dislike each other so much?

## Objectives

▶ **Describe** the reasons for conflict in Wales.

▶ **Examine** the different factors.

▶ **Evaluate** the relative importance of the factors and make links between them.

## England and Wales

After William the Conqueror became King of England in 1066 he spent the following few years securing his power in his new kingdom. This included much of Wales. Although Welsh lords (often referred to as princes) were still technically in charge of most of their country, they were answerable to the English king and owed him homage. The king ensured their loyalty through the **Marcher lords**. These were trusted English barons who controlled the buffer zone between England and Wales. This system worked well until, in 1233, one Welsh prince began to gain more power. Llywelyn the Great declared himself Prince of Wales and others recognised him as their overlord, rather than swearing direct homage to the English king. His grandson, Llywelyn ap Gruffudd, went even further in 1265, when he interfered in English politics by supporting Simon de Montfort when he rebelled against King Henry III. Montfort officially recognised Llywelyn ap Gruffudd as Prince of Wales, much to the king's anger. After Montfort was killed in 1267, Henry III signed the Treaty of Montgomery, which again confirmed Llywelyn's title. Llywelyn was recognised as the most senior Welsh prince but was still expected to pay homage to the English king. When Edward became king he was determined to assert his authority over the Welsh.

## Edward and Wales

It soon became clear that war in Wales was coming, and in 1277 Edward launched his first conquest of the country. The political system that had been accepted by Edward's father had worked, however, so how did war come about?

▼ **SOURCE A** *An illustrated manuscript showing Llywelyn the Great, Llywelyn ap Gruffudd's grandfather*

## Key Words

Marcher lord

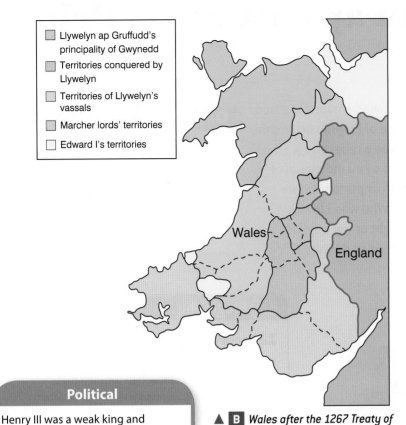

Legend:
- Llywelyn ap Gruffudd's principality of Gwynedd
- Territories conquered by Llywelyn
- Territories of Llywelyn's vassals
- Marcher lords' territories
- Edward I's territories

Wales

England

▲ **B** *Wales after the 1267 Treaty of Montgomery, signed by Henry III and Llywelyn ap Gruffudd*

## Work

1 Who were the Marcher lords and what was their purpose?

2 Explain how Llywelyn the Great changed the established system in Wales.

3 Look at the map of Wales opposite. Why might Edward be concerned by what it shows?

4 Why was Edward angry that Llywelyn ap Gruffudd refused to pay homage?

5 Explain an economic cause of conflict in Wales.

6 Turn the spider diagram into a large Venn diagram to show the links between causes.

7 Why was there conflict in Wales during Edward's reign? Explain your answer in detail and refer to all three factors shown in the spider diagram.

## Political

Henry III was a weak king and had faced numerous rebellions throughout his reign, most notably the Second Barons' War. Edward needed to show that he was strong and would not tolerate opposition from his nobles. Wales presented a particular problem. The Welsh princes remained officially loyal to Edward but the power of the Prince of Wales was dangerous. Could Llywelyn be trusted? He had, after all, supported Montfort against Henry III and was due to marry Montfort's daughter, Eleanor. When Llywelyn refused to pay homage to the new king, Edward saw it as vital that he force him to do so. He could not allow himself to be seen as weak.

## Why was there conflict in Wales?

## Personal

Edward and Llywelyn's rivalry became very personal. Edward could not easily forget Llywelyn's support for Montfort and was reluctant to come to any sort of compromise. It did not help that Llywelyn was going to marry Montfort's daughter. Edward demanded that Llywelyn do homage to him but he refused to make the journey to visit the king. The king responded by allowing two of the prince's enemies, including his brother Dafydd ap Gruffudd, to live in England under his protection. He also captured Llywelyn's fiancée, Eleanor de Montfort. Llywelyn refused to pay homage before his bride was returned, while King Edward refused to free her until Llywelyn did homage. Neither man was willing to show weakness and back down.

## Economic

Edward needed money and the best way to do this was to establish trade. Wales had much to offer in the way of natural resources, most notably wool, the single most important product in medieval England. By securing control of Wales, Edward would gain access to these important resources but the country needed to be at peace for the goods to be successfully transported. He could not afford for rebellious Welshmen to disrupt his trade routes. Edward was also keen for more English people to move into Wales. The more towns that were built, the more taxes could be collected and paid directly to him rather than going to the Welsh princes.

# Llywelyn ap Gruffudd, Prince of Wales

To his followers Llywelyn ap Gruffudd was a hero. He stood up for Wales and its people in the face of English attempts to take over. To Edward I, Llywelyn was a rebel and a traitor. It is certainly true that he was a key individual of the first half of Edward's reign and an important figure in the history of Wales and England. Who was Llywelyn? Why did he choose to take on the might of the English king? What happened to him when he was defeated?

## Objectives

▶ **Describe** the story of Llywelyn ap Gruffudd.

▶ **Recall** the key events of his life.

▶ **Explain** why he was an important figure during Edward's reign.

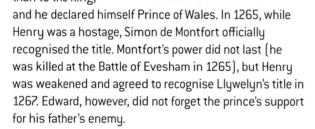

▶ **A** *The statue of Llywelyn ap Gruffudd in Cardiff City Hall, made in 1916; there are very few accounts of what he looked like*

## Llywelyn, Prince of Wales

Llywelyn ap Gruffudd helped to reunite North Wales, which Henry III had worked hard to split, fearing too much power in the hands of one prince. In 1258, the other Welsh princes officially began to pay homage to Llywelyn, rather than to the king, and he declared himself Prince of Wales. In 1265, while Henry was a hostage, Simon de Montfort officially recognised the title. Montfort's power did not last (he was killed at the Battle of Evesham in 1265), but Henry was weakened and agreed to recognise Llywelyn's title in 1267. Edward, however, did not forget the prince's support for his father's enemy.

## The other Welsh prince

Llywelyn wasn't the only member of his family with ambition; his younger brother, Dafydd ap Gruffudd, was equally determined to gain power in Wales and the relationship between the brothers played as big a role in Llywelyn's life as his conflict with King Edward. While his older brother gained power and influence at a young age, Dafydd spent time as a child hostage to Henry III in England as part of a peace agreement between his uncle, then ruler of Gwynedd and Prince of Wales, and the English. When his uncle died, Dafydd's older brothers Llywelyn and Owain inherited the land, leaving the younger man with nothing. Dafydd was ambitious and when the opportunity for power arose he took it. In 1255, he joined Owain in an attack on Llywelyn. It failed and he was arrested. Dafydd was forgiven by Llywelyn, but he later joined King Henry in attacking his brother again in 1263. Llywelyn forgave him once more, but a few years later, in 1274, Dafydd joined King Edward in another attack on his brother! Once peace returned, much of Llywelyn's land was given to Dafydd by the English king.

## Key Biography

### Llywelyn ap Gruffudd (c1233–82)

- He was the grandson of Llywelyn the Great who had first established the idea that the Prince of Gwynedd was senior to other Welsh princes.

- In 1258, other Welsh princes officially began to pay homage to him as their overlord.

- He supported Simon de Montfort in the Second Barons' War.

- He was engaged to marry Eleanor, Montfort's daughter. They finally married several years later.

- He led two unsuccessful rebellions against King Edward.

- He was killed in battle in 1282.

## Llywelyn backs up his little brother

Despite everything that had passed between them, when Dafydd rebelled against the English in 1282 Llywelyn joined in support of his younger brother. Perhaps this was because he saw an opportunity to force the English out of Wales, perhaps out of brotherly loyalty. Llywelyn's death in battle in December 1282 gave Dafydd the title Prince of Wales but his rule was short lived. He was captured, arrested and executed by Edward on 3 October 1283.

▼ **SOURCE B** *A contemporary illustration of the death of Dafydd ap Gruffudd; having been dragged through the streets of Shrewsbury by horse, Dafydd became one of the first prominent figures to be hanged, drawn and quartered*

## The death of Llywelyn

Llywelyn may have avoided the public humiliation and grisly death of his brother but his end was certainly not for the faint-hearted. He was killed in battle on 11 December 1282. Although there are different accounts of exactly how he died, it is believed that having been seriously wounded he revealed his identity and was beheaded by the English troops. Having been shown to the king, his head was sent to London where it was placed on a spike at the Tower of London. It remained there for 15 years.

▼ **INTERPRETATION C** *A description of the fate of Llywelyn's head from* Llywelyn ap Gruffudd: Prince of Wales *by J. Beverley Smith (University of Wales Press, 2014):*

> With an iron spike thrust through it, the severed head was raised on the Tower of London, displayed for the derision of the crowd and adorned with a crown of ivy in mocking fulfilment of a prophecy which said, so the English were led to believe, that one of the Britons would be crowned in London.

▼ **INTERPRETATION D** *The death of Llywelyn from* Cassell's History of England *(c1890)*

▼ **INTERPRETATION E** *From the website castlewales.com by the historian Frank Stephens, first published 24 September 2014:*

> From the outset, Llywelyn seemed almost to go out of his way to court Edward's anger. In particular, he refused to yield the homage and money payments owing to the king under the terms of the Treaty of Montgomery. He tempted fate further by arranging to marry Eleanor, daughter of rebel baron Simon de Montfort, an act destined to strain Edward's patience to the limit.

### Work

1. Who was Llywelyn's grandfather and why was he important?

2. Look at **Image A**. Why do you think there is a statue of Llywelyn in Cardiff City Hall?

3. Look at **Source B** and **Interpretation C**. Why do you think Edward was so brutal in how he dealt with the brothers?

4. a Look at **Interpretation E**. What impression does the historian give of Llywelyn and his attitude towards King Edward?

   b How fair is this interpretation?

5. 'Llywelyn's relationship with his younger brother Dafydd played a key role in his eventual defeat by Edward.' How far do you agree with this statement? Explain your answer.

# How successful were Edward's wars in Wales?

In 1277, Edward launched an attack on Wales. His plan was to force Llywelyn to back down as quickly as possible using his vastly superior forces. Success was never going to be that easy. The terrain was difficult and most of the Welsh were loyal to their prince. Despite his superior army, Edward faced a huge, and expensive, challenge. How successful was Edward's invasion? Why were the Welsh so difficult to put down? And what strategies did Edward develop for dealing with the Welsh?

**Objectives**

▶ **Describe** Edward's Welsh campaigns.

▶ **Explain** the key events.

▶ **Assess** the success of Edward's policies in Wales.

## The first Welsh campaign, 1277

- Llywelyn's centre of power, Gwynedd, was well protected by the terrain. Despite the challenges, Edward was much stronger than the Welsh who were lightly armed. The key difference was in cavalry: the Welsh were outnumbered when it came to knights mounted on horses. Edward imported more than 100 top quality French war horses to increase his advantage further. Realising his weaknesses, Llywelyn chose to use the terrain to his advantage, rather than confront the English in open battle.

- Before his invasion, Edward sent his Marcher lords to secure the area around Gwynedd.

- On 1 July 1277, Edward began his march towards the enemy. Perhaps realising what he was facing, Llywelyn finally offered to negotiate but was turned down.

- By 29 August, Edward had reached the Conwy River. Rather than attack directly, he sent a force of 2000 to attack the island of Anglesey by ship. The men took control of the island and destroyed the crops. Surrounded, and facing starvation without Anglesey's crops, Llywelyn surrendered on 1 November.

- In the Treaty of Aberconwy Llywelyn lost his title as Prince of Wales (instead becoming Prince of Gwynedd) and his brother Dafydd was awarded much of his land.

## The second Welsh campaign, 1282–83

Edward may have won but he handled his victory badly. The English nobles' treatment of the Welsh princes who had supported him was poor and there was a second rebellion, this time led by Dafydd. On 21 March 1282, Dafydd took control of key locations and, after careful consideration and in the belief that his brother stood a chance of victory, Llywelyn joined the rebellion. Determined to deal with the Welsh problem once and for all, Edward set out to conquer Wales and crush the rebels.

Llywelyn acted quickly, attacking the castle of Builth, a valuable link between the English forces in the north

▼ **A** *A ring of stone: Edward's castles in Wales*

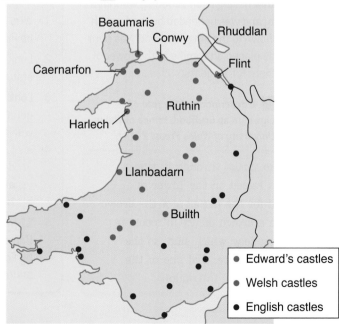

Legend:
- ● Edward's castles
- ● Welsh castles
- ● English castles

and those in the south, eventually taking control of a bridge on the River Irfon. In August, an English force led by John Gifford found another river crossing. They were able to surprise the disorganised Welsh and totally destroy them. They had been leaderless: Llywelyn had been killed before the battle by one of the Marcher lords. His head was sent to Edward who had it placed on a spike at the Tower of London.

By June 1283, Edward's troops had destroyed the Welsh defences and captured Dafydd, who was hanged, drawn and quartered. Edward had conquered Wales and shown that he would not tolerate opposition.

▼ **INTERPRETATION B** *A painting of Conwy Castle; notice the location of the castle next to the river (to allow easy access) and the bastide*

## A permanent solution

Edward was aware that the Welsh threat had not disappeared completely and money was running out. He needed to find a cheaper, longer term solution. In 1284, the **Statute of Rhuddlan** established that Wales was subject to English laws and under the control of the English king. Edward divided the country between himself and loyal lords (answerable to him as overlord). He then began a huge building programme in which he created new towns and encouraged English people to move there. Welsh peasants were forced to leave particular areas and were banned from entering the English settlements at night.

Edward was well aware that the cheapest way to control an area was through castles. Under the supervision of his master builder, James St George, a ring of imposing castles was built around Snowdonia, Llywelyn's old heartland in North Wales. The castles were designed to be intimidating individually as well as creating a ring of stone. Many of the castles included a bastide, or walled town, which was filled with English settlers. These castles required very few soldiers but were strategically placed to allow easy access by the English. Their presence reminded local residents who was in charge.

## Key Words

Statute of Rhuddlan

## Work

1   Explain one advantage Edward had over Llywelyn and one that Llywelyn had over Edward.

2   In pairs create a news report on Edward's first Welsh campaign. Explain what happened and who was involved.

3   What was the Statute of Rhuddlan and why was it important?

4   What was Edward's strategy when it came to building castles? Refer to the map in your answer.

5   Look at **Interpretation A**. What makes Conwy an effective castle?

6   How successful were Edward's policies towards Wales?

### Practice Question

Write an account of Edward's wars to defeat the Welsh rebels.     **8 marks**

### Study Tip

Remember to include castle building in your answer as well as the military campaigns.

# 7.4 Historic Environment: Medieval castles

Edward's castles in Wales were designed with two things in mind: to intimidate and control. The castles, which made up a ring of stone around the rebellious Snowdonia, were some of the most defendable and effective ever built and relied on two centuries of castle building expertise. What made Edward's castles so effective? What was new about their design? What were their key features?

## Objectives

▶ **Describe** the features of medieval castles.

▶ **Explain** what made a castle effective.

▶ **Relate** your knowledge to a specific site: Caernarfon Castle.

## Early castles

The first castles, as we might think of them today, were built by William I as part of his plan to secure control of England after his invasion. They were to create a stronghold for those loyal to the new king that could be easily defended and would remind the English who was now in charge. Early castles were simple, wooden structures, although soon replaced by stone, and each new method of attack was met with a change in design. Edward's Welsh castles were the most secure that had ever been built.

## What made an effective medieval castle?

The most important decision was location. A good castle builder would use the landscape to his advantage: building next to a river or on the coast allowed food and supplies to be delivered by water even if the castle was under attack or under **siege**. It also allowed for reinforcements to be brought or for the important residents to escape if the castle was going to be lost. Medieval ships were not strong enough to attack a castle, so the water also made one side of the castle safe. The castle would be built from strong stone and many were surrounded by a **curtain wall** or a moat, which offered protection. The number of entrances was limited and would often include a **barbican**, or gatehouse, and a drawbridge. This would be extremely well defended, with features like the **portcullis** and small slots known as murder holes in the ceiling through which to pour boiling oil onto attackers! Round towers replaced earlier square ones making them harder to climb or undermine (when attackers dug under the castle to force it to collapse).

Edward's Welsh castles were almost all **concentric**, a circular design inspired by Middle Eastern castles seen in the Crusades. They featured rings of stone walls of different heights, which enabled defenders to fire over the heads of others and created several barriers to attackers. The living area was at the centre, where the baron and his family lived or where the king stayed when visiting.

## Caernarfon Castle

Caernarfon Castle formed part of Edward's ring of stone that encircled the former lands of Llywelyn ap Gruffudd (see map on page 127). It was designed by the master builder James St George to dominate the landscape and to act as the main English seat of power in conquered Wales. The Statute of Rhuddlan made it the capital of Gwynedd and Edward visited the castle at least twice. His first son, also called Edward, was born there in 1284 and given the title Prince of Wales (the monarch's eldest son still holds this title today). Due to its importance, the castle was always defended by at least 30 men, even in peacetime.

Building began in around May 1283 and the site was chosen because it was in the heartland of anti-English feeling but was also a good castle location (it was not the first to be built on the site). All materials were brought by sea to avoid clashes with the local inhabitants. Just two years later, a working castle was established, but in 1294, a group of Welsh rebels got inside and burned much of the castle. When the English regained control they made it even more secure by building a great northern wall and the strong King's Gate under the new master builder, Walter of Hereford.

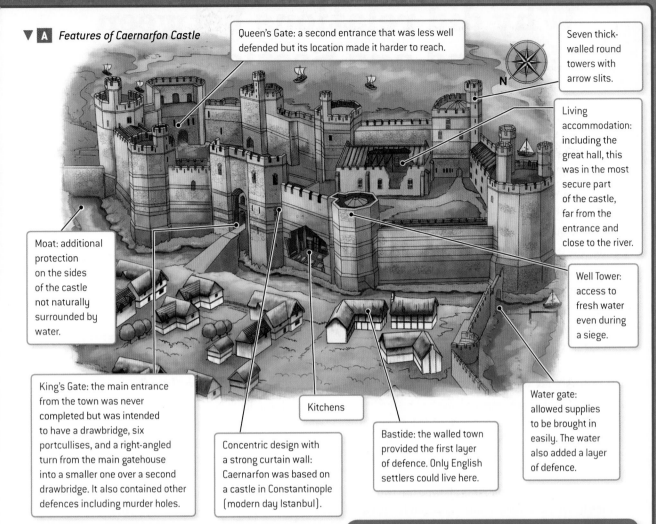

▼ **A** *Features of Caernarfon Castle*

**Queen's Gate:** a second entrance that was less well defended but its location made it harder to reach.

Seven thick-walled round towers with arrow slits.

**Living accommodation:** including the great hall, this was in the most secure part of the castle, far from the entrance and close to the river.

**Moat:** additional protection on the sides of the castle not naturally surrounded by water.

**Well Tower:** access to fresh water even during a siege.

**King's Gate:** the main entrance from the town was never completed but was intended to have a drawbridge, six portcullises, and a right-angled turn from the main gatehouse into a smaller one over a second drawbridge. It also contained other defences including murder holes.

Kitchens

**Concentric design with a strong curtain wall:** Caernarfon was based on a castle in Constantinople (modern day Istanbul).

**Bastide:** the walled town provided the first layer of defence. Only English settlers could live here.

**Water gate:** allowed supplies to be brought in easily. The water also added a layer of defence.

▼ **B** *A view inside the castle as it looks today; none of the internal buildings have survived*

## Key Words

siege    curtain wall    barbican
portcullis    concentric

## Work

1   Explain three defensive features common in medieval castles.

2   Why was it useful for a castle to be built near water?

3   Why was Caernarfon considered to be an important castle?

## Study Tip

Edward I located his castles carefully. What advantages did the location give? The design of Edward's Welsh castles was the most up-to-date for the time. Which features would have given the castle its formidable strength and deterred attackers? A castle like Caernarfon, and others that Edward built in Wales, had a bastide. What was its function and what does it tell us about Edward's aims in Wales?

# 8.1 Why did relations between England and Scotland get so bad?

England and Scotland were separate countries with their own royal families. As neighbours sharing the same island it was understandable that the two countries would become involved in each other's affairs and that there would be questions over whose monarch was the more senior in the feudal system. What was the relationship between the countries when Edward became king? Why did Edward become so heavily involved in Scottish politics? And why did war eventually break out between the two nations?

**Objectives**

▶ **Explore** the reasons for England and Scotland's poor relations from the 1290s.

▶ **Explain** why the countries ended up at war.

▶ **Evaluate** the long term consequences of the events of 1296.

## The problem of authority

Edward believed that he was owed homage by the King of Scotland but he was not keen to cause conflict. Scotland's King Alexander III did not want war either and so a compromise was reached. Alexander would pay homage to Edward for the lands he owned on the English side of the border. This allowed the two countries to live peacefully. Problems began to appear in the 1280s, however, when Alexander and all of his children died. Edward would become increasingly involved in Scottish politics from this point.

▼ **INTERPRETATION A** *King John Balliol pays homage to Edward in a late fourteenth-century French illustration*

## Edward and Scotland

When Alexander III died in 1286, the heir to the throne was his three-year-old granddaughter, Margaret. It was agreed at the Treaty of Birgham that she would become engaged to Edward's one-year-old son. This would guarantee peace between the two countries. Margaret was the daughter of the King of Norway and had to make the long voyage to Scotland, which she did in 1290. Unfortunately, she became ill and died on her journey, which left Scotland without an obvious heir. This crisis became known as the Great Cause.

## Edward's arbitration

There were many claims to the Scottish throne but just two real contenders: John Balliol and Robert de Brus. Both men were powerful lords and had wide support across the country. The Scottish **magnates** (the most powerful nobles) wanted the matter settled without a civil war and turned to King Edward to **arbitrate** (help end the disagreement). After much discussion, John Balliol was declared the rightful heir on 17 November 1292 and crowned king.

Edward continued to involve himself in Scottish affairs and tried to show his authority in the country. He heard and settled disagreements between Scottish magnates and at one point even demanded that King John appear before the English Parliament. When Edward called for Scottish magnates to send men to fight in his war against France, John felt that Edward had become too involved in Scotland's business. John declared support for France.

## War!

Edward was keen to teach the Scots a lesson. On 30 March he led his troops to Berwick-upon-Tweed, a key Scottish trading town, and captured it, killing thousands. Edward remained in Berwick for a month before launching the next stage of his invasion: the capture of the Earl of March's castle at Dunbar 30 miles further north. Although March himself supported the English, his wife had let Scottish soldiers occupy the castle. Edward sent an army with the Earl of Surrey, an English nobleman and King John's father-in-law, to attack the castle. The Scots at Dunbar sent a message to John and he sent a large part of his army to help them. The scene was set for battle.

▲ **C** *Locations of some of Edward's battles in Scotland*

## Key Words

magnate    arbitrate

## The Battle of Dunbar, 27 April 1296

Accounts suggest that the battle was fought between cavalry and that there were relatively few casualties compared with later battles. The Scots arrived first and positioned themselves at the top of a hill. Their advantage was short-lived, however, as they misinterpreted the English movements, believing that they were retreating. In their excitement the Scots charged downhill and were met by a strong English force. The battle was over quickly and a number of important Scottish lords were taken prisoner.

After the battle, the English swiftly took control of the rest of Scotland. John was captured and officially stripped of his kingship. Having destroyed the Scots, Edward returned to England, taking with him the Stone of Scone, an important symbol of the Scottish nation. For the Scottish, the humiliation made them determined to seek revenge.

## Fact

### The Stone of Scone

This ancient rectangular stone block, also known as the Stone of Destiny, was where Scottish kings sat to be crowned. When Edward took it to London, it was built into a special throne for the coronation of English monarchs. In 1996, it was returned to Scotland, but it will return to London whenever a new British monarch is crowned.

## Work

1  What was the Great Cause?
2  Explain Edward's role in settling the dispute.
3  Explain why Edward invaded Scotland in 1296.
4  How important was the lack of discipline among the Scots in their loss at the Battle of Dunbar?
5  a   Why do you think Edward brought the Stone of Scone back to England?
   b  What might be the long term consequences of Edward's actions in 1296?

## Extension

Some might argue that Edward's actions in Scotland were directly affected by his experiences in Wales. Challenge yourself by answering the following question: 'How far did Edward's experiences with Llywelyn ap Gruffudd in Wales affect his approach to Alexander III and John Balliol in Scotland?' Use Chapter 6 to help you.

# 8.2A Historic Environment: The Battle of Stirling Bridge

Medieval battles were extremely unpredictable. Defeat or victory could often come down to a single factor or decision. Having the most men or the best equipment was no guarantee of success, and while tactics played an important role so did the terrain and the weather. One of the most famous battles ever fought between the English and the Scots was the Battle of Stirling Bridge on 11 September 1297. Despite being just a few months after the English had humiliatingly defeated the Scottish, it was the Scots who left the field victorious. What happened in the Battle of Stirling Bridge, and what made medieval battles so unpredictable?

## Objectives

▶ **State** the events and outcome of the Battle of Stirling Bridge.

▶ **Describe** what made medieval battles unpredictable.

▶ **Assess** how far the Battle of Stirling Bridge reflects this.

## The build-up to battle

After the clear English victory at the Battle of Dunbar and the capture of the Stone of Scone it seemed that Edward had established his power over Scotland once and for all. He had, however, miscalculated the Scottish determination to control their own country and the fact that they could not accept the lack of respect he had shown them. With other problems to deal with in France, Wales and in England itself, Edward took his eyes off Scotland. This was a mistake.

By August 1297, two Scottish leaders, William Wallace and Andrew Moray, had taken control of almost all of the country north of the River Forth. Only the town of Dundee remained in English hands. Although they were initially rivals, the two men had joined forces and were ready to take on the might of the English. With the aim of reaching Dundee, which was under siege, the Earl of Surrey and his men marched north. They reached the town of Stirling, on the edge of the area under Scottish control. Here they planned to cross the River Forth.

▲ **A** Key location in the build-up to the battle

## The battle

The only place where it was safe to cross the river was a small wooden bridge, only wide enough to allow two mounted soldiers to cross at a time.
Wallace, Moray and their army watched from a nearby hill as the English set up camp.

The Scots were outnumbered, particularly when it came to cavalry, and it seemed like it would be another English victory.
The English were arrogantly confident of success and had a low regard for the Scottish troops based on their recent experience at Dunbar.

The English commander, the Earl of Surrey, ordered his men to cross the bridge the following morning, which they began to do at first light. Unfortunately, Surrey had overslept! When he finally arrived at the battlefield he recalled his men.

After giving the Scots the chance to surrender, Surrey ordered his cavalry to begin crossing the river again and to wait in the bend in the river on the other side.

The Scots just watched before taking action at the right moment. They charged down the hill and blocked the English cavalry's escape back across the bridge, and trapped those who had crossed into a small area in the bend of the river. They attacked the trapped men, cutting many of them down and forcing others into the deep water where many drowned. Some managed to escape by swimming despite their armour.

The battle only lasted an hour but with devastating English losses: 100 knights and 5000 men. The horses were useless in such a tight space. To try to limit the damage and protect his remaining men, Surrey destroyed the bridge. The defeat was crushing and humiliating.

## What made medieval battles unpredictable?

Medieval battles were unpredictable affairs and most kings and other leaders tended to avoid them if they could.

- Leadership and strategy – Armies were always led by nobles who planned the strategy; an effective commander who instilled discipline on his men and had the right strategy could make a significant difference. At the Battle of Stirling Bridge, the late arrival on the battlefield of the English commander, the Earl of Surrey, and his confused orders about crossing the bridge stood in contrast to the clear strategy followed by the Scottish leaders, William Wallace and Andrew Moray. Leadership and strategy were just two factors, however, and other factors were less easily controlled.

- Terrain – It was usually better to be on higher ground as this gave you a good view of the battlefield and it was much more difficult to fight uphill. Geographical features like rivers could also be used to one side's advantage: they would have to be crossed before any fighting could take place. At Stirling Bridge, the Scots had the higher ground and the English had to cross the River Forth using the narrow bridge there.

- Communication – For large armies, communication was difficult. Once an order was given, a messenger had to deliver it to the men. This took time and could lead to delays, as was the case at Stirling Bridge leading to confusion about when to cross the bridge.

### Work

1. Why had the situation in Scotland reached crisis point in August 1297?

2. Explain two factors that could make medieval battles unpredictable.

3. Why do you think the English lost the Battle of Stirling? Explain your answer.

# Historic Environment: The Battle of Stirling Bridge

▼ **INTERPRETATION A** *From an article written by the historian Ewan J. Innes in 1989. Published on Scottishhistory.com:*

The tactical positioning had obviously been worked out well beforehand and the planning of the battle had, it would seem, taken up a large part of the Scots' time. The timing of the rush down the causeway was crucial to the success of the Scots as, had too many English troops been allowed to cross, the final outcome could have been drastically different. It should also be pointed out that the troops who had beaten this large semi-professional English army – a balanced force of cavalry, archers and heavy foot [infantry] – were the landless peasants and not the great Scottish lords.

## The aftermath of the battle

The Scottish had shown they were a force to be reckoned with. The English had been better equipped and had many more men but it was the Scots who won. The only consolation for the English was that Andrew Moray was fatally wounded. Any satisfaction that this brought was short-lived, however, as Wallace quickly emerged as the leader of the Scottish people. He was declared **Guardian of Scotland** and became a symbol in the struggle against the English.

> **Fact**
>
> At the Battle of Stirling Bridge, the English army had between 200 to 300 cavalry and 10,000 infantry. The Scottish had 36 cavalry and 8000 infantry.

## The Scottish victory at Stirling Bridge: More luck than judgement?

▼ **B** *The Battle of Stirling Bridge*

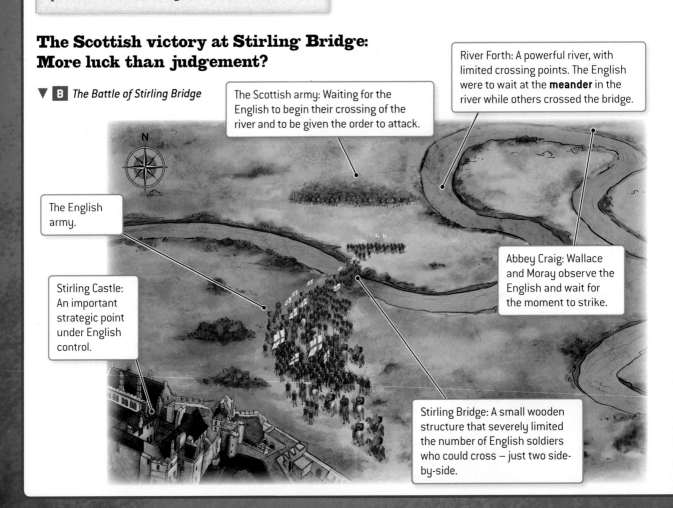

The Scottish army: Waiting for the English to begin their crossing of the river and to be given the order to attack.

River Forth: A powerful river, with limited crossing points. The English were to wait at the **meander** in the river while others crossed the bridge.

The English army.

Stirling Castle: An important strategic point under English control.

Abbey Craig: Wallace and Moray observe the English and wait for the moment to strike.

Stirling Bridge: A small wooden structure that severely limited the number of English soldiers who could cross – just two side-by-side.

## Why did the Scots win the Battle of Stirling Bridge?

| Scottish tactics | English mistakes |
|---|---|
| • The Scots arrived first. They predicted where the English would attempt to cross the River Forth. | • The Earl of Surrey overslept while his men began crossing the river and then called them back when he arrived on the battlefield. This gave the Scots time to formulate their plan. |
| • They positioned themselves on top of a hill, which allowed them to view all of the English movements. | • By slowly moving his cavalry across the bridge, Surrey was placing them in a trap on the bend in the river. It was much easier for the Scots simply to cut them down. |
| • They timed their attack perfectly, waiting for the cavalry to cross the bridge. If they had attacked too early, most of the English would still have been safe on the other side and could have regrouped. | • The difficult, marshy ground made it impossible for the English cavalry to move effectively. They were therefore at a disadvantage to the Scottish infantry. |
| • When they attacked, the Scots blocked the bridge. There was no escape for the English and no reinforcements could come. | • Destroying the bridge stopped the Scottish from crossing but also removed any hope of English victory. Surrey panicked and gave up. |
| • They successfully removed the two major advantages of the English: their superior numbers and the cavalry. There was not enough room for the horses to be useful. | |

▼ **C** *An aerial photograph of the battle site today; the original bridge was a much weaker structure*

### Work

1  Copy and complete this table:

| Features of the battlefield | Impact on the battle |
|---|---|
| River Forth | |
| The bend in the river | |
| The small bridge | |
| The higher ground on the Scottish side | |

2  Imagine you were the Earl of Surrey. What would you have done differently? Do you think victory was possible for the English?

3  Look at **Interpretation A**.
   a  What reasons does Innes making for the Scottish victory?
   b  How far do you agree with his assessment?

### Study Tip

What decided the outcome of Medieval battles at this time? Did a combination of factors lead to the English defeat at Stirling Bridge? You should consider the terrain over which the battle was fought. Who had the advantage? What were their plans? Did William Wallace show better leadership? Think about the decisions made at different points in the battle. Were the mistakes of the Earl of Surrey decisive? How did the troops on each side compare? Were they equally matched? Lastly, think about the element of luck. Was the battle decided by something neither side could have predicted or prevented?

### Key Words

Guardian of Scotland
meander

# The Battle of Falkirk

Defeat at the Battle of Stirling Bridge had humiliated the English, and in August 1298, Edward himself marched north ready to take on William Wallace and his men. The two armies clashed in the Battle of Falkirk. Once again, it was a bloodbath. What problems did Edward face as he marched north to fight Wallace? What exactly happened at the battle? And what were the consequences for both the winners and the losers?

### Objectives

▶ **State** the events of the Battle of Falkirk.

▶ **Explore** the reasons for the English victory.

▶ **Assess** what Falkirk tells us about medieval battles.

## Edward takes control

Edward had been fighting against the French in Flanders when Surrey's men were defeated at the Battle of Stirling Bridge. Once he was able to return to England in March 1298, he immediately began preparations to invade Scotland. He moved his government to York and held a council of war there to plan the attack. He called for the Scottish magnates to show their loyalty by attending the council but none came and he declared that they were all traitors. He formed a formidable army that included a cavalry of 2000, an infantry of 12,000 and thousands of other volunteers, including a large group of Welshmen. They began the march into Scotland on 25 June.

### Fact

#### Kingston-upon-Hull

Edward had seen the need to have supply towns for expeditions to Scotland, and in 1293 he had bought a settlement from an abbey and established a town he called 'King's town upon Hull' on the Yorkshire coast. From its harbour he would be able to supply his army by boat as it ventured north.

▲ **A** *Key locations in the build-up to the Battle of Falkirk*

## Wallace's strategy

Wallace knew that his army would be no match for the mighty English force and so he adopted a clever strategy. His army retreated, destroying all supplies as they went. This left Edward's men with little food. Wallace hoped that the English would become so weakened they would be forced to retreat, at which point the Scots would attack as they marched home.

The strategy seemed to be working. By the time Edward's forces were close to Edinburgh, morale was very low. A group of Welshmen became involved in a drunken riot that had to be broken up by the cavalry. As many as 80 Welshmen were killed. Retreat seemed inevitable. While Edward was considering returning to England he heard that Wallace was only 13 miles away, in Callendar Woods, near Falkirk. Edward ordered his army to meet the Scots on 22 July.

## The battle

As the English approached, the Scottish army got into its most successful defensive position by forming four giant schiltrons. This was a special battle formation where hundreds of men carrying long spears or pikes formed huge circles or rectangles, with their weapons pointing outwards. A schiltron was almost impossible to attack, as Edward's cavalry soon discovered when his men and horses were impaled on the pikes. As the English cavalry attacked, the Scottish horsemen seemed to panic and rode away from the battlefield. The Scottish archers stayed but were cut to pieces by the English. Only the schiltrons remained, but Edward's men simply couldn't get past them.

Edward called his men back and prepared a new type of attack. He ordered his longbowmen, a new English weapon, to focus their fire on the schiltrons. It worked.

While it had been impossible for the cavalry to get through, the schiltrons were helpless against the rain of arrows coming from above. Once enough damage had been done, and men in the schiltron began to die, the English cavalry charged again and killed the remaining Scots. Wallace and a few others managed to escape but the Scottish army had been totally destroyed.

▼ **INTERPRETATION B** *The Bishop of Durham, one of the commanders of the English cavalry, charges at the Scottish defences; from* Cassell's Historical Scrapbook *(c1880)*

▼ **INTERPRETATION C** *A twentieth-century illustration of Edward fighting the Scots*

## The aftermath

Although it would take a number of years to finally put down rebellions in Scotland, the Battle of Falkirk had done irreparable damage to Scotland's forces. William Wallace resigned as Guardian of Scotland and his successors were never able to come close to his achievements. Wallace continued to work for the Scottish cause for a number of years before his arrest and brutal execution on King Edward's orders in 1305. Edward continued to make his presence felt in Scotland and dealt swiftly and brutally with uprisings, gaining the nickname the 'Hammer of the Scots'. When Edward died in 1307, Scotland was once again on the rise under the leadership of Robert the Bruce.

### Work

1  Explain Wallace's strategy for defeating the English as they marched into Scotland.
2  a  Look at **Interpretation B**. How accurately do you think this picture shows what happened at the Battle of Falkirk?
   b  Do you think **Interpretation C** is more accurate? Explain your answer using your knowledge of the battle.
3  Create a storyboard that tells the story of the battle.
4  'Without the longbow, England would not have won the battle.' How far do you agree? Explain your answer.
5  Does the Battle of Falkirk challenge or support the idea that medieval battles were more about luck than judgement?

### Extension

Edward's conquest of Scotland led to the creation of new towns in the north of England to help supply his army and secure the area from Scottish raids. Challenge yourself by researching the towns that Edward created – Hull is mentioned opposite. Use pages 96–97 to remind you of the features of medieval towns.

# Was William Wallace a hero or a traitor?

For thirteenth-century Scots, William Wallace was not just a heroic military leader but also a symbol of their struggle to be independent from England. For Edward I and his supporters, Wallace was a rebel and a traitor who challenged Edward's right to be the overlord of Scotland. Who was William Wallace? Why was he such an important figure? Was he a hero or a traitor?

## Objectives

▶ **Explore** the life and career of William Wallace.

▶ **Compare and contrast** different opinions about him.

▶ **Explain** why different opinions about him exist.

## From unknown to Guardian of Scotland

Very little is known about William Wallace's background. It is thought he came from a lesser noble family and some historians believe that he must have had some military experience as a young man in order to have been such an effective commander. There are some suggestions that he fought for Edward in Wales as a mercenary. What is not in doubt is that he was a key figure in the First Scottish War of Independence.

His first known involvement was the assassination of an English official, William de Heselrig, in May 1297. He went on to fight in the rebellion in Scone before joining forces with another rebel, Andrew Moray, at Stirling Bridge. After an unexpected victory, Wallace became Guardian of Scotland, the leader of the Scottish army and Protector of the Scottish people.

## Fall from power

Defeat at the Battle of Falkirk in 1298 damaged Wallace's reputation and he soon resigned as Guardian of Scotland. He continued to work hard for the Scottish cause but was betrayed by some of the nobles and his previous supporters. He was handed over by them to the English on 5 August 1305. He was taken to London and put on trial for treason and war crimes against civilians. Refusing to accept that the court had any power over him, he said that he was not a subject of King Edward and so could not have committed treason.

Having been found guilty, Wallace was dragged naked through the streets of London by horse, before being hanged, drawn and quartered. His head was displayed on a spike on London Bridge while his body parts were sent to Newcastle in the north of England, and Berwick, Stirling and Perth in Scotland.

## Hero or traitor?

Very little is known about Wallace other than his two major battles and his arrest and execution. This means that his life has been open to wide interpretation.

▼ **INTERPRETATION A** *A twentieth-century illustration of William Wallace at Stirling Bridge from a children's history magazine*

▼ **INTERPRETATION B** *A nineteenth-century illustration of Wallace protecting priests, taken from a book about the history of England*

▼ **INTERPRETATION C** *From the website of the National Wallace Monument, a tower built on the site of the Battle of Stirling Bridge to commemorate Wallace:*

Over 700 years ago tyranny and terror were the tools being used by England to rule Scotland. Occupied and oppressed, the Scottish nation sought a hero to challenge the cruelty of King Edward I. Someone to take the campaign for freedom into battle, and on to victory. When the two countries faced each other at the Battle of Stirling Bridge in 1297, Scotland was led to victory by a figure destined to become a national hero – William Wallace. Sir William Wallace, a hero of Scotland and a true patriot, had a burning desire for peace and freedom which united the country's clans, gained the loyalty of its people, struck fear into his enemies and defied the cruel hand of an evil, warring and invading King – Edward I of England.

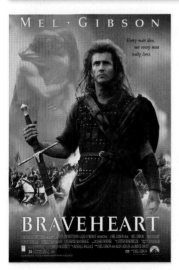

MEL · GIBSON

*Every man dies, not every man really lives.*

BRAVEHEART

◄ **INTERPRETATION D** *A poster for the 1995 film* Braveheart *about William Wallace*

▼ **INTERPRETATION E** *An extract from the novel* Rebel: The Bravehearts Chronicles *by Jack Whyte (Sphere, 2012):*

By the living God, he had terrified enough within his lifetime for his name to live on, in Scotland at least, long after his death, a grim reminder of the punishment for disloyalty, treachery and disobedience. William Wallace's time had passed and he had fallen from grace in the eyes of the people he had led and inspired just a few years earlier. He had become an embarrassment; a source of discomfort to all of them.

## Work

1 Why do you think Edward had Wallace executed in the way that he did? Why did he send parts of his body to other towns?

2 In your own words, describe how Wallace is portrayed in **Interpretations A** and **B**.

3 a **Interpretation D** shows the film from which most people know the story of William Wallace. Based on the poster, how do you think Wallace is portrayed in the film?

  b **Interpretation E** is also a modern retelling of the story. Do you think this interpretation appears to be more or less accurate than the film? Explain your answer.

4 Hold a debate in your lesson about whether William Wallace should be considered a hero or a traitor.

5 Why do you think there are different interpretations of Wallace? Explain your answer.

### Practice Question

How convincing is **Interpretation C** about the life and career of William Wallace?

Explain your answer using **Interpretation C** and your contextual knowledge.  **8 marks**

### Study Tip

Include your wider knowledge about Wallace and your study of the Battles of Stirling Bridge and Falkirk.

# 8.5 The death of the king

When King Edward I died in 1307 he left a clear **legacy**. For some he was a brave warrior-king who earned back the respect that his father had lost; for others he was the great reformer, the man who had completely reorganised England's legal and economic systems. However, for the Welsh and the Scots, Edward was a brutal tyrant who was unwilling to accept any challenge to his authority. What happened in the final weeks and days of Edward's life? What were his final wishes? And how should he be remembered?

## The last days of Edward Longshanks

Edward spent his final months dealing with a new threat in Scotland: Robert the Bruce. On 10 February 1306, Bruce had murdered his main rival and crowned himself King of Scotland. Edward, too ill to fight, sent his son (the future Edward II) north. The English recaptured territory, forced Bruce into hiding and dealt with his allies harshly. Bruce's sister was locked in a cage hanging over Roxburgh Castle for four years while his brother was hanged, drawn and quartered. The brutality backfired and support for Bruce grew.

This would be a problem that Edward's son would have to face. Edward I died on 7 July 1307, probably of dysentery, while attempting to march to Scotland. He was buried in Westminster Abbey on 27 October.

▼ **A** *Edward's tomb at Westminster Abbey with the inscription 'Here is Edward I, Hammer of the Scots, 1308. Keep the vow' in Latin; some historians believe this was not added until the 1600s*

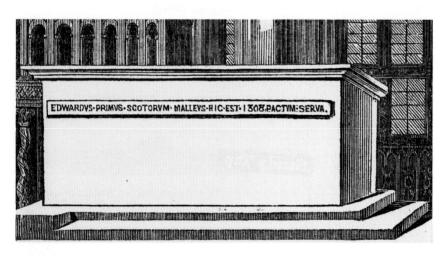

## Edward's final wishes

There are various stories about Edward's wishes. One story is that he asked for his heart to accompany a new Crusade to the Holy Land, while another says he wanted his bones to be carried by any English army that fought the Scots. A more likely story tells how he gathered senior nobles around him as he lay dying to ask them to look after his 23-year-old son, whom he felt was immature and reckless. We will never know the truth!

## Edward's legacy: England

In the centuries that followed, Edward's reputation as a great warrior grew. Stories of the crimes of William Wallace and others and Edward's skills as a leader became well established. In the seventeenth century, historians began to focus on Edward's other accomplishments like his changes to land and criminal law as well as the Model Parliament. He was given the nickname the 'English Justinian' after the ancient Byzantine emperor famous for his changes to Roman laws. Although modern historians recognise that Edward made mistakes, it is widely accepted that he was a successful medieval monarch and a significant figure in English history.

**Fact**

Edward's tomb was opened in 1774 by the Society of Antiquaries. They found his body well preserved and took the opportunity to find out his height. He was 1.88m (around 6 feet 2 inches), which was very tall for his time and certainly deserving the nickname 'Longshanks'.

▼ **INTERPRETATION B** *From the introduction of an article on Edward by Eric Niderost, first published in the American magazine* Military History *in December 1995:*

> A case can be made that Edward I was the greatest English king of the Middle Ages. A strong ruler, he was a man blessed with a strong sense of duty. Although he was no democrat, he believed the king should promote the general welfare and place himself above class or faction – a revolutionary concept in the 13th century. Although he has been called 'the English Justinian' because of his legal codes, Edward was first and foremost a military man, one of the great generals of the medieval world.

▼ **INTERPRETATION C** *An illustration from a twentieth-century children's history magazine showing Edward removing the Stone of Scone, an important symbol of the Scottish nation*

## Edward's legacy: Scotland and Wales

Scottish and Welsh popular history paints Edward in a different light. In Wales, Llywelyn ap Gruffudd is recognised as a national hero with monuments commemorating him as the last true Prince of Wales. Edward has been portrayed as the English conqueror who ended Welsh independence. In Scotland the view of Edward is even more negative. He has been portrayed as a war criminal and a tyrant who treated the Scottish with brutality in order to increase his own power – the 'Hammer of the Scots'.

# How to... analyse interpretations

▼ **INTERPRETATION A** *From the website of the National Wallace Monument, a tower built on the site of the Battle of Stirling Bridge to commemorate Wallace.*

Over 700 years ago tyranny and terror were the tools being used by England to rule Scotland. Occupied and oppressed, the Scottish nation sought a hero to challenge the cruelty of King Edward I. Sir William Wallace: A hero of Scotland and a true patriot, had a burning desire for peace and freedom which united the country's clans, gained the loyalty of its people, struck fear into his enemies and defied the cruel hand of an evil, warring and invading king – Edward I of England.

## Practice Question

How convincing is **Interpretation A** about William Wallace? Explain your answer using **Interpretation A** and your contextual knowledge.   **16 marks**

## Study Tip

What do you know about the event? How far do you agree with this interpretation?

## Over to you

This type of question wants you to decide how **convincing** an interpretation is. In other words, how far does the interpretation fit with what you know about the history of the event, person or issue?

1. You could usefully begin by showing that you understand the main points of the interpretation by summarising the interpretation *in your own words*. For example, you could consider what impression it gives of Wallace and of Edward's campaign in Wales.

2. You may not be totally convinced by the interpretation: this means you may not believe that the interpretation is completely correct or you may not agree that the interpretation is the best way to understand the events. Can you suggest a different interpretations or different ways the issue can be seen? For example, can you think of an argument that suggests Wallace was wrong?

3. Finally, do you agree with the interpretation? In other words, did you find the interpretation convincing? (Even if you agree with the interpretation that Wallace was a hero, you could still try to describe the alternative point of view.) Try to write a few concluding sentences in which you make a judgement about how persuasive or accurate the interpretation is compared to any alternative interpretation.

4. What are the strengths and weaknesses of the following essay introduction to the question?

In Interpretation A, the writer states that Wallace was a 'hero of Scotland' who brought the people of Scotland together. It is true that Wallace was able to unite the different factions that existed and became the unopposed leader of the Scottish rebellion. King Edward certainly saw him as key figure as is clear from his eventual brutal execution. Many accounts of Wallace suggest that he took a brutal approach to his enemies, ordering that Hugh de Cressingham be flayed alive. His actions before the Battle of Falkirk suggest that he was more than happy to avoid battle where possible and the fact that he lost power so quickly after one defeat brings into question how far he had truly gained the loyalty of his people. Overall, I think that the interpretation is not convincing as it ignores the more brutal and questionable actions of Wallace's career.

Now try to answer the question yourself!

# How to... tackle the Historic Environment question

**Over to you**

Before your exam, you will have learned a lot about a specific historic site or building. This type of question asks you how your knowledge of a particular site helps you understand a key feature of the Medieval period. In other words, what can a study of the **historic environment** tell you about people or events at the time? The environment may have influenced the outcome of the battle or conflict, so you could consider:

1 *Motivation*: Why was the battle fought?

2 *Location*: Why was it fought in that particular place? What are the main landscape features?

3 What happened at the battle? Why was the battle fought in the way that it was? What were the battle plans and how were forces deployed? How did the battle develop, and what were the key moments?

4 Who fought in the battle?

5 Questions 1 to 4 will be helpful for battle sites, but if you are studying a building, such as Stokesay Castle, you could consider different questions such as:

   a *Motivation*: Why did someone want to build this specific building?

   b *Location*: Why did they build it in that particular location?

   c *Function*: Why was it built in that particular way? Consider the shape and design of the building or its layout. People design buildings to work and look in particular ways. Firstly, buildings have to function in a particular way, for example for safety, defence, comfort, or pleasure. Can you identify and explain specific building features, and the job they do?

   d Purpose: What would the building be used for? Who lived or worked there?

6 Note that you don't need to use all the knowledge from your answers to questions 1 to 5 in order to answer the Practice Question. Select relevant information from the answers to write a response to the specific aspect of the historic environment you are asked about. The question asks 'how far' the battle shows that Medieval battles were often decided more by luck than judgement, so you will need to say whether the outcome of the Battle of Falkirk was decided more by luck or by planned tactics.

7 Now try to answer the Practice Question yourself!

# 1.1 Who was Elizabeth I?

This topic focuses on the last 35 years of the reign of Queen Elizabeth I. To understand this period, you need to begin by exploring Elizabeth's childhood and what England was like before she became queen. In 1558, Elizabeth, the daughter of Henry VIII and Anne Boleyn, became Queen of England. As the king's youngest daughter she did not seem destined for the throne yet Elizabeth would become a long-reigning and important monarch. She **inherited** a country that was divided and troubled after the uncertain years of her predecessor's reign and faced many challenges.

## Objectives

▶ **Explore** who Elizabeth was and how she became queen.

▶ **Explain** why most people believed she would never be queen.

▶ **Consider** how Elizabeth's childhood experiences may have affected her approach to ruling England.

▼ *The Tudor family tree*

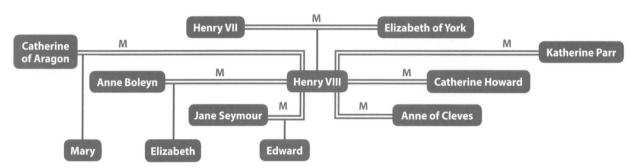

## A new princess...

Far from being a cause for celebration, Elizabeth's birth was a disappointment to her father. Henry was desperate to have a son and heir to continue the Tudor line and he had gone to great lengths to try to make this happen. Henry had divorced his first wife, Catherine of Aragon, and married Anne Boleyn, who gave birth to Elizabeth in 1533.

Anne Boleyn was accused of committing adultery with several men in court and was executed for **treason** in 1536, shortly before Elizabeth's third birthday. Henry married Jane Seymour 11 days later and she gave birth to Edward, the male heir that Henry had wanted all along.

## Family or threat?

For the rest of her father's reign Elizabeth was well looked after and educated in various subjects and languages. She was being prepared for life as a member of the **royal court**, the large group of advisors and other figures that surrounded the monarch. This would involve attending important events and, as a princess, most likely being married off to an important foreign figure to help form an alliance. Like other women, Elizabeth would have no role in decision making but would certainly play a valuable role as the king's daughter.

When Henry VIII died in 1547, Edward, aged just nine, became king. Elizabeth went to live with her father's sixth wife, Katherine Parr, and her new husband, Thomas Seymour, the king's uncle. After Katherine's death there were accusations made that Seymour and Elizabeth were to marry so that he could gain more influence over the young king. Seymour was executed for treason and Elizabeth's loyalty remained under suspicion through both her brother's and her sister Mary's reigns.

## From princess to queen

Edward died in 1553 and Henry's eldest daughter, Mary, became queen. Mary spent much of her reign feeling paranoid about threats and rebellions. She saw her younger sister as a potential symbol or leader for her enemies and even had Elizabeth imprisoned in the Tower of London in 1554 after she was accused of supporting a rebellion. Due to religious differences, many of Mary's enemies wanted Elizabeth to replace her sister on the throne. These five years gave Elizabeth time to grow as a future leader. She saw the mistakes her sister made and was often surrounded by powerful figures. She was forced to think in a political way for the first time. When Mary died in 1558, Henry VIII's youngest daughter became Queen Elizabeth I of England.

▼ **INTERPRETATION A** *An illustration of Elizabeth's christening from a children's book published in 1966*

When Elizabeth became queen she needed to establish her authority. When she was crowned, at the age of 25, she already had many enemies. She was also surrounded by powerful men, many of whom had served in the court of her father. Elizabeth had a difficult childhood, to say the least. Her mother had been executed on her father's orders and she had seen one stepmother die in childbirth and another follow her mother to the executioner's block. She then spent years under suspicion. It seems likely that these experiences would have had an impact later on when she made decisions about marriage or how to deal with her cousin, Mary, Queen of Scots.

▼ **SOURCE B** *A portrait of Elizabeth in 1546, painted by William Scrots*

## Key Words

inherit    treason    royal court

## Work

1 In your own words, explain the meaning of the following terms:
   a    royal court
   b    treason.

2 Who was Elizabeth I's mother?

3 Why was it considered unlikely that Elizabeth would ever be queen?

4 Look at **Sources B** and **C** and **Interpretation D**. What can they teach us about Elizabeth's childhood?

5 How might Elizabeth's experiences as a child have affected her approach to ruling England? Try to explain your answer using specific events and experiences.

▼ **SOURCE C** *Adapted from a letter to Henry VIII's Chief Minister Thomas Cromwell from Margaret Bryant, Elizabeth's governess; it was written after the birth of Edward, the long awaited male heir, in 1537:*

> I beg you to be good to her and make sure that she has clothing, for she has neither gown, nor petticoat, nor handkerchiefs, sleeves, nightdresses, corsets, nor nightcaps.

▼ **INTERPRETATION D** *Adapted from an article by Ashlie Jensen* On the Tudor Trail, *a history website focusing on the life of Anne Boleyn:*

> Even in toddlerhood Elizabeth was documented by multiple sources to be a vibrant, precocious and eloquent child. Those who encountered Elizabeth in her early years, particularly foreigners with no previous experience of her character, describe her as an exceptionally captivating young lady who had taken them by surprise.

# Who was powerful in Elizabethan England?

Although she was queen, Elizabeth did not have complete freedom to do as she pleased. Elizabeth's court of advisors and other figures had a clear structure but government was dominated by a small number of powerful men who at times had great influence on the queen.

## Objectives

▶ **Examine** the structure of Elizabeth's court and know some of the significant figures.
▶ **Explain** how the court and government worked and the difference between the two.
▶ **Assess** who held the power in Elizabeth's court.

## Parliament

Parliament was made up of the House of Lords (lords, bishops and other members of the **nobility**) and the House of Commons ('common' people, although still wealthy and educated). It was much less powerful than the modern UK Parliament but it did have influence over tax and was responsible for passing laws. The queen decided when to call Parliament and how much of their advice she should listen to.

## Privy Council

Took responsibility for the day-to-day running of the country. Its members were Elizabeth's main advisors. Technically Elizabeth could choose who was on the Council but in reality she had to appoint the most powerful landowners to avoid the risk of rebellion. The Council could be called upon to deal with almost any issue, including military and foreign affairs, religion and the queen's security. If the Privy Council agreed on a particular issue, it was hard for Elizabeth to refuse it. Luckily for her, privy councillors were rarely united. The Council was led by the **Secretary of State**.

### Who had the power in Elizabethan England?

## Justices of the Peace (JPs)

Each county had several Justices of the Peace to ensure order was kept. They were always selected from the local **gentry** and their main role was to ensure that the laws passed by Parliament were properly enforced. A single JP had the power to send somebody to prison but more than one JP was required to sentence a criminal to death. On taking office, JPs swore to treat everyone who they dealt with equally, whether they were rich or poor.

## Lord Lieutenants

Appointed by the queen to take administrative responsibility for a particular area of the country. This involved settling disputes and collecting taxes. They were also responsible for raising a **militia** to fight for the queen if needed. Many Lord Lieutenants held other important roles in court, most notably **privy councillors** (if they served on the Privy Council, their day-to-day work would be carried out by a deputy – someone who did the job in their place). The position of a Lord Lieutenant could lead to great power and influence.

### What was the royal court?

The royal court and the government were not the same thing. The court was made up of the government officials, ladies-in-waiting, servants and advisors who surrounded Elizabeth. Elizabeth's court consisted of around 1000 people from the highest nobles down to servants. It was the centre of political power but also the source of trends and fashions for the country. The Privy Council was a key part of the court but other important positions like Justices of the Peace were external to it. The real power lay with around 12 men who were close to the queen. Along with Elizabeth herself, this group could be described as the government.

## Significant court figures

Throughout Elizabeth's reign, various men became influential in her court. They often served on the Privy Council, in Parliament or as Lord Lieutenants but in reality their relationship with the queen was more important than the title they held. One way in which the queen could ensure loyalty was through **patronage**. This involved giving titles, power or other rewards to ensure individuals' support. Banishment from court was considered disgraceful, so patronage was highly desired.

### Key Words

nobility    Secretary of State    militia
privy councillor    gentry
patronage    Poor Laws

### Work

1  What was the role of the Privy Council in Elizabethan England?

2  Create a two-column table in your book. In the first column, write a list of the key jobs in Elizabethan government. In the second column, make a list of bullet points that explain the responsibilities of each job.

3  Who do you think had the most influence: the Privy Council, Parliament, the Justices of the Peace or the Lord Lieutenants?

4  How much freedom did Elizabeth have to make her own decisions? Explain your answer.

### Practice Question

Explain what was important about the Privy Council.    **8 marks**

### Study Tip

Remember that in an 'explain' question you should aim to go beyond describing what the Privy Council is. Include specific details about its role or who the members were.

### Fact

Historians sometimes add a 'c' before dates. This stands for 'circa', which means 'around' or 'approximately'.

# 2.1 Why was it difficult to be a female ruler?

When Elizabeth became the Queen of England in 1558, she **succeeded** her elder sister, Mary. Her father, along with many others, had been convinced that no woman could successfully rule a country, and Mary had done nothing to change people's view.

**Objectives**

▶ **Explore** some of the challenges that Elizabeth faced during her reign.

▶ **Explain** why she faced these challenges.

▶ **Evaluate** the significance of these challenges.

## What problems did Elizabeth face in the first ten years of her reign?

When Elizabeth came to the throne in 1558 aged 25, she was surrounded by men, many of whom had been powerful figures during the reigns of her father, Henry VIII, and both Edward VI and Mary. From the beginning and throughout her reign, Elizabeth faced challenges as a female ruler in a world where men had always held the power. Elizabeth was keen to assert her authority over Parliament and was not afraid to arrest those who questioned her policies.

One big problem Elizabeth faced was who would succeed her. Her heir, when she came to the throne, was her cousin Mary,

▼ **INTERPRETATION A** *Queen Elizabeth in Parliament from The Journals of All the Parliaments during the Reign of Queen Elizabeth by Simonds D'Ewes (1682)*

Queen of Scots. For many Englishmen, the prospect of the Scottish Queen Mary, a Catholic who had once been married to the King of France, becoming queen was something to be avoided at all costs. The way to avoid this was for Elizabeth to marry and give birth to a son, who could succeed her.

▼ **SOURCE B** *Adapted from The First Blast of the Trumpet against the Monstrous Regiment of Women by John Knox (1558); Knox was a Scottish Protestant who wrote the book during the reign of Mary I of England:*

> To promote a woman to rule and have superiority over any nation is insulting to God because it goes against His design for order and government. It is the overturning of good order and all principles of justice. For no man ever saw the lion bow down to the lioness.

▼ **SOURCE C** *An assessment of the state of the nation made by one of Queen Elizabeth's privy councillors, Armagil Waad, in 1558:*

> The Queen and the nobility are poor and the country is exhausted. There is a lack of good leaders and soldiers. The people are disorderly. The law is not properly enforced. All things are expensive. There are wars with France and Scotland. The French king threatens the country, having one foot in Calais and the other in Scotland. We know who our enemies are abroad, but we are not sure who our friends are.

## Succession

Henry VIII had done all he could to ensure the future of the Tudor line but Edward VI and Mary had died childless and Elizabeth had yet to produce an heir. In the past, there had been wars when people were not sure who would become ruler after a monarch's death. In 1562, Elizabeth contracted smallpox and nearly died. This drew attention to how uncertain the future was. Parliament and others were keen for Elizabeth to marry and have a child as soon as possible.

## Mary, Queen of Scots

Without a direct heir, the next in line to the throne was Elizabeth's Catholic cousin Mary. In 1568, Mary was **exiled** from Scotland to England and became a real threat to Elizabeth's rule. Catholics now had an alternative queen to fight for.

## Ireland

Like her predecessors, Elizabeth considered herself to be Queen of Ireland. Unfortunately, many of the Irish disagreed. A major problem was a revolt in northern Ireland in 1559, the first of several during her reign. She spent thousands of pounds and sent many of her best soldiers to try to limit Irish rebellion but nothing seemed to work in the long term.

## Elizabeth's problems

## Taxation

The government needed money and one of the few ways to get it was through taxes. Unfortunately, at a time of great **poverty** taxes would be very unpopular with the people of England, so raising taxes would be very dangerous for a new monarch.

## Key Words

succeed    exile    poverty    Pope

## Religion

Elizabeth's father had broken from the Catholic Church in order to obtain a divorce. After Henry's death, Edward continued to establish the Protestant faith. When Mary came to the throne she tried to undo what had gone before and re-establish Catholicism. Elizabeth was a Protestant but she was also practical. She did not want to make her enemies angry immediately. She allowed Catholics to follow their faith privately, but many Catholics remained unhappy, with some believing she had no right to be queen as they did not recognise Henry's second marriage to Elizabeth's mother, Anne Boleyn. In addition, the growing popularity of Puritanism, an extreme version of Protestantism, was seen as a threat.

## Foreign policy

Elizabeth had to deal with powerful countries that wanted influence over England. France and Spain, which were both Catholic and had the support of the **Pope**, saw Protestant England as a target. One major area of disagreement was the Netherlands. The mainly Protestant population was in conflict with the Catholic Spanish who ruled most of the area. Elizabeth would eventually need to decide how to deal with these concerns but initially her priority was keeping England secure.

## Practice Question

Write an account of the problems Elizabeth faced in the first ten years of her reign.    **8 marks**

## Study Tip

Remember to include plenty of specific detail, including any key dates.

## Extension

Historians need to be able to evaluate the relative importance of issues in the past. For example, they might make judgements about Elizabeth's problems. Which problem do you think could be the biggest threat to Elizabeth's rule? Give reasons for your choice.

## Work

1  When did Elizabeth I become queen?

2  Look at **Source B**. Why is John Knox so opposed to the idea of a female ruler?

3  Look at **Interpretation A** and **Sources B** and **C**. What problems did Elizabeth face?

4  Create a poster to illustrate Elizabeth's problems. You can use a maximum of ten words and one image for each problem.

# Elizabeth and the importance of marriage

**2.2A**

One of the biggest issues facing Elizabeth was that of marriage. Without an heir, the Tudor line would come to end. So from the day she became queen, her advisors were keen to find a suitable husband for her. Marriage also had another purpose. It was a way to secure alliances and increase influence at home and abroad.

## Objectives

▶ **Recall** why the issues of succession and marriage were so important.

▶ **Explain** the arguments for and against Elizabeth's potential marriage, particularly in relation to succession.

▶ **Assess** Elizabeth's possible suitors and evaluate the arguments for and against marriage.

▼ **INTERPRETATION A** A still from a 2005 television drama about Elizabeth; *The Virgin Queen* focuses on her relationship with Robert Dudley and suggests that the two were in love

## Why was marriage so important?

In Elizabeth's time, marriage, particularly for royalty, was less about love and more about making political deals between families and nations. As a young princess and then queen, who Elizabeth chose to marry could have a huge impact on England. She could choose to marry an Englishman and secure the support of an important family or she could marry a foreign prince and join two royal families together, and then their son would rule two countries. However, her choice was not quite so straightforward. If she married a foreign royal she risked losing control of England to her husband. Marrying an Englishman would avoid this but would lead to its own complications. As queen she would have authority over her husband but as a wife she must promise to obey him.

### Arguments for marriage

- Marriage could create an alliance with a foreign country or win the support of a powerful English family.
- By marrying, Elizabeth could produce an heir to succeed her and continue the Tudor line.
- Marriage and children would prevent Mary, Queen of Scots (a Catholic and Elizabeth's cousin), from ruling England after Elizabeth's death.

### Arguments against marriage

- Marrying a foreign prince or king could lead to England falling under their control.
- Marrying an Englishman could create problems over who had authority.
- Remaining unmarried meant that Elizabeth kept her independence. Marriage in the sixteenth century was not a partnership, as the husband legally had authority over the wife. It is possible that Elizabeth did not want to be answerable to her husband.
- Giving birth was risky for women at this time, often resulting in the death of the mother.
- Her sister Mary's marriage to King Philip of Spain was widely seen as a disaster and failed to produce an heir.

▼ **SOURCE B** *Elizabeth replies to a call from Parliament for her to get married in 1566:*

At present it is not convenient; nor never shall be without some peril unto you and certain danger unto me.

# Who could be worthy of marrying a queen?

Throughout her reign, many men became potential husbands to Elizabeth. Some would be entirely political matches but others were more personal. There were three suitors who were particularly notable.

## Robert Dudley, Earl of Leicester

As the queen's childhood friend and one of her favourites throughout her reign, many assumed that they would marry. When his wife died after a fall he was free to marry once again, but the scandal of her death (some thought he killed her deliberately) meant that marriage became almost impossible. Dudley was also a key figure in the royal court. As a Privy Councillor he wielded great power and influence in government.

## King Philip II of Spain

As King of Spain, Philip was one of the most powerful men in the world, as well as one of the wealthiest: Spain's control of South America and its resources had made the country very rich. Philip was in fact Elizabeth's  brother-in-law having been married to Queen Mary I, but had spent very little time in England. The biggest barrier between Elizabeth and Philip was religion: Philip was a Catholic and Elizabeth was a Protestant. This created many problems, not least of which was the issue of which religion their children would be raised in.

## Francis, Duke of Anjou and Alençon

As the French king's brother, marriage to Francis could lead to influence in France. As his brother was childless, Francis was also heir to the throne. The risk, however, was significant. By the time their marriage was considered, Elizabeth was 46 and most assumed she was beyond having children. If she died childless while married to the French heir, England could fall under French control. For this reason, and the fact that Francis was a Catholic, many influential people and the public were against the marriage.

## Work

1 What were the main arguments in favour of Elizabeth getting married?

2 Look at **Source B**. What possible 'peril' is Elizabeth describing?

3 Consider the three suitors on these pages. Create a dating website profile for each of the men. Do the same for Elizabeth. Who do you think is the best match for her?

4 Write a letter to Elizabeth explaining which (if any) of the suitors she should marry. Give reasons for your choice.

5 Look at **Interpretation A**. How convincing do you think the idea of a love story between Elizabeth and Dudley is based on what you know so far?

## Practice Question

Explain what was important about Elizabeth's decision regarding her marriage. **8 marks**

## Study Tip

Use specific examples of possible marriages to explain your points: for example, 'Marrying Francis, Duke of Anjou and Alençon, could lead to an alliance with France.'

# Elizabeth and the importance of marriage

Queen Elizabeth's marriage was not simply a matter of personal choice; it was about securing the future of the country. It was everyone's concern, from members of her Privy Council to Members of Parliament. How did Elizabeth react? What does this tell us about Elizabeth and her Parliament?

## Parliament as matchmakers?

After Elizabeth almost died of smallpox in 1562, Parliament became increasingly concerned about the lack of an heir. Many in Parliament saw it as their duty to find a match for Elizabeth and guarantee stability for England. The smallpox scare was not the only concern. By the time of her illness, the queen was almost 30, by no means old, but the likelihood of her producing an heir was getting smaller. By 1566, Parliament began to openly discuss potential matches. Elizabeth was furious with what she saw as an unacceptable interference and she banned Parliament from ever discussing the issue again. One politician, Peter Wentworth, ignored Elizabeth's orders and argued that Parliament should be able to discuss what it liked. Realising how the queen might react, the rest of Parliament had him arrested and placed in the Tower of London before Elizabeth blamed them all for his opinions. No matter how important the issue of marriage was to the country, it was clear that Elizabeth considered it a decision that she alone should make. This is an example of how Parliament and the queen clashed over the role Parliament should take. Elizabeth believed that there were certain matters that were entirely hers to consider, without any interference from Parliament. Marriage was one of these.

## Why didn't Elizabeth get married?

Despite the best efforts of Parliament and the Privy Council, Elizabeth never married. Historians have argued over why this was. At the time, some people felt that she was not doing her duty to her country while others felt that her decision was very clever indeed. The sources and interpretations opposite show some of the arguments and explanations that were put forward at the time.

▼ **INTERPRETATION A** *The Commons Petitioning Queen Elizabeth to Marry*, painted by Solomon Joseph Solomon in 1911; the subtitle reads: 'with this ring I was wedded to the realm'

▼ **SOURCE B**  *Sir James Melville, Scottish ambassador to England, in conversation with Elizabeth, 1564:*

> You will never marry. The Queen of England is too proud to suffer a commander. You think if you were married, you would only be Queen of England, and now you are king and queen both.

▼ **INTERPRETATION C**  *Written by the historian Hugh Oakeley Arnold-Forster, in A History of England (1898):*

> Who was the queen's husband to be, and what power was he to have over the government of the country? If he were a foreigner there was no knowing what power he might get over the queen, power which he would very likely use for the good of a foreign country, and not for the good of England. On the other hand, if he were an Englishman, he must be chosen from among the queen's subjects, and then it was certain that there would be jealousy and strife among all the great nobles in the country when they saw one of their number picked out and made king over them.

▼ **INTERPRETATION D**  *Elizabeth and Dudley were very close friends and many believed that they were in love. This description of the death of Dudley's wife Amy is from Spartacus Educational, a history website:*

> Amy Dudley insisted that everyone in the house attend a local fair in Abingdon. When her servants returned that evening, they found her lying dead at the foot of the staircase, her neck broken. Rumours began to circulate that Dudley had murdered his wife so that he could marry Elizabeth. It was now politically impossible for Elizabeth to marry Dudley.

▼ **SOURCE E**  *Queen Elizabeth in a letter written to Parliament, 1564:*

> I have already joined myself in marriage to a husband, namely the kingdom of England.

▼ **INTERPRETATION F**  *From a newspaper interview with Alison Weir who wrote a novel based on Queen Elizabeth's life:*

> Although Elizabeth loved Dudley she certainly did not want to marry him, or any other man. The reason goes back to a childhood that would have been considered highly dysfunctional in modern terms. Elizabeth hated the idea of marriage. This is understandable when you consider that her father was Henry VIII and her mother was his second wife Anne Boleyn whom her father ordered beheaded when Elizabeth was just three. Her stepmothers didn't fare so well either. At the age of eight she declared she would never marry.

## Work

1  Why was Peter Wentworth arrested?

2  Look at **Interpretation A**. What do you think is meant by the painting's subtitle?

3  Look at the sources and interpretations on these pages. What different reasons do they give for Elizabeth not getting married?

4  If Elizabeth was in love with Robert Dudley, why didn't she marry him?

5  What would be the advantages of Elizabeth getting married? Answer in as much detail as you can.

### Practice Question

How convincing is **Interpretation C** about the reasons why Elizabeth did not get married?

Explain your answer using **Interpretation C** and your contextual knowledge.  **8 marks**

### Study Tip

The interpretation puts forward a reason for Elizabeth not getting married. Aim to say whether you think this gives a fair and full explanation of why she never married or whether there are reasons that it does not mention.

# Norfolk's rebellion

It is clear that Elizabeth faced opposition throughout her reign. One major figure who rebelled against her rule was the Duke of Norfolk. He was involved in not one, but two plots against her. Who was the Duke of Norfolk? Why did he become involved in both rebellions?

## Objectives

▶ **Examine** the events of the Northern Rebellion and the Ridolfi Plot.

▶ **Explain** the causes of the rebellions.

▶ **Assess** the significance of the rebellions and what it can tell us about Elizabeth's authority.

## Challenges to Elizabeth's rule

After Elizabeth's coronation, she faced particular opposition from Catholics who felt that she had no right to be queen. Many believed that her father's marriage to her mother, Anne Boleyn, was illegal because Henry broke sacred laws by divorcing his first wife, the Catholic Catherine of Aragon. Increasingly, these opponents looked to Elizabeth's Catholic cousin, Mary, Queen of Scots, as an alternative monarch.

## The first rebellion: the Northern Rebellion, 1569

Despite the official religious changes, many people in northern England retained their Catholic beliefs and there was support for the idea of Mary, Queen of Scots, replacing Elizabeth on the throne. Although many northerners were torn between loyalty to Elizabeth and their religious beliefs, they nonetheless questioned her right to rule. Elizabeth was fully aware of the threat. She kept Mary under a close watch to prevent a possible rebellion while she debated how to deal with her. She even stopped her marrying the Duke of Norfolk. Norfolk left the royal court without permission and headed north. Taking this as a sign, a group of northern lords led by Westmorland (Norfolk's brother-in-law) and Northumberland began a rebellion against Elizabeth. They took control of Durham Cathedral and celebrated an illegal Catholic **mass**. They then began a march south with around 4600 men. Elizabeth struggled to gather an army to resist them but eventually one of her loyal lords, the Earl of Sussex, raised an army and the rebels disbanded. The leaders of the rebellion fled to Scotland where Northumberland was quickly captured and executed. Westmorland escaped to France, where he lived until he died in poverty.

## The rebels

### The Duke of Norfolk

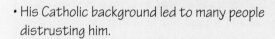

- He became the Duke of Norfolk after the death of his grandfather in 1554.

- He was Queen Elizabeth's second cousin and the leading English nobleman.

- He was raised as a Protestant despite being from a Catholic family.

- His Catholic background led to many people distrusting him.

- He was made Lord Lieutenant of the North.

### The Earl of Northumberland

- His father was executed for leading a rebellion against Henry VIII.

- He was not allowed to inherit his father's title until the reign of Mary I.

- He was a Catholic but was treated well by Elizabeth.

## The Earl of Westmorland

- A Catholic who had become powerful under Mary I's rule.

- He lost influence when Elizabeth was crowned.

- He remained powerful in the north.

- His wife was a member of the powerful Howard family to which three of Henry VIII's wives had ties.

## The second rebellion: the Ridolfi Plot, 1571

Norfolk spent ten months in the Tower of London but was eventually released and kept under house arrest, meaning that he was forced to stay inside his home at all times. He quickly became involved in another plot, this time led by a Catholic banker from Florence named Roberto Ridolfi. Having seen the Northern Rebellion fail, Ridolfi felt that foreign support was needed. In 1570 the Pope had commanded Catholics in England not to obey Elizabeth, giving English Catholics the dilemma of choosing between their religion or their country. As a banker, Ridolfi was able to travel freely across Europe building support. The plan was for the Netherlands to invade England at the same time as another northern rebellion. Elizabeth would be murdered and replaced by Mary, Queen of Scots, who would then marry Norfolk.

Elizabeth's network of spies proved too much for the plotters and a bag of gold coins with some coded

### Roberto Ridolfi

- An Italian banker who travelled widely across Europe.

- It is believed that he sent money to support Catholic rebels in England.

- It is likely that he worked as a spy for the Pope for many years.

## Key Words

mass

letters was discovered on its way north. The code was cracked when the cipher key (secret instructions) was discovered under a doormat at Norfolk's house. Norfolk confessed to his involvement and was executed on 2 June 1572.

### Extension

Historians are interested in evaluating the importance of particular events and comparing them with each other. For example, they might look at the two rebellions and consider which posed the biggest threat. Challenge yourself by answering the question: 'Was the Northern Rebellion or the Ridolfi Plot the biggest threat to Elizabeth's rule?' Think about the details of each plot: for example, one took place entirely in England, while the other involved the possibility of foreign invasion.

### Work

1 Why were some people keen to replace Elizabeth with Mary?

2 How was the Duke of Norfolk involved in the two plots?

3 Why do you think an Italian banker wanted to become involved in a plot against the English queen?

4 Working with a partner, study the two plots carefully. One of you should look at the Northern Rebellion and the other the Ridolfi Plot. You need to record:
   - when the plot happened
   - how it occurred
   - the reasons behind it (why did they want to overthrow Queen Elizabeth?)
   - why it failed and what happened to the rebels.

Now share your notes with your partner.

5 Why do you think Norfolk became involved in a second rebellion having failed in his first attempt to overthrow Queen Elizabeth?

The rebellions that Elizabeth was forced to deal with in her early reign did not disappear. Towards the end of her reign she faced a rebellion led by a man who was at one time considered as a potential husband for her, the Earl of Essex. Although the cause of many rebellions against Queen Elizabeth focused on religion, Essex's rebellion was all about power and influence.

### Objectives

▶ **Recall** the events of Essex's rebellion.

▶ **Explain** the causes of the rebellion.

▶ **Assess** what the rebellion tells us about Elizabeth's authority.

## Most beloved Essex

Robert Devereux was born in 1566 and inherited his title of Earl of Essex in 1573 when his father died. His father had been a loyal and respected member of the royal court who had helped to put down the Northern Rebellion in 1569. When Essex's mother remarried it was to the Earl of Leicester, who introduced Essex to the queen in 1587. Although more than 30 years older, Elizabeth took an immediate interest in the young earl. Essex made the most of being Elizabeth's latest favourite and in 1595 she made him a privy councillor. Essex's power grew further when the queen gave him the **monopoly** of sweet wine in England. This meant that by law anyone who wished to bring in sweet wine from abroad would have to pay him a tax, which made Essex lots of money. During this time, Essex developed a rivalry with another young man at court, Robert Cecil, who was a member of a very powerful family. Cecil, with his crooked back, could not have looked more different from the handsome Essex; this may well have played a role in Essex gaining the queen's attention. Essex won Elizabeth's further respect and admiration with his military success against the Spanish in 1596.

**▼ SOURCE A** *A portrait of the Earl of Essex from 1596; the handsome Essex was particularly well known for his legs!*

## A quarrel with the queen

Essex returned to England a hero but things soon began to go wrong for the queen's favourite. In 1598, he became involved in an argument with Elizabeth during a Privy Council meeting about Ireland. In a fit of anger, Essex turned his back on the queen and she retaliated by hitting him on the side of his head. He almost drew his sword, but was stopped by the other privy councillors. Elizabeth put him under house arrest but he still refused to admit he was wrong. However, Elizabeth took no further action against him. Many contemporaries thought that he had been lucky to escape with his life.

## Essex in Ireland and his return to England

In January 1599, Elizabeth made Essex the Lord Lieutenant of Ireland. He was reluctant to go at first, fearing that Cecil would become more powerful while he was away, but he eventually agreed. It was his job to crush the rebellious Irish, but not only did he fail to defeat the Irish rebel leader, he also made a truce with him, completely against the queen's orders. He knighted some of his army leaders in Ireland, which the queen had forbidden him to do.

To make matters worse, when Essex returned to the queen's palace, dishevelled and dirty, he rushed into her private quarters and caught her without her wig! Essex experienced a spectacular and rapid fall from Elizabeth's favour and she did not renew his sweet wine monopoly. This caused him problems as he had large debts.

His position, wealth and all of his influence gone, Essex faced financial ruin. Angry, and with little left to lose, Essex was determined to remove his long-term rival, Robert Cecil, from power. In February 1601, he began to gather supporters.

# Essex's rebellion

1. Essex took four of the queen's privy councillors hostage and with 200 followers marched to his London house with them.

2. Robert Cecil responded quickly; he labelled Essex a traitor and many of the rebels abandoned the march.

3. Essex returned to his house where he found that the hostages had been released by supporters who had abandoned his cause.

## Key Word

monopoly

4. Essex and his remaining supporters were arrested.

## Executing Essex

Two weeks after the disastrous rebellion, Essex was put on trial for treason. In an attempt to save his soul (although not his life) he agreed to identify many other members of the rebellion, including his sister, Penelope. He was executed on 25 February 1601. In exchange for his information, Elizabeth allowed Essex to be executed in private, rather than suffer a public beheading. Several other rebels were executed but most of them were simply fined.

## Work

1 Retell the story of Essex's rebellion in the most creative way you can. You could create a play, a giant storyboard, a newspaper article or something else.

2 Create a table in your book to show the reasons for the rebellion's failure. In one column list the mistakes and failings of Essex and in the other list the strengths of Elizabeth's court.

3 What does Essex's rebellion tell us about the authority of Elizabeth and her court?

4 Look back at your work on the Norfolk rebellions. Do you think Essex was more or less of a threat than Norfolk? Explain your answer.

## Practice Question

Write an account of the career of the Earl of Essex.

**8 marks**

## Study Tip

Remember to explain why Essex was such an important figure; don't just tell the story of his life.

# Why did rebellions against Elizabeth fail?

During her reign, Elizabeth faced many challenges and a number of rebellions. There were rebellions from Catholics who questioned her right to be queen and there were rebellions from nobles who wanted to increase their own power. Despite these challenges Elizabeth not only remained in power until the end of her reign, but her position never really looked vulnerable. How was this possible?

### Objectives

▶ **Recall** several rebellions that Elizabeth faced during her reign.

▶ **Explain** how these rebellions and plots were foiled.

▶ **Assess** why none of the challenges were ever successful.

▼ **INTERPRETATION A** *A portrait of Elizabeth in old age, painted nearly 20 years after her death*

## A tired queen and a weary nation

By the end of her reign many people's attention had moved on from Elizabeth and become focused on the future. After four decades people were ready for a change. Whether at the beginning of her rule as a young and inexperienced monarch, in the middle at the height of her powers or at the end, Elizabeth still needed to control and command the loyalty of her subjects. In her 45 years as queen she faced a number of rebellions.

## Why did the plots and rebellions against Elizabeth fail?

For a plot or rebellion to succeed, secrecy is needed. Messages need to be sent and plans made without any outsider knowing what is intended. The problem for those who tried to plot against Elizabeth was that she had the largest and most effective network of spies and informers that England had ever seen. These were not spies in the modern sense; they were employed through much less formal arrangements. Francis Walsingham, Elizabeth's Chief Minister, oversaw the network. Everyone from nobles, who might have the trust of plotters, to innkeepers and servants, who could overhear whispered conversations, could potentially be kept in Walsingham's pay.

The second thing necessary for a plot to succeed is popular support. All of the rebellions relied on others seizing the opportunity and joining the fight. The problem was that most people were happy with the way things were. For the first time in many years people were able to live in relative religious freedom. The brutality of Mary I's reign was something that no one wished to return to and even many Catholics preferred an English queen over Mary, Queen of Scots, or a foreign ruler like Philip of Spain. For many in England, it seemed that they had never had it so good. There simply was not the general appetite to change things.

## Spies

The network of spies headed by Walsingham meant that very few plots ever got beyond their earliest stages.

## Religious settlement

Elizabeth's religious policy kept most of the population happy. Although things became tougher for Catholics as her reign went on, there remained a level of tolerance. In areas where Catholicism was more popular, the new settlement was often not enforced to the same extent.

## Unconvincing alternatives

Regardless of their religion, most people preferred an English queen over the alternatives: Mary, Queen of Scots, or a foreign king like Philip. Mary was not only a former Queen of France but was also blamed by many for her second husband's death. Philip had been King of England before and had shown little interest in the country, while his wife oversaw the brutal execution of hundreds of Protestants.

## Why did plots against Elizabeth fail?

## A skilled politician

Elizabeth dealt with her most difficult relationship, the one with her Parliament, very effectively. She was skilled at getting her own way while still allowing Lords and MPs to feel influential. The issue of marriage and succession is a perfect example of this. She would listen to Parliament's advice but was clear where its power ended.

## Punishments

Elizabeth took swift action against traitors. Rebels were tortured and put to death. Her former favourite, Essex, whose plot never aimed to remove her from the throne, was beheaded and her own cousin, Mary, Queen of Scots, was kept locked up for many years before she was executed. For those who challenged Elizabeth, the consequences of failure were plain to see.

## Extension

An important skill for a historian is comparing factors that caused things to happen and deciding which factor played the largest role. Challenge yourself by using the information in this chapter to decide which of the factors in the spider diagram was the most important in stopping a successful rebellion against Elizabeth from ever taking place. In your answer, remember to say *why* one factor is more important than others by *directly comparing* them.

## Work

1 Look at **Interpretation A**.
   a Describe what you can see in the painting. Look carefully at what surrounds the queen, as well as the queen herself.
   b Look at **Source B** on page 145. How does this image of Elizabeth compare to **Interpretation A** opposite?
   c This painting was created 20 years after her death. Can you suggest reasons why it was not created while she was alive?

2 Explain two reasons why rebellions against Elizabeth failed.

3 Look back at the Northern Rebellion earlier in the chapter. Explain why this failed with reference to the factors in the spider diagram above.

4 Would a successful rebellion ever have been possible? Explain your answer.

5 Working with a partner, choose one of the rebellions that you have studied and create the script for a television news report about it. You should explain what happened, who was involved and then give a detailed account of why it failed.

## Practice Question

Write an account of a rebellion you have studied that took place in Elizabeth's reign. **8 marks**

## Study Tip

You could consider including the following: the causes, the key people involved, the events of the rebellion itself and both the immediate and longer term consequences.

# Wealth and fashion in Elizabethan England

In Elizabethan society, everyone knew their place. The queen was at the top as the most important and the peasants were at the bottom. In the sixteenth century, wealth and owning land meant power. Nobles owned huge amounts of land and held positions of power but the Elizabethan age saw the growth of a new group of wealthy people. Known as the gentry, they did not have the social status of the nobles but they became increasingly wealthy, and therefore powerful. Who were the nobility and gentry?

**Objectives**

▶ **Describe** the structure of Elizabethan society.

▶ **Explain** the positions, roles and daily lives of the nobility and gentry.

▶ **Judge** whether the gentry or the nobility had the most influence and power.

## The Great Chain of Being

Elizabethan society was based on an idea called 'the Great Chain of Being'. In the Great Chain, God is at the top, followed by his angels and other residents of Heaven. Human beings are beneath, followed by animals and plants. The Elizabethans broke the chain down further by having subdivisions (or categories) of humans. The monarch was at the top, followed by the nobility, the gentry and then the peasants. It was almost impossible to move between the human divisions.

▼ **SOURCE A** *'The Great Chain of Being' from 1579*

**Fact**

**The population of England**
In 1558, the population was around 2.8 million but by 1603 it had increased to 4 million. This was a huge increase in such a short time.

## The rich and the powerful

Two groups made up the wealthier members of Elizabethan society: the nobility and the gentry. If someone made money through trade or some other means they would use it to buy land. Land could provide a source of income from rent or growing crops to eat or wool to trade. Land made money and raised social status.

The nobility was made up of the most respected members of society, second only to the queen herself. The highest noble title was duke but others included earl and baron. Their average income was £6000 per year (equivalent to about £1 million today). A member of this group was born into it or awarded a title by the queen (which was very rare). Nobles had special privileges, including protection from torture. A noble who committed treason would always be beheaded and never hanged, avoiding public humiliation. Most nobles had large amounts of land, which was passed down from father to son. The richest in society were members of this group. It is estimated that 14 per cent of all the country's income went to just over 1 per cent of the nobility. Any influence they had was the queen's to give and take away.

The gentry were the landlords of the countryside. They lived on the rents of their tenants and did no manual labour themselves. The income of a member of this group could vary between £10 and £200 per year (around £1700 and £34,000 in today's money). Some members were wealthier than the poorer nobles. They had significant influence and power over their lands with many filling important roles such as Justice of the Peace (JP), and serving in Parliament. Some were given the title of knight and others had the title esquire. As the country was more stable and secure after the unpredictable years of Elizabeth's predecessors, people were able to settle and make money from trade. The gentry grew as a result.

▼ *Nobility: most powerful and (usually) wealthiest; held titles that were passed from father to son; held the most senior positions such as privy councillor*

▼ *Gentry: often wealthy landowners; held important positions like JP; might be richer than some nobles but still below them in society*

▼ *Peasantry: the poorest members of society, worked as farm labourers; often struggled for work: rising population made this even more of an issue*

▼ **SOURCE B** *The Cobham family portrait, dated 1567; Frances (standing on the right) was best friends with Bess of Hardwick (see page 162)*

(see page 162)

## What was it like to be wealthy in Elizabethan England?

Rich Elizabethans were proud to show off their wealth. They often built fine houses in the countryside. One area in which the gentry could show their wealth was through food. Rich Elizabethans tended to have meals made up almost entirely of meat and drank mainly wine. For the richest, banquets were an important way to show off the fact that they could afford lots of the very best produce. Fashion was also important. Women often paired fine clothes with whitened faces. This was intended to show that they did not have to work outside and get a tanned face. The effect was often created using lead-based make-up. A key element of both men's and women's fashion was the elaborate **ruff** worn around the neck. The fashions and wealth formed part of what became known as the Elizabethan 'golden age'. The wealthy, Protestant or Catholic, were free to live their lives and enjoy their success while the country was secure and stable.

**Work**

1  Explain the term 'the Great Chain of Being'.

2  Split a section of your book in half. On one side describe a member of the nobility, on the other describe a member of the gentry. You are limited to ten words but can use as many pictures as you like.

3  Why do you think Elizabeth and the nobility were so keen to maintain the strict structure of society?

4  a  Look at **Source B**. Which social group do you think this family are part of?

   b  What evidence in the image supports your conclusion?

5  Which do you think had the most power and influence: the nobility or the gentry? Explain your answer.

# Historic Environment: Elizabethan country houses

Many great houses were built during Queen Elizabeth's reign. These homes would not only show the wealth and power of the owners, but also demonstrate that the inhabitants were cultured, fashionable people. What were the features of great Elizabethan houses? Who built them, and how did they show the prosperity of their owners?

## Objectives

▶ **Describe** the features of an Elizabethan house.

▶ **Explain** how the houses demonstrated the prosperity of the owners.

▶ **Investigate** how a specific house, Hardwick Hall, reflected the status and prosperity of its owner.

## A culture of comfort

The Elizabethan period saw growing prosperity amongst the gentry in a time of stability in England, and houses reflected this. A country house was no longer the communal centre of a village (such as in the medieval period), but a private residence for a cultured noble. Architects, such as Robert Smythson, who designed Hardwick Hall, one of the grandest houses of the period, could focus on how the house looked and its comfort, rather than the security of the owner.

## What was the Elizabethan style?

During the **Renaissance**, it was the height of fashion to be inspired by ancient or classical civilisations, since it demonstrated a cultured mind and refined taste. The design of the building was symmetrical, usually built around an E or an H shape, which allowed for open courtyards as opposed to closed, secure ones. Rich oak wood panelling and geometric plasterwork set off walls hung with colourful tapestries. Glass was expensive and only affordable for the wealthy, so walls full of windows allowed the owner to show their wealth on the inside and outside of the building. Chimneys were based on classical columns and were often in stacks of two or three.

## What was it like to live in an Elizabethan house?

The medieval hall was replaced by a **great chamber** as the main room in Elizabethan houses. Houses still had a hall, but guests passed through it to go up to the great chamber and the other rooms. With the move to greater privacy, servants' quarters were set away from areas for the owner. The number of rooms in a house showed the family's importance and wealth, and Elizabethan houses had more rooms which allowed individual privacy. Rooms were accessed by a great staircase: they were made comfortable by the heat of a fireplace, and lit by light from the many glass windows.

▲ **A** *Hardwick Hall in Derbyshire, built by Bess of Hardwick, also known as Elizabeth Shrewsbury, between 1590 and 1597*

## Timeline

| 1527 | 1557 | 1565 |
|---|---|---|
| **Bess of Hardwick born:** Bess was born into the gentry but had risen in status and power through her four marriages to become the richest woman in England after Queen Elizabeth. | Bess' second husband, Sir William Cavendish, whom she married in 1547, was a wealthy key figure in King Henry VIII's court. When he died in 1557, Bess became a much wealthier woman. | Bess third husband was Sir William St Loe, who was from a well-established family and a favourite of the queen. This marriage gave Bess a place at court. When he died in 1565, Bess inherited his fortune. |

Elaborate geometric plasterwork reflected the latest Renaissance fashions.

Straight chimney columns reflected classical design. Chimneys were often on the side of a house, but at Hardwick, they were placed within the internal walls to ensure the house would be symmetrical.

Decorative stonework reflecting fashionable Italian design. The letters 'ES' stand for Elizabeth Shrewsbury, the house's owner. In the centre, is the Hardwick coat of arms.

The high great chamber: a place to receive guests. The decoration in this room includes beautiful images of Queen Elizabeth.

Large glass windows with **lattice** frames (large pieces of glass were not yet possible to make). Contemporary accounts describe Hardwick Hall as being 'more window than wall'.

Portraits and other features showed family connections. Oak panelling on walls could be carved to tell classical stories as well as keeping warmth in. Hardwick Hall features a carved **overmantel** which references the Hardwick and Cavendish families.

Long gallery: a place for entertaining guests and winter exercise. Two massive chimney pieces contain statues of Justice and Mercy.

The **loggia**, or open walkway, at the front was inspired by Italian Renaissance architecture.

▲ **B** *Hardwick Hall: details of the interior and exterior*

## Work

1  Conduct research about why and how Bess Hardwick built Hardwick Hall. Do you think its status as 'one of England's greatest Elizabethan houses' is justified? Why or why not?

2  Compare the features of Hardwick Hall with other Elizabethan houses (such as Speke Hall in Liverpool or Burghley House in Lincolnshire), and create a list of the architectural features they have in common.

## Key Words

great chamber    lattice
overmantel    loggia    Renaissance

## Study Tip

Compared with Medieval buildings, Elizabethan country houses, like Hardwick Hall, had many new technological and design features. What were they? What can we learn about the people who built and lived in such buildings from their external appearance and internal features?

### 1590–97

In 1567 Bess married the Earl of Shrewsbury and became nobility. Bess arranged the marriage of her daughter, Elizabeth, to Charles Stuart, Mary, Queen of Scots' distant cousin. Any children they had would have a claim to the throne. A daughter was born and Queen Elizabeth was enraged. Bess returned to her old home at Hardwick Hall without her husband and built a new house. Hardwick Hall was a home fit for a noblewoman.

# 3.3 The role of theatre in Elizabethan England

During Elizabeth's reign, one of the most popular forms of entertainment was the theatre. Every week everyone, from the queen down to the ordinary people, would come and watch performances of comedy, tragedy and history plays. Many of these plays proved so popular that they are still performed to this day. What made the Elizabethan theatre so popular?

## Objectives

▶ **Explore** the key features of Elizabethan theatre.

▶ **Explain** why there was some opposition to the theatre.

▶ **Assess** the importance of theatre during Elizabeth's reign.

## All the world's a stage

During Elizabeth's reign, rich and poor alike visited public theatres. These audiences had a huge appetite for new plays and many writers became very successful trying to keep up with the demand. Playwrights, including William Shakespeare, produced many new plays every year and their work was performed by theatre companies such as the Lord Chamberlain's Men and the Admiral's Men. The companies were usually named after the person who provided their funding: the **patron**. Acting was an entirely male profession with the female roles performed by boys. The most successful and popular actors could become very famous and would often return to roles they had played before or have parts specifically written for them in new plays.

## A day at the theatre

At the beginning of Elizabeth's reign, a visit to the theatre generally meant visiting an inn and watching a performance inside or out in the yard. By the end of Elizabeth's reign, a number of purpose-built theatres existed and visiting one became a popular way to spend an afternoon. Performances

### Fact

Shakespeare's history plays tended to suit the Tudor view of the past. For example, in *Richard III*, the king is portrayed as an evil hunchback – probably because Elizabeth's grandfather (Henry VII) defeated Richard III in battle, so Shakespeare wanted to show Richard in a negative way.

### Key Biography

**William Shakespeare (1564–1616)**

- The most celebrated playwright of all time, Shakespeare was the principal writer for the Lord Chamberlain's Men, a theatre company.
- He wrote 38 plays, which can be divided into three categories: histories, tragedies and comedies. Histories included plays like *Julius Caesar* and *Henry V*. History plays often followed each other chronologically with the same characters and actors appearing in them. Tragedies included *Romeo and Juliet*, and comedies such as *A Midsummer Night's Dream* were designed to keep the audience laughing and coming back for more – common features included mistaken identity and endings involving marriage.

### Key Biography

**Richard Burbage (1568–1619)**

- Burbage was one of the most celebrated actors of the Elizabethan period. As a leading member of the Lord Chamberlain's Men, he was the first to play many famous roles including Hamlet and King Lear.
- As well as acting, Burbage was a theatre owner.

usually began at 3:00pm and continued into the evening. Prices varied, depending on where you sat (or stood). The performance itself was often more like a circus than what we might expect at a modern theatre. Audience members would push and shove to try to get a better view and heckling was not uncommon. The theatre became an important part of life during Elizabeth's reign, particularly among the nobility. Being the patron of a theatre company was an important way to show how cultured you were and also a good way to please the queen. For ordinary people, a trip to the theatre offered a cheap afternoon's entertainment. Although they occupied very different parts of the theatre building, the rich and the poor watched and enjoyed the same performances.

▼ **SOURCE A** *The writer George Gascoigne presents Elizabeth with his latest work in this sixteenth-century engraving*

▼ **INTERPRETATION B** *A description of Elizabethan theatre-goers adapted from* The Facts about Shakespeare *(1913):*

> These people who watched with joy the cruel torment of a bear or the execution of a Catholic also delighted in the romantic comedies of Shakespeare. These people were so appallingly gullible and ignorant, so brutal and childish compared with Englishmen of today, yet they set the standard of national greatness.

## Opposition to theatre

Although very popular, some saw theatre as sinful and campaigned to have it banned. Theatres were seen as dangerous places where drunkenness, crime and other immoral behaviour took place. Many were concerned that such large gatherings of people might spread disease (although they had no understanding of germs). Religious groups such as the Puritans

**Key Word**

patron

**Work**

1. What were the three main types of play performed in Elizabethan theatres?
2. Why were Shakespeare's history plays popular with Elizabeth and her supporters?
3. Imagine a visit to the theatre in Elizabethan times. Write a diary entry to describe your afternoon. You should include what you saw and what it was like, where you sat and who else was there. Use the information on this page to help you.
4. Look at **Interpretation B**. What opinion does this give about Elizabethan theatre-goers? How fair do you think it is?
5. In what ways did theatre play an important role in Elizabethan society?
6. Look at **Source A**. What does this image suggest about Elizabeth's view of the theatre?

**Practice Question**

How convincing is **Interpretation B** about the Elizabethan theatre?

Explain your answer using **Interpretation B** and your contextual knowledge. **8 marks**

**Study Tip**

What impression of Elizabethan theatre is given in this interpretation? Do you think it is fair? Use your own knowledge to explain why.

wanted the theatres closed down completely as they saw them as a distraction. They believed that people should be spending their free time praying and studying the Bible rather than watching plays. Attending these entertainments may have made them less willing to sit through a sermon! Although restrictions were put in place at various times, the theatre's popularity continued, largely due to Elizabeth I's enjoyment of it. The opposition that theatre faced shows just how influential and important it had become.

# Historic Environment: Elizabethan theatres

During the reign of Elizabeth I, theatre was transformed from something that took place in the small backroom of pubs to the most popular form of entertainment. Rich and poor gathered to watch the latest plays from writers like William Shakespeare and Christopher Marlowe, performed by their favourite actors. These popular performances needed venues, so new theatres were built across the country but particularly in London. The chance to see performances at theatres like the Globe was not to be missed.

## Objectives

▶ **Recall** features of Elizabethan theatres.

▶ **Explain** what theatres tell us about Elizabethan society.

▶ **Investigate** this in relation to a specific theatre, the Globe.

## Tudor entertainment

When Elizabeth came to the throne there was a clear difference between the entertainment enjoyed by the rich and powerful and that experienced by ordinary people. The rich, including the monarch, enjoyed great banquets complete with music and dancing. The ordinary people attended events ranging from cock fights to dances. The only real plays were religious, showing stories from the Bible. Increasingly popular amongst the poor, however, was the performance of plays by travelling acting **troupes**. Companies, usually of only four or five people, would perform traditional plays in inns and pubs around the country. The plays would often be funny and the audience was encouraged to get involved in the action. Although the wealthy might enjoy a performance at a feast or banquet, theatre was largely something for ordinary people. The Elizabethan era changed this. The support of nobles, such as the Earl of Leicester, provided not only funding for more plays but also made them more respectable.

## Permanent theatres

As theatre became more popular amongst both the rich and poor, inns were no longer large enough for performances and it became clear that more dedicated venues were needed. England's first permanent theatre, the Red Lion, was opened in London in 1567. It provided a place in which touring theatre companies could perform.  It was

a financial failure and closed less than a year later but the idea did not go away. The Theatre was opened in Shoreditch in London in 1576 by James Burbage. It was a huge success and was followed by a number of other theatres including the Rose in 1587 and the Globe in 1599. Outbreaks of the plague had led to the Lord Mayor banning plays in the City of London (for fear of spreading the disease), which meant that all the new theatres were on the outskirts of the city. The new theatres were used by rich and poor who all watched the same performances. As the theatres became permanent, so did the theatre companies. Troupes such as the Lord Chamberlain's men performed regularly and the actors became well known to the audience.

▼ **INTERPRETATION A** *The reconstruction of the Globe that was completed in 1997; it is based on evidence of the original theatre's layout and is considered quite accurate although it is smaller (its capacity is 1400)*

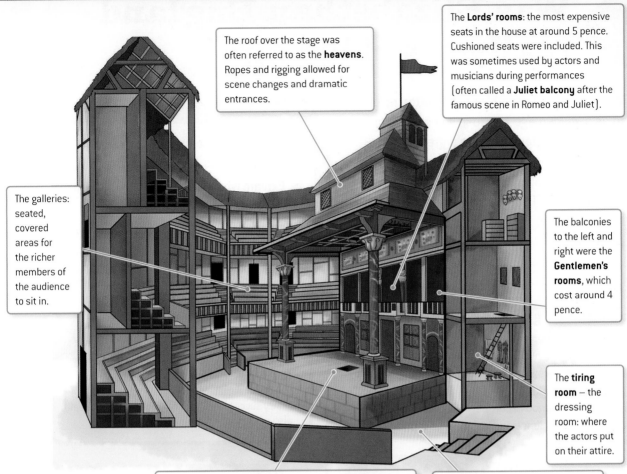

The roof over the stage was often referred to as the **heavens**. Ropes and rigging allowed for scene changes and dramatic entrances.

The **Lords' rooms**: the most expensive seats in the house at around 5 pence. Cushioned seats were included. This was sometimes used by actors and musicians during performances (often called a **Juliet balcony** after the famous scene in Romeo and Juliet).

The galleries: seated, covered areas for the richer members of the audience to sit in.

The balconies to the left and right were the **Gentlemen's rooms**, which cost around 4 pence.

The **tiring room** – the dressing room: where the actors put on their attire.

▲ **B** *The inside of the Globe Theatre*

The stage: where the actors performed. There would often be scenery and there was almost always a trapdoor to allow for special effects such as smoke. The wall at the back was called the **Frons Scenae** and included a door were actors made their entrances and exits.

The pit: this was where ordinary people stood to watch the performance. People in the pit often heckled the actors. This area was completely open to the weather.

## The Globe Theatre

The Globe was built by the Lord Chamberlain's Men, William Shakespeare's theatre company, in 1599 in Southwark, London. Members of the company were shareholders in the new theatre with James Burbage taking a majority. Although there are different accounts, the Globe was almost certainly big enough to accommodate up to 3000 spectators. It was circular in shape (a polygon of up to 20 sides) and was three storeys high. The Globe saw the first performance of many of Shakespeare's plays but was destroyed by a fire that started during a production of *Henry VIII* in 1613.

### Key Words

troupe    pit    Frons Scenae    Juliet balcony
heavens    tiring room    Lords' rooms
Gentlemen's rooms

### Study Tip

The Elizabethan theatre was immensely popular with many people at all levels in society. Why was this? How were theatres designed for the public performance of plays? Can you think of ways in which theatre contributed more than just entertainment to Elizabethan society and culture?

### Work

1  Describe two features of a typical Elizabethan theatre.
2  Explain how entertainment for rich and poor people was different at the beginning of Elizabeth's reign.

# Was Elizabethan England really a 'golden age'?

The period of Elizabeth's reign is often referred to as a 'golden age' because it is seen as a time when England became a great country. Elizabeth's reign was an era of new scientific experimentation, technological development and new ideas in the arts. Did people at the time think that they were living through a golden age?

## Objectives

▶ **Describe** the key features and developments of the Elizabethan era.

▶ **Explain** why many would argue that it was a golden age.

▶ **Evaluate** whether 'the golden age' is an accurate description of the Elizabethan era.

## A time of great accomplishments

The phrase 'golden age' is used to describe a time of great achievement. There is certainly no doubt that the Elizabethan era saw new ideas and accomplishments in many areas. Elizabethan England falls within the Renaissance period in Europe, a key time in history when art, medicine, science and literature developed greatly.

### Peace, power and pride

Before Henry VII became king, England had spent many years in chaos with different men claiming the throne. Elizabeth's long reign established peace and order, while military success and the country's growing wealth also made people proud to be English.

### Art

Portraits became very popular and were much more than just representations of the sitters. They often included a lot of symbolism: for example, Elizabeth was painted with her hand on a globe to show her power. The miniature portrait was popular. These were very small, detailed paintings intended for personal possession rather than public display. Other forms of art included decorative silverware and highly detailed textile patterns.

### Science and technology

There were some significant breakthroughs in navigation and astronomy and a growing understanding of how magnetism worked. Elizabeth's reign also saw more effective printing presses, which produced books and **pamphlets**. These allowed ideas to spread much faster.

### Education

Education was seen as increasingly important during Elizabeth's reign. Although still focused on wealthy boys, some girls also received a limited education.

### Exploration

Europeans discovered new lands and peoples, and England began to become a major power at this time.

## Elizabethan accomplishments

### Literature

In addition to the great plays written during Elizabeth's reign, poetry became very popular. Shakespeare wrote many sonnets but several respected nobles also wrote poems. A lot of Elizabethan poetry made references to stories of Ancient Greece and Rome.

### Theatre

Theatre was hugely popular during the Elizabethan era. Many theatres were built and the period produced plays that are still performed and studied today.

### Buildings

The Elizabethans built many of the stately homes that still stand today. These houses were built to impress the queen and other nobles. For the first time houses were not designed specifically with defence in mind.

▼ **INTERPRETATION B** *An alchemist in his workshop, painted c1650*

**Key Words**

pamphlet    alchemy
Gloriana

**Work**

1 Why is the Elizabethan era often described as a 'golden age'?

2 a In what ways does **Interpretation A** support the idea of a golden age?

   b How useful is it in telling us whether people *at the time* saw it as a golden age?

3 Look at **Interpretation B**. What does this source suggest about the Elizabethan period?

4 Split a page in two. On one side list the arguments for it being a golden age and on the other list the arguments against.

## Was it really a golden age?

Although Elizabeth's reign is often seen as a time of great advancement and success, it could be argued that this is myth and that, in fact, England was the same brutal place that it was before Elizabeth came to the throne. Blood sports like dog fighting and bear baiting remained popular, and cruel torture and punishments continued to be used. The population was very much divided too: a small minority lived in luxury while most people were very poor and grew just enough food or made just enough money to survive. Life expectancy was low and illnesses that would not kill us today were lethal. While it was a time of scientific experimentation, much of it was questionable. **Alchemy**, the attempt to turn cheap metal into gold, was very popular, as was astrology (using the planets to predict the future).

The idea of a golden age was certainly present at the time. There was a deliberate attempt to spread the idea of great success and advancement as a way of securing Elizabeth's position on the throne. This way of presenting the Elizabethan age was known as **'Gloriana'** and was achieved through plays and festivals as well as the printing of special pamphlets.

**Practice Question**

Write an account of the ways in which Elizabeth's reign could be seen as a 'golden age'.

**8 marks**

**Study Tip**

This type of question is not just asking you to describe the features of a particular period but also to explain how and why it could be described in this way. Think about whether people at the time would have seen it as a golden age.

# Why was there so much poverty in Elizabethan England?

The lives of the wealthy during Elizabeth's reign often involved great luxury. They had power and influence, lived in grand and beautiful houses and followed all the latest fashions. At the other extreme were the very poor. Those lucky enough to find regular work earned very little and others were left to beg on the streets. Who were the poor and what were their lives like?

## Objectives

▶ **Describe** who the Elizabethan poor were.

▶ **Explain** why poverty increased.

▶ **Evaluate** the importance of different factors in the increase in poverty.

▼ **SOURCE A** *A woodcut from 1569 showing a rich man giving money to a beggar; giving charity to the poor was seen as a good, Christian thing for the wealthy to do.*

## The life of the poor

Look back at 'the Great Chain of Being' on page 160. At the bottom of the human section, just above the animals, were ordinary people. For some lucky members of this group life could be straightforward. As long as they kept on the right side of their lord, they could provide for themselves and their families. For those without this security, however, life was much harder. Those without work were known as **paupers**, who relied on charity. This meant either begging or going to the local church for help.

## The Tudor approach to poverty

Elizabeth's grandfather, Henry VII, wanted to limit the threat of uprising among his nobles so he limited their right to have their own **retinues** (private armies). This left many soldiers without work. One of the most significant changes of the Tudor era was the **Reformation** during Henry VIII's reign. Between 1536 and 1540, Henry closed all of the **monasteries** in England and many people who had worked for the Church were evicted. In addition to causing unemployment, there was a huge impact on the poor. Before the Reformation, monks and nuns had played a vital role in looking after the sick and the poor, giving them charity and caring for them. The evicted poor had nowhere to go and this was still the case when Elizabeth came to the throne.

As Henry VIII's reign went on, economic problems increased and the cost of war was great. In order to save money, from 1542 he began to debase coins: this means that he mixed in less valuable metals with the gold and silver allowing coins to be produced much more cheaply. The problem with this was that foreign traders came to expect more coins for their goods. This damaged trade and jobs, and the cloth trade collapsed completely during his son Edward VI's reign. Elizabeth inherited a country that was in an economic mess. Unemployment and poverty were high, and as Elizabeth's reign began things became even worse.

## Failures in agriculture

England was hit by bad harvests between 1594 and 1598, which led to food shortages and some people died of starvation. In addition, a new system of farming was developing. More and more landowners began to keep sheep on their land rather than renting it out to farmers who had traditionally grown crops on it. This system, known as land **enclosure** (as opposed to the open fields that had existed before), meant fewer workers were needed and left many people jobless and homeless. A significant number headed to the towns and cities to try to find work but there were not enough jobs to go around. London's population went from around 60,000 in 1500 to over 200,000 in 1600. Norwich, Bristol and York had populations between 8000 and 12,000.

## The population and prices go up

During Elizabeth's reign the population of England grew from 2.8 million to 4 million. This was the result of both an increased birth rate and a falling death rate. Limited places to live gave power to landlords who unfairly increased rents (known as **rack renting**). As a result of the bad harvests, there was less food, which led to price **inflation**. A terrible outbreak of flu in 1556 had killed around 200,000, including many of the workers who were involved in producing food. All of these factors contributed to creating a very poor group of people at the bottom of Elizabethan society.

▼ INTERPRETATION B  *From Spartacus Educational, a history education website:*

> Unemployment was a major cause of poverty. When large landowners changed from arable to sheep farming, unemployment increased rapidly. The closing down of the monasteries in the 1530s created even more unemployment. As monasteries had also helped provide food for the poor, this created further problems. Unemployed people were sometimes tempted to leave their villages to look for work. This was illegal and people who did this were classified as vagabonds.

## Key Words

poverty  pauper  retinue  Reformation
monastery  enclosure  rack renting  inflation

## Work

1  Explain what is meant by 'debasing' coins. Why did Henry VIII do this and what were the consequences?

2  Explain the term 'enclosure'.

3  Look at **Source A**. What does it suggest about the different parts of Elizabethan society?

4  Create a spider diagram to show the reasons for the increase in poverty in Elizabethan times.

5  'The rise in population led to the increase in poverty in Tudor England.' How far do you agree with this statement? Remember to consider all of the factors and make comparisons between them based on their relative importance.

## Practice Question

How convincing is **Interpretation B** in explaining the causes of poverty in Elizabethan England?

Explain your answer using **Interpretation B** and your own knowledge.  **8 marks**

## Study Tip

The interpretation gives a number of factors for the increase in poverty. Are these factors accurate? Is there anything that is missed out?

# How did Elizabethans respond to poverty?

It is clear that poverty and the poor became a major issue during Elizabeth's reign. There were a lot more poor people than there were rich and there was always the potential for the poor to rise up and rebel. In the towns and cities finding a job was difficult, but the same thing was occurring in the countryside where changes in farming led to high levels of unemployment. Bad harvests meant that many poor people were close to starvation. In these pages, we will explore how wealthier Elizabethans responded to the poor.

## Objectives

▶ **Describe** the different groups of pauper.

▶ **Explain** why so many wealthy people had a negative view of the poor.

▶ **Evaluate** the effect of contemporary publications on public opinion of the poor.

## A sympathetic approach

Their belief in 'the Great Chain of Being' made it clear to Elizabethans where they were positioned in society. In the views of the time, the wealthy (nobles and gentry) were simply 'better' than the peasants. However, just as God looked after his people and the queen looked after her subjects, the wealthy were expected to offer some help to those below them. In practice, this might mean making the odd charitable donation, but not something that was going to solve the problem completely. Before Elizabeth, attitudes to the poor were largely unsympathetic. There was certainly recognition that some poor people could not help their situation, because of injury or ill health, so it was seen as correct that charities should help them. If someone was able-bodied, however, it seemed logical to the wealthy that the person could find work if they chose to.

As unemployment and poverty grew under Elizabeth there was a change in attitude. People began to recognise that many able-bodied paupers, particularly in **urban** areas, could not find work. They wanted to help themselves but they were not able to. These people were seen as the **deserving poor**. The response to this change in attitude was that many wealthier people worked hard to provide more help and charity to those in need. Archbishop Whitgift established **almshouses** in Croydon in south London. Almshouses were buildings that provided accommodation and food for those in need.

## The undeserving poor

While more people began to recognise the idea of the deserving poor, they also saw a group that was

▼ INTERPRETATION A *A painting from 1911 of an almshouse built by Archbishop Whitgift in 1596*

undeserving. These were untrustworthy beggars who had no interest in honest work. In 1567, Thomas Harman published a book that drew attention to some of the scams and tricks used by these conmen and women. The book was very popular and hardened some attitudes towards the poor. Many wealthy people began to question the honesty of all beggars they encountered.

## Common vagabonds in Elizabethan England from Thomas Harman's *Warning Against Vagabonds*

**The Counterfeit Crank** would bite on soap so that he frothed at the mouth and then pretend to have a fit. The idea was that people would feel sorry for him and give him money.

**The Baretop Trickster** was a woman who would trick men into following them, and perhaps buying them a meal, by removing items of clothing. The man would then be beaten and robbed by the woman's accomplices.

**The Clapper Dudgeon** would cut himself and tie dirty bandages around the wound. People would feel sympathy and give him money.

**Tom O'Bedlam** would pretend to be mad in order to get money. He might bark like a dog for hours, follow people around or stick a chicken's head in his ear. The money people gave him may have been out of sympathy or perhaps just to get rid of him!

▼ **SOURCE B** *Adapted from* A Description of England *by William Harrison (1587):*

> The vagabonds abide nowhere but run up and down place to place; idle beggars cut the fleshy parts of their bodies to raise pitiful sores and move the hearts of passers-by so they will bestow large gifts upon them. It makes me think that punishment is more suitable for them than generosity or gifts. They are all thieves. They take from the godly poor what is due to them.

## The idle poor

Harman's book was based on the idea of beggars being criminals but his view was not unique. Many believed that the best way to deal with begging was to threaten severe punishment. Beggars were often seen as idle or lazy and unable to change their ways.

▼ **SOURCE C** *This illustration shows the same man in normal dress (left) and disguised as a cripple (right)*

### Extension

As a historian it is important to know the background information of any source that you use. In order to make use of Thomas Harman's book we need to understand who he was and how he went about writing it. Spend some time researching Harman. Who was he? What did he do? How did he get the information for his book?

## Work

1 Explain the term 'deserving poor'.

2 What was an almshouse?

3 Create a poster warning visitors to your town of the dangers of Elizabethan vagabonds.

4 Look at **Source B**. What kind of vagabond is Harrison describing?

5 a Why do you think Thomas Harman's book and the picture in **Source C** were produced?

  b What effect do you think these publications might have had on how people viewed the poor?

6 Explain how attitudes to poverty in Elizabethan England changed.

# The government's treatment of the poor

As poverty increased, it became clear that the government needed to do more to combat it, so cities around England began to take new approaches to the problem. Inspired by these new ideas, in 1601 Elizabeth went further than any of her predecessors when she backed a fresh approach: the Poor Law. However, this was not the first new method of dealing with poverty as a number of towns and cities had already begun their own schemes. How was poverty dealt with in English cities?

## Objectives

▶ **Describe** the approaches to poverty in Elizabethan England.

▶ **Compare** the new approaches to how poverty had been dealt with before.

▶ **Evaluate** the success of the new approaches.

## The Tudors and poverty

Henry VIII and Edward VI passed laws to try to deal with poverty, but not only did the problem remain, it actually grew more serious as time went on. As far back as 1495, beggars were being punished in the **stocks** and sent back to their home towns if they had gone to another area. From 1531, with a few exceptions (who were given licences), beggars were publicly whipped. If they were caught for a second time they would have a hole burned in their ear and a third offence would mean they were hanged. Some laws were abandoned because they were seen as too harsh but most of the 1531 laws remained in place for most of Elizabeth's reign. The 1576 'Act for setting the poor on work' placed the responsibility for finding work for the poor in the hands of the local authorities while the national policy still focused on punishment.

## How did different towns and cities deal with poverty?

Different approaches to poverty were taken in various areas of the country. The problem was particularly felt in urban areas. In London, for example, Bridewell Palace was used as a shelter for the homeless; a new hospital, known as Bedlam, was established for the mentally ill; and other hospitals were opened for orphans and the sick. However, conditions in these institutions were harsh and the problem of poverty in the city continued to grow. With more and more paupers coming from the countryside, many of whom turned to crime, the

▼ **SOURCE A** *A beggar is publicly whipped in 1567*

authorities struggled to cope. Look at how three cities dealt with the problem of poverty:

## York

In the early Tudor period, York had become very prosperous and large numbers of poor people from the countryside moved into the city to try to find work. As a result, the city saw an increase in the number of beggars. In 1515, the York Corporation had begun issuing beggar licences, 16 years before other cities. Licensed beggars were required to wear a badge so that they could be identified. From 1528, a Master Beggar was appointed, whose job it was to keep a check on the rest. During Elizabeth's reign, many beggars were expected to work; weaving and spinning in particular helped increase the city's growing industry. Those who refused were sent to the **House of Correction** (a type of prison for those who refused to work) or were returned to the town or village that they had come from.

## Ipswich

In 1569, Ipswich introduced a licensing system for beggars and increased support for the poor. It also became one of the first towns to open a hospital specifically to help the old and sick who could not afford treatment. A youth training scheme was introduced, designed to help children learn a trade that would lift them out of poverty. The town was also one of the first to build a House of Correction.

## Key Words

stocks    House of Correction

## Norwich

In 1570, the authorities in Norwich conducted a survey which found that 80 per cent of the population lived in poverty. They separated the poor into two categories: 'idle poor' and 'unfortunate poor'. The 'idle poor' were given work such as knitting or sewing while the 'unfortunate poor' were given food and other forms of care and support. This system was effective in limiting the numbers who received poor relief, as the poor had to be officially identified. Norwich taxed its rich citizens to pay for the care of the vulnerable.

## Practice Question

Write an account of the different ways in which towns and cities dealt with poverty in Elizabethan England.    **8 marks**

## Study Tip

For this type of question you should aim to write about more than one example. Try to compare and contrast the towns and cities and consider how effective their methods were. Did they have an influence on national policy?

## Work

1 Create a warning poster for beggars in Tudor England that tells them what could happen if they are caught.

2 Look at **Source A**.
   a What is happening in this image?
   b How far does it reflect the Tudor approach to poverty?

3 a Explain how Norwich dealt with poverty.

   b In what sense did this represent a change to what had gone before?

4 Which of the measures taken by these towns would have done the most to deter vagabonds?

5 'Cities like York and Ipswich took a much more sympathetic approach to poverty.' How far do you agree with this statement?

# The government's treatment of the poor

## A new direction from Elizabeth?

In 1601, right at the end of her reign, Elizabeth and her government introduced the first ever Poor Law. The law said that in each area of the country, the wealthy should be taxed to pay for the care and support of the vulnerable, including the old and the sick. The fit and healthy poor were to be given work. This reflected the change in attitude that had taken place during this period. These kinds of taxes had existed before but never on this scale. This was not a total change in direction, however. Those who were deemed able to work, but who did not, were still dealt with harshly. They were whipped and then placed in a House of Correction. The box opposite shows how different groups were dealt with.

### The types of poor in Elizabethan England

**The helpless poor:** The sick and the old were provided with food to live on and placed in special homes where they could be cared for.

**The able-bodied poor:** Those who were considered fit, including children, were expected to work. They were given food and drink as payment and, in some cases, somewhere to sleep.

**The idle poor:** Those who were seen as lazy were whipped and then sent to a House of Correction where they would be forced to work. Those who went beyond begging into a life of crime might be dealt with even more harshly.

▼ **INTERPRETATION B** *A late seventeenth-century sketch of Bridewell House of Correction in London, opened in 1553*

29th March. At Harrow on the Hill in Middlesex, on the said day, John Allen, Elizabeth Turner, Humphrey Foxe, Henry Bower and Agnes Wort, being over 14 years and having no lawful means of livelihood, were declared vagabonds and sentenced to be **flogged** severely and burnt on the right ear.

## How effective were the Poor Laws?

The success of places like York, Ipswich and Norwich helped to convince Elizabeth and her government that a new approach was needed nationwide. Simply punishing the poor did not work. The 1531 laws did attempt to recognise the difference between the genuinely poor and those who were **vagrants**, but they remained focused on punishing the majority. Various attempts were made by individual MPs to introduce new Poor Laws but it was not until the end of Elizabeth's reign that things really began to change.

The aim of the 1601 law was to help those who were genuinely poor, but it still maintained the clear threat of punishment for those who were considered lazy. Initially, the Poor Law seemed to work but it was inconsistently used and many areas did not fulfil the requirements. Over the following few years instances of begging did seem to decrease but this may have been as much due to the threat of the House of Correction as the increased help available.

Some argue that the 1601 Poor Law was not entirely successful. As it made each area responsible for its own poor, there were arguments over which area paupers belonged to. Without a clear home, some paupers were simply sent from one area to another. Despite criticism, the Elizabethan Poor Law remained in effect until it was reformed in the nineteenth century.

### Fact

The Poor Law was finally reviewed in 1834. Many of the debates about who deserved to be helped and who did not were revisited and argued about at this time.

### Key Words

flogged    vagrant

### Work

1  a  Describe the punishment that would have taken place at the location in **Interpretation B**.
   b  Why do you think such harsh punishments were used?
2  How did the Poor Law change the way poverty was dealt with?
3  Imagine you are responsible for the changes that have been introduced. Create a presentation to explain how the poor should now be dealt with. You can use ideas from these pages and earlier in the chapter.
4  How far could the 1601 Poor Law be considered successful?

### Extension

Significance is a key concept for historians. Something that is significant had a big impact on people at the time and continued to have a big impact long after it happened. How significant do you think the 1601 Poor Law was?

### Practice Question

Write an account of how the Poor Law system changed under Queen Elizabeth I.    **8 marks**

### Study Tip

Remember that this type of question is asking how things changed. This means that you need to explain how systems to deal with poverty worked *before* Elizabeth's reign as well as during it.

# Drake and voyages of exploration

One of the most famous figures of the Elizabethan age is **Sir Francis Drake**, an explorer, adventurer and military leader. As we have seen, the reign of Elizabeth has often been described as a 'golden age' and a major reason for that is the exploration of new lands and the great new discoveries that were made during the period. In this chapter we will look at some of these discoveries and the adventurers and traders who made them, beginning with Drake himself.

**Objectives**

▶ **Explain** how and why the Elizabethan period is described as an 'age of discovery'.

▶ **Investigate** the life of Sir Francis Drake.

▶ **Analyse** what Drake's voyages tell us about Elizabethan England.

## The age of discovery

The Elizabethan period was a time of great discovery and exploration. Several European countries, most notably Spain, played a major role in this but in many areas it was England that led the way. At the forefront of exploration was Francis Drake, who **circumnavigated** (sailed all the way round) the world between 1577 and 1580. The discoveries of Drake and others led to a completely new understanding of the world.

Drake and his cousin, John Hawkins, made one of the first voyages to Africa to capture people as slaves to sell in the 'New World' of America. They sold the slaves at a Spanish port (San Juan de Ulúa in the Gulf of Mexico) and made lots of money, but were betrayed. Spanish warships attacked them and destroyed many ships. Drake and Hawkins escaped but wanted revenge on the Spanish. Drake became a **privateer**, attacking enemy ships (mostly Spanish) and taking their cargo. This made him (and Queen Elizabeth) a fortune.

▼ **SOURCE A**   *A map from 1590 showing Drake's circumnavigation; with more exploration, Europeans were gaining a greater understanding of how the world actually looked*

## Key Biography

### Francis Drake (c1540–96)

- Became an English hero but the Spanish saw him as a pirate and nicknamed him 'El Draque' or 'the Dragon'.

- Although he circumnavigated the globe he didn't set out to do so – but rather to get revenge for what the Spanish did at San Juan de Ulúa. When he returned he had so much gold on board that the half he gave to the queen was more than the entire royal income of the previous year!

- Knighted in 1581.

- In 1588, he led the successful defeat of the Spanish **Armada**.

▼ **B** *Drake's great journey*

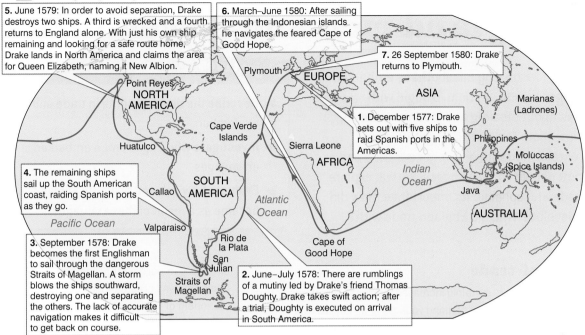

**5.** June 1579: In order to avoid separation, Drake destroys two ships. A third is wrecked and a fourth returns to England alone. With just his own ship remaining and looking for a safe route home, Drake lands in North America and claims the area for Queen Elizabeth, naming it New Albion.

**6.** March–June 1580: After sailing through the Indonesian islands he navigates the feared Cape of Good Hope.

**7.** 26 September 1580: Drake returns to Plymouth.

**1.** December 1577: Drake sets out with five ships to raid Spanish ports in the Americas.

**4.** The remaining ships sail up the South American coast, raiding Spanish ports as they go.

**3.** September 1578: Drake becomes the first Englishman to sail through the dangerous Straits of Magellan. A storm blows the ships southward, destroying one and separating the others. The lack of accurate navigation makes it difficult to get back on course.

**2.** June–July 1578: There are rumblings of a mutiny led by Drake's friend Thomas Doughty. Drake takes swift action; after a trial, Doughty is executed on arrival in South America.

*Map labels: Plymouth, EUROPE, ASIA, Marianas (Ladrones), Point Reyes, NORTH AMERICA, Cape Verde Islands, Sierra Leone, AFRICA, Philippines, Molùccas (Spice Islands), Huatulco, Indian Ocean, Java, SOUTH AMERICA, Callao, Atlantic Ocean, AUSTRALIA, Pacific Ocean, Valparaiso, Rio de la Plata, San Julian, Cape of Good Hope, Straits of Magellan*

---

▼ **INTERPRETATION C** *A nineteenth-century engraving showing Drake being knighted by Queen Elizabeth aboard his ship the* **Golden Hind***; knighting Drake angered Philip of Spain, which may have been exactly why Elizabeth did it!*

## How was all this possible?

The main reason for the increase in exploration was new technology. Ships built at this time were of higher quality, with new **lateen** (triangular) sails making them faster and easier to steer. Improved defences and weapons made sailing through hostile waters much safer. Advances in navigation also played a significant role. The **astrolabe** allowed sailors to judge how far north or south they were and better compasses made navigation more accurate. But voyages remained dangerous. Drake's circumnavigation, for example, began with five ships and 164 men but ended with just one ship

### Key Words

circumnavigate   privateer   Armada
lateen   astrolabe

and 58 men. However, men like Drake embarked on them knowing that success would bring wealth, influence and respect for themselves and for England.

### Work

1. Why might the Elizabethan period be referred to as an 'age of discovery'?

2. Create a comic strip to show the key events and problems during Drake's journey around the world. Write your own captions for each panel.

3. What does Drake's journey suggest about the reasons for voyages? Think about why he set off rather than what he achieved.

4. How did improved technology help voyages like Drake's?

5. Look at **Interpretation C**. Why do you think Queen Elizabeth chose to knight Francis Drake?

### Extension

Look at **Source A**. What does this map and Drake's voyage tell you about Elizabethan England?

# 5.2A  Did voyages abroad make England rich and powerful?

One major reason why Elizabethans embarked on voyages was to get rich. To begin with, this was about stealing and looting. However, over time more formal trade agreements were established with different countries and different people. In these pages, we will explore this trade and consider its importance. How did trade develop? Who did England trade with?

> ## Objectives
> ▶ **Describe** the developments in trade and exploration.
> ▶ **Investigate** why English men embarked on voyages.
> ▶ **Evaluate** how rich and powerful England became as a result of these voyages.

## The age of trade

The actions of explorers certainly increased the queen and the country's income (indeed the purpose of many voyages of discovery was to make money) but the real prize lay in trade, the buying and selling of goods. Before Elizabeth's reign, the majority of English trade was with other European countries but people began to look further afield, in particular the Far East where spices could be bought. Initially it was necessary to go through middlemen, traders who bought the spices and then sold them to the Europeans, making a big profit. The English were keen to cut the middlemen out by finding direct routes to India and the Far East in order to raise their own profits.

## Trade with the East

Several attempts were made to find a direct route to India and China. The first notable ones were those of Sir Martin Frobisher who tried on three occasions but failed each time. Attempts to reach the East led to the exploration of other areas including the Americas. Companies began to be established with the purpose of trading in particular areas. The Muscovy Company was created in 1555 and given the monopoly of trade with the city of Moscow in Russia, so that no other company could trade in this area. A similar model was followed elsewhere with the Eastland Company (1579) in Scandinavia and the Baltic, and the Levant Company (1581) in Turkey and the Middle East.

The biggest prize lay further east, however, and in 1582, Queen Elizabeth sent Ralph Fitch to India and the Far East and when he returned he told the queen that profitable trade was more than possible. The East India Company was established in 1600 to oversee this trade. Although English trade in the Far East was limited compared to that of other European countries, this period saw the foundations laid for dominance in later centuries. These companies brought products to England that had rarely been seen before, such as spices, silks and porcelain.

▼ **SOURCE A**  *The official seal of the Muscovy Company*

▼ **SOURCE B**  *Ralph Fitch's account of what he saw in India:*

They have a very strange order among them – they worship a cow, and esteem much of the cow's dung to paint the walls of their houses. They will kill nothing – not so much as a louse: for they hold it a sin to kill anything. They eat no flesh but live by roots and rice and milk. And when the husband dieth his wife is burned with him, if she be alive: if she will not, her head is shaven and then is never any account made of her after.

# The human trade

In 1564, with the authorisation of the queen and accompanied by his cousin Francis Drake, **John Hawkins** kidnapped several hundred West Africans. They were taken by ship to the South American coast where they were sold as slaves. This was not the first case of Europeans enslaving Africans, but it was the first time an Englishman had carried out the entire process (Hawkins had captured some slaves from a Portuguese ship two years previously). Throughout Elizabeth's reign, England's involvement in the slave trade grew and many more slave traders made their fortune. Demand grew for slaves to work the land in the Americas and produce materials to be returned to England.

▼ **SOURCE C** *John Hawkins' coat of arms, awarded in 1568*

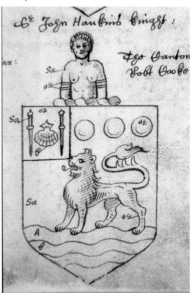

## Practice Question

Explain what was important about exploration and trade in Asia for Elizabethan England.

**8 marks**

## Study Tip

You could explain how trade developed with India and the Far East and why it was considered a priority. What was the impact on Elizabethan England?

## Key Biography

### John Hawkins (1532–95)

- Key figure in Elizabeth's court, even working as a spy joining the Ridolfi Plot against the queen and passing information about the plot to the authorities.

- Hawkins was responsible for building up the Royal Navy and was a respected military leader, playing a major role as a commander in the battle against the Spanish Armada. He was also a successful privateer, raiding Spanish ports and ships.

- From 1562 he became involved in the African slave trade, first seizing slaves from the Portuguese and then capturing them himself.

- He is believed to be responsible for introducing tobacco to England after discovering it during one of his voyages.

## Work

1  What is meant by the term 'trade'?

2  What made John Hawkins an important figure during the reign of Elizabeth?

3  Why were the English so keen to find a direct route to the Far East?

4  What does **Source B** suggest about European sailors' impressions of the East?

5  Look carefully at **Source C**. How does Hawkins' coat of arms demonstrate the way in which he made his money?

6  Design the cover of a book about John Hawkins. You need to decide what should go on the front, what the title should be and then write a blurb (the short piece of information on the back) that summarises his life.

## 5.2B Did voyages abroad make England rich and powerful?

### The New World

In addition to the Far East and Africa, English and other European sailors crossed the Atlantic Ocean to the Americas. Like elsewhere, these voyages were about gaining wealth and influence, but they were also about establishing **colonies**. Where and why were European countries so keen to establish colonies? Where was the New World and why did it prove such a challenging place for the English?

### Raleigh's New World

In 1584, Elizabeth gave **Sir Walter Raleigh** permission to explore, colonise (take ownership of) and rule any land that was not already ruled by a Christian. In return he had to give the queen one fifth of all the gold and silver that he found there. The aim was to increase England's influence and gain the country more wealth. Raleigh, who was a respected, famous explorer and adventurer, did not set sail for North America himself but rather sent others to form the first English colony in what is now the United States.

▼ **INTERPRETATION D** *An engraving from 1618 that shows the establishment of a colony in North America*

## Key Biography

### Sir Walter Raleigh (1552–1618)

- Born into a Protestant family and had struggled to survive the reign of Mary I.
- Very loyal to Elizabeth and spent years in Ireland fighting Catholic rebels.
- Became a favourite of the queen when he returned to court.
- Embarked on voyages to South America in search of a legendary city of gold: El Dorado.
- Funded an attempt to establish a colony in North America.
- His secret marriage to one of the queen's ladies in waiting led to a jealous Elizabeth banishing him from court for five years in 1592.

A colony was established at Roanoke but did not last. A second was established in 1587 and seemed set to succeed. However, when the colony's leader, John White, returned after a trip to England, the other colonists had disappeared. The only clue was the word 'CROATOAN' carved into a tree, the name of a local tribe. No trace of the colonists was ever found. It would not be until the reign of James I, Elizabeth's successor, that a colony was successfully established in North America.

## How did the voyages of exploration benefit England?

Elizabeth was a great supporter of the voyages of exploration that set sail from England during her reign. Their aim was clear, to increase the wealth, power and territory of England – but how successful were they in doing this?

### Wealth

By raiding Spanish ships and ports, English sailors like Sir Francis Drake brought riches back to England. Sailors like John Hawkins made his fortune and added to the country's wealth by trading in African slaves. However, other countries like Spain and Portugal also made huge amounts of money at this time by trading in spices and taking gold from South America. Despite this, England did build the foundations of the great trading empire it later became, with many of the trading companies established under Elizabeth becoming very important in the following century.

### Power

English naval power was a growing force under Elizabeth. It was clear that England could hold its own in any sea battle and was able to exert its influence over many weaker countries.

## Key Words

colony

### Territory

England failed in its first attempt to build a colony in America – and other countries

beat England in the race to colonise South America. However, English explorers and settlers persevered and over the next few centuries England began to build up more and more territory overseas.

### Work

1   In what ways did Walter Raleigh's religion play a role in his rise in Elizabeth's court?

2   What does the attempted colony in North America suggest about Elizabethan England?

3   Look back at John Hawkins' coat of arms. Design one for Walter Raleigh that reflects his life.

4   Explain how exploration made England wealthier.

5   Look at **Interpretation D**.
    a   What does this engraving suggest about the North American colony it is depicting?
    b   How far does this picture show the reasons for voyages of discovery?

### Practice Question

Explain what was important about voyages of discovery in the reign of Elizabeth I.   **8 marks**

### Study Tip

This type of question is asking you to explain consequences. Make sure you say how voyages had an impact on England. Think about wealth, trade and the country's reputation.

# How did England's religion change under Elizabeth?

Before the arrival of the Tudors, little had changed in England's religious practices and beliefs for hundreds of years. However, the Tudors made huge changes to religion which had a dramatic impact. When Elizabeth became queen she had to make some very difficult decisions about which religious direction England should take.

## Objectives

▶ **Examine** the religion of the country that Elizabeth inherited.

▶ **Describe** the decisions that Elizabeth made about religion in England.

▶ **Analyse** why Elizabeth made her decisions.

## Why was religion a big issue for Elizabeth?

The Reformation of Henry VIII's reign had officially made the country **Protestant** but in reality little had changed. Most **Catholic** practices were still followed. It was during Edward VI's reign (1547–53) that England became much more of a Protestant country. As Edward was only nine when he became king, the country was governed by groups of men, known as Regency Councils. During these six years there were drastic changes, including the introduction of the Book of Common Prayer which firmly established a more Protestant approach.

Edward's death brought his sister Mary to the throne. She spent the following five years returning the country to the Catholic faith. She made the Pope head of the Church once again, brought back the Latin Catholic mass and punished those who refused to return to the old religion. Almost 300 Protestants were martyred by being burned alive on her orders. Mary was desperate to have a child who would succeed her and keep England Catholic but this did not happen. When she died in 1558, Mary left a scarred and religiously divided country to her younger sister, Elizabeth.

▼ **SOURCE B** *An illustration from John Foxe's* Book of Martyrs, *published in 1663; it shows the burning of three Protestant bishops in 1556, including Thomas Cranmer.*

▼ **SOURCE A** *A painting from around 1575 showing Edward surrounded by his advisors, his dying father and the Pope*

## Catholic beliefs and practices

The Pope is the head of the Church and has final say on all religious matters.

The Bible and Church services should be in Latin.

Priests should not marry. Churches should be decorated with paintings, statues and stained glass windows.

Priests are ordinary people's link with God. The bread and wine taken in services literally transforms into the body and blood of Jesus. This is called transubstantiation.

## (Shared beliefs)

Priests are ordinary people's link with God.

God created the world and everything in it.

Jesus was God's son.

Those who challenge the true faith must admit their error or be punished by the true believers.

## Protestant beliefs and practices

The monarch should be head of the Church and have final say on all religious matters.

The Bible and church services should be in the language of ordinary people – English.

Priests are allowed to marry. Churches should be kept plain and simple with little decoration.

Ordinary people can connect to God through personal prayer.

When the bread and wine is taken in services it represents the body and blood of Jesus.

## Key Words

Protestant    Catholic

### Extension

Elizabeth was Protestant yet she chose not to enforce her beliefs in the same way as her brother and sister had. Why do you think she did this?

▼ **INTERPRETATION D** *Adapted from the Royal Museums Greenwich website describing Elizabeth's aims when she became queen. The 'statement' mentioned is the one in Source C:*

> The message was very clear: that they were all, including Elizabeth, members of the same team, working together for a common goal — that of a united, prosperous England. Extremes were to be avoided in order to unite, not divide. In this statement, Elizabeth very deliberately disassociated herself from the unpopularity of Mary's regime by signalling how hers would be different.

## Elizabeth's religious settlement

Elizabeth was a Protestant but she was also practical. She set about a compromise to bring aspects of both faiths together in a 'religious settlement'. Elizabeth allowed priests to marry, services were held in English and she brought back the Book of Common Prayer. However, she declared herself 'governor' rather than 'head' of the Church. Importantly, Elizabeth allowed Catholics to worship in their own way in private. Church services were designed to allow people of either faith to understand and participate in their own way. Elizabeth appointed a moderate Protestant, Matthew Parker, as Archbishop of Canterbury to oversee the English Church.

▼ **SOURCE C** *From the statement read out in Parliament after Elizabeth's coronation in 1559:*

> [The Queen's aim is] to secure and unite the people of this realm in one uniform order to the glory of God and to general tranquillity

### Work

1  a  Explain three differences between the beliefs of Catholics and Protestants.
   b  Which difference between the two faiths do you think is more significant: the way in which they *practise* their religion or the *beliefs* that they hold?
   c  Which difference do you think would be the biggest barrier to compromise? Explain your answer.
2  Look at **Sources A** and **B**. Both were produced during Elizabeth's reign.
   a  What point do you think **Source A** is making about the reign of Edward VI?
   b  What point do you think is being made about Mary's reign by **Source B**?
   c  Why were these sources produced during Elizabeth's reign?

### Practice Question

How convincing is **Interpretation D** about Elizabeth's approach to religion in the first ten years of her reign?    **8 marks**

### Study Tip

Does the interpretation fully explain the reasons for Elizabeth's approach? Do you agree with the writer's conclusions, and why?

# Reactions to Elizabeth's religious changes: England

**6.2**

Elizabeth's church settlement was designed as a compromise to avoid more conflict between Catholics and Protestants, and for many it worked. However, not everyone was willing to come together in the name of unity and peace. A series of Catholic plots challenged Elizabeth throughout her reign and when, in 1570, the Pope excommunicated her from the Catholic Church, the situation grew more tense.

### Objectives

▶ **Describe** the reaction to Elizabeth's church settlement.

▶ **Explain** the impact of Elizabeth's excommunication.

▶ **Evaluate** the success of Elizabeth's church settlement.

## What was life like for most Catholics under Elizabeth?

When Elizabeth came to the throne, many Catholics feared Protestant retribution for the burnings and persecution of Mary I's reign. Instead they found that Elizabeth was determined to bring the country together. Elizabeth's religious settlement combined some Catholic practices with Protestant ones. England was Protestant but Catholics could attend church and see many of the traditions of their faith. The services were written to avoid anything that would cause direct conflict for Catholics, with the wording left open to some interpretation. **Recusancy** fines for Catholics who refused to attend Protestant services were also very low. Catholics kept their own beliefs private and in return the government would not seek out disobedience.

## The papal bull

On 27 April 1570, Pope Pius V issued *Regnans in Excelsis* ('Reigning on high'). In this special message, or **papal bull**, the Pope **excommunicated** Elizabeth from the Catholic Church and called on Catholics to end her rule.

▼ **SOURCE A** *From a public statement read by the Lord Keeper, Sir Nicholas Bacon, in summer 1570 outlining the queen's policy:*

> As long as people continue to openly follow her laws and do not wilfully and clearly break them, then her majesty will not enquire into their religious beliefs or conscience. She will treat them as her good and obedient subjects.

English Catholics were faced with a dilemma: should they be loyal to their queen or the Pope? Many chose to ignore the bull but some now saw it as their duty to rise up against Elizabeth, whom Pius had called the 'pretended queen of England'. Pius was well aware of the impact of his message.

## Plots and rebellions

The excommunication was designed by the Pope to stir up rebellions and was originally planned to coincide with the Northern Rebellion of 1569, but was issued late. It did, however, inspire other rebellions.

## A new policy from Elizabeth

Plots after the papal bull showed that Elizabeth could no longer rely on the loyalty of all her Catholic subjects. A new approach was needed to ensure that potential trouble makers were found and Catholics did not rebel. New laws were introduced to try to disrupt Catholic activities and show that challenges to the queen's rule would not be tolerated. Having allowed private Catholicism for the first 23 years of her reign, a law was passed in 1581 making it treason to attend a Catholic mass. Greater fines were introduced for those who failed to attend church services. These recusancy fines rose to around £20, a significant sum, even for the more wealthy.

A second Act was passed in 1585 making it treason to have a Catholic priest in your home. Priests were executed and noble Catholic families faced the loss of their lands and wealth if their loyalty to the queen was placed in doubt. A 1593 law said that Catholics could not travel more than five miles from their homes.

| Catholic plots and rebellions | |
| --- | --- |
| **The plot** | **What happened** |
| The Northern Rebellion, 1569 | Elizabeth refused to allow the Duke of Norfolk to marry the Catholic Mary, Queen of Scots. This act inspired two northern Catholic nobles to lead a rebellion against Elizabeth to replace her with the Catholic Mary. Westmorland and Northumberland took control of Durham Cathedral and held an illegal Catholic mass. They then began to march south with around 4600 men. The loyal Earl of Sussex raised an army and the rebels disbanded. Northumberland was captured and executed, Norfolk was imprisoned and Westmorland escaped to France. |
| The Ridolfi Plot, 1571 | This plot was led by an Italian named Ridolfi and also involved Norfolk. The plan was that an invasion from the Netherlands would coincide with another northern rebellion. Elizabeth would be murdered and replaced by Mary, Queen of Scots, who would then marry Norfolk. The plot was exposed before it could be completed. |
| The Throckmorton Plot, 1583 | Led by Sir Francis Throckmorton, the plan was to assassinate Elizabeth and replace her with Mary, Queen of Scots. Once Elizabeth had been killed, there would be an invasion by the French Catholic, Henry, Duke of Guise, and an uprising of English Catholics. The plot also involved the Spanish ambassador. When the plot was discovered, Throckmorton was executed and Mary, Queen of Scots, was placed under even closer guard. |
| The Babington Plot, 1586 | This was another attempt to murder Elizabeth and place Mary, Queen of Scots, on the throne. Led by Anthony Babington, it was the discovery of this plot that led to Mary's trial and execution when it was found that she had known about and agreed with the plot all along. |

▼ **SOURCE B** *From a letter by Sir William Cecil, December 1580:*

> There can be no good government where opposition is allowed. The government can never be safe where there is toleration of two religions. There is no greater hatred between men than that caused by religious differences. People who disagree about God can never agree how to serve their country.

## Fact

Elizabeth's long reign saw no fewer than nine Popes at the head of the Catholic Church: Paul IV, Pius IV, Pius V, Gregory XIII, Sixtus V, Urban VII, Gregory XIV, Innocent IX and Clement VIII.

## Key Words

recusancy    papal bull    excommunicate

## Work

1  Explain what is meant by the term:
   a  religious settlement
   b  excommunicate.

2  How did most Catholics respond to Elizabeth's religious settlement?

3  Create a poster to show the major Catholic plots that Elizabeth faced. Try to show what happened by using up to ten words per plot.

4  What was the impact of the *Regnans in Excelsis* on Elizabeth's policies in England?

5  Look at **Sources A** and **B**. How do the sources show a change in policy for Elizabeth? Use the sources and your own knowledge to explain your answer.

# 6.3 Reactions to Elizabeth's religious changes: abroad

It was not just in England that Elizabeth faced opposition from Catholics. Powerful Catholics around the world also saw Elizabeth as a problem and her Protestant rule as something that should be challenged. Would Catholic countries like Spain and France see it as their duty to attack Elizabeth?

## Objectives

▶ **Describe** the opposition Elizabeth faced from outside England.

▶ **Explain** how other European countries reacted to Elizabeth's religious policies.

▶ **Evaluate** the effect of religion on relations between England and other countries.

▼ **SOURCE A** *Adapted from the papal bull issued in 1570 by Pope Pius V:*

> Elizabeth, the pretended queen of England and the servant of crime, has followed and embraced the errors of the heretics. We declare her to be deprived of her pretended title to the crown. We charge and command all the nobles, subjects, peoples that they do not dare obey her orders, mandates and laws.

## The college at Douai

In 1568, an English Catholic cardinal named **William Allen** established a **seminary** at Douai in the Spanish Netherlands to train priests. Allen, who had the full backing of the Pope, aimed to educate priests who would then travel to England as **missionaries** to convert the English back to the Catholic faith. The first priests arrived in England in 1574, just as Elizabeth's fear of Catholic rebellion was growing.

## The Jesuits

The Society of Jesus was created in 1540. It was part of what is known as the **Counter-Reformation** and hoped to bring people back to the Catholic religion. The Jesuits, as its members were known, first arrived in England in 1580. Their aim was to convert the Protestant population to the Catholic faith. Jesuit priests were seen by Elizabeth as a threat to her rule and those who were caught were treated harshly. The 1585 Act against Jesuits and Seminary Priests called for all Jesuits to be driven out of England and many were executed. Those who sheltered them could be arrested.

## Key Biography

### Cardinal William Allen (1532–94)

- An English Catholic who was made a Cardinal on the recommendation of King Philip II of Spain in 1587.
- A key figure in the Pope's plan for England to return to Catholicism.
- Involved in the Throckmorton Plot and the Spanish Armada.
- It is likely that had England become Catholic he would have been Archbishop of Canterbury and responsible for re-establishing the religion in the country.

## The Catholic powers in Europe

Although the Protestant faith was now widespread across Europe, the two most powerful countries remained firmly Catholic. Taking their lead from the Pope, the kings of France and Spain began to support challenges to Elizabeth's rule. To begin, it was hoped that a Catholic prince or perhaps Philip II himself might marry Elizabeth, but as it became clear that this would not happen, relations between the countries came under strain. Although he felt a duty to respond to the Pope's excommunication of Elizabeth, Philip was not yet in a position to launch a full-scale attack on England so he used other methods to try and undermine the English queen.

Although war was avoided, France and Spain supported the Jesuit missionaries and also gave financial support to those who wanted to get rid of the queen. Philip II even helped set up the seminary at Douai in the Netherlands, an area that was a source of conflict between the two countries. Elizabeth always showed her strength and determination when faced with threats from powerful Catholic countries, but the threats never went away. However, the death of Mary, Queen of Scots, and the failure of the Spanish Armada represented significant blows to Spanish, and papal, hopes of removing Elizabeth from power.

▼ **SOURCE B** *The 'Bishops' Bible published in 1568*

### Work

1  Who is the Pope and why was he so important in the 1500s?

2  Look at **Source A**.
   a  What does the Pope mean by 'her pretended title'?
   b  Working with a partner, rewrite the Pope's message in your own words.

3  Look at **Source B**. What does it suggest about religion in England in 1568?

4  Why did Elizabeth see the Jesuits as a threat?

5  Create a guide to England for a Jesuit priest. What does he need to know to stay safe? Which part of the country should he head to? How could he blend in?

▼ **INTERPRETATION C** *From a school History textbook, published in 2015:*

> Elizabeth was also concerned about the reaction from abroad. Both France and Spain were Catholic powers and could pose a threat to the settlement. In the event neither showed much inclination to be critical. Philip of Spain was prepared to give Elizabeth the benefit of the doubt. Neither he nor the Pope saw the changes in England as permanent and hoped that England could be persuaded to return the Church to Rome.

### Practice Question

Write an account of Elizabeth's changing policy towards Catholics.     **8 marks**

### Study Tip

Remember to include plenty of specific detail about how and why Elizabeth's policies changed.

# Elizabeth and the 'Catholic threat'

For the first twenty years of her reign, Elizabeth's policy towards Catholics was one of tolerance. The country was Protestant and, as long as they kept their personal practices private, Catholics would be left alone. In the 1580s this policy changed drastically. New laws made life extremely difficult for Catholics, forcing them to conform to Protestantism or face torture and even death. Catholic life was severely restricted and penalties were brutal. Why did Elizabeth's attitude to Catholics change so dramatically at this time? What laws did Elizabeth introduce and what was their effect on England's Catholics?

## Objectives

▶ **Recall** the change in Elizabeth's policy towards Catholics.

▶ **Explain** how and why the change came about.

▶ **Evaluate** how far Campion's mission was responsible for the change in policy.

## Why did Elizabeth's policy change?

In the 1580s, tolerance of Catholics declined sharply. Elizabeth and her government felt increasingly under threat at home and abroad. In England, there were a number of important Catholic families who still held a lot of power, particularly in the north. With the Catholic Church in Europe determined that England should return to Catholicism it is easy to see why Elizabeth felt vulnerable.

▼ **INTERPRETATION A** *An engraving of Saint Edmund Campion from 1819*

## Key Biography

### Edmund Campion (1540–81)

- He became a scholar at Oxford University during the reign of Mary I.
- As his Catholic views became known and less acceptable, Campion left England.
- He travelled alone and by foot to Rome to join the Jesuits in 1573.

## Campion's mission

The Jesuits had spent the years since 1540 sending missionaries all over Europe, often at risk to their lives, spreading their religious message. In 1580, they began a mission to England. The men chosen to lead the mission were two exiled Englishmen: Robert Parsons and the charismatic **Edmund Campion**. On arrival in England on the 24 June, Campion, disguised as a jewel merchant, began to preach to the ordinary English people. He travelled the country spreading his message. News of his presence reached the authorities and Campion became a wanted man. Parsons kept a much lower profile. The authorities were certain that Campion's aim was to encourage a rebellion.

## Campion is caught

Campion was arrested on 14 July in Berkshire and taken to the Tower of London. Under questioning by three members of Elizabeth's privy council, Campion maintained that he had no wish to overthrow the queen. He was held for four months and tortured several times on the **rack**. He was found guilty of treason on 20 November 1581. On 1 December, Campion was dragged through London before being hanged, drawn and quartered. Parsons escaped from England, never to return.

## Elizabeth's new laws

Elizabeth's stance on Catholics became tougher after 1580. The table below shows four of the important laws that were passed during her reign.

| Date | Key points of law |
|---|---|
| 1571 | Recusancy fines for Catholics who did not take part in Protestant services. They could be fined or have property taken from them. However, the rich could afford to pay and Elizabeth did not enforce the law too harshly; when Parliament tried to increase the fines, Elizabeth resisted. <br><br> It became illegal to own any Catholic items such as **rosary beads**. |
| 1581 | Recusancy fines were increased to £20 – more than most could afford; this law was strictly enforced. It became high treason to convert to Catholicism. |
| 1585 | Any Catholic priest who had been ordained (made a priest) after 1559 was considered a traitor and both he and anyone protecting him faced death. <br><br> It became legal to kill anyone who attempted to assassinate the queen. |
| 1593 | The 'statute of confinement' – Catholics could not travel more than five miles from their home without permission from the authorities. |

### Key Words

rack     rosary beads

▼ **SOURCE B** *Campion's reaction to being sentenced to execution, according to contemporary reports. The 'see of Peter' refers to the Roman Catholic Church (Saint Peter is believed to have been the first Pope):*

> In condemning us, you condemn all your own ancestors, all our ancient bishops and kings, all that was once the glory of England — the island of saints, and the most devoted child of the See of Peter.

▼ **INTERPRETATION C** *From the blog 'An Historian Goes to the Movies' written by Andrew Larsen. This entry is from October 2015:*

> Elizabeth did persecute Catholics in the later part of her reign, but she did so largely in response to Pius V's excommunication of her, which had the unfortunate effect of meaning that a devout Catholic could not be trusted to support Elizabeth as monarch (which is not to say that all Catholics opposed her, only that they almost automatically came under suspicion).

## Work

1. Explain how Elizabeth's policy towards Catholics changed in the 1580s.

2. Look at **Source B**. Explain what Campion means in your own words.

3. Look at **Interpretation A**.

   a. What do you notice sticking out of Campion's chest?

   b. Why do you think this has been included?

   c. What does it suggest about the person who created this image?

4. What does **Interpretation C** suggest caused Elizabeth's change in policy? How far do you agree?

5. Which of the two statements below do you think is more accurate and why?

   - 'Campion's mission was the reason for Elizabeth's change in policy towards Catholics.'
   - 'The way Campion was treated shows that Elizabeth's attitude towards Catholics had already changed drastically'.

## 6.5 Puritans and their beliefs

The aim of Elizabeth's religious settlement was to offer a compromise that both Protestants and Catholics could accept. While most people accepted it, a small of group of extreme Protestants known as Puritans were angered. Who were they and why could they not accept Elizabeth's church settlement?

**Objectives**

▶ **Describe** the ideas of the Puritans.

▶ **Explain** Elizabeth's policy towards Puritans.

▶ **Assess** the threat that Puritans posed to Elizabeth's religious settlement.

### Who were the Puritans?

The Puritans were Protestants who were unwilling to compromise in how their faith was practised. They had been influenced by more extreme Protestants in Europe, like John Calvin in Geneva, and argued for the removal of all Catholic elements from the English Church. Puritans hoped that Elizabeth would bring about the England they had dreamed of. Elizabeth's Church settlement was a huge disappointment to them.

Early in her reign Elizabeth appointed a number of bishops who had similar views to the Puritans. A big area of contention was what they wore. Puritans preferred ordinary, plain clothing but bishops of the Church of England were required to wear a white gown, or **surplice**, during services. Despite initial arguments most bishops ultimately accepted the clothing, especially after 1566 when it was made clear that refusal would cost them their jobs. By 1668, most Puritans accepted Elizabeth's changes and reluctantly conformed. A small dedicated group, known as **Presbyterians**, refused to give in and continued to argue against what they saw as a **popish** Church. They didn't like the idea of bishops at all and wanted them removed completely as had been done in Geneva.

▼ **SOURCE A** *A depiction of a sixteenth-century English Puritan family learning to sing hymns together; Puritans believed in the sombre and strict upbringing of children with much time spent on religious instruction and Bible study*

### How much of a threat were the Puritans?

In the 1570s, meetings known as **prophesyings** became popular. Prophesyings involved members of the **clergy** meeting for prayer and discussion and would often include strong criticism of Elizabeth's Church. The Archbishop of Canterbury, Edmund Grindal, encouraged these meetings but the queen saw them as very dangerous.

Grindal was suspended as Archbishop by the queen when he refused to ban prophesyings. More and more Puritans separated themselves totally from the mainstream Church and there were a number of attempts to establish new churches. In 1580, a new **separatist** church was established in Norwich. Its leader, Robert Browne, was arrested but later released. A second church was set up in London in 1592 and again the leaders, Henry Barrow and John Greenwood, were arrested. Unlike Browne, however, they were hanged.

### Powerful Puritans

Parliament included a number of Puritan MPs, including Sir Peter Wentworth and Anthony Cope, who tried to introduce new laws that would change the Church but failed to gain enough support. The queen's childhood friend and potential husband Robert Dudley was a Puritan, but the most prominent Puritan in government was Sir Francis Walsingham. He was well aware that Puritanism had little support among the majority of Protestants and so never made a serious effort to support the cause. He did, however, offer some protection to Puritans by limiting the extent to which Elizabeth cracked down on them.

## How did Elizabeth and her government deal with Puritans?

With the deaths of Dudley and Walsingham in 1588 and 1590, Puritanism lost powerful supporters at court, and Elizabeth took a harsher approach towards Puritans. Their refusal to accept her religious settlement was a challenge to her authority and something she was not prepared to allow. In 1583, with the queen's support, the new Archbishop of Canterbury, John Whitgift, had introduced rules to crack down on Puritanism. Among other things, the rules banned unlicensed preaching and enforced attendance at church by imposing recusancy fines. A new High Commission was given the power to fine and imprison Puritans who did not conform. Hundreds were dismissed or imprisoned, including Thomas Cartwright (in 1590). Dudley and Walsingham both urged more tolerance but Elizabeth backed her Archbishop completely. Puritans were producing increasingly extreme publications calling for the reorganisation of the Church and the persecution of those they saw as having Catholic sympathies, which lost them a lot of support. Elizabeth had Puritan printers punished, such as John Stubbs who had his right hand chopped off for criticising official marriage talks with a French Catholic prince. Whitgift's campaign broke the organisation of the Puritans.

▼ **INTERPRETATION B** *A seventeeth-century engraving of Thomas Cartwright*

### Key Words

surplice
Presbyterian
popish
prophesying
clergy
separatist

### Work

1 What is meant by the term 'Puritan'?

2 Why were Puritans so unhappy about the Elizabethan Church settlement?

3 Look at **Source A**. What does this source suggest about Puritans?

4 To what extent were Protestants a threat to Elizabeth's new Church?

5 How effective were Elizabeth and the mainstream Church in dealing with Puritanism?

### Extension

Many of the ideas of English Puritans were based on the teachings of John Calvin. Calvin established his ideas in the city of Geneva (now in Switzerland). Understanding what happened in Geneva will help you understand what Puritans were aiming for in England. Research and prepare a project or presentation on John Calvin's actions in Geneva in the sixteenth century.

### Key Biography

#### John Field (1545–88)

- He was a priest who became an important leader of the most extreme branch of Puritan thought in London.
- His outspoken criticism of the Church of England saw him banned from preaching for 8 years.
- In 1572 he wrote *A View of Popish Abuses yet remaining in the English Church* which was published with Thomas Wilcox's equally controversial *Admonition to Parliament*. Following the publication he was sent to prison for a year.
- After his release he attempted to bring more structure and organisation to the Puritan movement but he gained little support.
- He was later banned from preaching once again but escaped harsher punishment, perhaps as a result of the protection of powerful Puritans in Elizabeth's inner circle.

### Practice Question

Write an account of Puritanism during the reign of Elizabeth I.
**8 marks**

### Study Tip

Remember to include who the Puritans were, what they did and how Elizabeth responded. Try to explain how life changed for them during Elizabeth's reign.

# 7.1 Why was Mary, Queen of Scots, seen as such a threat?

A name that has come up many times when looking at threats to Elizabeth is that of Mary, Queen of Scots. Mary was Elizabeth's cousin and her closest living relative, so as long as Elizabeth remained childless, she was the heir to the throne. She was also a Catholic. How much of a threat was Mary, Queen of Scots?

**Objectives**

▶ **Examine** the story of Mary, Queen of Scots.

▶ **Explain** why Elizabeth saw her as a threat.

▶ **Assess** why Elizabeth waited 19 years before having Mary executed.

## Cousin Mary

Mary was Queen Elizabeth's cousin, her grandmother being Henry VIII's sister, Margaret, who married the King of Scotland. Mary had become Queen of Scotland in 1542 when she was just eight days old. She married the heir to the throne of France in 1558 and was briefly queen of two countries, Scotland and France, and the heir to the throne of a third – England. In fact, she maintained that she was the rightful Queen of England too!

The French king's death in 1560, however, was a turning point in Mary's life. The Catholic queen returned to Scotland to find that the Protestant faith had become more and more popular. Mary became increasingly unpopular, and after it was suggested that she had been involved in the murder of her second husband, Lord Darnley, she was forced to flee and seek safety in England. Her and Darnley's infant son James was crowned King of Scotland in 1567. Mary was now at Elizabeth's mercy.

▼ **INTERPRETATION A** *A nineteenth-century painting of Mary with her newborn son James*

▼ **SOURCE B** *Mary, Queen of Scots*

## A threat to peace in England

Many English Protestants reacted to Mary's arrival in England with shock and fear. They saw a potential Catholic queen and a possible return to the horrors of Mary I's reign, which had seen the burning alive of nearly 300 Protestants. The opinion in Parliament was clear: Mary was a threat to the security of the Protestant country. A number of Elizabeth's advisors in the Privy Council immediately called for Mary's execution but Elizabeth was hesitant. Executing a queen might give her enemies ideas! Instead, Mary was moved around the country as Elizabeth's prisoner for 19 years, although she was treated well.

For most of the 19 years there is not much evidence to suggest that Mary was directly involved in many plots to overthrow Elizabeth but it is clear that she was an inspiration to Catholic plotters and rebels. As you know, there were numerous attempts to overthrow Elizabeth and replace her with Mary, a number of which involved marriage to the Duke of Norfolk. In any case, Mary believed that she was the rightful Queen of England.

▼ **SOURCE C** *From a letter to Queen Elizabeth making charges against Mary, Queen of Scots, sent from Parliament in 1572:*

> Mary has plotted against Your Majesty. She has tried to persuade the Duke of Norfolk to commit treason and against your clear orders decided to marry him. She has stirred up the Earls of Northumberland and Westmorland to rebel against Your Majesty. She has tried to bring rebellion to the country and gain the help of the Pope and others from abroad. We, the members of the House of Lords and House of Commons, beg Your Majesty to punish her.

## The final plot

In 1586, there was one final plot to make Mary Queen of England. A rich, young, devoted Catholic named Anthony Babington came up with a plan to kill Elizabeth. He and five other men would kill her, rescue Mary from prison and place her on the throne. However, Babington needed to know if Mary supported his plan so he tried to contact her.

He managed to get Mary's servants to hide coded letters in beer barrels that were taken to her room. Mary replied saying she agreed to the plan. But in fact, Mary's servants didn't work for her at all, they worked for Elizabeth's chief spy, Sir Francis Walsingham, who took the letters straight to his queen.

When the code was broken, the message was clear: Mary was supporting a plot to kill the Queen of England. A group representing Parliament met with Elizabeth and called for Mary's arrest. Although Elizabeth remained hesitant, she had little choice but to act in the face of so much evidence. Mary, Queen of Scots, was about to go on trial for her life.

▼ **SOURCE D** *One of Babington's letters that was discovered*

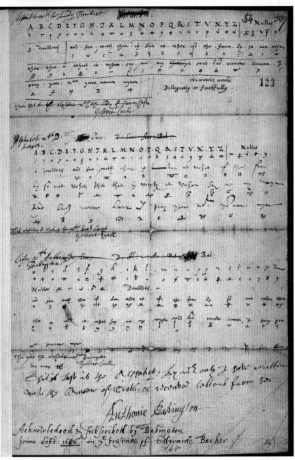

### Extension

Many historians agree that there was more to the Babington Plot than the official account suggests. It is thought that Walsingham was aware of the correspondence between Mary and Babington from the beginning. It is possible he allowed it to continue so that Mary would incriminate herself. Some even suggest that he had the letters planted! What does this suggest about the government's approach to opposition? Research Walsingham's involvement and include as much detail as you can in your answer.

### Work

1 Why did many see Mary as a threat to security in England?

2 Look at **Source C**. What does Parliament think should be done about Mary? Why?

3 Elizabeth kept Mary alive for 19 years. Why do you think the queen did not have her executed immediately? Include as many reasons as you can.

4 Working in a small group, write a script that tells the story of Mary's life up to her arrest in 1586. Perhaps you could perform it as a play.

# 7.2 Elizabeth's treatment of Mary, Queen of Scots

After the discovery of Mary's involvement in the Babington Plot, Elizabeth was left with little choice but to execute her. A trial was organised but its conclusion seemed inevitable. Elizabeth had resisted calls from Parliament for the execution of Mary. What might be the consequences of killing a queen?

## Objectives

▶ **Describe** the trial and execution of Mary, Queen of Scots.

▶ **Explain** why Elizabeth was hesitant to sign Mary's death warrant.

▶ **Assess** whether Mary's execution meant that she was no longer a threat.

## A queen on trial

In October 1586, Mary was put on trial before a court of 36 noblemen including Sir Francis Walsingham, the man who had found the evidence against her, and the queen's close advisor, Sir William Cecil. Mary argued her case strongly. She criticised the fact that she had not been allowed to look at the evidence against her and said that as a foreign queen, and not an Englishwoman, she could not be guilty of treason. But her protests made little impact and she was sentenced to death on 25 October.

Despite all the evidence, Elizabeth was reluctant to have her cousin executed. She even told the French ambassador that she had been in tears over the 'unfortunate affair'. She was worried that if a rightful monarch killed another then there might be terrible consequences. She was concerned that Mary's son, King James VI of Scotland, or even the Catholic Spanish might seek revenge. Eventually, though, she put these fears aside and signed the death warrant on 1 February.

▼ **INTERPRETATION A** *An illustration from* Cassell's History of England, *a book published in 1901, showing the trial of Mary, Queen of Scots, at Fotheringhay Castle*

## The death of a queen

Mary was executed at Fotheringhay Castle on the morning of 8 February. The execution was not held in public but was officially witnessed by the Earls of Shrewsbury and Kent. Elizabeth was said to have been angry about the execution and had the privy councillor who delivered the death warrant briefly imprisoned.

### Fact

Accounts of the execution suggest that it may have taken three blows with the axe: the first hitting the back of her head, the second almost cutting it clean off and the third finally severing it from her neck. The executioner supposedly held up Mary's head by the hair only to have her wig come off in his hands and her head fall to the floor! After the execution, her dog was found hiding beneath her skirts, covered in blood and terrified.

▼ **SOURCE B** *An illustration of the execution of Mary, Queen of Scots, from* Theatrum crudelitatum haereticorum nostri temporis *(Theatre of the Cruelties of the Heretics of our Time), published in 1588*

**Key Words**

martyr

▼ **INTERPRETATION C** *From* History of the Life of Mary Queen of Scots, *published in 1681 from the papers of a secretary of Sir Francis Walsingham:*

> Then lay she down and stretched out her body and her neck upon the block. She cried: 'Lord, into thy hands', and so she received two strokes. The people cried: God save the queen, and so perish all papists and Her Majesty's enemies.

## Did Mary's death solve Elizabeth's problems?

Parliament had spent years trying to convince Elizabeth to have Mary executed as a way to end the Catholic threat. Without Mary, Catholics had no obvious alternative monarch to replace Elizabeth. Should Elizabeth die or be killed her successor would be Mary's son, James, the Protestant King of Scotland. Yet it could be argued that in death, Mary remained a threat. Catholics had a **martyr** (someone who had died for their faith) and could now see that Elizabeth was the wicked heretic that they believed she was. Secondly, in killing Mary, Elizabeth had tried and executed a queen, a dangerous idea to give some of her less loyal subjects.

The French and the Scottish kings expressed outrage but took no action. Elizabeth wrote a letter apologising to James VI of Scotland for his mother's death.

▼ **SOURCE D** *A drawing from a book published in Germany in 1588; the book was written by Robert Turner who taught at the University of Ingolstadt, a centre of Jesuit activity; the first line of the caption said: 'Mary was Queen of Scotland and France and by law Queen of England and Ireland.'*

# Why was there conflict between England and Spain?

Tensions between Protestant England and Catholic Spain existed from the beginning of Elizabeth's reign. King Philip II of Spain was angry about England becoming a Protestant country. To make matters worse, Philip had been married to Elizabeth's Catholic elder sister Mary and had been at her side as she ruled England. Could the two countries ever find common ground? Would Elizabeth really consider marriage to Philip II? And how and why were the Netherlands involved in the conflict?

## Objectives

▶ **Describe** the changing relationship between England and Spain.

▶ **Explain** the factors that led to conflict.

▶ **Evaluate** the reasons for conflict and consider their relative importance.

## King, brother-in-law and potential husband

As King of Spain, Philip II was one of the wealthiest men in the world. Spanish explorers had returned from voyages to South America with vast treasures from Spain's new colonies. Philip II's conquests overseas had received the Pope's blessing so he saw it as his religious duty to expand his power and influence. In 1554, two years before he became king, Philip II married Queen Mary I of England. As long as they were married he would be joint monarch with her. The aim was to unite the Catholic world but Mary and Philip II had no children. Elizabeth became queen, Philip II did not waste time; he quickly issued a marriage proposal to Elizabeth. She did not refuse, but just kept him waiting. For a number of years England and Spain were at peace. But this was not going to last forever.

## Problems in the Netherlands

As well as being King of Spain, Philip II also ruled the Netherlands. In August 1566, there was a Protestant uprising in several Dutch cities. Although the initial disagreement was about taxes, it soon took on a religious dimension. There was an outbreak of **iconoclasm** when Catholic icons (images and sculptures) were smashed, and rioting took place. Philip II was ruthless in his response. He sent Spanish soldiers in to restore order. This led to even more resistance among the Protestant Dutch rebels. Although she did not want an all out war with Spain, Elizabeth agreed to send money to the rebels and allowed English volunteers to go and help. She also offered protection to rebel ships known as the *Gueux de Mer* (sea beggars) which she allowed to stay in English ports up until 1572, greatly angering the King of Spain.

▼ **SOURCE A** *A map showing the location of Spain and the Netherlands*

## Other priorities

Aiding the Protestant rebels in the Netherlands was not an easy decision for Elizabeth. In addition to the religious links, England had strong trade links with the Dutch, particularly the cloth trade. Conflict was bad for business. Philip II was also not keen to get involved with the rebellion, as he had more pressing matters to deal with closer to home in Portugal. He sent a powerful army led by the Duke of Alva to crush the rebellion but it just made the situation worse.

## A declaration of war

In 1584, the leader of the Dutch rebels, William of Orange, was assassinated by a Spanish Catholic. Things grew more chaotic in the Netherlands, and finally, in 1585, Elizabeth sent troops to support the Protestant rebels. She did not want Spain to get too powerful but she was also concerned about France becoming increasingly involved. She sent the trusted Robert Dudley and 7000 soldiers. Although Dudley achieved very little, this was a clear act of war against Spain.

> Philip had been married to Elizabeth's sister and wished to marry Elizabeth but she would not agree.

> England was Protestant and Spain was Catholic.

> The Pope called for all Catholics to challenge Elizabeth in 1570.

### Why was there conflict between Spain and England?

> Sir Francis Drake and other English sailors had spent years raiding Spanish ports in the Americas and stealing treasures in the 1570s.

> Elizabeth sent soldiers to help Protestants rebelling against the Spanish in the Netherlands.

▼ **SOURCE B** *A Dutch painting from 1585; it is a comment on the situation in the Netherlands, which is represented by a cow; Elizabeth is feeding the cow which Philip II is attempting to ride; William of Orange is holding onto the cow's horns; the man at the back is the French king's brother (and one of Elizabeth's suitors), the Duke of Alençon and Anjou*

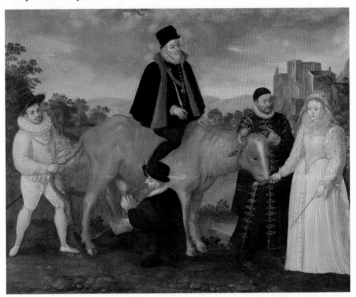

### Work

1. Who rebelled against Spanish rule in the Netherlands?

2. How did Philip II try to put down the rebellion?

3. Why do you think Elizabeth might not have been eager to send English troops to the Netherlands?

4. a. Create a spider diagram to show the reasons for conflict with Spain.
   b. Colour-code your spider diagram to show reasons to do with:
      - religion
      - power
      - other factors.
   c. Which factor do you think played the biggest role?

5. Look at **Source B**.
   a. Why is Philip II shown trying to ride the cow?
   b. Why do you think Elizabeth is feeding the cow? What might this be suggesting about her involvement?
   c. Why has the artist shown William of Orange holding the horns?

# 8.2 The importance of naval warfare

The sixteenth century saw great advances in naval warfare with new technology and stronger ships on the seas. It also saw the development of more effective tactics as countries sought to dominate the waves. The wealth of Spain, England and France relied upon the success of their ships. Whether raiding each other's supplies, exploring new worlds or at war with one another, the future was dependent on control of the sea. How did technology change sailing and battles at sea?

## Objectives

▶ **Consider** the changes in naval warfare in the sixteenth century.

▶ **Explain** why these changes took place.

▶ **Assess** the impact of greater sea power.

## Who ruled the sea?

Henry VIII had spent a fortune building a strong navy that could make England powerful at sea. As an island nation, England was vulnerable to attack by sea and so a strong navy had always been considered important. Before 1500, ships were seen as a way to get to a battle rather than as part of the fight itself.

The Tudor period in England saw ships being built with both attack and defence in mind. The navy had grown during Henry's time but it was under Elizabeth, or, more specifically, John Hawkins who she put in charge of the project, that England's navy reached its high point. England was not alone in building up its fleet, however. King Philip II of Spain was determined to build the most powerful navy in the world and he spared no expense in trying to achieve this aim.

## Piracy or good tactics?

The most common tactic of the sixteenth century was not to engage in all out sea battles but to raid and steal supplies. Sir Francis Drake, Hawkins and others took control of many Spanish ships and raided ports, most notably Cadiz in 1587 when Drake destroyed dozens of Spanish ships in what became known as 'singeing the King of Spain's beard'. Engaging head on was a huge risk whereas surprise attacks, as well as damaging the enemy's ships, could also provide opportunities to seize great treasures and wealth for the country. Elizabeth gave licences to her sailors to act as privateers. This allowed them to attack, raid and steal Spanish

▼ **INTERPRETATION A** *The* Henry Grace, *one of the great ships of Henry VIII's fleet*

possessions whenever they liked. The Spanish accused the English sailors of piracy but the tactic was certainly effective.

**Fireships** were a common weapon. An old or captured ship would be set on fire and sent into the middle of a fleet or harbour causing chaos, terror and huge amounts of damage. When full scale battles were fought, the **line of battle** tactic was used where ships would create a single line, arranged end to end, and then fire together on the enemy with the aim of sinking their ships.

▼ **SOURCE B** *A portrait of Elizabeth I, standing in front of paintings of the defeat of the Spanish Armada*

## Advances at sea in the sixteenth century

**Faster and more manoeuvrable ships** A new type of triangular sail known as a lateen allowed for much faster travel and new ships focused on both speed and manoeuvrability. This allowed greater distances to be travelled but was also perfect for raids and battles.

**More powerful weapons** Whereas previously sailors would have had to try and board enemy ships it was now possible to fire at them with cannons and try to sink them from a distance. Ships were built specifically for battle and for use in the 'line of battle' tactic. Stronger, sturdier ships allowed for heavier and more powerful weapons to be carried.

### New technology

**More accurate navigation** New inventions like the astrolabe allowed for greater accuracy when planning voyages and working out location. This allowed explorers to embark on journeys with a much higher level of accuracy and to be more prepared for passing through hostile waters.

## Key Words

fireship    line of battle

## Work

1 Who did Elizabeth put in charge of building her navy?

2 What was a 'fireship'?

3 Explain some of the tactics used by the English navy.

4 Discuss with a partner: 'Why did the English navy prefer raids over direct battles?'

5 Look at **Source B**.
   a What references can you see to the sea and naval power in the picture?
   b What does this portrait suggest about Elizabeth and her views on England's navy and power at sea?

## Extension

GCSE

The sixteenth century saw huge advances in naval technology. A historian would want to know exactly how these developments made the English navy more effective. Challenge yourself by researching the new technology and then answering the question: 'How did new technology lead to a more effective navy?'

## Practice Question

Explain what was important about the navy for Elizabethan England.

**8 marks**

## Study Tip

Try to explain how naval warfare worked in the Elizabethan period, how it was different from what went before and, most importantly, why success at sea was considered so important.

# Historic Environment: The Spanish Armada

For many years, there had been tension between England and Spain. English soldiers had been helping Protestants in the Netherlands to fight the Spanish, and English sailors had been raiding Spanish ships and stealing their gold. England was becoming a great *Protestant* naval power, too. It seemed inevitable that these two great powers would come into conflict on the seas. With the blessing of the Pope, Philip II decided to launch an attack on England. Does what happened to the Spanish navy – the Armada – show that a powerful and well organised navy was not enough – that it also needed luck?

## Objectives

▶ **Describe** the Spanish attempt to invade England.

▶ **Explain** why the Armada failed.

▶ **Analyse** what the English victory tells us about Elizabethan sea battles.

## King Philip's plan

Philip's plan was simple. He was going to send a great Armada (or fleet) of Spanish warships through the English Channel to anchor off the Dutch coast. Spanish soldiers in the Netherlands, under the command of the Duke of Parma, who had replaced the Duke of Alva in 1578, would then come aboard. The ships would land on the Kent coast and the soldiers would march on London. If things went as planned, victory would be assured.

## The Great Armada

The Spanish Armada consisted of 151 ships, 7000 sailors and 34,000 soldiers, along with 180 priests and monks who delivered the Catholic mass every day. They had enough supplies for four weeks, longer than they intended to be at sea. The commander was the **Duke of Medina-Sidonia**, a man with no maritime experience, but each ship was commanded by an experienced captain.

The assumption was that the Armada was not going to face much opposition from the English navy and so most of the weapons on board were for the final land attack.

## The English strike first

By 6 August 1588 the Armada had anchored off the Dutch coast as planned, ready to invade England. The first problem arose when the Duke of Parma was not there waiting with his troops. Tired of waiting for the Armada, he had sent his troops inland to mend canals and the Armada was then delayed by several days. The English chose this moment to strike first. Early on 7 August, in an attack led by Sir Francis Drake, eight fireships were sent into the Spanish fleet. The Spanish captains panicked and cut their anchor ropes to get away from the danger quickly. The well-disciplined fleet was now plunged into chaos and the Spanish crescent formation broken.

## Key Biography

### The Duke of Medina-Sidonia (1560–1615)

- He was a Spanish noble from a powerful old family. He had a reputation for being well organised and loyal, and was a devout Catholic.
- He was appointed by Philip II as commander of the Armada after the death of the previous commander.
- Historians cannot agree as to why Philip II chose him but it is thought that he wanted someone whom he could influence.
- Despite his lack of experience, he worked hard to ensure the Armada was well prepared, and reorganised much of the fleet.
- English **propaganda** has suggested that he was a fool and a coward.

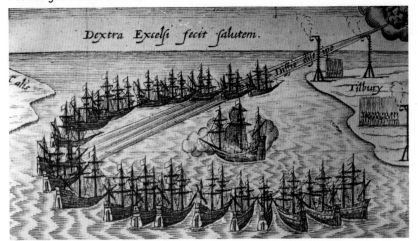

**Key Words**

propaganda

**Work**

1 Explain Philip's plan in your own words. Refer to **Source A** in your answer.

2 Design a story board which shows the complete journey of the Armada.

3 Discuss with your partner: at which point do you think the Spanish Armada was defeated?

▼ **B** *The route taken by the Armada*

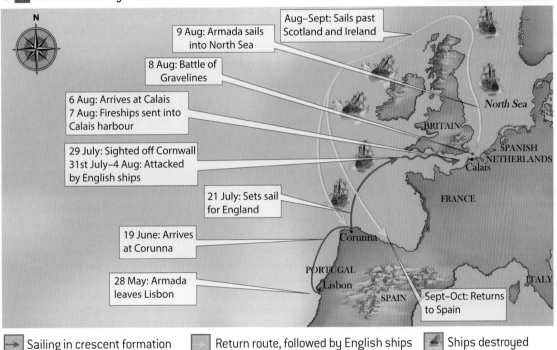

9 Aug: Armada sails into North Sea

Aug–Sept: Sails past Scotland and Ireland

8 Aug: Battle of Gravelines

6 Aug: Arrives at Calais
7 Aug: Fireships sent into Calais harbour

29 July: Sighted off Cornwall
31st July–4 Aug: Attacked by English ships

21 July: Sets sail for England

19 June: Arrives at Corunna

28 May: Armada leaves Lisbon

Sept–Oct: Returns to Spain

→ Sailing in crescent formation    → Return route, followed by English ships    Ships destroyed

## A great battle

The day after the fireship attack, the Battle of Gravelines began. The English fired constantly from a distance of around 100m, causing huge amounts of damage but not sinking any ships. The Spanish, poorly prepared for a sea battle, could barely defend themselves. With the Armada scattered, Medina-Sidonia attempted to lead his battered fleet home. The English gave chase, and continued to pound the Spanish ships with cannon fire.

## The end of the Armada

It was the weather that finally destroyed the Armada. The ships were battered by storms that blew them completely off course. Their water was polluted, their food rotten and they had no maps of the waters around the north of Britain. Ultimately, many ships were wrecked and some of the survivors were slaughtered by the Scots, the Irish and groups of English soldiers stationed in Ireland. Of the 151 ships that set sail, just 65 returned safely to Spain.

Philip was humiliated and Elizabeth saw the encounter not only as a great victory but evidence that God was on the side of Protestantism. The English admirals even received medals with the inscription: *'Flavit Jehovah et Dissipati Sunt'* ('God blew with his wind and they were scattered').

# Historic Environment: the Spanish Armada

## Why did the Spanish Armada fail?

The defeat of the Armada was hugely significant for Elizabeth and for England. It had a clear impact at the time but also affected England's global standing for many years. Spain was a superior naval power yet it had lost badly. Elizabeth had proved that a Protestant country, led by a woman, could defeat the most powerful and richest country in the world.

▼ **SOURCE C** *Part of Elizabeth's speech to her soldiers at Tilbury, Essex, on 9 August 1588. By this point the Armada was on its way home but the message that the threat was over was only just getting through and the troops were still ready for action:*

> I am come amongst you, as you see, at this time, not for my recreation, but being resolved, in the midst and heat of the battle, to live or die amongst you all, to lay down my life for my God and for my kingdom and for my people, my honour, and my blood, even in the dust. I know I have the body of a weak and feeble woman, but I have the heart and stomach of a king, and a king of England too, and think foul scorn that Parma or Spain, or any prince of Europe should dare to invade the borders of my realm; the which, rather than any dishonour shall grow by me, I myself will take up arms, I myself will be your general, judge, and rewarder of every one of your virtues in the field.

### English tactics

The use of fireships worked brilliantly. It broke the tight formation of the Spanish fleet and made individual ships vulnerable to attack. The constant bombardment by the English cannons made it impossible for the Spanish to regroup. Commanders like Francis Drake were good tacticians and leaders. The English ships were also faster than the Spanish.

### Why did the Armada fail?

### Spanish mistakes

The Spanish had some of the most effective warships in the world but they were designed for the Mediterranean and struggled to cope with the English Channel and the North Sea. They were slow and much less manoeuvrable than the English ships. The delay in getting soldiers on board from the Netherlands was disastrous for the Spanish but their biggest mistake was not being fully prepared for a sea battle. Most of the cannons they had on board were designed to be used once they had landed in England and they had also brought a number of the wrong cannonballs, making the cannons they did have for naval warfare useless. They were largely helpless as their ships were hit with English cannon fire. The commander of the Spanish fleet was inexperienced, although many of the ships' captains were very experienced.

### The weather

The Spanish ships had largely survived the battle with the English but many could not survive the journey home. They were battered by storms off the Scottish and Irish coasts and many were wrecked. They ran out of food and water and many of the sailors became too sick to sail.

## What made the defeat of the Armada so significant?

Having defeated the Armada, England was safe for the time being but it could not rest. The country had come very close to being invaded and it was important to ensure that did not happen again. Elizabeth continued to build up the navy for the rest of her reign. One significant consequence of the defeat of the Armada was that England had proved it could be a major naval power and it quickly set about making this the case.

Defeated but not yet ready to give up, Philip immediately began planning for a second Armada but there was little appetite for this in Spain. When Philip died ten years later he was no closer to achieving his aim of invading England.

The defeat of the Armada was significant because of the unity it brought to England. Most Catholics placed their loyalty with Elizabeth. She may have been a Protestant but they were English above all else and did not want the country to ruled by a Spaniard. Elizabeth showed herself to be a great leader and the victory added to the idea that her reign was a 'golden age'.

▼ **SOURCE E**  *The commander of the Spanish fleet, the Duke of Medina-Sedonia:*

> My health is not equal to this voyage. I know from my experiences at sea that I am always seasick and always catch a cold.

## Work

1  What does **Source E** suggest was the reason for the Armada's defeat?

2  Create a mind-map of the reasons for the defeat of the Armada. Use the spider diagram opposite as a starting point but then use your contextual knowledge to explain the factors that fit into the three main categories.

3  Look at **Source C** and **Interpretation D**.
   a  Why do you think Elizabeth visited the troops and made this speech?
   b  How much of an impact do you think it made on the outcome of the battle?

▼ **INTERPRETATION D**  *An eighteenth-century engraving of Elizabeth addressing the troops at Tilbury*

▼ **INTERPRETATION F**  *A Spanish galleon*

## Study Tip

What decided the outcome of battles at this time? When considering a sea battle like the Armada its unique location has a great impact. You should include the weather as a factor. Did a combination of factors lead to the English victory over the Spanish? How did the technology and equipment on each side compare? Were the two sides well matched? Who had the better leadership? How reliable were the plans of Medina-Sidonia? Did the English have superior tactics? Think about the decisions they made at different points in the battle. Lastly consider about the element of luck. Was the battle decided by something neither side could have predicted or prevented?

# How to... analyse interpretations

▼ **INTERPRETATION A** *An assessment of the threats to Queen Elizabeth, from* The Life and Times of Elizabeth I, *by Neville Williams (1972):*

There were other plots against Elizabeth's life in later years. However the revelations of the Ridolfi conspiracy, coming so soon after the Northern Rebellion, alarmed her most. That her own cousin, the Duke of Norfolk, should have plotted her downfall was the cruellest blow she had yet suffered.

## Practice Question

How convincing is **Interpretation A** about the threats to Queen Elizabeth I? Explain your answer using **Interpretation A** and your contextual knowledge.

**8 marks**

## Study Tip

This type of 'convincing' interpretation question in your Paper 2 British Depth Study exam is different from the 'how far' interpretation question in your Paper 1 Period Study exam.' This one is based on the writings of a historian or someone who has studied the event or period. Consider: what do you know about the event? How far do you agree with this interpretation?

## Over to you

This type of question wants you to decide how **convincing** an interpretation is. In other words, how far does the interpretation fit with what you know about the history of the event, person or issue?

1   You could begin by showing that you understand the main points of the interpretation by summarising the interpretation **in your own words**. For example, you could consider what you know about the history of threats to Elizabeth that matches or confirms the main point of the interpretation.

2   You may not be totally convinced by the interpretation: this means you may not believe that the interpretation is completely correct or you may not agree that the interpretation is the best way to understand the events. Can you suggest different interpretations of threats to Elizabeth, or different ways the issue can be seen? For example, do you think other threats to Elizabeth in her later reign were more alarming than the Ridolfi conspiracy? If yes, which threat was more alarming, and why?

3   Finally, do you agree with the interpretation? In other words, did you find the interpretation convincing? (Even if you agree with the interpretation that the Ridolfi conspiracy is the most alarming threat, you could still try to describe other threats and explain why they are less important.) Try to write a few concluding sentences in which you make a judgement about how persuasive or accurate the interpretation is compared to any alternative interpretation.

4   What are the strengths and weaknesses of the following essay introduction to the question?

> There were many plots against Queen Elizabeth I. In interpretation A the historian says that the Ridolfi plot, involving the Duke of Norfolk, was the one that upset Elizabeth the most. However, there were other plots during Elizabeth's reign, including the Throckmorton plot, 1583 and the Babington plot, 1586. These plots were far more alarming and threatening to Elizabeth and her government because they involved the assistance of foreign powers.

5   Now try to answer the question yourself!

# How to...tackle the Historic Environment question

**Practice Question**

'The main reason for building a stately home in Elizabethan times was to demonstrate the successful career of its owner.' How far does a study of Burghley House support this statement? Explain your answer. You should refer to Burghley House and your contextual knowledge.                    **16 marks**

**Study Tip**

You have studied other great houses in the Elizabethan period. Do more research into the details of Burghley House for this question. You could think about the key questions below to help you focus.

**Over to you**

This type of question asks you how your knowledge of a particular site helps you understand a key feature of the Elizabethan period. In other words, what can a study of the historic environment tell you about people or events at the time? You could, for example, consider the following:

1  *Motivation*: Why did someone want to build this specific building?

2  *Location*: Why did they build it in that particular location?

3  *Function*: Why was it built in that particular way? Consider the shape and design of the building or its layout. People design buildings to work and look in particular ways. Firstly, buildings have to function in a particular way, for example for safety, defence, comfort, or pleasure. Can you identify and explain specific building features, and the job they do?

4  *Purpose*: What would the building be used for? Who lived or worked there?

5  Questions 1 to 4 will be helpful for most sites, but if you are studying a battle, such as the defeat of the Spanish Armada, you should consider different questions because it is unlikely that there will be any physical remains for you to comment on. The environment may have influenced the outcome of the battle or conflict, so you could consider:

   a  *Motivation*: Why was the battle fought? Who fought in it?

   b  *Location*: Why was it fought in that particular place? What are the main landscape features?

   c  What happened at the battle?

6  Note that you don't need to use all the knowledge from your answers to questions 1 to 5 in order to answer the question. Select *relevant* information to write a response to the specific aspect of the environment you are asked about. Don't forget that this question asks '*How far*' houses demonstrated the greater prosperity and status of their owners, so make sure you give your evaluation of this.

7  Now try to answer the Practice Question yourself!

# A king without a country

This topic focuses on England between 1660 and 1685, but to understand this period properly, you need to go back a little further and examine what was happening in the years before this. Charles was born in 1630. As the eldest son of King Charles I, he was to be King of England, Scotland and Ireland. However, after a brutal civil war, his father was put on trial and executed. Charles fled to France, and England became a republic under the command of Oliver Cromwell. It seemed Charles would never rule over his kingdom…

## Objectives

▶ **Describe** England under Cromwell and the experiences of Charles in exile.

▶ **Explain** how England became a republic.

▶ **Assess** the impact of exile on Charles.

## The king loses his head

The English **Civil War** was one of the bloodiest conflicts England had ever seen. It centred on a disagreement between King Charles I and Parliament about who was to have power over England. Charles believed in **divine right**, which was the idea that God had chosen him as king and given him absolute authority. Members of Parliament saw themselves as the representatives of the people, there to ensure the king did not abuse his power. Making the situation more complex was the issue of religion. Parliament included many **Puritans**, who objected to the king's lavish lifestyle and what they saw as his **Catholic** ideas. Charles lost the war that eventually broke out with Parliament. Following a trial, he was publicly executed for **treason**. Charles's queen and children fled abroad and England was declared a **republic**: a country without a monarch. Instead, Parliament would have authority.

▼ SOURCE A *A Dutch woodcut showing crowds watching the execution of Charles I in 1649*

### Fact

Puritans were strict Christians who read the Bible closely as they believed it taught them how to live. They tried to live simply, following Jesus's example. They didn't like sports and entertainment, believing they distracted people from worshipping God.

## The new King of Scotland

By the time of his father's **execution**, Charles had already been abroad for several years. In the early battles of the Civil War, he had taken a direct role, despite being only in his mid-teens, but as time went on his advisors considered it too dangerous for the **heir** to the throne to remain in England. After his father was killed, Charles initially worked to try to take the throne.

He still had support, particularly in Scotland (his family had been ruling there for much longer than in England). Despite religious differences, Charles was crowned King of Scotland in 1651 but his supporters were soon defeated by Cromwell's men and Charles was forced to escape. It took him six weeks to flee England, including many narrow escapes from Cromwell's forces.

## A king in exile

In **exile**, Charles relied totally on others' help. He travelled without the grandeur expected of a king and had little money. He spent much of his time in France, in the **royal court** of his cousin, Louis XIV. Louis was an **absolute monarch**: he had complete control over his kingdom and did not have to answer to any Parliament. Charles had been brought up believing in divine right, and had seen how Parliament had destroyed his father's reign. He was haunted by what had happened to his father and keen to avoid a similar fate. However, Charles's experiences of how Louis ruled France made the need to compromise with England's Parliament particularly frustrating to him. King Louis was known as the Sun King and his court was famous for being grand and colourful. Charles's own royal court would have much in common with his cousin's. When it came, Charles seized the opportunity to return to England, even though it meant compromising, because it gave him the chance to live a more independent life than he had done in France.

After the execution of Charles I, England became a **Commonwealth** and was governed by the 'Rump Parliament', made up of the remaining MPs after the Civil War. In 1653, however, Parliament was disbanded and the country was governed by Oliver Cromwell, an important Civil War leader, who took the title Lord Protector. Cromwell and his supporters were Puritans

and introduced laws to encourage what they saw as a more Christian way of life, including more regular church attendance, plainer clothes and a more serious attitude to religious holidays. In Scotland and Ireland, Cromwell took a ruthless approach to those who challenged his authority, particularly Catholics. Stories of terrible slaughters committed by Cromwell's men spread quickly and many despised him.

▼ SOURCE C *An engraving of the 'execution' of Oliver Cromwell from around 1661*

# The Restoration of the English monarchy

**1.2**

In 1660, Charles II returned to London to huge celebrations and was crowned king. Eleven years after the beheading of Charles I, England once again had a monarchy. However, the country that Charles returned to was not the same one as he had fled. The Civil War and the years of Cromwell's **Protectorate** had left it divided. People were also wary of another King Charles on the throne after the tyranny of his father's reign. Was Charles really the man to reunite such a disunited kingdom?

## Objectives

▶ **Describe** the events that led to the Restoration of the monarchy.

▶ **Explain** the problems that Charles II faced.

▶ **Evaluate** which problems provided the biggest threat to Charles's reign.

## England after Cromwell

Oliver Cromwell died in September 1658. His successor was his son, Richard. Richard was not able to command the same respect that his father had, and just seven months after becoming Lord Protector a group of senior officers forced him from power. The Rump Parliament, which Oliver Cromwell had dissolved, returned. On Christmas Eve 1659, the MPs who had been forced to leave Parliament in 1648 were allowed to return in what was known as the Long Parliament. This included some MPs who were more sympathetic to the monarchy.

## Timeline

| 1658 | 1659 |
|---|---|
| **3 Sept** Death of Oliver Cromwell | **25 May** Richard Cromwell is forced from power |
| **7 May** Return of the Rump Parliament | **24 Dec** The Long Parliament returns |

## The return of the king

On 4 April 1660 from his base in the Netherlands, Charles issued the **Declaration of Breda**, which pledged to pardon the majority of those who had fought against his father. A special meeting of Parliament was organised and on 8 May it was proclaimed that Charles II had been the rightful king since his father's death in 1649. Charles returned from exile and rode into London on 29 May. This event is known as the **Restoration** of the monarchy and the period of Charles's reign is commonly known as the Restoration. Supporters lined the streets and the day was made a public holiday. After the unhappy years of Cromwell and the disorder that followed his death, many in England saw Charles's **coronation** as a return to the natural order of things.

## A divided kingdom

Although Charles II's reign was backdated to his father's death, he was far from being able to continue where his father left off. In 1660, England was a divided country. The horrors of civil war remained in people's memory, the Protectorate had brought religious and political division and Cromwell's army remained a powerful force loyal to Parliament. Charles faced many difficult challenges.

▼ **INTERPRETATION A** *A depiction of the Restoration of Charles I from a twentieth-century children's book*

## The effect of the Commonwealth

Parliament and Cromwell had completely changed the way England was governed. The country had a powerful professional, or standing, army, which remained loyal to Parliament. It was clear what would happen to a monarch who failed to govern fairly. Charles would need to ensure that his position was secure without appearing to repeat the actions of his father. After careful negotiation, the army was disbanded (no one wanted to risk another civil war) but the king's relationship with Parliament remained a delicate one.

### Charles's challenges

### The aftermath of war

The Civil War had divided England between supporters of the king and supporters of Parliament. Communities and families had been split and these wounds would not heal quickly. As well as emotional scars, thousands had died in battle and homes had been destroyed. Supporters of the king had been punished by having their land confiscated. It was now up to Charles to heal the wounds of war. One of his first acts was to return some of the confiscated land to **royalists**. Charles's decision to be a 'public' monarch was also seen as an important part of this healing process.

### Religious divisions

One of the major causes of the Civil War was religious difference. Although King Charles I had always said he was a **Protestant**, many saw his actions (marrying a **Catholic**, decorating churches, the people he chose to hold important Church positions) as evidence that he was really a Catholic. There was also division with the Protestant faith – a growing number of Nonconformists disliked **Anglicanism** (the Church of England) almost as much as they did Catholicism. There were different types of nonconformist but all wanted greater religious freedom and mistrusted the Anglicans in Parliament. England in 1660 was hugely divided and a religious settlement would be needed from Charles.

## Work

1. Who succeeded Oliver Cromwell as Lord Protector and how long did his rule last?

2. What was the main difference between the Rump Parliament and the Long Parliament?

3. a  List all of the problems facing Charles II when he became king. With a partner, put these problems in order of importance, starting with the one that would be the biggest threat to Charles's rule.
   b  Write a brief paragraph explaining your order.

4. Why do you think the regicides were excluded from the pardon given to other enemies of Charles I?

## The king killers

One major dilemma facing Charles was how to deal with those who had fought against his father in the Civil War and, in particular, those who had put him on trial and executed him. The **Indemnity and Oblivion Act** of 1660 put into law what the Declaration of Breda had promised. The prominent **regicides**, those involved in Charles I's trial and execution who had not fled abroad, were put on trial and then hanged, drawn and quartered. Cromwell's body was dug up so that the same punishment could be carried out on him.

### Practice Question

Write an account of the ways in which the Restoration of the monarchy affected England at this time.     8 marks

### Study Tip

Remember to include how Cromwell's rule came to an end and how Charles attempted to show that he was willing to compromise and forgive.

# How did Charles work with Parliament?

Charles II's relationship with Parliament was never going to be an easy one. The rule of his father, Charles I, was certainly in people's minds and the new king would have to deal with Parliament carefully, particularly over the key issues of religion, money and foreign policy. What was Charles's relationship with Parliament like? Did Charles learn from his father's mistakes?

## Objectives

▶ **Describe** the rise and fall of the Clarendon Ministry.

▶ **Explain** the actions of the Clarendon Ministry and the Cavalier Parliament.

▶ **Assess** the success of the Clarendon Ministry.

## Parliament under Charles II

Charles's first Parliament was known as the Convention Parliament. It was fairly evenly split between committed royalists and Parliamentarians who were unsure about the return of the king. This meant that Charles would have to work hard to gain the support of half of his Parliament. A major cause of the Civil War had been the issue of tax. In order to avoid more conflict, it was agreed that the king would be given a sum of money each year to run his government. Once Charles was crowned, the Cavalier Parliament (after the name used to describe the royalists during the Civil War) was formed. This new Parliament was overwhelmingly royalist and very supportive of Charles.

## The Cavalier Parliament

The Cavalier Parliament was formed on 8 May 1661 and lasted 18 years, overseeing a number of significant events and changes. Although Charles had the support of much of this Parliament, their relationship was far from smooth, especially over money, religion and foreign policy. The Cavalier Parliament period can be roughly split into three parts, in which different individuals and groups became powerful: the **Clarendon Ministry**, the **Cabal Ministry** and the **Danby Ministry**.

### Key Biography

#### Lord Clarendon (1609–74)

- As an MP before the Civil War he became a close advisor to King Charles I and continued to advise him during the war.

- He served Charles II in exile and became a very loyal, close advisor.

- His daughter married the king's brother, the Duke of York.

- As Charles II's Chief Minister he led the Clarendon Ministry until 1667.

▼ **INTERPRETATION A** *From* King Charles II *by the historian Antonia Fraser (Weidenfeld & Nicolson, 1979):*

> One outstanding question was of course religion. That wonderfully open, peaceful desire of Breda that no one should be 'disquieted or called into question' for their religious opinions so long as they did not disturb the peace, still remained to be implemented. What finally emerged as a religious settlement – the Clarendon Code – was as far from the heady heights of Breda as could be imagined.

### Work

1   a   When was the Cavalier Parliament formed?

   b   Why was it given this name?

2   Explain two ways in which the Clarendon Code tried to make the country completely Anglican.

3   Explain why the Clarendon Ministry came to an end.

## Money

The Clarendon Ministry aimed to increase Britain's wealth and influence in the world. It was made illegal to sell British raw materials, such as wool, abroad and the import of some manufactured goods like lace from overseas was banned. The plan was to build new **colonies**, such as those in North America, as places where raw materials could be produced and then brought to Britain. Other laws placed heavy taxes on foreign merchants and gave advantages to British farmers.

Parliament was responsible for paying Charles his annual **grant**, but in the early years the Cavalier Parliament struggled to raise the necessary amount (£1.2 million). Unpopular taxes, including one based on the number of fireplaces each house had, and restrictions on **paupers** began to make Parliament unpopular. Other than the issue of the annual grant, Parliament and the king's relationship during the Clarendon Ministry was relatively good.

## Religion

Under the influence of the Clarendon Ministry, Parliament passed a series of laws making it harder to follow a religion other than that of the Church of England (Anglicanism). These became known as the Clarendon Code. Charles was not pleased; he believed in much more freedom for Catholics and Nonconformist Protestants, but accepted the laws to avoid conflict with Parliament. The Clarendon Code was a clear attack on the freedom of nonconformists. The Cavalier Parliament made clear that Anglicanism was the only form of Protestantism that was acceptable.

## The Clarendon Ministry 1660–67

## Foreign policy

The Second Anglo-Dutch War began in March 1665 and was very unpopular with much of Parliament and the public. Charles had run out of money to fight and was reluctant to ask Parliament for more. In 1667, the problem reached crisis point when the Dutch raided the Medway at the mouth of the River Thames. The Clarendon Ministry was now associated with an embarrassing attack from a foreign rival. The king acted decisively. He did not want to be personally blamed and so the Clarendon Ministry was removed from power and Parliament forced Clarendon himself into exile. By removing his old friend Clarendon from office, Charles showed his willingness to do as Parliament wished but also avoided taking the blame for the disaster himself.

### The Clarendon Code

| 1661 | Corporation Act | Everyone holding public office had to swear allegiance to the Crown and the Church of England. |
|------|-----------------|--------------------------------------------------------|
| 1662 | The Act of Uniformity | The Anglican 'Book of Common Prayer' had to be used in all services – a clear statement that only Anglicanism was acceptable. |
| 1662 | The Licensing of the Press Act | Limited the freedom to publish anything that challenged the Church of England. |
| 1664 | Conventicle Act | Other than Anglican ones, no religious meeting could involve more than five people. |
| 1665 | The Five Mile Act | **Nonconformist clergy** could not go within five miles of their parish. |

### Practice Question

How convincing is **Interpretation A** about the Clarendon Code?

Explain your answer using **Interpretation A** and your contextual knowledge.

**8 marks**

### Study Tip

The interpretation suggests that the Clarendon Code was harsh. Consider how far you agree with this.

# How did Charles work with Parliament?

## The Cabal

In the past, 'the government' had tended to centre around one trusted advisor, or favourite, of the king. They, quite literally, helped him 'govern' the country. When the Clarendon Ministry came to an end in 1667, for the first time a collection of **nobles** became the most powerful group in the country. Baron Clifford, the Earl of Arlington, the Duke of Buckingham, Baron Ashley and the Duke of Lauderdale now held power. The group's initials spelled the word 'CABAL', which became the name by which the group was known.

The Cabal Ministry had control over all government policy. Some saw the Cabal as a threat to the king's authority but most people saw it as a challenge to Parliament. The fact that the group was so powerful but also quite secretive made many believe that they had been responsible for bringing down the Clarendon Ministry in order to gain power themselves.

▼ **SOURCE B** *This painting by Sir John Baptist de Medina (1659–1710) is believed to show the Cabal Ministry of King Charles II*

### Divisions within the Cabal

Although from the outside the Cabal looked like a united group, in reality it was made up of five men with different political ideas who were willing to work together to hold power and influence. Buckingham was the most powerful, as he was a close friend of the king. It was said that the members of the Cabal hated each other and spent as much time arguing as working together.

### Key Biography

#### The Duke of Buckingham (1628–87)

- He fought in the Civil War for Charles I before living in exile with Charles II.
- He returned to England in 1657 and was imprisoned by Cromwell.
- He was part of the royal court but his rivalry with Clarendon stopped him from gaining much power and led to him falling out of the king's favour.
- After Clarendon's fall he returned to the king's favour and led the Cabal Ministry.

## Party time

Unlike today, in the 1660s the most powerful House of Parliament was the **Lords** rather than the **Commons**. The influence of the Cabal, who were all members of the Lords, began to change this. MPs in the Commons began to be more independent and some challenged the ideas and policies of the Cabal. In 1669, Sir William Coventry formed a group in the Commons known as the Country Party. This was opposed to the power of the Cabal which it saw as corrupt and also questioned its foreign policy decisions. In response, a rival group known as the Court Party was created to defend the royal court. Party politics was born! The parties later became more organised, with the Country Party becoming the **Whigs** and the Court Party becoming the **Tories** in 1678.

## Key Words

noble   Lords   Commons   Whig   Tory

| The Country Party/The Whigs | The Court Party/The Tories |
|---|---|
| Challenged what they saw as corruption in the king's court. | Supported the king and his ministers' policies. |
| Disliked power being held by small groups (such as the Cabal) and felt that power should be with Parliament. | Believed in the defence of the Church of England. |
| Believed in freedom of religion for all Nonconformists | Believed that James, Duke of York, should succeed his brother as king. |
| Believed in individual freedom for all of the king's subjects. | Accused the Whigs of being republicans (not wanting a monarch to rule the country), extreme Protestants and warmongers. |
| Opposed James, Duke of York, the king's Catholic brother, ever becoming king. | |

### Money

Parliament controlled the country's finances, giving it a huge amount of power. MPs were unwilling to give money to a government whose actions they did not support. Lack of money from Parliament forced Charles to issue the Stop of the Exchequer in 1672, officially stating that the Crown could not pay any of its debts. This resulted in humiliation for Charles and was a show of power for Parliament.

### Charles, the Cabal and Parliament, 1667–73

### Religion

In 1672, Charles issued the Declaration of Indulgence. This royal order stated that Catholics and Nonconformists should be allowed to freely practise their religion. Charles's willingness to give freedom to nonconformists, which included Puritans, can be seen as evidence of his fear of opposition and even rebellion or civil war. This directly went against the Clarendon Code and angered the Anglicans in Parliament. Parliament put pressure on the king and his supporters and Charles backed down, a huge victory for Parliament. A year later, in 1673, Parliament passed the Test Act, which banned all Catholics from holding any position of authority. This forced some of the king's most trusted ministers to resign, including members of the Cabal.

### Foreign policy

Despite the previous disaster, Charles had entered another war with the Dutch. Once again Parliament was angry that the king was supporting Catholic France against a fellow Protestant nation. Members were concerned that the war was part of a larger plan to return England to the Catholic religion. The fact that the alliance with France was based on a secret agreement between the two kings – the Secret Treaty of Dover (1670) – only made Charles's actions seem more suspicious. Charles needed Parliament's financial support to fight the war and it was not willing to give him what he wanted. The war had to be abandoned.

### Work

1  What do the letters CABAL stand for?

2  Explain one difference between the Country Party and the Court Party.

3  In what ways did the Declaration of Indulgence go against the Clarendon Code? (Use your prior knowledge to help you.)

4  Look at **Source B**. What does it suggest about the Cabal Ministry?

5  Why could 1672 be seen as a turning point for the relationship between Parliament and the king?

## The end of the Cabal

The disasters of the Third Anglo-Dutch War (1672–74), the Stop of the Exchequer and the Test Act divided and then destroyed the Cabal. Although no longer in government, the Cabal's members remained active as members of the House of Lords.

## 1.4 Why did Charles fall out with Parliament?

After the fall of the Cabal, Charles's relationship with Parliament never completely recovered. The final period of the Cavalier Parliament, the Danby Ministry, was once again occupied by the same issues of religion, foreign policy and money. By 1679, it was clear that the Cavalier Parliament and Charles had reached the end of their strained relationship. Could the king and Parliament ever see eye to eye? Why did the Whigs and the Tories fight three elections in three years?

### Objectives

▶ **Describe** the end of the Cavalier Parliament and what happened next.

▶ **Examine** why Charles's relationship with Parliament deteriorated.

▶ **Analyse** the reasons for the deterioration.

### The Danby Ministry

When the Cabal fell, it was Lord Danby who became the new Chief Minister of Charles II. As an Anglican, Danby was popular with many in Parliament but former members of the Cabal were suspicious of him. Baron Ashley, who had been given the title Lord Shaftesbury, became very powerful in the House of Lords and worked with the Country Party in the Commons in opposition to the government.

### Key Biography

#### Lord Danby (1632–1712)

- He worked with Buckingham and others to oppose the Clarendon Ministry.
- He rose to a senior position under the Cabal Ministry before leading the government himself in the Danby Ministry.
- He had strong anti-Catholic views and supported the Test Act.
- He was forced to compromise to stay in power when he entered negotiations with Catholic France on the king's orders.

### Parliament under the Danby Ministry, 1673–9

Shaftesbury's group, who were all Anglicans, dedicated their time to making life difficult for those who failed to follow Anglicanism. They introduced bills that limited the freedom of Catholics and Nonconformists. The king opposed them but Danby, as Chief Minister, struggled to control the increasingly confident Parliament.

Despite previous disasters, Charles was keen to once again become involved in the war between France and the Netherlands. Parliament said it would fund this, providing the king supported the Dutch. Charles agreed but Parliament delayed giving the king the money he needed until it was too late. France and the Netherlands made peace and Britain had failed to gain anything from it.

Danby and the king were humiliated by their foreign policy failures but things quickly got worse. In October 1678, a damaging secret was revealed. On the king's orders, Danby had been negotiating with the French since 1676, and had promised that England would not help the Dutch. He was concerned that if the Dutch were defeated, the French might turn on England and he wanted to avoid this at all costs. Parliament was furious and tried to put Danby on trial. In order to avoid this, Charles called elections, bringing to an end the 18 years of the Cavalier Parliament.

## Fact

A direct link can be drawn between the Country and Court parties and two modern day political parties in Britain. The modern day Liberal Democrats can trace their history back to the Whigs and the modern day Conservative Party can trace its origins to the Tories.

## Key Words

Interregnum    dissolve
Habeas Corpus Parliament
Oxford Parliament

## Key Biography

### Lord Shaftesbury (1621–83)

- Anthony Ashley Cooper, first Earl of Shaftesbury, was an important and influential politician during both the **Interregnum** (from the execution of Charles I on 30 January 1649 to his son's return to London on 29 May 1660) and the Restoration.

- He had been a member of the Convention Parliament that had asked Charles to return and went on to become one of the five members of the Cabal Ministry.

- After the Cabal fell, he became the leader of the opposition in Parliament founding the Whig Party.

- As an Anglican, Shaftesbury was always wary of Catholicism and became one of the main critics of James, the king's brother, and a key supporter of the Exclusion Bills, by which Parliament tried to pass a law to exclude James from succeeding Charles.

## The Exclusion Parliaments, 1679–81

After 18 years of the Cavalier Parliament, the final years of Charles's reign saw three short-lived Parliaments. All were dominated by the succession issue: whether James, a Catholic, should be allowed to be king after Charles. Each time the Exclusion Bill was about to be passed, Charles **dissolved** Parliament. No matter how powerful Parliament became, the king always had this right. The three elections were the first that were fought, in a fevered atmosphere, between the two political parties: the Whigs and the Tories.

| Three Parliaments | | |
|---|---|---|
| The **Habeas Corpus Parliament** | March–July 1679 | The exclusion of James, Duke of York, from the throne was considered for the first time when Lord Shaftesbury introduced the Exclusion Bill. |
| The Exclusion Parliament | July 1679–January 1681 (although it was not allowed to meet until October 1679) | Money would be given to the king only if a second Exclusion Bill was passed, but Parliament was dissolved before it could be passed. |
| The **Oxford Parliament** | 21–28 March 1681 | A final attempt was made to pass an Exclusion Bill. |

After the end of the Oxford Parliament, Charles chose to rule alone. He had the money he needed and Parliament could no longer be trusted. It was not recalled until his brother became king in 1685.

## Work

1  Who did Lord Shaftesbury work with in the Commons?
2  Explain why the Parliaments after the Cavalier Parliament were so short.
3  a  Explain what the Exclusion Bill aimed to do.
   b  Why did the Whigs support the bill?
4  What do the following events suggest about Charles's relationship with Parliament?
- The problems over the funding of the war between France and the Netherlands
- The fall of Lord Danby and the end of the Cavalier Parliament
- The three Parliaments that followed.

Try to make reference to the key issues of money, religion and power.

# How successfully did Charles work with Parliament?

Charles initially enjoyed a high level of loyalty from the Cavalier Parliament before things began to go wrong. Parliament started to become more independently minded and had a direct influence in the falls of Clarendon, the Cabal and Danby. By the end of the Cavalier Parliament, it had shown itself more than willing to challenge, question and even embarrass the king. The three Parliaments that followed showed that Charles could no longer depend on their loyalty. When and why did the relationship between the king and Parliament go wrong?

## Objectives

▶ **Describe** the relationship between Charles II and Parliament.

▶ **Explain** the major issues that caused tension.

▶ **Evaluate** the importance of the different factors.

## Was conflict inevitable?

When Charles became king he found himself in a position that no King of England had ever been in before. Up until his father's reign, Parliament was loyal to the king. Charles had been brought up to believe in divine right and had watched his father fight a civil war in its defence. Parliament had executed the previous king and Charles was fully aware that he could not simply ignore it. His time in exile, however, must surely have also had an impact, in particular time spent in the court of King Louis XIV of France, which was still an absolute monarchy. Parliament had invited the king to return but it was certainly not prepared to allow him to behave as his father had. In addition to these tensions, the horrors of war and the Interregnum were fresh in people's minds. The alternative to working together was unthinkable; they simply had to find a way to co-operate.

## The big issues

The three major issues of money, religion and foreign policy dominated the relationship between Charles and Parliament.

▼ **SOURCE A** *A contemporary portrait of Charles II in the ceremonial robes he wore to the annual State Opening of Parliament; painted by John Michael Wright c1661*

### Fact

Historians sometimes add a 'c' before dates. This stands for 'circa', which means 'around' or 'approximately'.

### Extension

Using the information on this and the previous pages, create a timeline of Charles's relationship with Parliament. Colour-code it to show which events and problems were to do with money, religion and power. Do you think there was a turning point at which the relationship started to go wrong? When was it? Why?

## Religion

- As Anglicans, Charles II and his supporters were Protestants but were much closer to Catholicism in how they practised their religion. Despite this, they tended to argue for tolerance.
- In the Cavalier Parliament, Anglicanism was the dominant religion. This was complicated by the fact that Charles's brother became a Catholic and many suspected that Charles had sympathies for this religion too. Perhaps more concerning for the Cavalier Parliament was the growing number of Nonconformist groups; they wanted Anglicanism to be the only accepted form of Protestantism in England and Nonconformists were a threat to this.
- The Clarendon Code showed that a majority in Parliament was determined to deal with Nonconformists. Charles and his ministers, including Clarendon himself, felt that Parliament's laws went too far but accepted them. Later, the Declaration of Indulgence made the differences even clearer.
- In forcing Charles to back down and then passing the Test Act, Parliament showed that it was willing to challenge the king. Many in Parliament began to believe that Charles was planning to make the country Catholic. The **Exclusion Crisis** showed that Parliament was so determined to limit Catholic influence that it was willing to stop Charles's brother becoming king.
- The major foreign policy issues of Charles's reign also were dominated by religion.

## Foreign policy

- The ongoing war between Catholic France and the Protestant Netherlands was a major issue.
- In the Second and Third Anglo-Dutch Wars, Charles came to the aid of the French. Parliament was unhappy that England was supporting a Catholic country.
- When the first war went badly wrong the Clarendon Ministry fell, and failure in the second war played a major part in the fall of the Cabal. On both occasions, Parliament's decision not to give more money to the king played a significant role.
- In 1678, Parliament went a step further when it embarrassed the king by delaying funding for an army to support the Dutch. This was done for political reasons: Parliament wanted to demonstrate how much power it held.
- Once the truth was revealed about Danby's secret negotiations with the French, trust between Parliament and king was destroyed.

## Money

- As part of the Restoration agreement that saw Charles ascend to the throne his government would be funded by an annual grant from Parliament.
- The agreed sum of £1.2 million was generous, but it was never met and Charles's government was always underfunded.
- Parliament had control of finances and whenever Charles needed money he had to ask for it. His main expense was foreign policy.
- In order to secure money for the Anglo-Dutch Wars he was forced to allow Parliament to pass anti-Catholic laws such as the Test Act.

## Work

1 Explain one way in which religion caused conflict between Parliament and the king.
2 Identify and explain a link between the issues of money and foreign policy in Charles's relationship with his Parliament.
3 Look back over the whole of this chapter. Do you think there was a key moment, or turning point, when Charles and Parliament's relationship changed?

## Practice Question

Explain what was important about the Cavalier Parliament's control of finance with regard to its relationship with Charles II. **8 marks**

## Study Tip

Aim to think about the relative importance of money. Is it more or less important than foreign policy or religion? How are the three concepts connected?

# Historic Environment: Restoration stately houses

The Restoration period saw many great houses built across England but it also saw huge changes to the houses that already existed. Culture and fashions from France and the Netherlands along with new Eastern influences from India, China and Japan dominated the look and style of English homes. What can the houses of the wealthy tell us about the changing fashions of the Restoration?

## Objectives

▶ **Describe** the features of a Restoration stately home.

▶ **Explain** how great houses reflected the fashions of the time.

▶ **Investigate** how a specific house, Ham House, reflects the fashions of the Restoration period.

## The Restoration style

As the seventeenth century began, stately homes were becoming larger and grander than ever. Elizabethan houses had become less concerned with security and by the time of the Stuarts there was little need for thick stone walls, battlements and moats. Houses were about comfortable living and demonstrating that you were a cultured and wealthy person. After the Restoration of the monarchy in 1660, houses became even more extravagant as styles and influences from abroad were brought to England.

## The appeal of the foreign

The grandeur was not limited to the house itself – some houses were surrounded by parkland while others had ornate gardens in the popular European style. Before and after Charles II's coronation, the style of houses was influenced by French and Dutch design. Symmetry was important on the outside of the building and large windows showed wealth – glass, although more widely available, was still expensive. There were often many rooms. Special state rooms would be reserved for royalty, should they decide to visit. Rooms were decorated with French-style ornate carvings and tapestries, usually showing floral and fruit designs. Charles II's exile in France had given him a taste for French design and people quickly followed this trend. Increasing trade in Asia was often

▼ **A** *'The Queen's Closet', one of the state rooms at Ham House; this room was designed especially as a private space for Charles II's wife, Catherine of Braganza; as with the other rooms, it is elaborately decorated*

The ceiling features a painting of a Greek myth – 'Ganymede and the eagle'.

A decorated alcove hung with red damask (a woven fabric, Arabic in origin) with plaster to resemble white marble and gold.

'Sleeping' chairs: upholstered with silk and silver thread. The backs of the chairs are able to recline adding to the luxury of the room.

Scagliola (imitation marble) fireplace decorated with a floral design and the Lauderdales' personal cipher.

Tall, square chimney stacks were increasingly popular in the seventeenth century and were constructed more to maintain symmetry than for practical reasons.

Busts of Roman emperors reflect the fashion for the ancient world. Other classical statues can be found in the gardens. In front of the building is a large statue of 'Father Thames', another ancient, mythical character.

**Loggia:** a covered walkway; based on the Roman style, this was common in Italian buildings of the period.

Servants' quarters: the entire basement was for servants. Hidden passageways all over the house allowed servants to move around without using the main rooms and hallways.

▲ **B** *The exterior of Ham House, by the River Thames in Richmond, Surrey*

reflected by ornaments and decoration in Japanese, Chinese and Indian styles.

## Ham House pre-Restoration

Ham House was built in 1610 on royal lands by Thomas Vavasour, an important figure in the court of James I. In 1626, the house became the home of William Murray, a close friend of the future Charles I. It was built close to the River Thames to allow Vavasour to travel to the royal court easily by river. As a committed royalist, Murray was forced into exile after the Civil War but his eldest daughter, Elizabeth, and her husband, Lionel Tollemache, moved into the house and were its residents when Charles II was crowned.

## The Lauderdales

The Tollemaches made few changes to the house in the 1660s and Elizabeth spent much of her time in London. Soon after Lionel's death, she began to spend time with the Duke of Lauderdale, causing rumour and scandal in the

court. They eventually married in 1672. Lauderdale was a key figure in government throughout the king's reign; most notably, he was a member of the Cabal. The location of Ham House was perfect for Lauderdale. The duke and duchess, and Ham House, were at the heart of political life. The house was expanded for its now powerful occupants by the architect William Samwell. He remodelled the garden side of the house, filling in part of the 'H' shape to make it double pile (two rooms deep). Ham House was now comparable with other great country houses of the Restoration, such as Belton House in Lincolnshire.

### Study Tip

Stately houses of the Restoration period, like Ham House, included many new features in their design. What were they? What can we learn about the people who built and lived in these buildings from the external appearance and internal features? Before the Restoration of Charles II he had spent much time abroad. Think about how this might influence the fashions of the period.

### Work

1  Describe two common features of a Restoration stately house.
2  Why do you think French and Dutch design became so popular?

# What was the Popish Plot?

On 16 August 1678, while Charles was out walking, he was approached by a man named Kirby who told him of a murderous plot. When Charles demanded proof, Kirby named Israel Tongue, a clergyman, who he said knew all about the plot. Tongue appeared before Lord Danby and told him of a **conspiracy** involving over 100 **Jesuits** (a group of Catholics who aimed to convert Protestants). The plot was to kill the king either by shooting or by poisoning. He produced a document as evidence but said he did not know who had written it. Who was behind the plot? Was Charles really in danger?

## Objectives

▶ **Describe** the Popish Plot.

▶ **Explain** how and why the plot developed.

▶ **Assess** what these events can tell us about England in 1678.

## Catholic conspiracies?

Parliament was dominated by Anglicans whose aim, through the Clarendon Code, was to ensure that no other religion could gain influence. Religious division had caused great upheaval since the reign of Henry VIII and Parliament wanted stability. Fear of Catholic conspiracies did not disappear and there was even concern, raised by Charles's allegiance with the French, that the king himself might want to return the country to the old religion. Israel Tongue's revelation was therefore taken very seriously.

▼ **INTERPRETATION A**  *A nineteenth-century illustration of Kirby warning Charles about the plot*

## The Popish Plot

After hearing Tongue's evidence about a plot to kill him, the king was dismissive. He decided that there was no threat and ordered that it be kept secret to avoid inspiring similar ideas. However, when Charles's brother James heard about the plot he called for an investigation. The name Titus Oates soon came up; when Oates was questioned, he gave an account of secret Catholic meetings and conspiracies. The evidence he gave was so detailed that it had to be taken seriously. In September, Oates appeared before the **Privy Council** where he made 43 allegations against Catholic groups or individuals, including some in very senior positions such as the queen's doctor. He also claimed that the plotters had been in contact with the French royal court, producing letters that supported what he was saying. Under Oates's direction, arrests were made.

## Murder and mass panic

On 17 October, the Protestant MP Sir Edmund Godfrey's mutilated body was discovered. Godfrey, a magistrate, had taken down Oates's evidence. London began to panic. It seemed clear that Catholics were involved and when Oates accused five Lords the country began to become hysterical. The Lords were tried for treason and many other Catholics were arrested. Anti-Catholic feeling in the country was widespread and violence was commonplace. There was even a search of Parliament in the belief that there might be another gunpowder plot!

## The plot unravels

Although believed by many, there were holes in Oates's story from the beginning. It slowly became clear that he was lying about the whole plot. The document and the letters that had been his main evidence turned out to be forgeries and it emerged that the accusations that he had made had no substance whatsoever. Oates was eventually arrested and imprisoned, but 22 innocent people had been executed and countless others imprisoned. The Popish Plot was a lie but it had very serious consequences for England's Catholics.

## The consequences

The hysterical reaction to Oates's accusations showed that anti-Catholic feeling had been present all along and, despite being proved false, it led to much less tolerance from Parliament. Lord Shaftesbury in particular was keen to introduce more and more anti-Catholic measures. The events led directly to the passing of the Test Act, which made it impossible for Catholics to serve in positions of authority, and the Jesuits in particular faced violence and **persecution**. One of the most significant consequences was that it set off the Exclusion Crisis, and the argument for exclusion gained a lot more support. With anti-Catholic feeling running so high, could England's next king really be a Catholic?

▼ **INTERPRETATION B** *Adapted from the website of the Jesuits in Britain association:*

> Lord Shaftesbury had been stoking the fires of religious hatred against Catholics in a long game to end absolute monarchy and to depose a king. Charles II openly favoured religious toleration of Catholics. This meant a significant minority in parliament always voted with the king. The Whigs therefore wanted to eliminate the Catholics in parliament. The Plot was constructed against the Catholics at court – the Queen, the Duke and Duchess of York, and their clergy, many of whom were Jesuits. The King could not defend all the accused despite the clearly absurd nature of the accusations.

▼ **SOURCE C** *From a set of playing cards produced in 1679; here, Oates receives the letters that were supposedly sent to the French court*

## Key Words

conspiracy    Jesuit
Privy Council    persecute

▼ **SOURCE D** *From a ballad written by 'A Lady of quality', c1679:*

> Whether you will like my
>     song or like it not,
> It is the down-fall of the
>     Popish Plot;
> With characters of plotters
>     here I sing,
> Who would destroy our good
>     and gracious King;
> Whom God preserve, and give
>     us cause to hope
> His foes will be rewarded
>     with a rope.

## Work

1  Working in a group, create the script for a television news report. You could include some 'breaking news', for example: the murder of Godfrey. How did this event change things?

2  Look at **Sources C** and **D**. What do they suggest about people's reaction to the Popish Plot? Think about *what* the sources are as well as their content.

3  Read **Interpretation B**. Who does it hold responsible for the Popish Plot? What does it suggest was their motive?

4  Explain three consequences of the Popish Plot.

5  Why do you think people were so ready to believe the Popish Plot was genuine?

# The Exclusion Crisis

When Charles returned as king in 1660, it was assumed that he would quickly produce an heir to succeed him. Although Charles had numerous children with his many mistresses it became clear that he was not going to have a **legitimate** child with his wife, Catherine of Braganza. This meant that Charles's younger brother, James, Duke of York, was heir to the throne. This was not a matter of great concern until it was revealed that James had secretly become a Catholic in 1668. How did Parliament – and Charles – respond? And if James couldn't be king after Charles's death, then who would be?

## Objectives

▶ **Describe** the events of the Exclusion Crisis.

▶ **Explain** why some Anglicans were opposed to James becoming king.

▶ **Assess** what the Exclusion Crisis tells us about Charles's authority.

## Plenty of children but no heir

Charles II had at least 20 children outside of his marriage but only a legitimate child could succeed him on the throne. The king and queen had no children of their own and, without an heir, the next in line was Charles's brother, James.

## A secret Catholic

Like Charles, James had spent years living in exile and had returned to England in 1660. He played a key role in Charles's government, particularly during the Clarendon Ministry. On the surface he seemed a reasonable king-in-waiting. However, in 1673 it was revealed that James had secretly converted to Catholicism in 1668. He had still attended Anglican services and kept his beliefs private but it was the Test Act that had forced him to reveal his religion. He chose to give up his role as Lord High Admiral rather than give up his faith.

## James the conspirator?

The Popish Plot, although proved false, had raised fears that there was a plan to return England to Catholicism, perhaps with James on the throne. On 15 May 1679, Lord Shaftesbury introduced a bill into Parliament that, if passed, would mean that James would be excluded from becoming king. (See page 217 for the Exclusion Parliaments 1679–81.)

### Fact

After it was captured from the Dutch in 1664, the port of New Amsterdam on the east coast of America was renamed in James's honour. It still carries the name today: New York.

### Extension

As a historian, it is important to have background knowledge of an event or issue. The experiences of Charles and James while living in exile in France had a clear impact on their later lives. Working with a partner, research the court and country of King Louis XIV. Try to find out: what his rule was like; how his court worked; and what was happening in France while Charles and James were there.

---

### How could James be stopped?

There were three options open to those who wanted to stop James becoming king:

1 Charles could divorce his wife and marry a Protestant princess. Their children would be above James in the order of succession.

2 Charles's eldest son, James Scott, Duke of Monmouth, could be declared legitimate. This would make him the rightful heir.

3 James could be excluded by an Act of Parliament. The challenge would then be deciding who should rule in his place. Would his Protestant daughter accept the throne while her father was still alive?

## Key Biography

### James, Duke of York (1633–1701)

- As Charles I's second son, James had a similar childhood to his older brother.
- He was nine when the Civil War began and left England in 1648 after escaping from St James's Palace in London where he was being held captive.
- Like his brother, he spent most of his exile in France but unlike Charles he served in the French army rather than staying at the court of Louis XIV.
- He played an important role in Charles's government holding a number of positions.
- He married twice, firstly to the Protestant daughter of Lord Clarendon and secondly to the Italian Catholic princess, Mary of Modena.

## Fact

Diana, Princess of Wales, was descended from two of Charles's illegitimate sons. This means that her son, Prince William, will become the first descendant of Charles II to occupy the British throne, if he succeeds as expected.

## Key Words

legitimate    prorogue    illegitimate

### The First Exclusion Bill

On 16 May 1679, a bill was introduced to Parliament that would exclude the Duke of York from the line of succession. The Parliament, the second of Charles's reign, was known as the Habeas Corpus Parliament. This Parliament's relations with Charles were problematic, but Charles believed that he had enough support for the bill to fail. He was wrong. The bill passed its initial votes and was on the verge of becoming law in May 1679. Charles took action. He immediately brought Parliament to a halt (**prorogued** it) and then dissolved it on 3 July.

The problem had not disappeared, however. Both Shaftesbury and Charles's eldest **illegitimate** son, the Duke of Monmouth, were members of the Privy Council and so still held influence. Monmouth supported exclusion as he felt that he would have a strong claim to succeed his father. But as long as there was no Parliament there could be no exclusion of James. Recognising him as a threat, Charles sent Monmouth into exile and forced Shaftesbury to leave the Privy Council. Aware of public opinion, Charles sent James into exile too, first to Flanders and then to Scotland.

## Work

1  In what ways were James's experiences in exile similar to those of his brother? How were they different?

2  What job did James hold in Charles's government?

3  Look at the three options for stopping James from becoming king.
   a  Make a list of arguments for and against each option.
   b  Which do you think would be the best option?
   c  Why do you think the exclusion option was chosen?

4  Why do you think it was seen as such a problem that James was a Catholic?

### The Second Attempt: The Exclusion Bill Parliament

Elections were held in the summer of 1679 for a new Parliament and the Whigs did very well. Knowing that they were in support of exclusion, Charles delayed the meeting of Parliament as long as he could. While Parliament was prorogued, Shaftesbury spent his time accusing the Duke of York of working for the **Pope** and gathering signatures for a petition to allow Parliament to meet. Monmouth returned to London and the king invited his brother back too.

When Parliament did meet, in October 1680, another Exclusion Bill was introduced. This was defeated but Shaftesbury and others continued to call for James's exclusion and, increasingly, openly criticised the king. When Charles once again dismissed Parliament in January 1681, people began to consider the possibility of another Civil War. Parliament and the king seemed completely unable to work together.

▼ **SOURCE A** The Solemn Mock Procession of the Pope, Cardinals, Jesuits and Friars through the City of London, November the 17th, 1679; *an engraving from 1680 showing an event held by Whigs in which they would burn an* **effigy** *of the Pope*

### The Oxford Parliament and the arrest of Shaftesbury

After new elections, Parliament met again in March 1681, this time in Oxford. With relations worse than ever and Shaftesbury still arguing that James was a traitor, a final Exclusion Bill was introduced and, after just a week, Charles dissolved Parliament. In July, Shaftesbury was arrested for high treason and placed in the Tower of London. Members of the public were outraged and there was no real evidence against him, so he was later released. Tensions were running extremely high when, in May 1682, Charles became ill. Although the king recovered it was clear that the issue of succession had to be dealt with soon. With no Parliament, Shaftesbury began to plot rebellions and even considered an attempt to assassinate both Charles and James. Unable to build enough support, Shaftesbury fled England in November 1682 and died in January 1683.

Charles suffered a stroke on 2 February 1685, and died, aged 54, four days later, having converted to

### The Exclusion Crisis: key dates

| 1678 | 1679 |
|---|---|
| The Popish Plot. Anti-Catholic hysteria reaches a height. Senior members of the court are named in connection with the plot | March 1679 The Habeas Corpus Parliament meets for the first time<br>21 April 1679 Charles appoints Shaftesbury Lord President of the Council (cabinet minister overseeing the Privy Council) believing this might make him less likely to rebel<br>11 May 1679 The First Exclusion Bill is introduced<br>27 May 1679 Charles prorogues the Habeas Corpus Parliament (he dissolves it on 3 July)<br>Oct 1679 The Duke of York moves to Scotland and Shaftesbury is removed from the Privy Council<br>27 Nov 1679 Monmouth rides back into London |

Catholicism on his deathbed. He was succeeded by his brother who became James II. Although Shaftesbury had failed in his aims, the crisis had been significant and the possibility of another Civil War had been very real indeed.

**Key Words**

Pope    effigy

▼ **INTERPRETATION B** *Adapted from a modern university English Literature textbook by Penny Pritchard:*

> Charles's failure to produce a legitimate heir, coupled with the fact that James had by now openly converted to Catholicism, were strong factors which added to some people's growing unease about the probable return of a Catholic monarch. The possibility was a strong one: both Charles and James had much sympathy for their mother's religion and the French court which had protected them after their father's execution. More significantly, and not to be revealed until his death, was the fact that Charles had secretly signed the Treaty of Dover with his first cousin, Louis XIV, in 1670.

**Fact**

The Licencing of the Press Act, 1662, placed restrictions on what could be printed. However, the act had to be renewed regularly, and with Parliament barely active during the Exclusion Crisis, the act was allowed to lapse. The press could therefore get away with printing all sorts of things, and the atmosphere in the country became even more fearful.

**Work**

1   When was the first Exclusion Bill introduced?

2   Explain the term 'prorogued'.

3   Working with a partner, imagine a debate between a Whig (supporter of Shaftesbury) and a Tory (supporter of Charles). Write a script where they explain their views. How might they explain the events of the Exclusion Crisis?

4   Why were there three Parliaments between 1678 and 1681?

5   Why did Charles appoint Shaftesbury as Lord President of the Council?

6   Look at **Source A**.
   a   What does this image show?
   b   What do you think the purpose of this event was?
   c   What do you think the effect was?

**Practice Question**

How convincing is **Interpretation B** as a summary of the causes of the Exclusion Crisis?

Explain your answer using **Interpretation B** and your contextual knowledge.    **8 marks**

**Study Tip**

Try to identify what Proitchord believes caused the Exclusion Crisis. Can you find facts that support or challenge the points in the interpretation?

| 1680 | 1681 | 1682 | 1685 |
| --- | --- | --- | --- |
| 26 June 1680 Shaftesbury accuses James of working for the Pope | Jan 1681 Charles dissolves the Exclusion Bill Parliament | 2 Dec 1682 Shaftesbury flees England | 6 Feb 1685 On the death of Charles II, the Duke of York becomes King James II |
| 21 Oct 1680 The Exclusion Bill Parliament meets (over a year after the election) | Feb 1681 The Oxford Parliament | | |
| 15 Nov 1680 The Lords vote against the second Exclusion Bill | 2 July 1681 Shaftesbury is arrested for high treason | | |

# What was the Rye House Plot?

By the early 1680s, there was still a lot of opposition to both King Charles and his brother, James. On 1 April 1683, Charles and James planned a trip to the horse races at Newmarket. Plotters decided to use this trip as an opportunity to kill them both in an ambush on their return. So who were the plotters and how exactly was the plan going to work? Why were they so intent on killing the royal brothers? And how close did they actually come to succeeding?

## Objectives

▶ **Outline** why there was opposition to Charles and his brother.

▶ **Explain** the Rye House Plot and its consequences.

▶ **Evaluate** the importance of the Rye House Plot.

## Why didn't people trust Charles?

After the Popish Plot, distrust of Catholics was high and by the end of Charles's reign people were even questioning whether he was being honest when he said he was an Anglican. His loyalty to his brother and opposition to policies that restricted Catholic freedoms were seen as evidence that, even if not a Catholic himself, he had sympathies for the religion. His support for France in the wars with the Netherlands also placed him under suspicion. The problem for all Catholics and indeed for Charles was that, for many, Catholicism and absolute monarchy were one and the same thing. Many people were concerned that Charles would follow the same path that King Louis XIV had in France if Catholics gained influence. Charles had spent many years in the Sun King's court while in exile and seemed to have a fondness for France. The Whigs in particular wondered if Charles had a plan to copy his cousin Louis's absolute rule.

## The plot

The Rye House Plot was planned by a small group of men and centred on a mansion in Hertfordshire. Their aim was to kill Charles and James and inspire a rebellion that would place the Duke of Monmouth, Charles's illegitimate eldest son and a Protestant, on the throne.

### The Rye House Plotters

Duke of Monmouth
Earl of Essex
Lord William Russell
Algernon Sidney
Sir Thomas Armstrong
Robert Ferguson
Lord William Howard
Earl of Argyll

▼ **A** *The gatehouse of Rye House; this is all that remains of the house today*

The plan was to ambush and murder the king and his brother as they passed Rye House on their way home from the races at Newmarket. While the plot unfolded, the Earl of Argyll was to launch a rebellion in Scotland. Charles and James were due to reach Rye House on 1 April 1683, but unfortunately for the plotters, the royal party left Newmarket early. The assassination was never even attempted, and the planned rebellion in Scotland did not occur either.

## The consequences

The consequences of the failed assassination went far beyond the plot itself. The king wanted to make an example of the plotters but also used it as an excuse to treat Protestant opponents more harshly. A number of Protestants, some involved in the plot and some not, were executed as traitors while others were forced to leave England to avoid the same fate. The king and his supporters spent the following months and years arresting and executing Protestant opponents. The plot gave Charles the chance he was looking for to destroy once and for all the opposition to his reign and his brother's succession to the throne.

▼ **SOURCE B** *An official account of the plot written in 1685, after James became king, by Thomas Sprat, a bishop and close supporter of both Charles and James; the Duke of Monmouth was still alive at this point and there was still much opposition to James's rule*

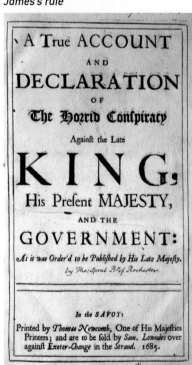

▼ **INTERPRETATION C** *Lord Russell, one of the plotters, says goodbye to his children before he is executed; a painting from around the end of the 1700s by Thomas Stothard*

## Fact

Although James became king when his brother died, his reign did not last. After three years of facing opposition across the country he was forced from power after Parliament invited the Protestant William of Orange to come and take the throne. William married James's eldest daughter, Mary, and they became joint monarchs of England, as William III and Mary II.

## Work

1 Explain the term 'absolute monarchy'.
2 Why were people concerned about Charles's links with King Louis of France?
3 Explain what the Rye House plotters planned to do.
4 Look at **Source B**.
   a Why do you think this was published?
   b What does it suggest about the new king?
5 What impression does **Interpretation C** give of Lord Russell?
6 Do you think **Source B** or **Interpretation C** tells us more about the Rye House Plot and its consequences?

## Practice Question

Explain what was important about the Rye House Plot in securing Charles's reign and his brother's succession. **8 marks**

## Study Tip

You might like to consider whether the importance of the Rye House Plot is not so much the plot itself but what it allowed Charles to do in terms of the Protestant 'threat'.

# Was Charles the 'merry monarch'?

After the Puritan years of the Interregnum, many hoped that the Restoration of Charles II would bring a more colourful and exciting era to England. Theatres were reopened, celebrations and festivals took place and a young king was on the throne. Charles certainly made the most of his wealth and power and was described at the time as the 'merry monarch'. How accurate was this nickname? Why did Charles feel the need to live so much of his life in public view?

**Objectives**

▶ **Describe** some of Charles's characteristics.

▶ **Explain** why he was given the nickname the 'merry monarch'.

▶ **Evaluate** the extent to which the nickname was deserved.

## A new era

When Charles rode into London to claim his throne in 1660, he was met with huge celebrations and very high expectations. Many hoped that the Restoration would bring a new golden era. Charles was well aware of what was resting on his shoulders but he also wanted to enjoy his return from exile. The question for historians is whether Charles was just having fun or whether the 'merry monarch' was a carefully planned public image.

### Work

1 Why did Charles and Catherine have two weddings?

2 Explain three reasons why Charles was described as the 'merry monarch'.

3 What point do you think is being made by **Source A**? What image of Charles do you think it is trying to put in people's minds?

4 Look at **Interpretation B**.
   a What does it suggest about Charles and his reign?
   b How convincing is it? Use the interpretation and your knowledge.

5 Look at **Interpretation C**. How accurate is this picture?

6 How accurate is the description of Charles as the 'merry monarch'? Use the information on these pages and your prior knowledge to help you.

▼ **SOURCE A** *Charles is presented with a pineapple, an exotic fruit prized by the wealthy in the 1600s, in this painting from around 1677*

▼ **INTERPRETATION B** *Adapted from a Daily Telegraph review of a book about Charles I by Malcolm Gaskill, first published 4 October 2009:*

Energies suppressed in state matters ran wild in the bedroom. Charles liked riding and tennis, and lapped up jokes and gossip. But his passion was women and plenty of them. Nell Gwyn, sloe-eyed and streetwise, everyone knows. What, though, of Barbara Castlemaine, the peer's wife who bore Charles four children in as many years. This sleazy decadence, and the court's eye-popping extravagance, harmed the king's image.

## Marriage

▼ **INTERPRETATION C** *A twentieth-century illustration of Catherine's arrival in Portsmouth*

When Charles returned to London, the need for an heir meant that a suitable bride needed to be found quickly. In 1662, Charles married Catherine of Braganza, a Portuguese princess – twice. There was a public, Anglican ceremony but also a secret, Catholic one. As a Catholic, Catherine was distrusted by many in England, and was even accused of treachery during the Popish Plot. She had at least three miscarriages and no heir was ever produced. Meanwhile, her husband had affairs with many women! Catherine knew about these but remained faithful. Charles insisted that his wife was treated with respect and refused calls to divorce her and marry a Protestant who might produce an heir.

### Fact

Queen Catherine was a 'trendsetter'; it is believed that it was her enjoyment of drinking tea that first made it popular in England.

### Key Words

Royal Society    patron

### Sports, arts and sciences

Charles dedicated much time and money to arts and sciences. He founded the Royal Observatory and was a major supporter of the **Royal Society** (an important scientific organisation). He took an interest in theatre and architecture, acting as a **patron** to the famous architect Christopher Wren. In 1682, he founded the Royal Hospital Chelsea, a home for retired soldiers. Charles also greatly enjoyed horse racing and spent a lot of time at the races.

### Party time

Charles became famous for his parties and banquets. Meals would usually begin mid-afternoon and often involved hundreds of dishes. Elaborate table decorations occasionally included a centrepiece of a fountain flowing with wine. The parties and banquets were intended to establish Charles as the centre of attention and show off his and the country's wealth.

## The merry monarch?

### Mistresses and illegitimate children

Charles fathered at least 20 children with his many mistresses. Far from hiding them, he acknowledged them, giving them titles and government roles. This would cause him major problems in the case of the Duke of Monmouth who many Whigs supported as an alternative king! Some of Charles's mistresses became high profile figures. These included the actress Nell Gwynn and Louise de Kéroualle, a French woman who is thought to have encouraged Charles's decision to become officially Catholic on his deathbed. One mistress, Lady Castlemaine, held so much sway over Charles that she was known as the 'uncrowned queen'.

### The visible king

People wanted to see Charles and he dedicated a lot of time to public appearances. These were carefully managed to maintain his image as dignified and royal but also relaxed and informal. Charles was very aware of the importance of performance. It could be said that he was the very first celebrity! His court seemed much less formal than any that had existed before but behind this was a very well thought-out public image.

▼ **SOURCE D** *A painting by Hendrick Danckerts from 1674–75 showing Charles walking in St James's Park*

# How did Charles's court work?

The royal court of King Charles was the centre of Restoration life. It was where Charles and his Privy Council governed the country, as well as where Charles entertained foreign royals and their ambassadors and where he held parties and banquets. Like other monarchs, Charles was rarely in one place for long and when he moved between his palaces his court of around 1300 people moved too. What was it like in Charles's court? How was Charles inspired by the court of his cousin, Louis XIV of France?

## Objectives

▶ **Describe** the court of King Charles and its key positions.

▶ **Explain** who held the power.

▶ **Assess** the similarities between Charles's court and that of Louis XIV.

## The court of King Charles

The royal court was where the public and private life of Charles met. It was the centre of English social life and the source of fashion, but it was also the centre of government and included all of the key offices of state and individuals who were responsible for running the country. The royal court was the access point to the monarch. The king had his favourites and they had influence over his decisions. Their opinions carried weight and they could wield great power because of this. Favourites could include ministers, mistresses and friends. When it came to influence, what the king thought of you was more important than your job. For someone who was outside the court the only way to affect decision making was through one of those in Charles's inner circle. The Restoration saw some positions of government become increasingly powerful. The combination of politics and social life meant that Charles's court was always full of rumour, scandal and the occasional conspiracy!

## Who had the power?

The king was at the centre of power but other offices and groups had significant influence over the king and his decisions. Chief Ministers under Charles usually held the position of Lord Chancellor or Lord Treasurer. It is important to remember that the king was not an absolute monarch; he had to answer to Parliament, which controlled the country's money.

## The impact of the French court

In many ways, Charles based his court on that of his cousin, King Louis of France. The official positions like Lord Chancellor and the Privy Council had been present in England for many years but the style of government and the way the court worked had much more in common with the French court than previous English ones. The problem for Charles was that, unlike Louis,

▼ **SOURCE A** *King Charles and his court painted by the Flemish artist Hieronymus Janssens, c1660*

### Fact

The royal court was not a building, but a collection of influential people. It was a group of advisors and important people, including the monarch and their family and friends.

## The Privy Council

The key advisors to the king. 'Privy' meant 'private', as these men were usually trusted with all sorts of private matters. The Council was made up of men who held other positions in government or Parliament. During Charles's reign there were an average of 60 members. They advised the king but could not force him to do anything. However, Charles was unlikely to go against their advice.

## Lord Chancellor

The chief legal officer of the country and therefore a very senior post in government. Lord Clarendon held this position for the first part of Charles's reign, followed by Lord Ashley (later Lord Shaftesbury) during the Cabal Ministry.

## The king

Had the final say on all matters and appointed his ministers. Charles was not completely free to do as he chose, however. He had to keep his opponents happy and avoid conflict with Parliament.

## The Lord Treasurer

Responsible for the kingdom's finances (although, of course, Parliament had overall control). Another senior role, held very briefly by Clarendon, by Lord Clifford in the Cabal Ministry and by Lord Danby during his ministry.

## The Exchequer

Collected money owed to the king (taxes, rents, etc.). Although at times there was a head (or Chancellor) of the Exchequer, for the most part the king's finances were run by a committee.

he was not an absolute monarch; he could not just do as he pleased. As was the case in France, outsiders looked to the king and to members of his inner circle for the latest fashions and trends in clothing, decoration and hobbies. If someone in court was seen in a new style of dress, people would rush to recreate it.

▼ **INTERPRETATION B** *King Louis XIV of France, drawn by Maurice Leloir, a twentieth-century artist*

## Work

1  Explain the role of the Privy Council.

2  Explain the role of the Exchequer.

3  Look at **Source A**.
   a  Describe what you can see in this picture.
   b  How accurate do you think it is as a depiction of Charles's court?

4  Historians have long recognised that Charles's court was influenced by King Louis's. Look at **Interpretation B**. What evidence can you see in this picture that supports this? Use **Source A** and your own knowledge to help you answer.

## Extension

Conduct some research and explain the ways in which Charles's court was similar to that of King Louis.

## Practice Question

Explain what was important about the royal court in Restoration England.     **8 marks**

## Study Tip

In your answer give thought to how the royal court allowed access to the king and how it might have affected government policy.

# What was the Great Plague?

In 1665, England and Charles faced a great crisis and this time it was nothing to do with religion or Parliament. This time the crisis was a deadly outbreak of **plague**. Thousands died across the country. In London alone, 100,000 residents were dead within a year, a quarter of the city's population. England had been struck by plague before, but this was a significant outbreak, and at a time of optimism in the country it hit people hard. What was the Great Plague? What did people think caused it and what was its actual cause? What did Charles and the royal court do in response?

**Objectives**

▶ **Describe** the Great Plague of 1665.

▶ **Explain** what people thought caused it and its consequences.

▶ **Assess** measures taken by the authorities.

## A terrible plague

Plague had first arrived in England in 1348 when it was known as the **Black Death**. Somewhere between a third and half the population of England was killed. In the following centuries there were numerous outbreaks in England of the same disease. Death from plague was very painful and the disease spread very quickly, wiping out whole families and villages. The plague was mainly spread by infected fleas that usually moved around on black rats and found a new human home when the rat died. Within a few days of the flea bite, the victim would be in agony, and most would be dead soon after.

**Symptoms of plague**

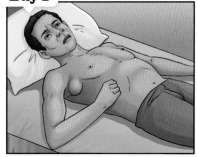

**Day 1**

Painful swellings called buboes appear in the victim's armpits, usually the size of an egg but could be bigger.

**Day 2**

Vomiting and fever.

**Day 3**

Bleeding under the skin causes dark blotches to appear all over the body.

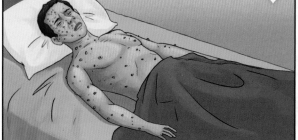

**Day 4**

The disease attacks the nervous system causing spasms and terrible pain.

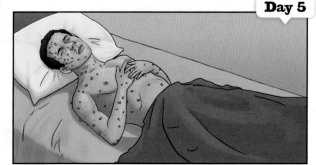

**Day 5**

If the buboes burst (producing a foul smelling liquid) the victim may survive, but if not they will suffer a painful death.

**INTERPRETATION A** *Adapted from the 1722 novel* A Journal of the Plague Year *by Daniel Defoe. Although Defoe was only a child when the plague struck, his book is one of the most important accounts of the Great Plague for historians:*

> One mischief was, that if the poor people asked these mock astrologers whether there would be a plague or no, they all agreed in general to answer 'Yes', for that kept up their trade. But they always talked to them of such-and-such influences of the stars, of the connections of such-and-such planets, which must necessarily bring sickness, and consequently the plague.

**INTERPRETATION B** *A 2009 painting of the Great Plague by Rita Greer*

## Key Words

plague    Black Death
astrology

## Work

1 When did plague first arrive in England?

2 Describe the symptoms of the plague.

3 What spread the plague?

4 a Summarise what people thought caused plague at the time.

   b Can you suggest reasons why people thought these things?

5 Look at **Interpretation A**.
   a What explanation for the Great Plague is Defoe referring to?
   b What is his opinion on astrologers?
   c Why do you think people were so ready to believe this and other explanations?

## Bad air

The smell in seventeenth-century London was terrible. Open sewers ran through the streets and animals lived in the city with their owners. Many believed that it was the bad smells that spread the disease. This was referred to as 'bad air'.

## God

Some saw the Great Plague as a punishment from God. Catholics may have seen it as a punishment for abandoning the faith; others saw it as evidence that the country was not Protestant enough.

## Extension

The Great Plague of London in 1665 was just one outbreak among many that took place in England and the rest of Europe during the 1600s. Research and produce a large learning poster about plague in seventeenth-century Europe. Where were the major outbreaks? How many died? What was the impact on the places where plague struck?

### What did people at the time think caused the Great Plague?

## The planets

There was a widely held belief in **astrology** in the seventeenth century and many believed that the alignment of the planets was the cause.

## Stray animals

London's streets were full of stray cats and dogs and some believed that they might be spreading the disease. All together around 40,000 dogs and 200,000 cats were killed on the orders of the Lord Mayor.

# What was the Great Plague?

## London in 1665

Seventeenth-century London was a crowded place of great poverty and filthy conditions. People and animals often lived in the same buildings and open sewers ran through many of the streets. This was the perfect breeding ground for black rats and their fleas. Unsurprisingly, most plague deaths were in the poorest areas.

## Cures and quacks

For every theory that existed for the cause of the plague, there was a suggested cure. Churchmen recommended prayer. Other people tried to cover up the bad air with perfumes, herbs or tobacco smoke. Conmen took advantage of the situation selling all sorts of potions and remedies to desperate people. These people of questionable medical skill were known as **quacks**.

| Measures taken by the city authorities to prevent the spread of the plague |
| --- |
| • Houses where the plague had struck were boarded up and marked with a large cross and the words 'Lord have mercy on us'. |
| • No one could leave or enter an infected house for a month after the last victim had died or recovered. Watchmen were appointed to enforce this. |
| • Searchers were given the job of identifying which corpses were killed by the plague. |
| • The dead were only to be buried at night in special plague cemeteries following strict regulations. |
| • Victims' clothing was burned. |
| • Fires were lit in the streets to try to remove the bad air. |
| • Pubs and theatres were closed. |
| • People had to sweep the streets outside their homes. |
| • Dogs and cats were killed and all animals were banned from the city. |
| • The Royal Society and other organisations stopped meeting. |

## Attempts to control the plague

The main reason that plague had caused such devastation in the past was that no steps were taken to try to prevent its spread. Although they did not know exactly what spread the disease, it was clear to many people that two things seemed to be present when someone caught the disease: a lack of cleanliness and a person who was already infected. If something could be done about these two things then perhaps the plague could be stopped. The Lord Mayor and the City Council of London passed a series of rules and regulations to try to halt the spread

of the plague. Other organisations also took precautions. King Charles, his court and most others who were able to left the city.

▼ **SOURCE C** *A drawing of a plague doctor from the seventeenth century; doctors dressed like this when visiting victims; every part of their body was covered and they would place perfume or spice inside their mask to avoid the bad air*

### Fact

The costumes worn by plague doctors often kept them safe because the thick leather protected them from fleas. They didn't know this at the time, however, and saw their survival as evidence that their theories were correct!

## The aftermath

Despite attempts to limit the plague's spread the number of dead quickly began to rise. Mass graves were dug and the call of 'Bring out your dead' was heard each night as new victims were collected from their homes. Prior to the plague, the authorities had not been strict when it came to reporting deaths but they began to insist this was done. **Bills of Mortality** (lists of deaths) showed people at the time, and reveal to historians, the numbers that died, the causes of death and where

**INTERPRETATION D** *A twentieth-century cartoon showing the Great Plague of London by Kitty Shannon*

they lived. People could see that the poorest areas had the highest death rate. The number of deaths began to fall by the end of the year, and in February 1666 the king and his government returned to the capital. The plague had devastated the poor of the city.

## Extension

**GCSE**

The Great Plague was devastating but it could be argued that the actions of the city authorities stopped it from being even worse. Consider the following questions: Which of these measures would have made much of a difference? Overall, how successful were the authorities in halting the spread of the Great Plague?

## Practice Question

Write an account of the impact of the Great Plague of 1665. **8 marks**

## Study Tip

Include specific details about the number of people who died and how the authorities responded.

## Key Words

quack   Bill of Mortality

▼ **SOURCE E** *A Bill of Mortality from 1665; it shows deaths from the plague as well as other causes of death including 'the King's Evil', a disease called scrofula, and a number of diseases that were spread because of poor conditions and diet, such as rickets*

### The Diseases and Casualties this Week.

| | | | |
|---|---|---|---|
| Abortive | 6 | Kingsevil | 10 |
| Aged | 54 | Lethargy | 1 |
| Apoplexie | 1 | Murthered at Stepney | 1 |
| Bedridden | 1 | Palsie | 2 |
| Cancer | 2 | Plague | 3880 |
| Childbed | 23 | Plurisie | 1 |
| Chrisomes | 15 | Quinsie | 6 |
| Collick | 1 | Rickets | 23 |
| Consumption | 174 | Rising of the Lights | 19 |
| Convulsion | 88 | Rupture | 2 |
| Dropsie | 40 | Sciatica | 1 |
| Drown two, one at St.Kath. Tower, and one at Lambeth | 2 | Scowring | 13 |
| | | Scurvy | 1 |
| Feaver | 353 | Sore legge | 1 |
| Fistula | 1 | Spotted Feaver and Purples | 190 |
| Flox and Small-pox | 10 | Starved at Nurse | 1 |
| Flux | 2 | Stilborn | 8 |
| Found dead in the Street at St.Bartholomew the Lfs | 1 | Stone | 2 |
| | | Stopping of the stomach | 16 |
| Frighted | 1 | Strangury | 1 |
| Gangrene | 1 | Suddenly | 1 |
| Gowt | 1 | Surfeit | 87 |
| Grief | 1 | Teeth | 113 |
| Griping in the Guts | 74 | Thrush | 3 |
| Jaundies | 3 | Tissick | 6 |
| Imposthume | 18 | Ulcer | 2 |
| Infants | 21 | Vomiting | 7 |
| Killed by a fall down stairs at St. Thomas Apostle | 1 | Winde | 8 |
| | | Wormes | 18 |

Christned ⎰ Males—83 Females—83 In all—166 ⎱   Buried ⎰ Males—2656 Females—2663 In all—5319 ⎱   Plague—3880

Increased in the Burials this Week——1289
Parishes clear of the Plague—34 Parishes Infected—96

*The Assize of Bread set forth by Order of the Lord Maior and Court of Aldermen. A penny Wheaten Loaf to contain Nine Ounces and a half, and three half-penny White Loaves the like weight.*

## Work

1   Name three measures taken to try to prevent the spread of the plague. How effective do you think they were?

2   Why do you think bodies were removed and buried at night?

3   Look at **Source E**.
    a   What percentage of the total deaths were due to plague?
    b   What does the number of plague deaths tell you about the outbreak?
    c   Why do you think the authorities wanted to record the number of plague victims?

# 4.2 Why did the Great Fire spread so quickly?

At 1am on 2 September 1666, a spark started a small fire at a bakery in Pudding Lane, London. Within five days one third of the city had been destroyed and around 100,000 people had been made homeless. The Great Fire of London was one of the most dramatic events of Charles's reign and it took 50 years to fully rebuild the city. How did such a small fire lead to so much damage? And how did the authorities, including the king himself, react to this disaster?

**Objectives**

▶ **Describe** the spread and consequences of the Great Fire.

▶ **Explain** why the fire spread so quickly.

▶ **Assess** what the Great Fire tells us about Restoration England.

## London's burning!

The fire spread quickly from building to building in the narrow streets. It grew so fast that Londoners just focused on escaping with as many of their belongings as they could. Some escaped by river, others headed out to the city limits and set up camp in the surrounding fields. A total of 13,200 houses were destroyed, yet fewer than ten people were killed.

▼ **INTERPRETATION A** *An extract from* London: A Novel *by Edward Rutherfurd (Century, 1997):*

> If any explanation of the fire's unstoppable growth were needed, the scene before them certainly provided it. The narrow street, the wooden and plaster houses (the orders to build in brick or stone were always ignored, every century), the upper storeys that jutted out, each one further than the one before until they practically touched the house opposite: this huddled mass of tenements, courtyards and wooden structures that leaned this way and that, sagging and stooping like a row of drunken old gossips, was in reality nothing more or less than a huge tinderbox[1].

1 A box containing dry material for lighting a fire

## Why did the fire spread so quickly?

The summer of 1666 had been hot and dry, perfect conditions for a fire. The fire spread quickly due to the tightly packed buildings and a strong wind blowing the flames from house to house. Many houses were wooden and the surrounding buildings were warehouses storing flammable materials like rope, oil and timber: a perfect combination of conditions for fire to engulf the city quickly. There were attempts to fight the fire by pouring on water, but this made little difference. The most effective way of stopping a fire was to demolish the buildings in its path to create a firebreak, leaving it nothing to burn. This required organised leadership but the Lord Mayor failed to fulfil this role. When demolitions did happen, even these had limited success. The wind was so strong that the fire was simply blown across the gaps. With the Lord Mayor unable to cope, the king stepped in and put his brother, the Duke of York, in charge. James ordered the demolition of whole rows of houses. Five days after the first spark the wind dropped and the firebreaks finally began to work.

▼ **INTERPRETATION B** *The spread of the Great Fire*

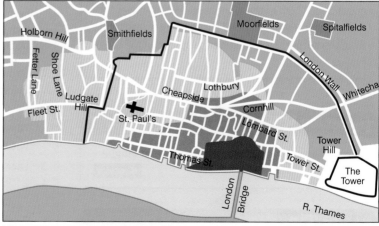

Key:

■ Sunday, 2 September   ■ Monday, 3 September

□ Tuesday/Wednesday, 4/5 September

> So I down to the waterside, and there saw a lamentable fire. Everybody endeavouring to remove their goods and flinging them into the river. Poor people staying in their houses as long as till the very fire touched them, and then running into boats or clambering from one pair of stair by the waterside to another. I did tell the King and Duke of York what I saw, and that unless his Majesty did command houses to be pulled down, nothing could stop the fire. At last met the Lord Mayor in Canning Street. To the King's message, he cried like a fainting woman, 'Lord what can I do? I am spent! People will not obey me. I have been pulling down houses. But the fire overtakes us faster than we can do it.' With one's face in the wind you were almost burned with a shower of firedrops.

## Work

1  When and where did the Great Fire start?

2  Why did the fire spread so quickly?

3  Create a newspaper article from the day after the fire ended to include: what happened; what damage was done; how people tried to fight it; some different opinions about who was to blame and the reaction of the authorities; an image to show the destruction.

4  Read **Source C**.
  a  How does Pepys describe residents' reactions to the fire?
  b  What is his suggestion for fighting it?
  c  What impression does he give of the Lord Mayor?

5  Look at **Interpretation D**.
  a  How is King Charles portrayed in this image?
  b  How accurate do you think it is?

## The aftermath

Angry at their terrible losses, and the lack of action from the authorities, people began to look for someone to blame. There were suggestions of a foreign, possibly Catholic, plot but there was never any evidence of this. For reasons that remain unclear, a French watchmaker named Robert Hubert confessed responsibility for starting the fire and was hanged on 28 September. However, he couldn't possibly have been responsible as he wasn't even in London during the fire! With the city devastated and unrest among the people, the king was concerned that there may be a rebellion. He quickly set about bringing order, setting up a special court to deal with disputes about who should pay for damage. Charles was determined that rebuilding should began as soon as possible and set about making grand plans for the city.

▼ **INTERPRETATION D**  *An illustration of Charles II among his people during the Great Fire, from a twentieth-century children's magazine*

## Extension

The reaction to the fire can tell us much about Restoration England. For example: where people laid the blame. Why do you think people were so ready to blame Robert Hubert for the fire? What does this suggest about Restoration England?

## Practice Question

How convincing is **Interpretation A** about the spread of the Great Fire of London?

Explain your answer using **Interpretation A** and your contextual knowledge. **8 marks**

## Study Tip

In this type of question try to include specific details from your own knowledge to back up what you say about the interpretation.

# How was London rebuilt?

The Great Fire destroyed a third of London and thousands of people lost their homes and businesses. England's capital needed to be rebuilt. The city had also lost 87 of its 109 churches, including St Paul's Cathedral. The easiest option would be to rebuild the city that had been destroyed but Charles had grander plans. London was to be a much safer city, with new regulations and wider streets to stop any future fire from spreading so quickly. A magnificent new city was to rise from the ashes. Things did not go quite according to plan, but why not?

## Objectives

▶ **Recall** the plans and the reality of rebuilding London.

▶ **Explain** why the plans were not fully carried out.

▶ **Assess** what the rebuilding of London tells us about Restoration England.

## A new London

Charles put out a call for designs for a new London and many were submitted, including plans by the architect Christopher Wren and the writer John Evelyn. London was to be more like Paris and other European cities, with great buildings, wide streets or avenues and grand open public squares like those in Italian towns and cities. A group of lawyers was appointed as the 'Commission to establish ownership' to investigate who owned what land so that people could be compensated to allow for the new designs to be built on their land.

▼ **SOURCE A** *The plan for London by John Evelyn with its well-ordered and wide streets; this illustration is from* **London in the Time of the Stuarts** *by Sir Walter Besant (A & C Black, 1903) but is based on Evelyn's design*

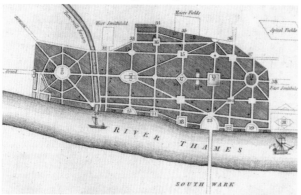

## The reality

Despite the grand plans, Charles's vision for a new London was not realised. Arguments over land ownership took too long to settle and many Londoners simply wanted to rebuild their houses and get on with their lives. Most of the business and commercial areas of the city were left untouched by the fire and so London's economy could continue to function even with all of the damage. There was also a lack of workers available for construction following the fire as many had fled the city. In the end much of London was rebuilt as it was, along the same street plans.

There were some improvements, however. New building regulations were put in place to try to prevent another major fire, streets were widened and houses were no longer built right next to the river. The devastation also led to the establishment of the first insurance companies. In exchange for regular payment by a building's owner, insurance companies would send a fire brigade to put out a fire and limit the damage. These were the forerunners of the modern day fire service. Most importantly, the new buildings were made from brick rather than wood. However, some of the new designs did become reality in public buildings such as churches. Most famous of these was the new St Paul's Cathedral designed by Christopher Wren, with its huge dome, which was built on the site of the old cathedral.

▼ **B** *A modern photograph of St Paul's Cathedral, designed by Christopher Wren*

### Sir Christopher Wren (1632–1723)

- The most celebrated architect of the Restoration.

- Responsible for designing 52 churches in London after the Great Fire, including St Paul's Cathedral, which was completed in 1711.

- His other work included the Monument to the Great Fire, the Royal Naval College and the Royal Observatory in Greenwich, a new section of Hampton Court Palace and numerous university buildings in Oxford and Cambridge.

- As well as an architect, Wren was a respected scientist and served as president of the Royal Society.

▼ *A portrait of Sir Christopher Wren painted by Joseph Smith in 1828*

▼ **C** *The Monument on the site of the Pudding Lane bakery where the fire started; designed by Wren on the orders of King Charles; if it fell, its top would land on the exact spot where the fire started!*

1 Describe King Charles's vision for London after the fire.

2 Look at **Source A**.
   a Write a sentence that describes the design.
   b How far does this design reflect Charles's vision?

3 Why could Evelyn's plan not be followed fully?

4 In what ways was London made safer after the fire?

5 Two of the most significant new buildings are shown in **Images B** and **C**.
   a What are the buildings and what is their purpose?
   b Why do you think Charles requested they were built?

6 What do you think the plans and the reality for the new London tell us about Restoration England?

# Theatre and playwrights

During the Interregnum, theatre, along with most other public entertainment, was banned. It was seen by the Puritans as immoral and a distraction from living a good Christian life. Plays returned to the theatre after the Restoration in a completely new style that quickly captured the public's imagination and interest. What was so new about theatre under Charles II? What new plays were written and by whom? And what would a trip to the theatre actually involve?

**Objectives**

▶ **Describe** theatre in the Restoration.

▶ **Explain** the key features and developments of Restoration theatre.

▶ **Evaluate** the role of women and their involvement in the theatre in the Restoration.

## A new king and new theatres

Soon after his return, King Charles, who loved the theatre, reintroduced it to England. Although many groups began to put on productions, not everyone was allowed to formally put on plays. Charles gave the exclusive right, or **patent**, to stage plays to two groups: the King's Company and the Duke's Company. This **royal patronage** meant that these two companies could quickly begin staging classic plays written before the Civil War.

Two new large and elaborate theatres designed by Sir Christopher Wren were built in London, and others followed. Lit by candlelight, theatres were fitted with the latest in movable scenery and included machinery that produced sound effects such as thunder and lightning. At the Dorset Gardens Playhouse, actors could even be flown onto the stage on wires! Plays were designed to be spectacular events. The extravagant designs both inside and outside the theatres were attempts to outdo rival theatres and attract large audiences. Capacity at the new theatres was greater than it had ever been before.

## The battle for audiences

A visit to the theatre during the Restoration was one of the most popular forms of entertainment. The cheapest tickets could not be reserved and people would try to squeeze into the pit in front of the stage. Wealthier audience members could enjoy a much more relaxing environment seated further back and higher up in the theatre from where they could look down on the stage. Theatre became extremely fashionable among the upper classes, who started trends such as the wearing of masks by women and the eating of oranges during the play! The two patent theatre companies – the King's Company, run by Thomas Killigrew, and the Duke's Company, run by Sir William Davenant – battled over the right to perform new plays and to get audiences through the doors of their playhouses. This meant that it was necessary to produce plays that would be immediately popular with audiences.

▼ **SOURCE A** *A contemporary sketch of the Dorset Gardens Playhouse, London, built in 1671*

▼ **INTERPRETATION B** *An 1808 engraving of the Drury Lane Theatre, showing the layout of a Restoration theatre*

## Women and Restoration theatre

Women in the Restoration still did not hold positions of authority, could not vote and had very little say in who they married. While some upper class women did begin to have a little more freedom than before, ultimately it was still their fathers and husbands who held the power. Restoration theatre brought about a significant change, however. For the first time, women could appear on stage. There was no difference between what was acceptable for male and female actors, and women performed all kinds of roles. One common plotline involved women dressing and acting as men.

▼ **INTERPRETATION C** *Nell Gwynn, the most famous actress of the era (and one of Charles II's mistresses); an illustration by Kitty Shannon from 1926*

### Work

1. What were the two new theatre companies that were created when Charles became king?

2. Describe four key features of a typical Restoration theatre building.

3. Why was Aphra Behn such a significant figure?

4. Look at **Interpretation C**.
   a. Who is the woman in the picture and why was she an important figure?
   b. How has the artist portrayed her? What impression do you get of her?
   c. Why do you think she was still being painted in 1926?

### Key Words

patent    royal patronage    genre

### Key Biography

#### Thomas Betterton (c1635–1710)

Thomas Betterton was the son of one of Charles II's cooks who became one of the most successful actors of his age. He played a number of lead roles for the Duke's Company and became particularly popular with the king, who paid for him to study acting in Paris. Betterton went on to become an important theatre company manager for the Duke's Company and later the United Company (formed when the King's and the Duke's companies merged).

### Key Biography

#### Aphra Behn (c1640–89)

Aphra Behn was one of the first women to make a living out of writing plays. Very little is known about her early life but it is thought that she came from a relatively poor background, and was possibly the daughter of a barber. She briefly worked as a spy for King Charles in the Netherlands. After the death of her husband, and finding herself deep in debt, she took a job at a theatre and soon began writing plays. She wrote in all **genres** but her biggest successes came in comedy. Behn was very politically minded and often used her plays to criticise Whig politicians. Her work became extremely popular and when she died she was buried in Westminster Abbey.

# Why were Restoration comedies such a serious business?

**5.2**

Although Restoration theatre included a wide variety of genres, by far the most popular was comedy. A great many plays that criticised or mocked those in power were produced during Charles II's reign. In the Restoration, comedy could have a big impact on public opinion. How important was comedic theatre in Restoration society?

## Objectives

▶ **Describe** the features of Restoration comedies.

▶ **Explain** why comedies were important.

▶ **Assess** the impact that comedies could have on public opinion and politics.

## The power of comedy

In the early years of the Restoration, theatres needed to attract large audiences in order to compete with each other. Theatre managers quickly realised that comedies were the best way to do this. Theatres wanted to have the exclusive rights to the most popular plays so writers responded to what the audience liked. Plays were fast-paced and often had several complicated plots happening at once. These plays fitted the public perception of how the royal court functioned at the time, including lots of scandalous behaviour from lords and their mistresses. The plays usually involved plots that included sex, adultery and double entendre. Husbands were portrayed as unintelligent while their wives were shown to be clever and in control.

As time went on, comedies became more politically focused, making points in favour of or against issues of public concern. For example, during the time of the Popish Plot and the Exclusion Crisis comedies were produced that made fun of both Whig and Tory politicians. This **satire** became as important as anything said by the politicians themselves in shaping public opinion. Plays were written either by professional playwrights such as Aphra Behn and John Dryden or by courtiers and other wealthy people.

▼ **SOURCE A** *A scene from* Love in a Tub *by George Etheridge, a successful, professional playwright; it was first performed in 1664; in this scene, a man is wearing a barrel because he has lost his trousers; stupidity and the loss of dignity were common themes in Restoration comedies*

# The power of satire

One of the most famous satires of the Restoration was *The Country Gentleman*. It tells the story of a country family who travel to London and meet a variety of ridiculous characters, many of which are trying to follow French fashions and manners, something that was very popular at the time. They also meet a man called Sir Cautious Trouble-All, a politician who is shown to be incompetent and childish and who sees governing the country as a game. References in the play made it clear that the character was based on Sir William Coventry, a real-life politician.

Although the majority of the play was written by Robert Howard, the scenes involving Trouble-All were written by the Duke of Buckingham, a rival of Coventry's. Coventry was outraged and challenged Buckingham to a duel. For threatening the life of one of his ministers, Charles imprisoned Sir William but in order to avoid further scandal the play was banned. The damage to Coventry's image was irreparable. The power and influence that the comedies could have was significant and writers regularly used their plays to put across their own points of view.

▼ **INTERPRETATION B** *An illustration from a twentieth-century children's magazine showing an audience and performers at a theatre during the Restoration*

## Work

1 Why was comedy popular during the Restoration?

2 Why was Sir William Coventry upset about *The Country Gentleman*?

3 Why do you think politicians were so concerned about comedies?

4 Look at **Source A**.
   a What does this image suggest about Restoration comedies?
   b How far do you think this picture shows what Restoration comedies were like?

5 'A writer of successful comedies could have a huge influence on politics in Restoration England.' How far do you agree?

## Extension

For historians, plays can be really useful in understanding the society in which they were written and performed. In order to widen your knowledge and understanding, try to read a section of a Restoration comedy. Some plays are available online but there will also be some in your school or the public library. A good place to start would be *The Country Gentleman* as you already know some of its background. The website *dramaonlinelibrary.com* will help you find out about some of the plays that you might choose to read: search under 'Genres' for 'Restoration Comedy'. Try to spot any references to Restoration society, particularly if they are making fun of it!

## Study Tip

Don't just write down everything you know about Restoration theatre. Think about how it showed a change in society, for example, in the role of women.

## Practice Question

Explain what was important about theatre during the Restoration. **8 marks**

# Science and the arts in Restoration England

The Restoration was a time of new ideas and experimentation in the arts and sciences, which have been built on up to the present day. However, it also saw many 'wrong turns' in scientific developments and a reluctance from some people to move on from theories that had been disproved. The wider availability of the printing press led to the creation of great literature and music but there was also censorship. What was the new approach to science? Why did some cling to old ideas? And was the Restoration really a time of advancement?

## Objectives

▶ **Identify** some of the key features of science and the arts during the Restoration.

▶ **Explain** why the Restoration could be seen as a significant time for the arts and the sciences.

▶ **Evaluate** how far it can be seen as an 'age of advancement'.

## A new scientific age?

Although scientific investigation was not new when Charles was crowned, he was quick to encourage it. He established the Royal Observatory at Greenwich to investigate the stars and planets and was patron of the Royal Society. Although a group of people interested in science had been meeting since 1645, it was not until they were awarded a royal charter, giving the organisation special privileges, that the Royal Society was born. Attending Royal Society events was seen as an important part of being a respectable man during the Restoration. The group, which included leading scientific figures like Robert Boyle and Robert Hooke and architects like Christopher Wren, met weekly to discuss the latest developments in physics, botany (plants), astronomy, medicine and other sciences.

Members demonstrated experiments in front of an audience using the Society's state-of-the art laboratory. Charles attended Society meetings regularly but also had a laboratory built in one of his palaces. Experiments at the Royal Society were based on the clear scientific principles of fair experiment and proof, following the motto 'Nullius in verba' ('take nobody's word for it'). This approach was progress towards an evidence-based experimental method. The Society aimed to spread knowledge more widely by publishing books and articles. Despite new ideas, however, many people held to centuries-old ones. The new learning that was present in the Royal Society did not filter down to ordinary people.

## The coffee house

Official meetings at places like the Royal Society were far from the only place where new ideas took shape. A key part of London culture was the coffee shop. Over coffee, men would discuss the latest developments in science, politics, literature and philosophy.

Coffee houses attracted the brightest minds of the time who would spend hours in discussion over a cheap cup of coffee. The coffee cost a penny and the shops were nicknamed 'penny universities'.

## Key cultural and scientific events of the Restoration

| 1660 | 1661 | 1662 | 1666 | 1667 | 1673 |
|------|------|------|------|------|------|
| London theatres reopen. The Royal Society is founded | 'Boyle's law', an important principle in physics and chemistry, is published | No publishing is allowed without a licence | Isaac Newton publishes his theory of gravity | *Paradise Lost*, a very influential poem by John Milton, is published | Christopher Wren starts work on rebuilding St Paul's Cathedral after the Great Fire seven years before |

▲ **SOURCE A** *Charles II attempts to 'cure' people with scrofula, 'the King's Evil'; it was still believed by many that the touch of the king could cure the disease*

## Key Biography

### Samuel Pepys (1633–1703)

- He was a key figure in court and the Royal Society.
- He served as the Chief Secretary of the Admiralty.
- His real importance comes from his diary. Pepys's descriptions of daily life in the Restoration through the key events of Charles's reign, including the Great Plague and the Great Fire, are vital to historians in understanding the period. He also comments on society and politics.

## Key Biography

### Robert Boyle (1627–91)

- He was considered one of the founders of modern chemistry and the scientific method of experimentation.
- He discovered 'Boyle's law' – an important scientific principle. It states that if the volume of a gas decreases, its pressure increases in proportion.

## Key Biography

### Robert Hooke (1635–1703)

- Described by one historian as Britain's Leonardo Da Vinci, he organised experiments at the Royal Society.
- He was an early user of the microscope. His book, *Micrographia*, had the first drawings of nature seen under microscope.
- His studies touch on issues like evolution (based on his study of fossils), gravity and light.
- He was a successful architect and was heavily involved in the rebuilding of London after the Great Fire.

## Extension

Historians should consider changes and developments over longer periods. Challenge yourself by answering this question: 'How far can the Restoration be seen as an age of great advancements in science and the arts?' Remember to consider both sides of the argument.

## Work

1. When was the Royal Society founded?
2. Look at **Source A**. What does this suggest about medicine during the Restoration?
3. Why is Samuel Pepys important to historians?
4. Explain the importance of coffee houses.
5. a. Create a table in your book. On one side make a list of reasons why the Restoration was a time of scientific progress and on the other list reasons why it was not. You could add to your list by doing some additional research.
   b. Do you think that the Restoration was a time of scientific advancement?

| 1679 | 1682 | 1683 |
| --- | --- | --- |
| End of the printing licences; many political pamphlets are published | Christopher Wren starts work on Royal Hospital Chelsea | Henry Purcell appointed 'keeper of the King's instruments', employed to compose music for the king |

# Historic Environment: The Royal Observatory Greenwich

During the Restoration there was a growing desire to understand the world and beyond. Charles II was a great supporter of the latest 'scientific thought' and demonstrated this when he ordered the building of the Royal Observatory at Greenwich. The latest expertise and technology would come together to explore the stars. It was not just about curiosity, though. The observatory had a second, perhaps more important purpose: developing ever more accurate methods of navigation.

## Objectives

▶ **Describe** the features and purpose of the Royal Observatory Greenwich.

▶ **Explain** why Charles II ordered it built using your wider knowledge of the Restoration.

▶ **Assess** what the Observatory can tell us about the culture and interests of the Restoration.

## A great scientific age

The Restoration was a time of scientific experimentation and research. Old ideas were questioned and the basis of modern ideas in physics, chemistry and biology were formed. Charles II's establishment of the Royal Society allowed the great minds of the age such as Boyle, Hooke and the celebrated physicist, Isaac Newton, to share their latest theories and experiments. One area of particular interest was astronomy. The work of Galileo Galilei and Nicholas Copernicus in the 1500s had questioned accepted ideas about the universe and, despite opposition from the Catholic Church, their theories awakened a new interest in the sky.

## A place to observe the heavens

The building of an observatory at Greenwich in London was first proposed in 1674 by Jonas Moore. The location was perfect as it was close to the Naval College; the navy was increasingly important to trade and influence abroad. Moore was Surveyor-General of the Ordnance Board, responsible for managing land and buildings that were important to England's military success. Gaining knowledge of the stars was not just motivated by scientific curiosity; it was also about improving navigation for the growing navy. With permission from the king, Moore organised the building of the observatory and paid for its equipment himself. The building was designed by Sir Christopher Wren, probably with help from the scientist Robert Hooke. Built in 1675, it was the first purpose-built scientific building in Britain.

## Work

1. Look at the quotation within the Key Biography. What does it suggest Charles's reasons for establishing the observatory were?

2. Compare the Royal Observatory with other royal buildings of the period, such as Tilbury Fort, and list the features and ideas they have in common.

▼ **SOURCE A** *A 1676 engraving of the Royal Observatory Greenwich*

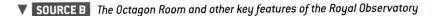

Flamsteed prepared some of the most accurate star maps ever produced.

Tompion clocks: these were vital to accurate astronomical observations.

The Octagon Room: This room was designed to observe the movement of stars and planets and housed many astronomical instruments and clocks.

**Quadrant**: Flamsteed used this for measuring **latitude**. The quadrant could be wheeled from window to window.

The **Greenwich Meridian** was first established in the 1670s and measured from a small building in the observatory grounds.

Increasingly powerful telescopes allowed for more accurate observations.

The Astronomer Royal's quarters: these were underneath the Octagon Room and served as Flamsteed's home for nearly 40 years.

## Key Words

quadrant   latitude   Greenwich Meridian   longitude

## New discoveries

On Moore's recommendation, Charles appointed John Flamsteed as the first Astronomer Royal to lead work at the observatory. Initially, this involved tracking and recording the movement of the stars and planets with increasingly powerful telescopes. This allowed Flamsteed and others to find patterns and make predictions about the movements of objects in the sky. This proved hugely useful for ships as they were able to more accurately work out their positions by using the stars. The observatory also contained two of the most accurate clocks ever made. Built by Thomas Tompion, they had a 13 foot pendulum and only needed winding once a year. The clocks' accuracy allowed Flamsteed to prove that the Earth revolved on its axis at a constant rate.

## Key Biography

### John Flamsteed (1646–1719)

- The first Astronomer Royal and director of the Royal Observatory Greenwich.
- Charles gave him the official job of 'rectifying the tables of the motions of the heavens, and the places of the fixed stars, so as to find out the so much desired **Longitude** of places for Perfecting the Art of Navigation'.
- He recorded and catalogued over 3000 stars and accurately predicted solar eclipses in 1666 and 1668. In 1690, he became the first astronomer to record a sighting of Uranus.

### Study Tip

The Restoration period was a time of great scientific curiosity and experimentation. It was also a time when trade and the navy were very important to the nation. Think about how a building such as the Royal Observatory demonstrates these features of the period. What was important about the choice of the location of the building?

# What was the East India Company?

One of the most important colonial gains during the reign of Charles I was the creation of the country's first colonies in India. Two hundred years later, India would be described as the 'jewel in the crown' of the British Empire but it all began as a wedding gift. Like other colonies, India was a business opportunity and the founding of the East India Company was intended to make money above all else. So what was the East India Company? What was Charles's great wedding gift and who was it from? Why was India such an important area for Britain?

## Objectives

▶ **Describe** the establishment of the trading post in Bombay.

▶ **Explain** why India was an important location for British colonies.

▶ **Evaluate** the effect of Indian colonies on Britain.

## Charles, his wife and Bombay

When Charles II married the Portuguese princess Catherine of Braganza, her family needed to provide a **dowry**. The gift they gave Charles was a growing port in India that they had owned since 1534. The Portuguese referred to it as Bom Bahia (the 'good bay') and the name stuck once the English arrived, with the slightly different pronunciation of Bombay.

Although it was in a good location for trade, particularly for spices (increasingly popular in Europe and therefore very lucrative), Charles was not particularly interested in his swampy new land. He agreed to rent it to a private company for 10 pounds of gold a year. The East India Company would have the exclusive right (**monopoly**) to trade from the port. The climate and swamps made Bombay a challenging place to live for the British (many died of diseases like malaria or of infections) and the constant threat of raids by other Europeans made it dangerous. To many, it appeared that the East India Company was never going to make much money from their investment, but within a few years Bombay was a successful and prosperous city.

## All about trade

Bombay was built as a port city to make money for the East India Company. Trading in goods like silk and spices, the company was allowed to trade not just with Britain and British colonies but also with its Portuguese neighbours and with China. The company was given complete control over the area, including the right to make and enforce laws and control an army to protect it.

Bombay was just one of the East India Company trading posts in India: with posts in Surat, Calcutta and Madras they were increasingly able to dominate trade in the area. Britain now had a firmly established foothold in Asia giving it control of the lucrative spice market. Traders and investors back in Britain made a fortune. Although this was limited to a relatively small number of people and goods during Charles II's reign it was the start of one of Britain's most successful trades and would play a key role in the growth of the Empire over the following centuries.

▼ *East India Company trading posts*

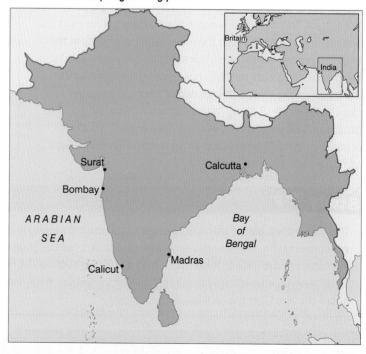

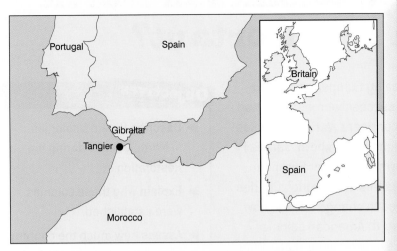

▲ *Tangier on the north coast of Morocco on the Straits of Gibraltar*

## Another wedding gift

In addition to the gift of Bombay, Queen Catherine's dowry also included the port of Tangier, another Portuguese colony. Like Bombay, it was ideally located but otherwise not seen as particularly useful. The Portuguese had spent years trying to maintain order with constant rebellions and attacks from the Moroccans who wanted the city back. The English faced the same problems and, with growing concern about the cost of the colony, Charles ordered that it be abandoned in 1683.

▼ **SOURCE A** *An engraving of the trading post at Surat, from around 1680*

## Key Words

dowry    monopoly

## Work

1 How did Charles first gain control of Bombay?

2 What did he give the East India Company the right to do?

3 Look at the map of India. Why do you think these particular places were chosen for trading posts? Hint: think about location in relation to the sea and other countries/colonies.

4 Why was Tangier less successful than Bombay as a colony?

5 Why do you think the East India Company wanted to establish a post in Bombay?

6 Look at **Interpretation B**.
   a Why does Dan Bogart think colonisation in India in the seventeenth century was important?
   b How far do you agree with him?

▼ **INTERPRETATION B** *From an article written in 2015 by Dan Bogart, a historian from the University of California. The 'corporate institutions' that he refers to are organisations like the East India Company:*

The emergence of regular trade between Europe and Asia in the seventeenth and eighteenth centuries is one of the most important developments in the history of the world economy. Its significance lies not in the value of trade which remained small, but rather in the corporate institutions which laid the foundation for European colonisation and influence in Asia.

# Why were colonies in North America so important?

Since the discovery of North America by Europeans around 200 years before Charles II's reign, successive monarchs had attempted to build colonies on the continent. Various colonies had been established during the reigns of Elizabeth, James I and Charles I with limited success, whereas other European nations had built settlements across this 'New World'. Charles and his government were determined to change this. So how successful was Britain in building North American colonies? How did Britain gain them and where exactly were they? Why did the country even want colonies?

## Objectives

▶ **Describe** Britain's colonies in North America during the Restoration.

▶ **Explain** why these colonies were established.

▶ **Assess** how much the country gained from its foreign colonies.

## The New World

The Spanish were the first to set up colonies in the newly discovered world of the Americas and bring back riches to their home country. Elizabeth I encouraged English sailors to look for new lands and riches too. There were several attempts to build colonies during Elizabeth's reign, but it was not until the time of James I (Charles II's grandfather) that any were successfully established. During Charles II's reign, Britain was becoming a growing power in North America.

▼ *Areas of North America controlled by European countries in the seventeenth century*

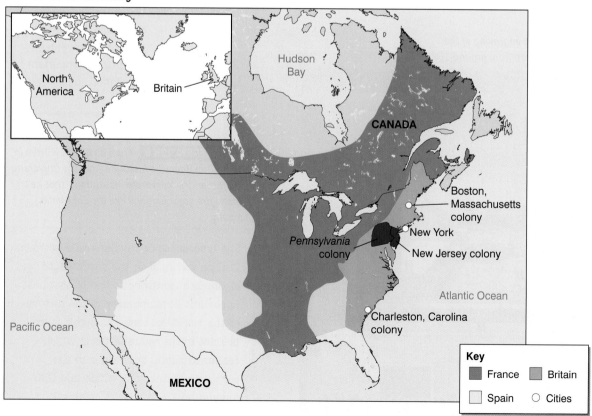

## England's existing colonies

The colonies that were established before the Restoration had been left alone and allowed to rule themselves during the Commonwealth. Once on the throne, Charles and his government attempted to gain more direct control over his lands in America. The people of Massachusetts in particular had become very independent in their way of thinking. As Nonconformists they were very resistant to the Anglican ideas of the new king. Of greater concern to Charles was their treatment of another group of Nonconformists: **Quakers**. The groups were unable to tolerate each other and the Quakers in particular were treated badly. Religious difference and tolerance was a key issue in America during Charles's reign. Despite some differences between the viewpoints of the colonists and that of their government in London, the main aim was to ensure that British territories were more successful than their European rivals. With this in mind, it was decided that British colonies should only trade with Britain or with each other.

## New colonies

Creating new colonies was seen as important but a real success was seizing one from a rival empire. When English troops took control of the Dutch colony of New Netherland and its city of New Amsterdam in 1664, they not only gained a useful port but also delivered a humiliating blow to the Netherlands. Charles gave the new land to his brother, the Duke of York, and it was quickly renamed New York in his honour. Although it was briefly recaptured it was firmly established as British in 1674. James gave part of his new land to a friend and New Jersey was created. Little changed in the colony for its residents; most of the Dutch people remained, but Britain now had control over a vital port.

Further south, another new British colony was formed in 1663. It was named Carolina, after Charles, and quickly became very prosperous. Carolina's climate and fertile soil allowed for huge amounts of rice to be grown. This could be traded with other colonies and with people in Britain. A third significant colony was at Hudson Bay where a company was created to trade beaver fur in 1668. Although building colonies was a way to show the power and influence of Britain, the main aim was to make money. The king ruled the colonies but they were owned and managed by those who had created them. Colonies were run like companies and the government made money through tax. Most North American colonies were first and foremost business opportunities.

## Key Words

Quaker

### A new home for Quakers

Not all colonies were created for financial gain. William Penn was a Quaker who wanted to build a land for other followers of his religion where they would be safe from persecution and free to live their lives as they wished. In 1682, Penn was given Pennsylvania by the king as a way to pay off a debt and it quickly grew as more and more Quakers moved there. Pennsylvania became wealthy but was also much more tolerant towards other religions than other colonies and, very unusually for the time, treated the Native Americans with a level of respect.

▲ **INTERPRETATION A** *A portrait of William Penn (1644–1718) by J. Hill from a painting by B. West, 1849*

### Work

1. a When was the colony of Carolina created?
   b Why was it given this name?
2. Why did New Amsterdam become New York?
3. Why did William Penn want to create a new colony?
4. What was the purpose of colonies in North America?
5. Look at the map opposite. Which country do you think has the most useful colonies? Think particularly about location.

# 6.3 British colonies in the Caribbean

Like the lands further north, the Caribbean was an area that Europeans were desperate to get their hands on. Its climate and fertile soil were perfect for producing materials like cotton, sugar and tobacco that could be traded to make a fortune. Unlike further north, however, there was significantly less land and the European nations had to fight for control of the valuable islands. Why were so many countries so keen to control the Caribbean?

## Objectives

▶ **Describe** the British colonisation of the Caribbean.

▶ **Analyse** the purpose of the British colonies.

▶ **Evaluate** the reasons for British colonisation of the Caribbean.

## Pirates in the Caribbean

Like South America, much of the Caribbean had been captured by the Spanish in the fifteenth and sixteenth centuries. Yet England did control some islands there, most significantly Barbados. Competition between the three European powers (England, France and Spain) over the Caribbean did not involve full scale battles. Instead they raided each other's ports, stealing what they could and then causing as much damage as possible to their rival's ships. The most famous of the British pirates was Henry Morgan who spent years attacking and raiding Spanish ships and ports. He was seen as a hero by the English but as a criminal by the Spanish.

By the time Charles II was crowned, the Spanish had begun to lose interest in the Caribbean, deciding to focus more on South America and the money that could be made there. In 1655, the British captured the island of Jamaica. Despite this, Morgan and others continued to lead raids against the French and the Spanish.

### Key Biography

#### Henry Morgan (1635–88)

Captain Morgan's daring raids of Spanish settlements and ships brought riches to Britain and embarrassed the Spanish. He became a legendary figure. In 1671, however, many thought that Morgan went too far. His burning of the Spanish-controlled city of Panama in Central America was seen as unnecessarily brutal at a time when relations with Spain were improving. He was arrested by Charles for breaking a peace treaty with Spain (the **Treaty of Madrid**, 1670) but was released when relations between the two countries worsened. He was later knighted and then made lieutenant (later governor) of Jamaica.

▲ **INTERPRETATION A** *'Henry Morgan – Pirate', an illustration from the front cover of a children's history magazine from 1978*

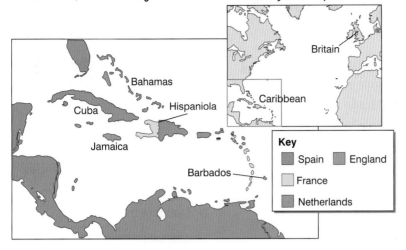

▼ *A map of the Caribbean in 1700 showing which countries controlled which islands; there were regular raids on the colonies of rival empires*

Britain

Caribbean

Bahamas

Cuba

Hispaniola

Jamaica

Barbados

**Key**

Spain

France

Netherlands

England

**Key Words**

Treaty of Madrid    plantation

## Why was the Caribbean so important to European countries?

When the Spanish first arrived in the Caribbean they were in search of gold but it was another valuable substance that made the islands valuable to Britain and its rivals: sugar. In the seventeenth century the amount of sugar consumed in Britain increased greatly and the Caribbean provided the perfect conditions to grow it. Sugarcane was grown on huge **plantations** and shipped to England where it was refined for sale. Bristol in particular processed large amounts of sugar in the 1600s and a number of men became very wealthy as they acquired the land cheaply and sold the produce for immense profit. The income from a 200-acre cane plantation in Barbados was enough to support the lifestyle of a duke in England. Those with land could live very comfortably. Many of the businessmen rarely, if ever, visited the islands, instead leaving it to agents to run their plantations and to black African slaves to do the work. Sugar and other Caribbean crops became a key part of British trade in the seventeenth century.

▼ **SOURCE B**   *An engraving showing a sugar plantation in the Caribbean in the seventeenth century*

**Work**

1   Why was the Caribbean an area of interest for Britain?

2   Why was Henry Morgan arrested in 1671?

3   Look at **Interpretation A**.
    a   What impression does this give of Henry Morgan?
    b   How accurate do you think this interpretation of Morgan is?

4   What does **Source B** suggest about how sugar plantations worked?

5   'The colonisation of the Caribbean was all about making money for the British.' How far do you agree?

**Extension**

A historian is always looking to make comparisons. Using the information in this chapter and additional research try to answer this question: 'Which colonies brought the greatest benefit to England and why?'

**Practice Question**

Write an account of the ways in which the expansion of British colonies affected Restoration England.    **8 marks**

**Study Tip**

This type of question is looking for a detailed account. This means that an answer should include specific information like places and dates and consider the ways in which developing colonies had an impact on England.

# What were the Navigation Acts?

Trade was one of the biggest concerns of the government during the reign of Charles II. If the country was going to be prosperous, it needed to make money and successful trade was the way to do that. In today's world, trade is very open – countries, people and companies buy and sell from each other, no matter who they are. But during the Restoration things were different; Britain had established colonies and gained control of **trade routes** all over the world. It was not willing to share with rival empires and nations, but rather trade should be kept within and between its territories at all costs.

## Objectives

▶ **Describe** the Navigation Acts and understand the term 'mercantilism'.

▶ **Explain** how the trade policies and the Acts worked.

▶ **Evaluate** their success.

## The importance of trade

As is still the case today, one of the ways a country could gain wealth in the Restoration was through successful trade. Countries needed to be able to sell the products that they produced and buy the products that they couldn't while making a profit in the process. Britain was able to produce a number of products that could be **exported** overseas but also needed to **import** a significant amount. Products like sugar, coffee, tea and cotton could not be grown in Britain and there was an increasing demand for them. One option was to buy these products from rival countries but this would simply increase those countries' wealth.

Before and during the Restoration, England had established colonies all over the world. Tea and silk were imported from Bombay, cotton from North America and sugar from the Caribbean. The money went to British businesses rather than foreign ones and

only British ships were allowed to transport goods. Laws were passed to ensure that this happened. This was part of a policy known as **mercantilism** that was adopted by most European countries. Governments saw it as their responsibility to encourage and protect their own country's trade.

▼ **SOURCE A** *This contemporary painting shows a British ship departing for trade with India*

# The Navigation Acts and their impact

The idea of passing laws to try to keep all trade within British territories was first introduced during the Commonwealth in 1651 but it was during the Restoration that it became firmly established. Acts of Parliament were passed in 1660, 1663, 1670 and 1673. The table below shows the rules that the Navigation Acts introduced. The aim of the Acts was to keep Britain's wealth in British hands. It was accepted that there was a limited amount of wealth and if a rival country was involved in British trade (tobacco, sugar, etc.) that meant that the wealth would move into foreign hands. The Acts were designed to stop this happening.

Although the Acts were obeyed, smuggling did take place between colonies and involving other European ships. After the Second Anglo-Dutch War ended in defeat for England in 1667, smuggling became even more common.

## The Navigation Acts: the key points

- Only British ships could transport goods between the colonies and Britain.

- Crews must be at least three-quarters British.

- Goods such as sugar, tobacco and cotton that were produced in the colonies could be exported only to Britain and its colonies.

- From 1663, all goods had to go via Britain in order to be taxed and colonies had to buy all their manufactured goods in Britain.

- The 1673 Act banned the direct trading of raw materials between colonies.

▼ **B** *Sugar cane, a major import for Britain that was grown in the Caribbean*

▶ **C** *A pair of Restoration sugar tongs; sugar was a valuable commodity*

## Key Words

trade route    export
import    mercantilism

## Work

1  Explain the term 'mercantilism'.

2  Explain one of the rules that the Navigation Acts introduced.

3  Explain how sugarcane would be affected by the Navigation Acts.

4  How convincing a description of European attitudes to trade is **Interpretation D**?

▼ **INTERPRETATION D**  Adapted from a chapter written by historian John J. McCusker in *The Cambridge Economic History of the United States, Volume 1* (Cambridge University Press, 1996):

> Mercantilism's desire to expand overseas trade was based on the idea that the promotion of one's own merchants reduced the power of foreign merchants. The increase of one's own overseas trade came at a cost to the overseas trade of other, competing nation-states. The gold in our own monarch's treasury and the gold in our own merchants' money chests was gold denied others. That, at least, is what mercantilists believed. Our gains were our enemies' losses.

# How did the slave trade develop during the Restoration?

As well as the growing trade in cotton, sugar, rice and other goods, the seventeenth century also saw the development of another trade: the trade in humans. The buying and selling of African men, women and children was not new but during the Restoration it became one of the most profitable businesses and vital to the success of other businesses. The American colonies would not have been able to function without slave labour. So how did the slave trade work? Who was involved and how was money made from it? And how important was the slave trade at this time?

## Objectives

▶ **Describe** the African slave trade in the seventeenth century.

▶ **Explain** how the trade developed.

▶ **Explore** the reasons for the development of the slave trade.

## The beginning of the slave trade

African people were first traded as slaves during the reign of Elizabeth I. Merchants and **privateers** (captains with royal permission to attack foreign ships) would capture them, or trade with tribal leaders and kings, and then take them to the Americas to trade for goods. The trade was on a small scale, however, and up to individuals to organise and make deals among themselves. As the British colonies in the Caribbean grew and developed during the Restoration, a larger workforce was needed to manage the plantations. African slaves were the answer. A more extensive operation was needed than had ever existed before.

## Slavery during the Restoration

As with other colonies, one company was given the exclusive right to trade in the British territories of West Africa. The Company of Royal Adventurers Trading to Africa was set up by Charles II in 1660 and was led by his brother, the Duke of York. Its initial purpose was to trade in the region's gold along the River Gambia. Like the East India Company, it was given the right to build forts and defend its monopoly. Profits were split 50-50 between the company and Charles.

After the end of the Second Anglo-Dutch War in 1667, the company fell into debt and was relaunched as the Royal African Company, complete with a new royal charter in 1672. This time, however, its interests went beyond gold. company had recognised the need for slave labour

in the Caribbean and began to fill this gap in the market. In the 1680s, the company was transporting around 5000 slaves a year across the Atlantic. Slaves were branded with either the company's initials (RAC) or the initials of its governor, the Duke of York (DY).

▼ **SOURCE A** *The charter given to the Royal African Company by Charles II in 1672; this gave it the monopoly on trade in West Africa, including the trade in slaves*

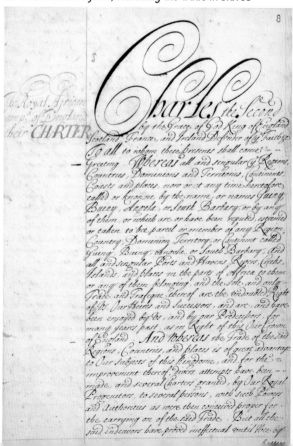

Trade

# A trade in people

When Europeans first arrived in North and South America, there were many native tribes already occupying the land. But the Europeans took the land anyway. The attitude of European settlers towards native people in the seventeenth century was that they had some use as workers but were otherwise largely unimportant. Millions of native people in South and North America were killed by diseases like smallpox that were brought over by the Europeans. Bringing in strong and healthy men and women from Africa to replace them seemed logical. Slavery was not a new concept; it is present in the Bible and most Europeans saw it as the natural order of things. The desire to build colonies and the policy of mercantilism meant that all the resources of a new territory could and should be used to make money. To the European businessmen, African men, women and children were simply another **commodity** (or product) to be bought and sold, and the trade in slaves became a key part of the success of English trade in general.

▼ **SOURCE B** *A painting from the 1670s showing slaves processing tobacco in Virginia, a North American colony*

▼ **INTERPRETATION C** *Adapted from* In the Balance: Themes in Global History *(McGraw-Hill, 1998) by the historians Candice Goucher, Charles LeGuin and Linda Walton:*

> The European entry into the world of the Americas had catastrophic effects on the indigenous peoples, who succumbed to diseases and genocidal policies of the Europeans; and in the wake of population decreases, other forms of coercive labour, including slavery, were exploited in the construction of the 'new world'. Central to the growth of Atlantic commerce were two commodities: sugar and slaves. The history of Atlantic commerce is inseparable from the history of slavery.

## Practice Question

How convincing is **Interpretation C** about the development of the slave trade in the seventeenth century?

Explain your answer using **Interpretation C** and your contextual knowledge.

**8 marks**

## Study Tip

Think about what the interpretation is arguing. What role does it suggest slavery played? You might want to look back at the previous chapter to remind yourself about American colonies.

## Key Words

privateer    commodity

## Fact

Between 1525, when the first recorded trade in African people took place, to its ban in the 1800s, it is estimated that between 10 and 12 million slaves were transported across the Atlantic.

## Work

1  What would a slave traded by the Royal African Company be branded with?

2  Explain how the slave trade worked in the seventeenth century. Where did slaves come from and where did they go?

3  Why were slaves needed in the Caribbean in the 1600s?

4  Look at **Source A**. What does the royal charter tell you about Charles's attitude towards slavery?

## Extension

Slavery was widely accepted in seventeenth-century England. Trying to understand why is a real challenge. Try to come up with as many explanations as you can. You could split them into three categories: religion, money and beliefs about race.

# What was the impact of the slave trade on Britain?

**7.3**

The trade in human beings carried out by the Royal African Company happened far from Britain and most British people would have had little knowledge of how it worked. They certainly knew it existed, however. As a direct result of the slave trade, many people in Britain became very rich. How did the slave trade affect the country's wealth? Who made the money and how? How did it affect the lives of ordinary people?

**Objectives**

▶ **Describe** how the slave trade affected Britain.

▶ **Explain** how people made money from the slave trade.

▶ **Assess** the impact of the slave trade on Britain and its people during the Restoration.

## Slavery brings wealth to Britain

**Who profited?**

### Slave ship owners
Up to 50 per cent profit could be made by ship owners who often never left Britain.

### Slave traders
The men who actually bought and sold the African slaves.

### Factory owners
Products like textiles could be sold in the colonies (half of the textiles produced in Manchester were transported to Africa and the other half to the West Indies!) and raw materials that had been grown by slaves were used in manufacturing, particularly in the north of England in Yorkshire and Lancashire. Ambrose Crowley, an iron merchant from County Durham, produced chains for use on the ships, and many of the ships themselves were built by the Pett family of Deptford who used timber grown on their land.

### Ports
During the 200 years of the trade, it is estimated that around half of the ships that carried slaves from West Africa to the Americas originated in Liverpool. In the seventeenth century, London was one of the most important trading places because of its transport links on the River Thames and the docks. Merchants based in Blackheath, Greenwich and Deptford dealt with around 75 per cent of the sugarcane imports from the colonies. Glasgow and Greenock were the main tobacco ports in Scotland.

### Plantation owners
Huge amounts of money could be made by using slave labour as it avoided the need to pay wages. Some owners became extremely wealthy. By the 1700s, a third of Jamaican plantations were owned by Scots, some of whom dressed their slaves in their clan tartan.

### Bankers
Merchants needed to borrow money to fund their long voyages and banks could earn from the interest on these loans.

### Ordinary people
The trade provided many jobs for people in Britain, particularly in the factories. Birmingham had over 4000 people making guns to sell to slave traders.

▼ **SOURCE A** *Liverpool c1680; the city would grow very quickly as a result of the slave trade in Africa*

## New fashions and the slave trade

An important effect of the slave trade was the wider availability of new products like sugar, cotton and tobacco. These became very popular with the English, particularly the wealthier classes. Sugar became widely used as the popularity of tea drinking (another import from a colony) grew. Coffee houses developed, where intellectuals gathered to discuss philosophy and politics, including new liberal ideas about freedom and individual rights. Customers would sit and drink coffee and smoke tobacco produced by enslaved African men, women and children.

## The plantations and their owners

The people who made the most out of the slave trade were the owners of the plantations in North America and the Caribbean. Rich English landowners would often buy or be given vast tracts of land in the New World to run for profit. Many would rarely visit the plantations, preferring instead to remain in England while a manager organised their business in the colonies. By using slave labour, costs could be kept to a minimum and huge profits could be made bringing the goods to Britain. The money from these plantations was often spent on building elaborate houses and gardens in this country that can still be visited today.

▼ **SOURCE B** *An illustration of Lloyd's Coffee House, opened in the 1680s, where those involved in shipping and trade would often meet; it eventually evolved into the Lloyd's of London Insurance organisation*

## Work

1 Approximately how many slave ships originated in Liverpool?

2 How did Ambrose Crowley make money from the slave trade?

3 Make a list of the ways in which slavery had an impact on British people's lives. How easy do you think it would have been for someone to argue against it?

4 Explain how new fashions encouraged the growth of the slave trade.

5 Look at **Source A**. Explain how the slave trade contributed to the development of Liverpool.

### Fact

Coffee had become an extremely popular drink in England and gathering for discussion in coffee houses was very popular. They were places for debate, political negotiation and plotting, trade and business deals; and other financial and intellectual meetings.

### Practice Question

Explain the economic impact of the slave trade on Restoration England. **8 marks**

### Study Tip

Use the spider diagram opposite to give your answer a structure (each branch could be the basis of a paragraph).

### Extension

Historians are interested in how a variety of factors can contribute to an event or change in history. Challenge yourself by answering the question: 'Why did the slave trade develop during the Restoration?' Use your knowledge about Britain, its colonies, trade and the effect of slavery on the country to help you answer the question.

# 8.1 How was war fought at sea?

The European powers of the seventeenth century aimed to expand their control and influence. In order for mercantilism to work, trade routes needed to be kept open and attempts had to be made to undermine the trade of other nations. So what were the latest developments, tactics and technologies in naval warfare? What was it like to be on board a navy ship in the seventeenth century? And which country had the most successful navy and why?

## Objectives

▶ **Describe** war at sea during the Restoration.

▶ **Explain** the tactics that were used.

▶ **Assess** the importance of a powerful navy in the late seventeenth century.

## The island nation

Being surrounded by water gave England a natural defence that its European neighbours did not enjoy. The failure of the Spanish Armada, one of the greatest naval fleets ever built, in 1588 proved how difficult England was to invade. The surrounding sea also meant that in order to expand their territory, the English needed to be successful sailors. By the Restoration, invasion of the country seemed less likely as its navy was more powerful than it had ever been. Charles is seen as the founder of the modern Royal Navy. Hundreds of ships had been built under Cromwell and in the early years of the Restoration, and Charles and his government used this to their advantage, sending ships far and wide to inflict damage on opponents and their ports.

Charles introduced the 'Blue Water' policy, which established that successful trade and a powerful navy were 'mutually sustaining'. This means that they were necessary for the success of each other. The navy provided protection of the trade that existed and allowed trade to expand while the taxes raised from trade in turn paid for the growth of the navy.

## War at sea

In the seventeenth century, battles at sea tended not to involve lots of ships in a direct battle. The most common tactic was to raid enemy ports or take individual, or small groups, of ships by surprise. Men like Henry Morgan had great success attacking Spanish ports in the Caribbean. Ships patrolled the trade routes on the lookout for enemy vessels that strayed into their territory. Despite favouring this type of warfare, larger scale battles did take place, particularly during conflicts like the Anglo-Dutch wars. The most common tactic used during these full scale battles was known as the **line of battle**.

▼ **INTERPRETATION A** *A Royal Navy battle ship, from around 1650, painted by William Frederick Mitchell for* Her Majesty's Navy Including its Deeds and Battles *by Lieutenant Charles Rathbone Low (Virtue & Co., 1890–93)*

## The line of battle

The line of battle tactic involved ships lining up in a row facing the enemy. The aim was to make the most of their fire power by ensuring that ships on the same side did not get in the way of each other's cannons. The fleet would create a wall of cannon fire that it would be almost impossible to withstand. Although it was not a new idea, the development of more powerful cannons during the Restoration made it increasingly effective. Previously, small ships had played their part. Now, however, increasingly specialised war ships that were able to hold their own under enemy fire were needed. These ships became known as **ships of the line**.

▼ **SOURCE B** *A sketch showing the line of battle tactic; this is from the Battle of Öland between the Danish-Dutch alliance and the Swedish navy in 1676*

## Life at sea

Life in the navy was hard, although it is fair to say that it was better than it had been in the past. Wages were higher and conditions had improved. This was mainly because the navy was much more organised and structured than ever before. The king's brother, James, served as Lord High Admiral for most of the Restoration but there were often skilled officers on board the ships making day to day decisions. The king still preferred to appoint nobles to senior positions but compulsory training and tests ensured that every ship had a good number of high quality officers. The navy administration was handled by the Chief Secretary to the Admiralty, Samuel Pepys.

▼ **INTERPRETATION C** *An illustration of a press gang from* Cassell's History of England *published in the nineteenth century*

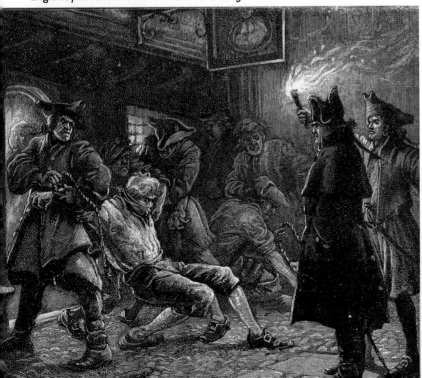

### Key Words

line of battle    ship of the line
press gang

During times of peace, men chose to join of their own free will but life on board ship was tough: months at sea, often poor treatment by officers and limited rations of food and water. In times of war, there were never enough sailors and men were **press-ganged** into joining. This was a form of conscription but much less formal. Men were forced to go to sea under a threat of violence. At times this involved men being 'recruited' directly from inns while they were out for a drink!

### Extension

'Press-ganging' was a technique that was used quite extensively in the seventeenth century. Research the technique, more formally known as 'Impressment'. What happened to those who were press-ganged?

### Work

1  Explain the term 'press gang'.

2  a  Explain the line of battle tactic.

   b  Why were specialist ships required for it?

   c  What made the tactic so successful?

3  What made life difficult for sailors?

4  'England's navy developed because of the need to protect trade routes.' How far do you agree with this statement?

5  Look at **Interpretation C**.

   a  Explain what is happening.

   b  How accurate a depiction of navy recruitment do you think this is?

# Conflict with the Dutch

England and the Netherlands were natural allies. They were both Protestant nations yet Charles's reign saw two disastrous wars against the Dutch. They were rivals when it came to empire and trade and this led to conflict. The wars are important not just because of their impact on England's international power but also because of how they affected English politics, particularly the difficult relationship between the king and his Parliament. What were the key causes of this conflict? What were the important battles of the war? And how did it end?

## Objectives

▶ **Describe** the events of the Second Anglo-Dutch War.

▶ **Explain** how the war went wrong for England.

▶ **Assess** the key turning points in the war.

## The Second Anglo-Dutch War (1665–67)

When war broke out in 1665 between England and the Netherlands it was the second conflict between them in ten years (the first took place between 1652 and 1654 and was fought for similar reasons to the later conflicts). It is therefore known as the Second Anglo-Dutch War. The war began mainly because of their rivalry over trade and colonies. The two key events that led to war were the English attack on the Dutch slave trading posts in West Africa in 1663 and the capture of New Amsterdam (renamed New York by the English) in 1664. Both countries had key interests in the same areas of the world and by 1665 relations had reached a low point.

## An English victory

The war began with a Dutch attack on a large group of English ships and the English retaliated with an attack led by the Duke of York. On 3 June 1665, at the Battle of Lowestoft, the English inflicted a heavy defeat on the Dutch who lost 30 ships, along with Jacob Opdam, one of their most respected admirals. As the remaining ships sailed away, James decided not to pursue them. His replacement as leader, Edward Montague, built on the success when, in August, he forced a Dutch **convoy** into a Danish harbour. The Danes were happy to destroy it.

## The tide turns

In January 1666, things became much harder for England because of France's entry into the war in support of the Dutch. As English ships sailed to where they mistakenly thought a French convoy was positioned, the Dutch were able to rebuild and prepare for battle once again. Between 1 and 4 June, Dutch and English ships engaged in one of the largest naval battles ever fought. The Four Days' Battle saw intense fighting, resulting in a terrible defeat for the English. With 20 ships lost they were forced to retreat to the Thames estuary.

The Dutch blockaded the Thames, trapping the English navy. The blockade was finally broken on 25 July, when in the Battle of North Foreland, 160 Dutch ships were destroyed. Following this, Charles felt confident as the long peace negotiations began – so confident that he allowed the ships to be moored and his sailors to go home. He believed the war was over. However, the Dutch were not finished. During the raid on the Medway, Dutch ships came within 20 miles of London and caused great damage along the riverbanks. Humiliated, Charles signed the **Treaty of Breda**, which gave the Dutch most of what they wanted.

## The view from England

In England the war was initially viewed with some unease. Many Members of

▼ **SOURCE A** *'The Battle of Lowestoft', painted by Isaac Sailmaker (1633–1721), a Dutch painter who lived and worked in England*

convoy    Treaty of Breda

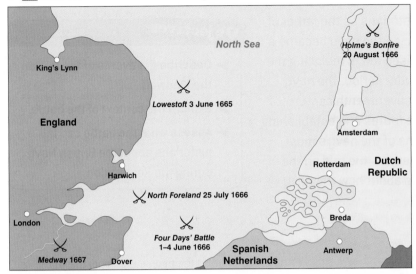

▼ **B** *Main sea battles in the Second Anglo-Dutch War*

King's Lynn

*North Sea*

Holme's Bonfire 20 August 1666

Lowestoft 3 June 1665

**England**

Amsterdam

Rotterdam

**Dutch Republic**

Harwich

North Foreland 25 July 1666

London

Breda

Four Days' Battle 1–4 June 1666

**Spanish Netherlands**

Antwerp

Medway 1667    Dover

▼ **INTERPRETATION C** *Adapted from heritage-history.com, a history education website:*

Like the first Anglo-Dutch war, the second war was provoked by the English, for essentially mercantile interests. Although Charles II did not particularly want war, some elements within his government had designs on Dutch colonies. Although the early war went in favour of the English, the Great Plague and Great Fire severely weakened the English war effort, and eventually, they were forced to appeal for peace.

## Timeline

| 1664 | 1665 | 1666 | 1667 |
|---|---|---|---|
| English raid Dutch slave trading posts in West Africa | English capture New Amsterdam (later renamed New York) | **1–4 June 1666** The Dutch win the Four Days' Battle and blockade the Thames; the blockade is broken in July | **June 1667** The Raid on the Medway |
| | **3 June 1665** English win the Battle of Lowestoft | **20 Aug 1666** English destroy 140 Dutch merchant ships in Vlie estuary | **21 July 1667** The Treaty of Breda |
| | | **Aug 1666** Peace negotiations begin | |

Parliament saw the Protestant Netherlands as potential allies but were willing to support their nation at war, especially when English victory seemed likely. Once the tide turned, however, opposition in Parliament grew. The Raid on the Medway disaster was the final straw. Bad decisions had put the country at risk. Charles reacted swiftly and removed his Chief Minister, Lord Clarendon. Clarendon took the blame for the disaster and the Cabal came to power in his place. One of the major reasons for the war's poor management was that many were distracted by the Great Plague of 1665 and the Great Fire of London of 1666. Indeed, it was the need to save money that had led to Charles taking a risk and sending his sailors home in August 1666.

## Work

1   When did the Second Anglo-Dutch War take place?
2   When was the Battle of North Foreland?
3   Create a graph in your book. On the *x* axis, write the key events of the war. On the *y* axis, draw an English flag at the top and a Dutch flag at the bottom. Now put a mark on the graph for each event to show whether it was good for England or the Netherlands. Join your line together. Was a Dutch victory inevitable from the start or was there a point at which the direction of the war changed?

### Practice Question

How convincing is **Interpretation C** about the Second Anglo-Dutch War? Explain your answer using **Interpretation C** and your contextual knowledge.

**8 marks**

### Study Tip

Work your way through the interpretation and think about how far each point accurately reflects the causes, events and result of the war.

# Historic Environment: The Dutch raid on the Medway

Charles II is recognised by many historians as the father of the British Royal Navy. During his reign the navy became a much more professional and organised force, replacing the much less structured navy of the Tudor period. The navy was key to Britain's success in the seventeenth century, playing a vital role in securing trade routes and establishing colonies. But the period also saw one of the navy's most disastrous and embarrassing moments – the raid on the Medway in 1667. What does it tell us about how the navy was led during the Restoration?

## Objectives

▶ **Describe** the events of the raid on the Medway.

▶ **Explore** the context of the battle.

▶ **Assess** what the battle can tell historians about the British Navy during the Restoration.

## What happened?

The Second Anglo-Dutch War (1665–67) had not been a success for the English. Charles and his government, led by Lord Clarendon, had hoped to gain control of trade routes but a series of errors led to failure. Success at the Battle of Lowestoft got the English off to a good start but by the time it came to negotiating a peace settlement it was the Dutch who had the upper hand.

With Parliament and the people unsupportive of the war, Charles could not afford to continue fighting or even to keep all of his ships in operation. Although peace was yet to be formally agreed, Charles believed that the war was all but over and decided to place a portion of his fleet on the River Medway in the estuary of the River Thames. By taking these ships out of operation, he would be able to save some money.

▼ **A** *A map showing the Dutch attack*

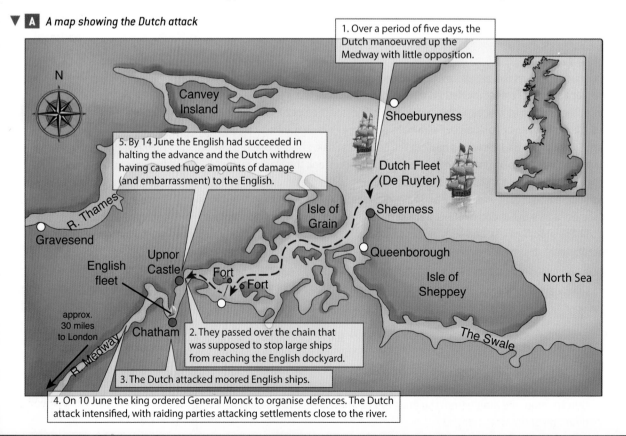

1. Over a period of five days, the Dutch manoeuvred up the Medway with little opposition.

5. By 14 June the English had succeeded in halting the advance and the Dutch withdrew having caused huge amounts of damage (and embarrassment) to the English.

2. They passed over the chain that was supposed to stop large ships from reaching the English dockyard.

3. The Dutch attacked moored English ships.

4. On 10 June the king ordered General Monck to organise defences. The Dutch attack intensified, with raiding parties attacking settlements close to the river.

Map labels: Canvey Insland, Shoeburyness, Dutch Fleet (De Ruyter), R. Thames, Isle of Grain, Sheerness, Gravesend, Queenborough, Upnor Castle, Fort, Fort, English fleet, Isle of Sheppey, North Sea, approx. 30 miles to London, Chatham, R. Medway, The Swale, N

## The Dutch prepare

Peace negotiations between the English and the Dutch began in March 1667 but were subject to many delays. Charles was reluctant to agree to anything because he was secretly in talks with the French, hoping that with their support he could once again go to war with the Dutch. The Dutch were suspicious of Charles's intentions. Johan de Witt, the Dutch politician who had been masterminding the war, decided that they needed a quick and decisive victory over the English before any alliance between France and England could be made. Despite misgivings among senior figures in the navy who thought the plan too risky, it was decided that Dutch ships would sail up the Thames estuary and attack the English ships that were moored there.

## The attack begins

The attack caught the English completely off guard. Their ships were poorly protected; in order to save money, guards and sailors had been sent home. None of the English commanders believed that Dutch sailors would have the nerve to sail into the Thames estuary. When the Dutch ships appeared there was panic. The English were disorganised and contradictory orders were given. Many of the English sailors had not been paid for months and so morale was

already very low. In addition the small English army was elsewhere and took days to reach the scene.

The Dutch were able to carefully manoeuvre themselves up the Medway to Chatham, where the English ships were moored, with almost no opposition. The only real defence was a huge chain across the water that was supposed to stop large ships passing. The chain was either broken by the powerful Dutch ships or it may even have been opened intentionally by unhappy English sailors. The king ordered General Monck to begin co-ordinating the defences on 10 June, but it took days to get equipment and men into positions. The whole area was in a panic as the Dutch attacked with cannons and sent raiding parties onto the land.

## The aftermath

The Dutch finally withdrew on 14 June but the raid cost the English 13 ships. The Dutch also took two of the navy's finest ships as trophies. It was not just disastrous (costing the modern equivalent of nearly £17 million!) but also humiliating. Enemy ships had been able to sail within a few miles of London and cause devastation. Many of the English ships had been unable to put up a fight as the crews abandoned the sinking vessels.

However, from the disaster came an opportunity. Determined never to allow a similar event to happen again, Parliament granted huge sums of money to build even greater, more modern ships, which played an important role in England's dominance of the sea in the following century.

### Work

1 Why did the Dutch decide to attack the Medway?

2 Explain why it was seen as such a disaster for the English.

### Study Tip

The Dutch raid on the Medway was a success for the Dutch and the humiliation of the English. How much was this due to good Dutch tactics and leadership? What part was played by poor English defence? How did the location affect the outcome? What was the long-term impact of the attack? Lastly consider about the element of luck. Did it play a part?

# Why was Charles's next Dutch war so unpopular?

Despite the humiliation of defeat, Charles quickly began planning another war with the Dutch. The Third Anglo-Dutch War between 1672 and 1674 was once again the result of an English attack on the Dutch and once again led to the devastation of the English fleet. There were, however, significant differences between the wars; most notably the position of France. Charles's war with the Netherlands was unpopular with Parliament and many ordinary people and caused great damage to his position. What were the key events, battles and turning points? And why was it so unpopular in England?

**Objectives**

▶ **Describe** the events of the Third Anglo-Dutch War.

▶ **Explain** the reasons for England's defeat.

▶ **Assess** how far the war damaged Charles's reputation.

## A secret treaty with Catholic France

The road to war began again in 1670 when Charles signed a treaty with France (known as the Secret Treaty of Dover). France was a much more powerful country and a more significant rival when it came to building colonies than the Dutch. As Charles knew that Parliament would be unhappy about an alliance with a Catholic country, the treaty was kept secret. It meant that the two countries would support each other in a war against the Dutch and that Charles would receive

financial support from the French king (remember that Charles was running short of money!). The treaty also stated that Charles would officially convert to Catholicism as soon as possible. It was this final clause that was kept secret when the treaty was revealed to the public later in the year.

France and the Netherlands had been at war for some time and the French welcomed English support. On 13 March 1672, English ships attacked a Dutch convoy and both sides began preparing for all-out war. At this point Charles made a political error. He issued the

**The Third Anglo-Dutch War**

Peace was made when the **Treaty of Westminster** was signed on **16 February 1674**. It had been an embarrassing defeat for England but, more importantly, a humiliation for Charles who had been shown to be powerless against his Parliament. The Cabal was forced from power shortly afterwards. The war had been hugely unpopular both in Parliament and with the wider public. France was a Catholic power and many saw Charles's support for France as a sign of a possible return to Catholicism in England.

Despite the lack of money, the war went on for two years. In the first major battle, the **Battle of Sole Bay** on **28 May 1672**, the Dutch inflicted great damage on the English, sinking dozens of ships and killing the Earl of Sandwich after the French fleet fled.

On **28 May 1673**, under the command of the king's cousin, Prince Rupert, the English launched an attack on a Dutch convoy, but the Dutch were well prepared and once again the English suffered heavy losses at the **Battle of Schoonveld Channel**, which began on the same day.

The English were defeated once again at the **Battle of Texel** on **11 August 1673**.

Declaration of Indulgence on 15 March 1672, which aimed to give Catholics and other non-Anglicans more religious freedom. Parliament was angry and, concerned about the king's possible Catholic leanings, refused to give any more financial support to the war. England now faced a war it could not get out of with no money to pay for it.

▼ **INTERPRETATION A** *The Earl of Sandwich refusing to leave his burning ship at the Battle of Sole Bay, from a nineteenth-century history book*

▼ **INTERPRETATION B** *The Battle of Sole Bay, painted in 1691 by Willem van de Velde II*

## Work

1 a What was the main difference between the contents of the Secret Treaty of Dover and the 'public' treaty?

  b Why do you think this was kept secret?

2 When did the Battle of Schoonveld Channel take place?

3 a How did Parliament respond to the Declaration of Indulgence?

  b Why did it respond in this way?

  c What were the consequences for the war?

4 Create a storyboard to show the key events of the Third Anglo-Dutch War.

5 How far do you think the Secret Treaty of Dover and the English defeat damaged Charles's reputation with Parliament and his people?

### Practice Question

Write an account of the Third Anglo-Dutch War. **8 marks**

### Study Tip

Remember to consider the impact of the Secret Treaty of Dover on Charles and Parliament.

# Relations with France and Spain

The two great world powers in the seventeenth century were Spain and France. Both were Catholic countries. England's relationship with France was one of the most significant issues of the Restoration. On the one hand, France was a close neighbour and much could be gained from an alliance. The court of King Louis had sheltered Charles during his exile after the Civil War and French fashions were all the rage in England. On the other hand, France was a trade rival and competitor for colonies around the world. Spain had fewer personal connections to England, but had to be dealt with carefully by Charles and his government, nonetheless. Why was England's relationship with France so difficult for Charles?

## Objectives

▶ **Describe** England's relationship with France and Spain.

▶ **Explain** the different views of Charles and his Parliament.

▶ **Assess** why the relationship with France and Spain was such an important issue.

## Charles, Louis and the issue of religion

Charles had a strong connection to France. He had spent many years in the court of his cousin Louis, and his mother was French. The French influence on Charles was plain to see from how he dressed to the way he conducted the business of his court. Charles's younger sister, Henrietta-Anne, was married to the French king's brother and had influence in the French court. She was also very close to Charles. She played a major role in the negotiations that led to the Secret Treaty of Dover.

The king was fully aware of the difficulties a relationship with France raised. Parliament was concerned about the Catholic threat to Anglicanism in England and Charles's dealings with France just added to this fear. He had to tread carefully. The Secret Treaty of Dover and

▼ **SOURCE A**  *A portrait by Jean Nocret (1670) of King Louis and his family dressed as ancient gods (the king is shown as Apollo); on the far left is Henrietta-Anne*

Parliament's refusal to fund the Third Anglo-Dutch War demonstrate the differences of opinion over France. Charles did not learn from this experience, however. After the disastrous war and facing a hostile Parliament, Charles needed money and Louis could provide this. From 1675, he began giving money to Charles (for Louis, this was a much cheaper option than war!). In 1677, Charles and Louis signed the **Treaty of Germaine-en-Laye**, designed to improve trade links between the countries. As Charles built friendship with the French, his Parliament and many others opposed it, fearing a Catholic plot, and instead called for alliance with the Dutch and war against France. King and Parliament could not have been further apart on this crucial issue.

## Another Dutch war?

Despite two defeats, Charles was keen once again to become involved in the ongoing war between the French and the Dutch, believing England could make significant gains from it. In 1678, Parliament agreed to fund the war on the condition that England supported the Netherlands. Charles agreed, a clear victory for Parliament, but ultimately the war came to an end before England could become involved. Despite his promise to support the Dutch, Charles had made a secret agreement with the French not to attack them. When in October the truth was revealed, Parliament was outraged and Charles quickly prorogued and then dissolved it.

## Religious refugees

The difficult relationship between the French and the English was illustrated in 1685 when Louis issued the Revocation of Nantes, which made all forms of Protestantism illegal in France. Previously, Protestants, known as **Huguenots**, had been allowed to practise their faith freely, but after 1685 they were left with no protection. Many were killed but an estimated 50,000 fled France and arrived as refugees in England and Wales. The Huguenots were given protection and the right to stay. For many in England, France's treatment of the Huguenots showed that the French could not be trusted. Charles's determination to make an alliance with France caused him significant problems and inflicted great damage to his popularity.

▼ **INTERPRETATION B** *An engraving from 1754 showing French Huguenots arriving in Dover in 1685*

### Fact

The Huguenots who came to England settled in communities across the country. Initially they tended to stay together, speaking their own language and setting up their own churches. As time went on, however, they began to integrate with the English population. Despite this, clear traces of the original refugees can still be seen in French street names, such as Fournier Street in east London, and in the style of some buildings. It is estimated that around a quarter of London's population has traces of Huguenot blood!

## The other Catholic power: Spain

Like France, Spain was a powerful rival to England when it came to trade and colonisation. However, Charles was not as determined to create an alliance with Spain

### Key Words

Treaty of Germaine-en-Laye   Huguenot

as he was with France. Spain was a constant enemy throughout the Restoration, particularly when it came to the Caribbean where Henry Morgan made a career of raiding Spanish ports. The one attempt at peace between the two nations was the Treaty of Madrid but this was very short lived and was barely observed while it existed. France and Spain made a number of alliances during this time. The two Catholic powers working together formed a formidable enemy.

▼ **SOURCE C** *A meeting between Louis XIV of France and Philip IV of Spain to sign a peace treaty in 1659; an alliance between Spain and France would be a very real threat to other colonial powers*

### Work

1   What was the official religion of France?

2   What did Parliament agree to in 1678?

3   a   Who were the Huguenots?
    b   Why did they have to leave France?
    c   Why did the arrival of the Huguenots in England further complicate the relationship with France?

4   Look at **Source A**. What does Henrietta-Anne's place in the portrait tell us about the connection between Charles and the French court?

5   Why was Parliament against an alliance with France?

6   Look at **Source C**. Does this source help us to understand why Charles was keen to make an alliance with the French?

# How to... analyse interpretations

**▼ INTERPRETATION A** *Adapted from a* Daily Telegraph *review of a book about* Charles I *by Malcolm Gaskill, first published 4 October 2009:*

Energies suppressed in state matters ran wild elsewhere. Charles liked riding and tennis, and lapped up jokes and gossip. But his passion was women and plenty of them. Nell Gwyn, sloe-eyed and streetwise, everyone knows. What, though, of Barbara Castlemaine, the peer's wife who bore Charles four children in as many years? This sleazy decadence, and the court's eye-popping extravagance, harmed the king's image.

## Practice Question

How convincing is **Interpretation A** about Charles II and his reign? Explain your answer using **Interpretation A** and your contextual knowledge.

`8 marks`

### Study Tip

Remember that this type of 'convincing' interpretation question in your Paper 2 British Depth Study exam is different from the 'how far' interpretation question in your Paper 1 Period Study exam. This one is based on the writings of a historian or someone who has studied the event or period. Consider: what do you know about the event? How far do you agree with this interpretation?

## Over to you

This type of question wants you to decide how **convincing** an interpretation is. In other words, how far does the interpretation fit with what you know about the history of the event, person or issue?

1   You could usefully begin by showing that you understand the main points of the interpretation by summarising it **in your own words**. How does the writer view Charles I and his actions? What does he believe were the consequences of Charles's actions?

2   You may not be totally convinced by the interpretation: you may not believe that it is completely correct or you may not agree that it is the best way to understand the events. Can you suggest a different interpretation or different ways the issue can be seen? For example, can you think of an argument that Charles's actions had a positive impact? If yes, explain the alternative argument.

3   Finally, do you agree with the interpretation? (Even if you agree that Charles's court was decadent and damaged his reputation, you could still try to describe the alternative point of view.) Try to write a few concluding sentences in which you make a judgement about how persuasive or accurate the interpretation is compared to any alternative interpretation.

4   What are the strengths and weaknesses of the following essay introduction to the question?

In Interpretation A, the writer describes Charles's lifestyle, including his love of various sports and women. It is certainly true that Charles spent much time pursuing his interest in sports, held numerous parties, had many mistresses and illegitimate children. The interpretation argues that Charles's lifestyle damaged his reputation and harmed his image. However, Charles's behaviour did not show a lack of care, but was in fact part of a carefully crafted public image. He was a 'public' and accessible monarch and his lifestyle was key to establishing this. Overall, the interpretation is not convincing as it suggests that Charles's behaviour had an entirely negative effect on his position whereas in reality this was not the case.

5   Now try to answer the question yourself!

# How to... tackle the Historic Environment question

## Practice Question

'The main reason for design of royal buildings was to demonstrate the new ideas and technology of the period.'

How far does a study of Tilbury Fort, during the Restoration period, support this statement? Explain your answer. You should refer to Tilbury Fort, during the Restoration period, and your contextual knowledge.   **16 marks**

## Study Tip

You have studied other royal buildings in the Restoration period. Do more research into the details of Tilbury Fort for this question. You could think about the key questions below to help you focus.

## Over to you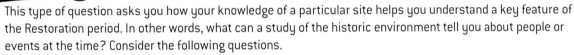

This type of question asks you how your knowledge of a particular site helps you understand a key feature of the Restoration period. In other words, what can a study of the historic environment tell you about people or events at the time? Consider the following questions.

1   *Motivation*: Why did someone want to build this specific building?

2   *Location*: Why did they build it in that particular location?

3   *Function*: Why was it built in that particular way? Consider the shape and design of the building or its layout. People design buildings to work and look in particular ways. Firstly, buildings have to function in a particular way, for example for safety, defence, comfort or pleasure. Can you identify and explain specific building features, and the job they do?

4   *Purpose*: What would the building be used for? Who lived or worked there?

5   Questions 1 to 4 will be helpful for most sites, but if you are studying a battle, such as the raid on the Medway, you should consider different questions as it is unlikely that there will be any physical remains to comment on. The environment may have influenced the outcome of the battle, so you could consider:

   a   *Motivation*: Why was the battle fought? Who fought in it?

   b   *Location*: Why was it fought in that particular place? What are the main landscape features?

   c   What happened at the battle?

6   Note that you don't need to use all the knowledge from your answers to questions 1 to 5 in order to answer the question. Select *relevant* information to write a response to the specific aspect of the environment you are asked about. The question asks '*How far*' houses show the change in fashions of the Restoration period, so you will need to say whether there is any continuity from what had gone before.

Now try to answer the Practice Question yourself!

# Practice Questions for Paper 2: British Depth Studies

The examination questions on the British Depth Studies will be varied but there will be a question on an interpretation (AO4), some questions on your knowledge and analysis of the period using historical concepts (AO1 and AO2), and an extended writing question on the Historic Environment (AO1 and AO2). Below is a selection of these different kinds of questions for you to practise.

## Norman England c1066–c1100

You are advised to spend 50 minutes on these four questions.

Use **Interpretation A** to answer question 1.

**Interpretation A**   An interpretation of the impact of the Normans on English monasteries.

Adapted from an article by Hugh Lawrence, in 'History Today' 1986.

> English monasticism after the Conquest was transformed by the aggressive building of new monasteries occupied by monks from France. This was deeply disturbing for English monks, who had to accept new Norman superiors. Tension was heightened by the lack of respect shown for English customs.  But the Normans breathed fresh intellectual life into the English monasteries through new learning from the continent along with different customs.

Answer **all four** questions below.

1   How convincing is **Interpretation A** about the impact of the Normans on English monasteries?

   Explain your answer using **Interpretation A** and your contextual knowledge.          **8 marks**

2   Explain what was important about land holding and lordship in Norman England.          **8 marks**

3   Write an account of the ways in which the lives of Anglo-Saxon villagers stayed the same under the Normans.          **8 marks**

4   'Luck was the main reason for the outcome of battles in this period.'

   How far does a study of the battle of Stamford Bridge support this statement?

   Explain your answer.

   You should refer to Stamford Bridge and your contextual knowledge.          **16 marks**

# Medieval England: the reign of Edward I, 1272–1307

You are advised to spend 50 minutes on these four questions.

Use **Interpretation B** to answer question 5.

**Interpretation B**    An interpretation of Edward I's use of castles in Wales.

Adapted from an article by Alan Rogers, in 'History Today', 1969.

> The castles of North Wales, with their defensive strength, were strongholds deep in enemy country but they had wider aims than just keeping down a hostile population. Although castles had military importance as permanent footholds, they were also safe places in a country where trouble could break out at any time. They were part of a process of civilisation, of changing the way Wales looked, and the minds of her people.

Answer **all four** questions below.

5   How convincing is **Interpretation B** about Edward I's use of castles in Wales?

Explain your answer using **Interpretation B** and your contextual knowledge.    `8 marks`

6   Explain what was important about relations between Edward I and the Church in England.    `8 marks`

7   Write an account of the work of Robert Burnell and the way in which government changed under Edward I.    `8 marks`

8   'Medieval battles were often decided more by luck than judgement.'

How far does a study of the Battle of Falkirk show this?

Explain your answer.

You should refer to the Battle of Falkirk and your contextual knowledge.    `16 marks`

# Elizabethan England c1568–1603

You are advised to spend 50 minutes on these four questions.

Use **Interpretation C** to answer question 9.

**Interpretation C**    An interpretation that questions the motives for Drake's round the world voyage.

Adapted from an article by David Cressy, in 'History Today' 1981.

> Was the real and secret purpose of Drake's voyage to raid the wealth of Spain as an authorised privateer, or was he sent to discover new lands and set up British colonies in the New World? Was it simply a trading voyage with the aim of finding a new and profitable route to the spices of the East and done in secret to protect any commercial gains? Probably there was a mixture of motives, with much left to chance.

Answer **all four** questions below.

9    How convincing is **Interpretation C** about the motives for Drake's round the world voyage?

Explain your answer using **Interpretation C** and your contextual knowledge.    **8 marks**

10    Explain what was important about the rebellion of the Earl of Essex for Elizabethan England.    **8 marks**

11    Write an account of the ways in which Queen Elizabeth dealt with the challenge of Puritanism.    **8 marks**

12    'The main reason for building a stately home in Elizabethan times was to demonstrate the successful career of its owner.'

How far does a study of Burghley House support this statement?

Explain your answer.

You should refer to Burghley House and your contextual knowledge.    **16 marks**

# Restoration England, 1660–1685

You are advised to spend 50 minutes on these four questions.

Use **Interpretation D** to answer question 13.

**Interpretation D**   An interpretation of the growth in power of the East India Company.

Adapted from an article by Bruce Lenman, in 'History Today' 1987.

> Charles II's restoration began a period of growth for the Company, bringing it prosperity, glory and war against the Dutch. It concentrated on India through heavily-fortified ports over which it had complete control. Its decision to keep infantry at its new headquarters at Bombay was an indirect challenge to Moghul authority and the power of local rulers was undermined. With Bombay already fortified, the new flashpoint would be elsewhere.

Answer **all four** questions below.

**13** How convincing is **Interpretation D** about the growth in power of the East India Company?

Explain your answer using **Interpretation D** and your contextual knowledge.    **8 marks**

**14** Explain what was important about the theatre in Restoration England.    **8 marks**

**15** Write an account of the ways in which the English Civil War and Commonwealth affected the Restoration of the monarchy.    **8 marks**

**16** 'The main reason for design of royal buildings was to demonstrate the new ideas and technology of the period.'

How far does a study of Tilbury Fort, during the Restoration period, support this statement?

Explain your answer.

You should refer to Tilbury Fort, during the Restoration period, and your contextual knowledge.    **16 marks**

[All questions, with the exception of Question 8, are taken from AQA 2016 Paper 2 specimen material.]

# Glossary

**abbess/abbot** the religious leader of an abbey

**abbey** a monastery under the supervision of an abbot or abbess

**absolute monarchy** the monarch has complete power without having to answer to Parliament

**Aethling** of noble birth

**alchemy** the 'science' of turning ordinary metal into gold

**allegiance** an agreement to be on someone else's side; often in war

**almshouse** charity building set up to provide food and rest for the poor

**Anglican** to do with the Church of England

**anti-Semitism** prejudice against Jews

**apologist** someone who puts forward a view designed to make a person or group appear more acceptable

**arbitrate** to help opposing sides come to a decision

**aristocracy** the highest-ranking people (except the monarch) in most societies

**Armada** the fleet of Spanish ships sent to attack England in 1588

**astrolabe** a navigation tool that allowed for much more accuracy at sea

**astrology** the study of stars and planets' positions in the belief that they influence human affairs

**bailey** an encircled area of land around, or at the base of, a motte

**bailiff** someone who collected tax for the landlord

**barbican** the outer defence of a castle or walled city, especially a double tower above a gate or drawbridge

**baron** a person at the lower end of the nobility who held land from the king

**bastide** a fortified town

**Bayeux Tapestry** an embroidered piece of fabric made in 1077; it depicts the events of the Battle of Hastings from the Norman perspective

**Benedictine** an order of monks that follows the Rule of St Benedict

**benefactor** a person who gives money or other help to a person or cause

**bill of mortality** a list of the dead and what killed them

**bishop** senior member of clergy

**Black Death** the name used for the bubonic plague that killed millions of people in Europe in the 1300s

**buffer zone** a neutral area serving to separate hostile forces or nations

**bubonic plague** a disease that spread quickly in England on numerous occasions including in London in 1665

**burgess** urban (town) dweller

**Cabal Ministry** group of ministers who held power between 1668 and 1674

**canon law** Church laws set up by the Pope in Rome

**Catholic** to do with the religion of Roman Catholicism

**cavalry** soldiers on horseback

**celibate** to refrain from sex or physical pleasure

**census** a government survey of the people

**Chancellor** a senior government position

**Chancery** Lord Chancellor's court

**chivalry** the respectful way for a knight to behave, with a sense of duty and fairness

**circumnavigate** to travel all the way around something

**civil war** a war between two groups of the same country

**Clarendon Ministry** government led by Lord Clarendon from 1610 to 1667

**clergy** members of a religious order, e.g. priests

**colony** land controlled by another country

**commodity** a product or a raw material that can be bought and sold

**Commons, House of** the elected Lower House of Parliament; it had power and influence but not as much as the Lords

**Commonwealth** a democratic republic, especially the period when Cromwell governed Britain

**concentric** design consisting of circles that share the same centre

**conspiracy** a secret plan by a group to do something unlawful or harmful

**convoy** a group of ships travelling together, usually for protection

**coronation** ceremony of crowning a monarch

**corrupt** showing a willingness to act dishonestly in return for money or personal gain

**Counter-Reformation** the reform of the Catholic Church in Rome in the sixteenth and seventeenth centuries, in response to the Protestant Reformation

**crenellations** battlements

**cruck** a type of peasant housing

**Crusade** a war fought for control of Jerusalem and the Middle East between Christians and Muslims in the eleventh, twelfth and thirteenth centuries

**curtain wall** the outer wall of a castle

**customs** taxes collected by the government on imported goods

**Danby Ministry** a government body led by Lord Danby from 1674 to 1679

**Danelaw** an area of land extending from the North East of England to East Anglia where most of the population were of Danish descent

**demesne** all the land owned by a particular lord

**demoralised** lost confidence or hope

**desertion** leaving an army without permission

**deserving poor** people who were poor through no fault of their own; the old, the sick or wounded or people who tried hard to find work but were not able to

**diocese** an area of land that is covered by a particular church

**dissolve** to break up Parliament

**divine right** (of kings) the belief that a king is chosen by God to rule

**Domesday Book** a census carried out by William I after the Norman invasion

**dowry** money and/or property that a wife or her family paid to her husband on marriage

**drawbridge** a bridge over a castle's moat, which is hinged at one end so that it may be raised to prevent people crossing

**duchy** an area controlled by a duke

**duty** a tax paid on a particular item

**earl** a member of the nobility

**ecclesiastical** issues concerning the Church and religion

**effigy** a model of a public figure that was often burned in protest

**enclosure** an area surrounded by a barrier

**estate** land owned in the feudal system

**Exchequer** the government office responsible for collecting taxes

**Exclusion Crisis** in Restoration times, the period in which Parliament debated bills that would stop James, Duke of York, from becoming king

**excommunicate** officially remove from the Catholic Church by order of the Pope

**exile** being sent to live in another country that is not your own, especially for political reasons

**export** to sell and send goods to another country

**fealty** a promise to be loyal to someone of higher social status in the feudal system

**feigned retreat** pretending to run away

**fief** land held in the feudal system

**fenlands** low area of marshy land

**feudalism/feudal system** the medieval social system in which the vassal gives fealty and military service to the monarch in return for land and title

**fireship** a burning ship sent into an enemy convoy or harbour

**fiscal feudalism** system under which land could be exchanged for military service or money

**flogged** to be whipped, a punishment used for begging and other crimes

**fortifications** defences in case of attack

**fortified** a place that is strengthened and has defensive measures as protection against attack

**franchise** an agreement to hold an event in a town for the purpose of business e.g. a market

**frankalmoign** transfer of lands to the Church as a gift

**freeman** peasant who paid rent to the lord instead of loyalty

**friar** a member of the clergy equivalent to a monk but who does not live in a monastery

**fyrd** a medieval army made up of peasants

**garrison** a strong building or fortress designed to defend the occupants

**geld** tax levied to pay for something specific e.g. a war

**General Eyres** travelling judges who could hear and settle cases in the name of the king

**gentry** high social class ranked below the nobility; they might be local JPs or hold similar office

**gonfanon** a type of heraldic flag or banner

**grant** a sum of money given by a government

**Great Cause** the name given to Scotland's succession crisis between 1286 and 1292

**guerrilla** a type of warfare where soldiers fight in small groups and hide in order to catch out the enemy

**guild** an organisation of craftsmen or merchants from a specific craft or industry

**Harrying** the devastation of the north of England in 1070

**heir** a person who has the legal right to receive the title or property of another on that person's death

**hide** an area of land

**Holy Land** the area in the Middle East in which most of the events described in the Christian Bible, the Jewish Torah and the Muslim Qur'an took place

**Holy War** a war fought either on behalf of God or with the support of God

**homage** the act of submission to a feudal lord; promising loyalty, respect and service

**honorial court** often in castles; where tenants could appeal against their landlord

**House of Correction** where beggars would be forced to spend the night as punishment

**housecarl** professional well-trained soldier hired by the king or an earl

**hue and cry** a loud cry calling for the capture of a criminal

**Huguenot** a French Protestant

**hundred** a subdivision of an Anglo-Saxon shire, which were 100 hides in size (a hide is c120 acres)

**Hundred Rolls** a census carried out by Edward, with specific detail about individual people and their property

**iconoclasm** the destruction of religious images and sculptures (icons)

**illegitimate** born outside of marriage; only the monarch's children from within marriage could become monarch themselves

**import** to bring into a country a product made in another country

**infantry** foot soldiers

**inflation** a currency becoming worth less, shown through rapidly rising prices

**inherit** to gain possessions after someone has died

**interest** money charged for delaying the repayment of a debt or loan

**Interregnum** 'between rule'; in Restoration times, the period between the death of Charles I and the Restoration of the monarchy

**Jesuit** a group within Catholicism whose aim is to spread the religion

**jurisdiction** the area in which somebody's power exists

**jury** members of the public who hear legal cases

**keep** secure or safe building to house Norman earls on the top of a motte

**lance** long wooden weapon with a pointed metal head

**lanteen** a triangular sail that was invented in the sixteenth century; it allowed ships to move much more quickly

**last rites** a Christian ceremony administered to a person who is about to die

**lay brother** person who worked in a monastery but was not part of the religious order

**legacy** something left or handed down by a person who died

**legitimate** born within marriage; only the monarch's legitimate children could become monarchs themselves

**line of battle** a naval tactic used in battle; ships line up to create a long wall of canon fire

**Lords, House of** the more powerful and unelected Upper House of Parliament

**Magna Carta** Great Charter; the agreement between King John and the barons in 1215 in which the king agreed to respect their rights; he later went back on the agreement

**magnate** one of the most powerful nobles

**manor** the area controlled by a lower lord or knight

**Marcher lord** the lords of the area of England that bordered Wales

**marchlands** an area of land on border between countries or territories

**Marshal of England** a powerful figure in the royal court; responsible for raising an army in time of war

**martyr** someone who has died for their religious beliefs

**mass** a Catholic church service

*mens rea* a legal term meaning criminal intent

**mercantilism** the main economic system used during the sixteenth to eighteenth centuries; its main goal was to increase a country's wealth by imposing government regulation on all trade

**mercenary** a soldier who can be hired to fight for money

**mesne lord** a middle lord who owes homage to another lord rather than directly to the king

**militia** a non-professional army raised to fight for a particular cause, e.g. to defeat a rebellion or fight a war

**minting** the process of making coins

**missionary** someone whose aim is to spread their religious faith

**moat** circle of water surrounding a castle as a form of defence

**mobilise** to prepare an army for war

**Model Parliament** a Parliament held in 1295 that was the most representative there had ever been

**monastery** a building occupied by monks

**monasticism** a religious way of life in which one renounces worldly pursuits to devote oneself fully to spiritual work

**monopoly** the exclusive right to trade in a particular product

**motte** a mound, either manmade or natural; in Norman times, utilised for castle building

**murdrum fine** the heavy fine payable to the king by an entire area where the criminal lived if a Norman earl was murdered

**nave** the central part of a church building, intended to accommodate those attending church service

**negotiation** to discuss affairs with the aim of coming to an agreement between opposing parties

**noble/nobility** the earls, dukes, lords and ladies; the most respected members of society; they were given special rights and privileges and owned most of the land

**Nonconformist** a Protestant who dissented from (did not comply with) the established Church of England

**novice** a trainee monk

*novissima verba* to be promised the throne upon a death bed

**outlaw** a person who is not under the protection of the law; if they were caught they would be punished for previous crimes, often by death

**overlord** the most senior lord; in medieval times, King Edward viewed himself as overlord of Wales and Scotland

**overmantel** an ornamental structure over a mantelpiece, typically of plaster or carved wood

**pamphlet** short document usually printed to spread a particular political or religious message

**Papal Banner** formal support given by the Pope to a king

**papal bull** special message issued by the Pope

**Parliament** country's law-making body; in medieval times, this was a meeting of important people, usually barons, who agreed on laws; its role became increasingly important during and after King Edward's reign

**patron** someone who funds the work of an artist or performing group

**patronage** land, titles or power given to ensure an individual's support

**pauper** the poorest members of society who were unable to find work

**penance** making a payment for sin in the form of either money, pain, prayer or a combination of these

**perpendicular style** an architectural style concerned with creating rich visual effects through decoration, mainly with vertical lines or pointed tops in stone windows

**persecuted** treated with hostility

**piety** reverence to God

**pilgrim** person who goes on a journey (pilgrimage) to a religious place in order to worship God

**plague** a contagious, deadly disease mainly spread by infected fleas on black rats

**plantation** a large area of land, especially in regions such as the Caribbean, where crops such as coffee, sugar and tea are grown

**plough** a machine used in farming to turn soil, moved by either man or ox

**pluralism** to hold more than one position in the Church

**Poor Laws** laws introduced from 1601 to deal with the growing problem of poverty

**Pope** the head of the Catholic Church

**popish** term for a supporter of the Pope

**portcullis** strong, heavy grating that can be lowered down on each side of a gateway to block it

*post obitum* a designation or bequest of a throne

**Presbyterian** a Protestant Church that believes bishops should be replaced by elders

**press-gang** to force someone to join the navy or army

**primogeniture** process by which the eldest son inherited all the land or titles from his father; younger sons or daughters would be left with nothing

**prior** the male head of a religious order

**priory** small monastery governed by a prior

**privateer** a ship's captain with royal permission to attack foreign ships

**Privy Council** a monarch's private counsellors

**propaganda** deliberately chosen information presented in order to influence people to think something specific

**prophesying** a meeting of Protestant clergy which usually involved criticism of the English Church under Elizabeth

**prorogue** to stop Parliament from sitting but not dissolving it

**protectorate** a period when a Protector is in power, especially that of Oliver Cromwell in England

**Protestant** general term describing Christians that left the Catholic Church

**Puritan** an extreme Protestant who believed that churches should be plain and that prayer and Bible reading should be a solemn activity undertaken every day

**quack** untrustworthy 'doctor' who claims to be able to cure illnesses such as the plague

**Quaker** Nonconformist Protestants who were greatly persecuted in Britain during the Restoration period

**quire** area of a church building were the choir or monks sat

*Quo Warranto* a legal process by which an individual's right to hold office could be challenged

**rack renting** demanding an excessive or extortionate rent from a tenant or for a property

**rampart** defensive wall of a castle

**ravaging** damaging or wreaking havoc

**recusancy** when a person refused to attend services of the Church of England

**reeve** a senior official such as a chief magistrate

**reform** to change for the better

**Reformation** the split of Protestantism from the Catholic Church beginning with Martin Luther in 1517; the English Reformation refers to Henry VIII's break from Rome

**regent** someone who rules a country in the absence of the monarch

**regicide** the act of killing a king or the person who does so

**remonstrance** forceful or angry protest

**Renaissance** the revival of European art and literature under the influence of classical civilisations in the fourteenth to sixteenth centuries

**republic** a country without a monarch; England was a republic between the death of Charles I and the Restoration of 1660

**retinue** a group of advisers or guards (i.e. private armies) accompanying an important person

**rhetoric** the art of persuasive speaking or writing

**Romanesque** style of architecture common in Europe from the tenth to the twelfth century

**royal charter** a formal document issued by a monarch granting a right to an individual, or for the establishment of towns or cities

**royal court** the nobles, advisors and others who surrounded the monarch

**Royal Society** the oldest and most important scientific organisation in Britain, formed by Charles II in 1660

**royalist** supporter of the monarch personally and the monarchy more generally

**ruff** an item of clothing worn around the neck

**salting** throwing salt over farmland to make it infertile

**satire** a method of criticising a person, idea or institution using humour, often in writing, to show their faults or weaknesses

**scholar** someone who dedicates their life to studying

**scriptorium** a room set aside for writing and copying manuscripts by hand in a monastery

**scutage** tax paid to the monarch instead of service

**scythe** a tool used in agriculture with a long curved blade

**Secretary of State** the leader of the Privy Council; a very powerful position

**secular** not connected to religion or the Church

**self-sufficient** to produce everything you need in order to survive without having to get products from anywhere else

**seminary** a training college for priests

**separatist** Someone who wants to break away from the mainstream

**serf** a person who had to give service to a lord and was transferred along with land

**sheriff** the king's chief legal official in an area

**shield wall** Anglo-Saxon defence strategy; soldiers interlinked circular shields with the aim of creating an impenetrable wall

**ship of the line** a sailing warship of the largest size, used in the line of battle

**shrine** a place or a casket associated with a saint

**sickle** a tool with a curved blade used for cutting grass

**siege** a form of attack on a castle; supplies were blocked forcing the inhabitants to either surrender or starve

**social hierarchy** a system with layers of classes

**solar** a private living area for a lord's family

**stocks** method of punishment for begging and other crimes; criminals would be held by the hands and feet while people threw things at them

**subinfeudation** the splitting of land with a social inferior by a lord who expected homage in return

**sub-regulus** deputy king

**substitution** transferring the ownership of land from one person to another

**succeed** to take over the throne

**surplice** a white gown worn by priests in the Church of England

**surplus** an excess of production or supply

**tenant-in-chief** someone who held land from the king

**thegn** a person who owned land but was not a noble

**tithe** a tax paid to the Church, normally 10 per cent of income

**Tory** political party formed to support the Duke of York becoming king; began as the Court Party

**treason** an attempt to kill or overthrow the monarch or betray the country; punishable by death

**undeserving poor** dishonest poor people who tried to trick others out of their money

**urban** relating to a town or city

**usury** charging interest on loans

**vagrant** a person without a settled home or work who wanders and lives by begging

**vassal** a lord who owes homage to a more senior lord

**vernacular** local language spoken by ordinary people

**villein** a peasant

**watchman** a person employed to keep watch in a town at night

**Whig** political party formed to block the Duke of York from the throne; began as the Country Party

**Witan** a group of leading earls and churchmen

# Index